D1917806

ALSOP'S TABLES

ALSOP'S TABLES

(Alsop, Alsup, Alsip, Allsop, Alsep,
Allsup, Alsopp, Allsopp, Alsept, Etc.)

Volume III
Part I

Jerry David Alsup, B.S., M.A.

iUniverse, Inc.
Bloomington

Alsop's Tables
Volume III Part I

Copyright © 2012 by Jerry David Alsup

Limited First Edition

All rights reserved. No part of this book may be used or reproduced by any means, graphic, electronic, or mechanical, including photocopying, recording, taping or by any information storage retrieval system without the written permission of the publisher except in the case of brief quotations embodied in critical articles and reviews.

iUniverse books may be ordered through booksellers or by contacting:

iUniverse
1663 Liberty Drive
Bloomington, IN 47403
www.iuniverse.com
1-800-Authors (1-800-288-4677)

Because of the dynamic nature of the Internet, any web addresses or links contained in this book may have changed since publication and may no longer be valid. The views expressed in this work are solely those of the author and do not necessarily reflect the views of the publisher, and the publisher hereby disclaims any responsibility for them.

Any people depicted in stock imagery provided by Thinkstock are models, and such images are being used for illustrative purposes only.

Certain stock imagery © Thinkstock.

ISBN: 978-1-4697-9830-1 (sc)
ISBN: 978-1-4697-9831-8 (hc)
ISBN: 978-1-4697-9832-5 (e)

Printed in the United States of America

iUniverse rev. date: 03/27/2012

Table of Contents

Preface

This is the third volume of the family history entitled Alsop's Tables which follows the first two volumes published in 1986 and 1994. The earliest book began with the oldest known records and information yet discovered on the Alsop family and followed the numerous branches as they settled in various countries after emigrating from their place of origin in England. The second book in this series followed the original work by eight years and started where the first book ended.

Volume III will begin where the previous book concluded and will treat families who originated in England and remained there or those who settled in Ireland, Scotland, Australia, Canada, United States, etc. When appropriate, the various branches of the family tree who immigrated to the United States will be separated into chapters beginning with the arrival of the immigrant ancestor.

There are several good systems for identifying and coordinating the members of a particular family. The Register System, the same system used in the first two volumes of Alsop's Tables, will again be the method for placing the descendants of the immigrant ancestor in recognizable order in those chapters having enough descendants to require it. When this procedure is used, the immigrant ancestor is given the Arabic numeral one and his children are given lower-case Roman numerals. For each child who appears later as the head of his or her own family group or as a member of a supplementary family, an Arabic numeral is placed in front of the Roman numeral. The names in parentheses following the head of a family unit trace the direct line of the individual back to the earliest known direct ancestor.

To the many family members, ancillary family individuals, and anyone else interested in the Alsop, etc. family history, I extend my genuine gratitude. Without you, there would be no need to put this family information into the form of a book. To those who have contributed information of historical merit, I recognize your valuable assistance.

As the days of "horse and buggy" genealogical research draw to a close and the era of computer investigation pushes it aside, I would like to express my sincere appreciation to providence for allowing me to have enough interest to start digging on my progenitors at a very early age. I was thus afforded the eventual opportunities to travel, work courthouse records, visit old homesteads, check cemeteries, and visit in person the present day descendants of my ancestors. This method of family research, while not available to everyone, is one that I have enjoyed as a way of life for the past four decades. I know that modern day technology has opened the door to genealogical pursuits for almost anyone who has the least bit of interest in their family heritage. I think it is marvelous that a vast amount of family information can be accumulated without going out the front door. This involves simply turning on the computer. However, my own years of genealogical research would not be half as meaningful to me (and I hope to you) if I had not gone there and done that.

Jerry D. Alsup

Dedication

Many sayings have evolved through the ages about brothers. There are numerous kinds of brothers, but the brother that I am dedicating this third volume of our family history to is my own blood kin and sibling; born when I was two years old. Memories of our boyhood days came flooding back as I picked thorough the available photos to find just the right ones to include. Baseball was our favorite sport, and as the older, wiser brother, I made him help me get ready for the big games by practicing sliding into his glove and hitting him fly balls to increase my long ball skills. I try not to remember the twelve stitches that were required for his leg when I actually used my baseball spikes for a more authentic practice session, or another trip to the emergency room to set his broken nose when my high fly ball found its way through his glove. Known by one and all as "Peaches" during his high school and college years, he and Elizabeth Ann Mullins (I claim credit for having gotten them together during his first year at Memphis State University) became a permanent item hailed by acquaintances as "Peaches and Moon." Although the nicknames have long since dissipated, the relationship was genuine; and it took an invitation from the Lord to separate this caring and responsible human being from his wife and two wonderful children, Tim and Beth.

Marshall Neal Alsup- 5 Nov. 1935-17 April 1996

View of the Alsop ancestral home and the caretaker's cottage

The Alsop manor house as seen from St. Michael churchyard

CHAPTER I

Have Dominion Over Every Living Thing That Moveth Upon the Earth

******

The Alsop family planted deep roots into the earliest history of Derbyshire. From their original location at the tiny village of Alsop-En-Le-Dale to a near worldwide dispersion, the numerous descendants of this family have had remarkable success in exerting their sphere of influence. In this chapter and the following ones can be found evidence of the dominance of many of the members of this family over their environment and circumstances. Even those who have not always been successful in mastering their surroundings have usually shown an indomitable spirit, just waiting for the development of the appropriate conditions to enable them to rise above their adverse situations.

******

Map showing portions of Derbyshire, Staffordshire, Cheshire, and Yorkshire

Several English Families - 1500's - 1600's.

Margaret Alsop and Giles Ivyto were married in Oxford Co., England, 25 October 1596 in the Parish of Banbury.

Gilbert Alsope and Judith Spurway were married 29 August 1602, Exeter - St. Petrock of Devon County.

John Francis and Magdalen Alsop obtained a marriage license in London in the year 1612.

Elizabeth Alsoppe, daughter of Lewis Alsoppe, was baptised in 1652 at St. James, Clerkenwell, London.

The High Court of the Admiralty was a court set up to handle problems on the seas. From its records we find that in October, 1654 the ship "Exchange" of which Wm. Wilkinson was master and part owner was scheduled for a voyage with passengers and goods for Virginia. Edward Alsop of St. Olave, Southwark, Surrey was listed as a 30 year old mariner who was signed on as the master's mate for the voyage. The captain employed a pilot, James Wareing, to guide his ship from the Thames to the Downs. The pilot proved to be a facetious man who cursed and stated that he wished to see the ship destroyed. At Reculver the ship went on the sands, received a broken rudder and could not continue the voyage. No mention was made of the final court decision concerning the dispute between the captain and his pilot.

On 16 July 1663, Anthony (X) Yates of Bpps. Cleeve, Gloucestershire, yeoman, age 30 and Elizabeth Assope of the same place, age 26 were married.

Thomas Wright of Norleech, Gloucestershire was married to Hannah Assips, also of Norleech, on 19 January 1679. The bondmaker was Francis Gardner and the apparitor was Mr. Stow.

On 7 October 1685, George Steavens of Bristol County, yeoman and Rosamond Alsobe of St. Stephen, Bristol County were married at St. Augustine or Cathedral. The bondmaker was Israel Contstant, Bristol Farrier.

The Gloucestershire, England marriage of Joseph (X) Alsop of Burton-On-The-Water, weaver, to Jane Egerton, also of the same location, took place on 1 June 1688. Richard Alsop, a weaver of Burton-On-The-Water, Gloucestershire, England and Mary Scotford of Notgrove, Gloucestershire, were united in marriage on 3 May 1694.

Mr. Alsop was listed as a clerk who emigrated from England to Jamaica on 3 Feb. 1701. This record is preserved in the Public Records Office of London and is filed under Money Book 16-17. Money books are lists of ministers or school teachers who emigrated to America from 1690-1811.

Anthony Alsop - Poetical Writer

Anthony Alsop was born ca. 1670, and educated first at Westminster, one of the oldest public schools of England, and then at Oxford University. Oxford is divided into many colleges, Christ Church being one of the colleges and the one from which he obtained his M.A. degree on 23 March 1696, and his B.D. 12 December 1706.

After graduation Anthony remained at Christ Church as a clergyman and teacher on the faculty and became censor of the college and tutor to the important noblemen and gentlemen who attended Christ Church. As a favorite of Aldrich, Dean of Christ Church, he was responsible for publishing the 1698 selection from Aesop entitled "Fabularum Aesopicarum Delectus, one of the series of classical works which the dean presented as new-year presents to his students. This work consisted of 236 fables in Latin verse with 158 of them in original Greek, the next 10 in Hebrew, Arabic of the next 8, and the remaining 60 in Latin only. In the preface of his "Aesop" Alsop refers to a man named Bentley, who had criticized the previous publication "Phalaris", as a man "in volvendis lexicis satis diligentem". He recounts the fable of the dog in the manger and hints of its applicability to Bentley. In addition the Christ Church wits verbally assaulted Bentley, who had alluded contemptuously to Alsop.

Thomas Warton, poet laureate of England, in an essay on Pope describes the sixty fables as "exquisitely written". Anthony Alsop was given a prebend (a stipend or maintenance granted by the church) in Winchester with the rectory of Brightwell in Berkshire by Bishop Trelawny.

Alsop was brought to court in 1717 by an action against him for breach of promise of marriage, and he was found guilty with the requirement that he pay damages of 2,000 L. Forced to leave the country for a while, he returned several years later only to be struck down by the hand of fate. He was walking in his garden on 16 June 1726, when a bank suddenly collapsed throwing Anthony into the river which flowed past his backyard, and he drowned.

Many Latin odes in manuscript were left by Alsop. Sir Francis Bernard proposed plans for publishing them in 1748, saying that Alsop has been "not unjustly esteemed inferior only to his master Horace." The odes were published in 1752 with a dedication to the Duke of Newcastle. Although the odes displayed a classical taste, the personality behind them was of a jovial college tutor who was as fond of smoking as his supporter, Aldrich, as one of the odes was written with a pipe in his mouth. In Alexander Pope's fourth book of the "Dunciad", verse 224 –

> Let Friend attest to speak as Terence spoke
> And Alsop never but like Horace joke -

the lines are intended to show satire and not compliment. The "Dunciad" by Pope was an attack on dunces and ridiculed certain writers, critics and overly scholarly professors. Some of Anthony Alsop's poems can be found in the "Gentleman's Magazine", Vols. V, VIII, IX and in Dodsley's collection.

Vincent Alsop - Celebrated Nonconformist Clergyman

Born in Northamptonshire ca. 1630, Vincent Alsop attended at an early age St. John's College of Cambridge University and earned his degree of

M.A. He received deacon's orders from a bishop which qualified him as a cleric in orders next below a priest. His first position was that of assistant master in the free school of Oakham, the county town of Rutlandshire.

During his early residence, Vincent was an active participant in the merry and convivial gatherings of the local society. Tradition describes him as a brilliant but broadly inclusive wit. A local minister of the Gospel, Benjamin King, slowly won him away from his trifling, leisurely, and unbridled ways. Eventually he married the minister's daughter, accepted his beliefs, and was ordained in the Presbyterian way. During the English Civil War and the Commonwealth (1642-1660) the Anglican clergy was replaced by some 8,000 non-conformist ministers and teachers. Parliament passed the Act of Conformity in 1662 which required all ministers and teachers to use the Book of Common Prayer. Those who refused were to be expelled from the churches and schools. Alsop was presented to Wilby in his home area of Northamptonshire, but he refused to accept the Act of Uniformity and along with two thousand other ministers was ejected from the church.

He was forced to preach semi-privately at Oakham and Wellingborough receiving for his efforts the typical curbs and penalties of the time. Vincent once was imprisoned for six months for praying with a sick person. The government believed that it was its duty to enforce a common form of worship on all the people.

In the year 1675, Vincent Alsop wrote a book entitled "Antisozzo" which criticized Sherlock. The book was written in a style which brought him fame as a wit and humorist exhibiting his ability in the natural use of the paradoxical and ridiculous. The new found fame which "Antisozzo" acquired for him also helped the author to secure a position as the head of a large nonconformist congregation at Westminister.

Alsop continued to take an important part in the ecclesiastical instead of the theological disputes of his day. He also wrote more books which continued to display his brilliant and abundant wit by use of firm conclusions disguised in a playful manner. His "Melius Inquirendum" in 1679, and "Mischief of Impositions" in 1680, combine to remain as historical milestones in nonconformist history.

Even though his church in Westminister was located close to King James II and his court, he was able to avoid fines and imprisonment. At an advanced age he was involved by a son in practices that bordered on treason, but the king liberally pardoned both. His feelings toward James II were very amicable from this point on. Alsop drew up "The Humble Address of the Presbyterians" for the "General Indulgence."

As he neared the end of his life, he gave fully of himself to both his pulpit and his ministerial duties. Even as a very old man he worked with tireless enthusiasm and great success. He preached every Sunday and continued to lecture at Pinner's Hall while his natural faculties and energy abated not at all. He died 8 May 1703, and his funeral was preached by Slater to a huge following.

Vincent Alsop put his considerable mental ability and wit into all of his writings. A study of his "Duty and Interest united in Praise and Prayers for Kings" written in 1695, and "God in the Mount" are still of value to today's readers. His "Faithful Reproof to a False Report" reveals unusual strength and energy while even his sermons of the "Morning Exercise" give evidence of extraordinary wit. Additional genealogical connections will be presented in a later volume.

Thomas Allsop - Astwith

Thomas Allsop, parents not known, born ca. 1761 at Astwith, Derbyshire, and Elizabeth Bowle, christened 8 Sept. 1754, daughter of Wm. and Clemence were married 5 October 1786 at Ault Hucknall. Thomas died 29 October 1809 at Astwith and Elizabeth died 5 May 1836 at Ault Hucknall, Derby. Their daughter Ann Allsop, born 26 January 1787 at Ault Hucknall, Astwith became the wife of Joseph Farnsworth, born 30 May 1794 at Heage, Derby, on 27 November 1816. Ann died 29 May 1854 at Heage, Belper, Derby and her husband died 10 April 1868 in the same location. Their son George Farnsworth had a son Arthur Farnsworth whose great granddaughter is Mrs. Gayle Turner, 2636 Sherwood Dr., Salt Lake City, Utah.

Samuel Allsop - Hognaston

Samuel Allsop was baptized ca. 1661 at Hognaston, Derbyshire, the son of parents who are unknown at this time. He was married to Elizabeth Brunt, the daughter of John Brunt of Bakewell, Derbyshire, who was baptized in Bakewell about 1665, on 6 May 1686 in her home village. Samuel was a yeoman farmer who lived the first couple of years of his married life at Bakewell, and then he returned to Hognaston where he lived the balance of his life. He was buried at Hognaston on 4 Feb. 1720, and his wife, Elizabeth, was buried in the same location on 5 July 1726. Their children were John, born 1687 at Bakewell; Samuel, born 1693 at Hognaston; Rebecca, born 1689 at Hognaston; Hannah, born 1696 at Hognaston, and Jonathan baptized 28 Aug. 1700 at Hognaston.

Jonathan, son of Samuel and Elizabeth married Hannah Storer, baptized 18 March, 1701, at Kirk Ireton, Derbyshire on 25 Feb. 1723 at Atlow in the same county. Jonathan lived at Atlow for the first couple years of his marriage where his first son, Jonathan was born in 1724. Finding a farming situation in his wife's birthplace of Kirk Ireton, he relocated there by 1726 when his first daughter, Hannah, was born. The rest of his children were also born at Kirk Ireton. They included: Mary, 1728; Elizabeth, 1730; George, 1732; Samuel, 1734; John, baptized 3 Sept. 1737; Ann, 1740; Millicent, 1742; and Rebecca, born and died in 1745. Jonathan and Hannah were buried at Kirk Ireton on 4 April 1759, and 1 Sept. 1761, respectively.

John, son of Jonathan and Hannah, was baptized on 3 Sept. 1737 at Kirk Ireton and married on 6 June 1758 at Wirksworth, Derbyshire, Maria Peat. John followed the trade of a cordwainer and specialized in making shoes from cordovan leather which is a soft, finegrained, colored leather. He began work at Ashleyhay, Derbyshire, but later lived at Ideridgehay and Kirk Ireton. His eight children were Hannah, baptized 1764 and died an infant death; Samuel 1767; Jonathan, born 1770, and died 1783; Thomas, 1772; Joshua, baptized 8 Nov. 1775 at Ideridgehay; Hannah, 1778; William, 1781, who died the same year; and Elizabeth, born 1782. John was buried at Kirk Ireton 19 Sept. 1815, and Maria was buried 22 Nov. 1811.

Joshua, the fourth son of John and Maria, and Elizabeth Alton were married 10 Feb. 1796. Elizabeth died ca. 1801, and he then married Lydia Eyre, baptized 1768, on 6 June 1802 at Duffield, Derbyshire. There were no children by the first marriage, but the four offspring by the second marriage were William, 1803; Samuel, 1805; George, 1808; and Joseph, baptized 10 June 1810. Joshua died at Milford on 29 June 1836, and Lydia was buried 18 Dec. 1836.

Joseph, the last child of Joshua and Elizabeth, wed Elizabeth Wigley at Muggington, Derbyshire on 21 Feb. 1830. He pursued the occupation of cotton spinner at 3 Chevin Alley, Milford, Derbyshire. Elizabeth and Joseph were the parents of Mary, 1831; Salome, 1832; Elizabeth, 1834; Harriet, 1838; Sabina, 1840; George William, born 1 Jan. 1843; Joseph, 1846; Elizabeth, 1848; Lydia, 1851; and Samuel, 1854. Joseph died at Milford, Derbyshire on 8 May 1890.

George William, born to Joseph and Elizabeth Wigley Allsop on 1 Jan. 1843 at 3 Chevin Alley in Milford, was married to Elizabeth Sophia Crofts on 11 Feb. 1865 at St. Mary's Church at Nottingham. She was also born at Milford in the year 1846, daughter of Samuel Crofts of New Inn, Milford. George William first worked as a joiner, a skilled woodworker who does the woodwork necessary for the finishing of buildings. Later he became the publican of the New Inn at Milford. The New Inn was a public house (combination of a hotel and a tavern) and George was the keeper. Their children were Samuel Crofts, born 1865 - died 1955, married Ada Greenall at Sheffield; George William, 1867-1950, married Sally Marshall at Killamarsh, Derbyshire; Fanny Mary, 1870-1926, married Arthur Lack at Duffield; Frederick James, born 5 Feb. 1872 at Milford; Elizabeth Sophia, 1875-1935 married Tom Botham; Edgar, 1878-1948, married first, Elizabeth Knifton and second, Edith Holmes; Emma, 1880-1962, married William Hy Carte who was later adopted by his employer and became known as William Hy Carte Hingley; Annie Winifred, born 1883 and died at Hendon in 1964; and the youngest child, Maurice Albert, 1890-1980, married Grace Brightman. The father died 26 Jan.1904, and the mother died just 11 days earlier.

Frederick James, son of George and Elizabeth Crofts Allsop, became the husband of Alice Foster, born 21 Mar. 1877 at Barnsley, Yorkshire on 16 Oct.

1900 at Wesleyan Chapel, located at her birthplace. Frederick entered the educational profession as a schoolmaster and his wife followed the same field as a schoolmistress. He died 29 March 1936 at Crindleford, Derbyshire and she 9 Dec. 1958 at Wandsworth, London. They both chose to be cremated, he at Sheffield and she at Putney Vale. The children born to Frederick and Alice were Fred 1901-1977, married Pat Milner of Kensington; Leslie, 1903-1981, married M. Fewtrell of Sunderland; Phyllis, born 5 Aug. 1907 at Tilney St. Lawrence, Norfold, married Cyril Alfred Reader of Eyam, Derbyshire, and is a retired school teacher; Joyce, born 1918, married J.K. McKay of Eyam; and Eric Allsop who submitted this family information and lives at Dadles, Gayton Road, Ashwicken, King's Lynn, Norfold PE 32 1LS. Eric, born 22 Aug. 1905 of Tilney St. Lawrence, Norfolk, married on 8 June 1935 at St. Mary's Church, Southtown, Great Yarmouth, Muriel Emilie Knight, born 25 June 1904 at Great Yarmouth. Both Eric and Muriel are retired school teachers.

Harold Alsop - Lincolnshire

Harold Alsop is thought to have come to the London area from Lincolnshire where he married and had a family. His children included several sons, one of which was Alfred Donald Alsop who died of cancer in August 1941. Alfred was the older brother of Betty Alsop who married a Montague and is still living. Harold's first marriage was a disaster, and he did not get along well with his daughter, Betty. He probably remarried in the 1930's, and it is believed that he died in Lancashire in the1960's.

Alfred Donald Alsop was the father of Anne Alsop who married Roger Graham Holloway 31 March 1962. She was born 1 Feb. 1942 after the death of her father. Anne and Roger Holloway have a daughter Victoria, born 8 Feb. 1963, and sons Adam, born 29 July 1965, Julian, born 24 June 1971, and Leo, born 1 July 1973. Victoria has a son, Alexander, born 31 Jan 1988, although she is not married to the father, David Durrant. Additional research should extend the ancestry of this family.

James Allsop - Derbyshire

Mary Coulton and James Allsop were married in Derbyshire about the middle of the nineteenth century although the exact date has not yet been determined. Two of their children were daughters Mary, baptized in Ripley on 29 April 1853, and Sarah, born Green Hillocks, Ripley on 14 Feb. 1855. Sarah Allsop and Samuel Clarke were married at Baptist Chapel, Swanwick, Derbyshire on 25 Nov. 1877 and had at least six children. James Allsop, Sarah's father was noted on the marriage certificate as being dead. The children were John, 1878, Thomas 1880, James, unknown, Mary, 4 Feb. 1885, and Samuel and George whose birthdates are unknown at this time. Samuel Clarke, Jr. died in an accident at work. Mary married John William Belton on 6 Nov. 1905, and died in February, 1955. John and Mary had twelve children, three of them dying in infancy and the other nine (who range in age from 60 to 82) are still living. Sarah Allsop Clarke died in the early 1900's at Treeton, near Sheffield, Yorkshire. Margarita Smith of 12 Marlborough Avenue, Tadcaster, North Yorkshire is the great granddaughter of Sarah and the granddaughter of Mary.

Berta Ivor Allsopp - Swansea, Wales

Berta Ivor Allsopp was born in the Swansea area of Glamorgan, Wales. He is said to have connections with the Derbyshire Allsopps but no definite proof has been discovered as yet. His children were Ivor, William, Sarah who married an Everson, Berram born 1915, Balil born 1919, and Gleny who married a Ball. All of these children were born at Pontycrommer, Glamorgan, Wales.

Berram had a son, Balil, born in Luton about 1942 and a daughter, Margaret, born about1949 in the same area. Balil, son of Berram, married Paula Groom and their children were Catherine, born 1966, in London and]eremy, born 1967, also in London. Margaret married Colon Wellard and they had a daughter, Hannah, born about 1971, and a son, John, born about 1974. They were born in Berkshire.

Balil Allsopp, son of Berta Ivor Allsopp, moved to Dunstable, Bedfordshire where all of his children were born. They were: Elizabeth J., born 1957, who married Glen Price and had two daughters, Bethany Sarah Anne, born 1984, in Luton, and Rebecca Elizabeth Lucy, born 1986, in Greenlothe; Rebecca H., born 1959, and married K. Snoudon and the children all born at Leeds were Jack William, born 1983, Kathy Elizabeth, born 1985, and Jenny, born 1987; Timothy J. born 1961; and David A., born in 1963, and married Sally Ross who had a son Owen William David, born in Luton in 1986.

John Forman Allsop - Liverpool, England

Born ca. 1815 in the Liverpool area, John married Elizabeth Evans in the middle 1830's. Family tradition indicates that John F. Allsop qualified as a master mariner and as such, he became Captain of a ship which worked out of Liverpool. Rumor has it that the ship was even used at times to transport slaves. Captain Allsop, according to other unconfirmed family tradition, was sailing his ship off of the coast of France north of Spain when a great storm caused the ship to sink in the Bay of Biscay and he drowned. A "Crimean War" jug became a family possession in the 1850's and was much treasured by several generations of the Allsop family. It disappeared along with some irreplaceable family photographs.

The known children of Captain John and Elizabeth Evans Allsop were John William, born 5 Oct. 1839, at Kirkdale, Liverpool and Ellen, baptized 25 June 1838, also at Kirkdale, Liverpool. John William Allsop was married twice, although the first wife is unknown at this time. His second marriage to Jane Price, daughter of a shoemaker, Robert Price, occurred on 12 Oct. 1881 at Liverpool. His three children were Thomas, Mary and Elizabeth. Research has yet to be completed on Thomas and Mary. Elizabeth, daughter of John William Allsop and wife, Jane Price, born 6 Nov. 1881 at Liverpool, was married on 22 June 1900 to Edward William Johnson, a woodcutter and machinist. Their first child was John Edward, born 1901, who served in the Navy where he died a diabetic with no issue. Ethel Johnson, born 4 Feb. 1903, second child of Elizabeth Allsop and husband Edward William Johnson had a granddaughter Eyvone Elizabeth O'Donald, born 1967, by their daughter Shirley and son-in-law, Alan O'Donald. Ethel's husband was Thomas Doyle.

Sidney Johnson, brother of Ethel and John Edward, was born 4 Apr. 1905, and married first Evelyn Mable Edgar by whom he had the following children: Dorothy, born 18 Feb. 1929; Edward William, born 6 July 1931;

and Joyce, born 6 Jan. 1937. Sidney married second Dorothy Worsfold August and a son, Peter, was born to this union on 8 July 1952.

Dorothy married first Brian Pugh and their issues were Steven, 1949, Edward W., 1950, and Reginald P., 1951. Secondly, Dorothy married William John Pritchard and had one daughter, Penelope Ann, 1966.

Edward William married Joan B. August by whom he had Terry Johnson, 1952, and Lorraine Johnson, 1954. He then married Julia B. Hall, and their only child was a son, Edward D. C. Johnson , 1964.

Joyce, the third child of Sidney and Evelyn, married Paul Orr and had children: Donald L., 1954; Paul Edward, 1955; David Phillip, 1960; and Christopher John, 1964. Peter, half-brother of Dorothy, Edward, and Joyce, married Erica and their children were Richard and Adam Johnson. Other children of Edward and Elizabeth Allsop Johnson were Percival James, born 1907, married Nellie and had children James, Elizabeth, Elaine, and Patricia; Evelyn who wed Charles O'Dowd and had no issue; William, born 6 May 1917, who married Anne Bolton and they were the parents of Reginald, William and Pauleen; Vera, born 1919, who married James Bell and their two children were Barbara and Vivian; Reginald, born 16 Jan. 1925, married Elizabeth Jones with issue being Linda and Valerie.

Percival and Nellie Johnson's daughter, Elizabeth married Joe Pankhurst and issue were Terry, John, Carol and Amanda. William "Billy" Johnson's son Reginald married Rose and known children were Annera and Paul. "Billy" Johnson's other son married Pauleen and his only daughter, Pauleen, married John Carrol, and their family consisted of Steven, David and Michael.

John Allsop - Birmingham, England

Very little is known about John Allsop (probably born near Birmingham ca. 1815) other than he was a silk weaver. John had a son named James Cornelius Allsop who was born in 1837 in Birmingham. James C. and Emma Perry were married 25 Dec. 1866. The marriage certificate lists Emma's age as 27. James' occupation was cattle dealer, and his address at the time of his marriage was Brearley St. in Birmingham. Thomas Allsopp, the first known son was born 26 Feb. 1861 at 20 Court Hospital Road,

Birmingham. This would indicate that Thomas was either a child of a previous marriage, or he was born prior to the actual marriage. Thomas seems to have been the first family member to use the double "P" in his surname. Thomas moved from Birmingham to Nottingham some time prior to his marriage to Priscilla Smith which occurred on 31 Dec. 1882. He and his wife were both age 21 at the time of the ceremony. Thomas was living on Davis street, and he described his occupation as laborer.

Thomas Alfred Allsopp was born to Thomas and Priscilla on 24 May 1883 at 20 Davis Street in Nottingham. Thomas A.and Lavinia Priestland Green were married on 26 Dec.1903, he age 21, and she 19. At the time of the wedding, Thomas lived at 11 Water Street and worked as a corporation clerk. The first child was born of this union on 7 June 1904 at 5 Crown Street in Nottingham. Thomas A. Allsopp died at the age of 70 in 1953. The first offspring of Thomas and Lavinia was Stanley Thomas Allsopp. He and Frances Irene Watts wed on 21 Nov. 1925 in Nottingham. Both husband and wife were 21 years of age and Stanley T. was living at 24 Hooton Street with the occupation of mechanical engineer. He died on 27 Oct. 1986, age 82.

The previous lineage is the direct ancestry of Maurice Brian Allsopp, born 10 Nov. 1934 in Nottingham. Maurice Brian and Margaret Holland were married on 20 Dec. 1958, and lived at 12A Dale Street, Ilkeston, Derbyshire. He was employed as a power station chargehand operator. They now live at 52 Carlton Road, Long Eaton, Nottingham. Their only son, John Nicholas Allsopp was born 13 Dec. 1961 and is single.

CHAPTER II

Allsops in Australia

(continued from Alsop's Tables, Vol. II, Chapter II, page 42)

THE CHILDREN OF MICHAEL AND ADA

1. Sarah Jane Allsop.
Sarah was born on 11. 4. 1874 at Anvil Creek, Greta. She never married and died from Tuberculosis at the age of 23 years. Sarah was buried at the Church of England Cemetery on 30. 3. 1898.

2. Arthur George Allsop.
Arthur was born at Westbrook, Singleton on 9. 11. 1875. At the age of 21, he had the great honour of being one of two New South Wales Light Horsemen to be chosen to represent Australia at Queen Victoria's Diamond jubilee. These men were chosen for their outstanding horsemanship. He returned from England, but went back to fight in the Boer War. After his return, he married Ethel Dennis at Singleton on 7. 6. 1915, and they had 3 children, David, Rowland and Lance. Arthur was a member of the Hunter River Lancers and died 30. 12. 1957.

3. Lucy Elizabeth Allsop.
Lucy was born at Westbrook, Singleton on 19. 4. 1878. As a young woman Lucy was a dressmaker, staying at the homes of people that wanted sewing

done. On 2. 7. 1902, she married Charles Beh at Singleton, and settled down to life on a farm, helping her husband with the dairy work. Lucy also grew all their own vegetables and took great delight in her flower garden and bush house. She had 3 children, Lucy, May and Charles. On Sundays she made time to continue teaching Sunday School, a job she enjoyed for many years. Lucy died on 20. 1. 1945.

4. Ada Ellen Allsop.
Ada was born on 23. 4. 1880 at Westbrook, Singleton. She worked as a cook on the property "Warramean", owned by Mr. P. Stacey. At the age of 38, Ada married John Keen and went to Gresford to live. She had 3 step-daughters. Ada died in Sydney on 23. 10. 1946.

5. Mary Louisa Allsop.
Mary was born at Westbrook, Singleton on 24. 10. 1882. She died at the age of 2 months on 27 .12. 1882 of Infantile Bronchitis.

6. Rowland Michael Allsop.
Rowland was born at Westbrook, Singleton on 14. 9. 1883. On 10. 9. 1913, he married Aileen Harris, and they had 1 child, Norma. Rowland worked for the Railways, and on 30. 10. 1918, he was involved in a fatal accident. "A coupling on an F waggon got jammed, and Allsop was attempting to attach it to an automatic coupling, using a hammer to release the jammed part.

According to Howard (Mr.), the train stopped, but the carriages bumped and Allsop was caught between the buffers." (Singleton Paper)

Daughters of Michael and Ada Allsop - l to r, Front Row: Sophia, Lucy; Back Row: Mabel, Ada, and Rhoda.

7. Rhoda Margaret Allsop.

Rhoda was born at Sedgefield, Singleton on 11. 10. 1886. She married Robert Crow at Singleton on 21. 4. 1909 and went to live at Scott's Flat, on a dairy farm. Rhoda helped her husband on the farm and had 3 children, Robert, Myra, and Myrtle. When her children were young she drove them to school in a sulky. Rhoda made all her own jams and pickles and was very interested in the local cricket. She died in Singleton on 4. 3. 1938.

8. Mabel Alice Allsop.

Mabel was born at Sedgefield, Singleton on 29. 5. 1889. She married Leonard Harris in a schoolroom at the local school in Singleton on 14. 2. 1911. They had 6 children, Una, Laurel, Iris, Russell, Donald, and Merton. Mabel died on 25. 8. 1965 at Bonalbo, but was buried at Lismore.

9. Amelia May Allsop.
Amelia was born at Sedgefield, Singleton on 3. 11. 1891. She died on 23. 11. 1891, at the age of 20 days, of Infantile Bronchitis.

10. Sophia Eliza Allsop.
Sophia was born at Westbrook, Singleton on 10. 10. 1893. She played the violin, and at the Theoretical Examinations held at Newcastle in 1911, she passed her theory exam with honours. Sophia worked as a housemaid for 27 or 28 years on the property "Warramean" owned by Mr. P. Stacey. During this time she was engaged to Mr. Wilfred (Jim) Leake, but he was killed during the First World War. Sophia died at Scott's Flat, Singleton on 9. 4. 1955.

11. Cyrus Clarence Allsop.
Cyrus was born at Sedgefield, Singleton on 17. 12. 1896. Early in life he changed the spelling of his surname from Allsop to Allsopp. The change was never made legally, but all his correspondence was spelt with the double "P". He enlisted in the lst Australian Imperial Force at Singleton, New South Wales on 23rd March, 1916. He served with the 9th Australian Training Battalion in England and 34th Australian Infantry Battalion in France and was twice wounded in action. Allsopp-Cyrus was issued with the British War Medal and the Victory Medal. After his discharge he married Florence McGrath on 31. 1. 1920 and they had 5 children, Francis, Alan, Donald, Gordon and Lola. Cyrus was employed by Mr. Vickery of "Bective Station", Tamworth, for 28 years. He died in Sydney on 9. 9. 1974.

Cyrus Clarence
Picture taken 20 Dec. 1918.

12. Myra May Allsop.
Myra was born at Glendon, Singleton on 11. 9. 1901, and died of croup and lung congestion at the age of 1 year and 3 months, on 23. 12. 1902.

ROBERT ROLAND ALLSOP AND ELIZABETH EVE IDSTEIN.

Robert Roland, the second son of Rowland and Jane Allsop, was born on 13. 3. 1852 at Williams River, near Maitland. At the time of his birth, Rowland was working as a labourer in Maitland.

Robert married Elizabeth Eve Idstein on 22. 2. 1876 at West Maitland. He spent the whole of his life in the Maitland district and served his apprenticeship as a cabinet maker with Mr. Robert Hyndes. He was employed by Mr. Hyndes firm until it relinquished business in the 1890's.

He then worked for the Maitland Brewing Co. and Tooth and Co. as a cellerman for the next 33 years.

Robert was one of the foundation members of the St. John's Branch of the A.H.C. Guild, also of the Holy Family Confraternity, and the records show practically an unbroken attendance during 40 years.

He took a keen interest in all things promoted for the good of the town and was an ardent supporter of all movements in connection with church matters.

Robert was associated with the old 4th Infantry Company of Volunteers, and was considered one of the best rifle shots in the district, and was awarded the long service medal.

Elizabeth has been described as a real homemaker. She made her own preserves, jams, butter, candles and beer and always helped with the suppers for local balls.

Robert died at the age of 73 years on 8. 12. 1925 of Diabetes Mellitus, and Elizabeth passed away on 22. 7. 1925 at the age of 77 years.

They had 8 children, 4 boys and 4 girls.

Robert Roland Allsop and wife
Elizabeth Eve Idstein Allsop.

THE CHILDREN OF ROBERT AND ELIZABETH

1. Elizabeth Ann Allsop.
Elizabeth was born on 3. 2. 1877 at Maitland. She was a school teacher, and on her retirement she was presented with a gold fountain pen and pencil and a crystal vase. Elizabeth never married and died on 19. 4. 1952. She is buried at the Campbell Hill Cemetery, Maitland.

2. Mary Genevieve Allsop
Mary was born at Maitland on 1. 1. 1879. She was a dress maker and used to sew for the "better off", staying at their homes whilst working for them. Mary took a keen interest in community life and was an active worker for the Roman Catholic Church. She was also a staunch supporter of the Campbell Hill Orphanage. Mary never married and died on 14. 5. 1930 in Maitland.

3. Alphonsus Charles Allsop.
Alphonsus was born in Maitland on 23. 2. 1881. He married Beryl Resleure on 16. 2. 1907 and they had 3 children Bernice, Yvonne and Richard. Alphonsus enlisted in the 1st Imperial Force at Sydney on 19th April 1918. He embarked for overseas service on HMAS "Medic" on 2. 11. 1918. Whilst on board ship he came down with Bubonic Plague. He recovered at the quarantine base on North Head. The troopship was recalled and disembarked again on 12. 12. 1918. He then caught pneumonia and suffered heart damage. He was discharged from the Army on 23. 12. 1918. Alphonsus was issued with the British War Medal. He died on 4. 7. 1920.

4. Catherine Lucy Allsop.
Catherine was born at Maitland on 18. 2. 1882, and was always known as Kitty. She was a lady of extraordinary beauty, engaged twice but never married. When her brothers established "Allsop Bros., Drapers and Mercers" in 1913, Catherine worked for them, running the "fancy side" of things. This included wools and knitting requirements, fancy work of all sorts, ladies underwear, gloves, buttons, etc. Catherine died on 30. 8. 1956 at Maitland.

5. Frederick John Joseph Allsop.
Frederick was born in Maitland on 5. 3. 1885. He was also very community minded and was president for both the St.Vincent de Paul Society and the Maitland Chamber of Commerce for many years. He was also on the committee for the Maitland Ambulance Service. Frederick was a "Justice of the Peace" from an early age. He was one of the founders of "Allsop Bros, Drapers and Mercers". Frederick married Monica Pogonoski on 3. 6. 1912, and had 4 girls, Joyce, Lorna, Aileen and Rita. He died on 12. 10. 1945.

6. Vincent James Allsop.
Vincent was born on 22. 7. 1887 in Maitland. He married Myra Bell, and whilst he was serving in France during the First World War, their only child was born. Vincent enlisted in the lst Australian Imperial Force at Newcastle on 16th March 1916. He served overseas in England and France with the 35th Australian Infantry Battalion. Vincent was killed in action in France on 29th May 1917. He was given the British War Medal and the Victory Medal. In a letter to Vincent's parents, Private Percy Nicholls wrote "We were camped in what is known as Ploegsteert Wood, just behind the third line of trenches, for a little over a week, and then we were ordered to take over the front line. It was here, a few nights after, where poor Vince met his death. He was killed by a shell outright, and so suffered no bodily pain. His body was laid to rest in a quiet little cemetery in Ploegsteert Wood. A neat little wooden cross was placed at the head, containing particulars."

7. Norbert Roland Allsop.
Norbert was born on 31. 3. 1889 at Maitland. He managed a department at "Grainger and Faulkiner" in Singleton in response to an invitation to take a position at "fifty shillings and start Saturday." He then worked for "Compton and Sheedy" in Maitland. After a little while he asked for a rise in wages and was told he had better find other employment if he thought he deserved better. So in 1913, he and his brother Frederick established "Allsop Bros, Drapers and Mercers." Norbert married Ann Atkinson and had 7 children, Kenneth, Marie, Shirley, Joan, Kathleen, Henry and Norbert. He died at Maitland on 14. 7. 1957.

Norbert Roland Allsop and son Henry Joseph Allsop. - 1931.

Norbert Roland and wife Ann Atkinson Allsop - Maitland, Australia - 1954.

8. Edith T. Allsop.
Edith was born on 27. 7. 1891 at Maitland. She helped keep the home with her mother and never married. In later years she did work with Catherine at "Allsop Bros." Edith died at the age of 70 on 31. 12. 1961.

DECENDANTS OF CYRUS CLARENCE AND FLORENCE MAY ALLSOPP

1. Francis Allsopp
Born 11-6-1919, Singleton, N.S.W., Australia, married Beryl Mcleod 31-3-1944 at Sydney, N.S.W. Their children were (a) Michael Mcleod, (b) Philip John, and (c) Frances Margaret.

a. Michael Mcleod
was born 14-5-1945 and married Elaine Jennifer Barrett on 8-11-1969.
Their four children were:

(1) Bradley Jason,	born 21-6-1971;
(2) Ashley Michael,	born 22-2-1973;
(3) Christopher Philip,	born 24-10-1977;
(4) Mari Anne Frances	born 9-10-1979.

b. Philip John
born 2-5-1959, at Sydney, N.S.W.

c. Frances Margaret
born 20-7-1961, at Sydney, N.S.W.

2. Alan Clarence Allsopp
born 8-11-1920, Singleton, N.S.W.,
married Evelyn May Poetschka, and they had one child.
a. Douglas was born 7-8-1948, and married Paula Frances Saunders.
Their two children were
(1) Brian Geoffery, born 14-9-1968, and
(2) Sonia Jacqueline, born 13-12-1971

3. Donald Allsopp

born 2-3-1922, Singleton, N.S.W.
died 2-1-1975, Newcastle, N.S.W.
Don was married three times
(1). Ida Clark (no family)
(2). Mary McGregor (one child) Adrian born 20-6-1952
and died 2-2-1972, and
(3). Doreen White (no family)

4. Gordon Allsopp

born 19-10-1926, Tamworth, N.S.W., married 13-3-1948, Aerial Millicent Goodman, who died 1-9-1969. Their three children are John, Cheryl & Mark.

(a) John Allsopp, born 10-6-1953, at Newcastle, N.S.W., married 8-6-1973, Elaine Elcin Bellingham, born Scunthorpe, England, no family.

(b) Cheryl Ann Allsopp, born 4-9-1955, at Newcastle, N.S.W., married 4-11.1972, Gordon Bruce Somerville, Tamworth, N.S.W., and their two children are
1. Justine Aerial, born 22-1-1975, Tamworth.
2. Jaimee-Lee, born 22-11-1976, at Tamworth.

(c) Mark Leonard Allsopp, born 31-5-1963, died 8-2-1983.

5. Lola Gwen Allsopp

born 9-5-1931, at Tamworth, N.S.W., married 11-8-1956, Edward Preston, St. Johns Church, Tamworth. Their three children are Terrance Lloyd, Wayne and Michael.
(1)Terrance Lloyd Preston was born 10-12-1957, at Tamworth, N.S.W., and married Julie Ann Di'Salvia, on 1-11-1980. Their children are Lucas Brent, born 29-11-1982, and Brett Marcus, born 19-8-1984.

(2)Wayne Preston was born 26-9-1962, and married 4-10-1986, Janelle Thompson at St. John's Church in Tamworth.
(3)Michael Preston, born 8-7-1965, Tamworth, N.S.W.

L to r Front Row: Gordon Allsopp, Len Goodman and Ted Preston. Back Row: Francis Allsopp, Wayne Preston, Bruce Somerville, Terry Preston and Michael Preston - 1986.

Joyce Allsop Byrne and Lola Allsopp Preston cut family reunion cake. Singleton - 30 Sept 1984.

Allsop-Allsopp family reunion held every two years at Singleton, New South Wales, Australia

Allsopp-Allsop Family Reunion-1984. Photo by E. J. (Ted) Allsopp

William Allsopp-Walsall, England

(continued from Alsop's Tables, Vol. II, Chapter II, pp 43-44)

From Doveridge, Edward and Amelia Cooper Allsopp moved to New Mills Farm which was located about three fifths of a mile along Wednesbury Road, Walsall. Edward was employed as a close plater, but the inhalation of acid fumes created a serious health problem. Edward Allsopp, Jr., son of Edward and Amelia learned to skate on the pool at the rear of New Mills Farm.

In 1893, Edward gave up his occupation as a plater and moved to the Delves Green Cottages where he eventually started a small dairy farm and sold milk in Walsall. He was allowed to graze his cattle on the Delves Green Common, having "Commoners Rights", to do so. The area of common land was 17-1/2 acres, and the right to use the area for grazing purposes was entrusted to the residents of the cottages. He retired from dairy farming about 1907, and bought the two cottages on Delves Green from the Charity Commissioners under the Hopkins Trust of 1681. The only drinking water supply for the cottages and the nearby church and school came from the well in Edward's garden. Rain water was collected off the properties for general use. House lighting was provided by candles or oil lamps and earth return sanitation was the method necessary to provide a healthful home environment.

Amelia Cooper Allsopp died in 1913, and was buried next to her daughter, Mary, who died in 1898. Edward Allsopp, Sr., died in 1925 and, under his will, he left one cottage to his son, Edward, Jr., and the other one to his daughter, Fanny.

Edward Allsopp, Jr., born 1868, married Hannah Bodley on 21 March 1896 at the Baptist Chapel Vicarage Walk, Walsall and began married life at 71 Highgate Terrace, Follyhouse Lane. Hannah, born 1863, was the daughter of James and Louise Bodley, one of the old established families of Walsall which is located between Birmingham and Wolverhampton. The two families had been neighbors at both New Mills Farm and at Delves Green Farm. It was at their first home that Edward's and Hannah's children were born. They were Edward (Teddy) who died at an early age, Thomas Cyril, born 1898, William, and Harold Sidney, born 3 January

1900. Next, the Allsopps moved to 174 West Bromwich Road and ca. 1904, went to Maw Green House.

Fanny Allsopp, sister of Edward, Jr., had married Frank Burton and also lived on West Bromwich Road. They had two daughters, Evelyn, born 21 March 1900, and Dorothy, born 16 April 1904. About 1912, they moved to the Delves Green Cottage next door to Fanny's father, Edward Allsop, Sr.

Edward, Jr., was taught the trade of saddletree making at a factory on Birmingham St. near St. Mathews Church. The saddletree is the framework on which riding saddles are formed, and it is necessary in order to assure that the saddle will fit properly on the horse's back. It is made with beechwood and reinforced with steelwork at the head and rear of the frame. After some time at the factory, Edward started his own business by opening a workshop at the rear of Caldmore Green. He employed several men to cut and carve the wood into the proper shape while he, himself, forged the metal into the appropriate form. When World War I started in 1914, work stopped for private saddles, and he closed the workshop down completely and sold his stock and tools in 1918.

In 1907, Edward assumed the ownership of his father's dairy cattle and kept them in the outbuildings at Maw Green. His sons each in turn helped in the farming activity, such as driving the cows back and forth between Maw Green and Delves Commons, which they recalled with fond memories.

William, eldest son of Edward and Hannah, was born about 1897, and worked at several jobs before moving back home and helping his father with the farm. After the war, jobs were almost non-existent, and many children in England who were unemployed had to be kept by their parents. Toward the end of 1923, "Bill" left his parents and moved to Victoria, Australia as the Maw Green Farm had been closed, and he was out of work again. He married and had two children and three grandchildren. Karen, one of his grandchildren visited her father's brother, Thomas Cyril Allsopp, in England in 1980, while touring Europe with friends. William died in Australia in 1985.

Thomas Cyril, son of Edward and Hannah, left school in 1912, and his father had him apprenticed to Walsall Electrical Manufacturing where he remained until 1935, except for his military service during 1914-18. He married Monica Price in 1922, and lived on Florence Street in Walsall. In 1924, they moved with their two sons, Stanley and Francis, to Cyril's parents' home as Monica was in poor health and his parents had a large house with plenty of room. Edward, Jr., inherited one of his father's Delves Green Cottages in 1925, and he and Hannah lived there until Edward's death in 1947. Hannah then went to live with Cyril until her death in 1950. Cyril moved from his parent's home at Maw Green Farm in November 1930 to 79 Willow Road which was near the Charlotte St. home of his wife's parents. When Cyril's son, Stanley, married in January 1948, he lived in the now very familiar Delves Green Cottage where his son, Martin was born in 1951. The cottage was finally condemned in 1959, forcing Stanley and family to move. The other son, Francis, married in 1947 and has five boys (two sets of twins), all of whom are married, and eight grandchildren.

Monica, wife of Cyril, died in October 1964, only a year after Cyril's retirement, and he remarried a family friend, Nellie Thursfield, in 1969. She died in 1984 after four years of poor health. Cyril is still living in Walsall, England, and is a valuable source of family history. He was contacted by Mrs. Beverly Kronk in January 1985, who is a great-great-granddaughter and descendant of his Uncle William in Bundaburg, Australia.

Harold Sidney Allsopp, the third son of Edward, Jr., and Hannah, served in the war and was seriously wounded in France from an exploding shell which showered his back with pieces of shrapnel. As he could not find work in England after the war, he immigrated to Australia in 1922, and lived, at first, in Melbourne where he found employment as a carpenter. Harold courted Winifred Minnie James who became pregnant and was banished from her home by the family. She and Harold sailed to Fremantle, Western Australia, near Perth after they were married in a church ceremony on 29 May 1925 at Dandenong, Victoria which was attended by some of her family. The baby was born in 1925, and died a few days later, unnamed.

A few years later Harold and Minnie were able to buy a ten acre farm outside Perth where they raised and sold vegetables, chicken and eggs. In this manner, along with an occasional supplementary job, the parents were able to care for six children through the depression years. Harold got a more permanent job with a large firm in Perth just before World War I began. However, he left this job to serve in the war effort as a cook and general helper in Western Australia. After returning to his job, he was given a position supervising the canvas department which made tents, water bags, canvas covers, etc. He retired from this job at age 65 and died eleven years later of a stroke. During his retirement years he utilized his artistic talents by making plaster casts of birds and animals suitable for wall decorations. His death occurred on 23 December 1976, and his wife died 3 Feb. 1979. Their children were: Myrtle Ellen, b. 23 Dec. 1926; Edward James, b. 23 March 1928; Donald Sydney, b. 11 July 1930; William Stanley, b. 6 Sept. 1932; Dorothy Eva, b. 18 Feb. 1935; and Reginald Cyril, b. 15 Dec. 1937.

Myrtle Ellen Allsopp, the oldest daughter of Harold and Minnie, married Joseph Frederick Starcevich, b. 20 Aug. 1926, on 14 Feb. 1948, and four children were born to them.

(1) Kevin John, b. 13 June 1949, married Wendy Joy Snook and had Michelle Leigh, b. 3 Dec. 1982, and Robert John, b. 30 June 1985.
(2) Colin Frederick, b. 8 Feb. 1952, married Andrea Joy Young, b. 2 Jan. 1957, and they were the parents of Diana Louise, b. 11 Dec. 1981, and Michael Joseph, b. 3 Apr.1987.
(3) Brian, b. 10]uly 1954, was united in marriage with Cynthia Yvonne Mouritz, and they were blessed with Craig Ashley, b. 21, Jan. 1978, Lauren Marie, b. l3 Oct. 1979, and Gary Benjamin, b. 11 Dec. 1982.
(4) Norma Ellen, b. 11 Aug.1956, wed Lino Sussa, b. 13 Aug. 1950, and they were divorced in 1988 with no issue.

Edward James Allsopp, oldest son of Harold and Minnie, was married to Eunice Lemon on 11 June 1955 at South Fremantle, Western Australia, and their children were Stephen James, b. 21 June 1959; Graeme Leslie, b. 4 June 1961; Wendy Louise, b. 16 Mar. 1964; and Rodney Allen, b. 27 June 1966. Stephen James Allsopp married Lorraine Longria at Inglewood, Western Australia on 28 Mar. 1981, and they had a son, David Graeme, born 17 April 1982, at Melbourne. Edward James died 14 Jan. 1984.

Donald Sydney Allsopp, issue of Harold and Minnie, born in Victoria Park, Western Australia and Sylvia Jean Counsel, b. 14 Jan. 1936 at Claremont, W.A., were wed on 16 Mar. 1955 at Cannington. Their children were Diane, b. 1955; Karen, b. 1957; Janet, b. 1959; Nan Lesley, b. 1964; and Trevor Don, b. 1969. Diane married Charles Cassey in 1977, and had Brandon 1978, Daniel 1980 and Simone 1985. Karen married 1980, Michaelle Gorman and their children were Michelle 1981, and Michael 1985. Janet Allsopp married James Cooke in 1981, and their two children were Jenson 1982, and Jayden 1984.

William Stanley Allsopp, born in 1932 to Harold and Minnie, married in 1956, Betty Colley and their five children, all born in Perth, were Gary John 1957, Judith Anne 1958, Christine Faye 1960, Nola Gaye 1962, and Kaylene 1964. There are no grandchildren yet.

Dorothy Eva, a daughter of Harold and Minnie, married 18 Feb. 1956, Bruce Graham Hayes who died 1 Mar. 1985, leaving daughters Kimberly 1956, Linda 1964, and a son Russell 1958. The children were all born in Subiaco, Western Australia. There are no grandchildren.

Reginald Cyril Allsopp, youngest child of Harold and Minnie, united in matrimony with Anna Maria Theresia Seitz on 3 Feb. 1962, and their children, all born in Perth, were Wayne Gregory 1962, Mark Warren 1964, Peter Dale 1966, and Darren John 1970. The only grandchild is James Edward, born 14 Sept. 1984, to Wayne Gregory and Tiria Hiri Allsopp, his wife, who was born in New Zealand.

William Allsopp, son of Edward, Sr., and Amelia Cooper Allsopp, arrived in Australia in 1885 from England and married 3 May 1888, Sarah Ann Arstall. Their children were William Edward, died 1964, Alice May, died 1966, Victor Thomas, died 1954, Daisy Amelia, died 1965, Violet Annie, died 1983, Harold, died 1983, and Myrtle Fanny. William died in 1940, and his wife, Sarah, died in 1935. Their great-great-granddaughter, Mrs. Beverly Kronk, is compiling a family history and has corresponded with Allsopp relatives in Walsall, England. Myrtle Ellen Allsopp Starcevich, daughter of Harold and Minnie is also researching the family history and submitted most of the information on the Walsall, England Allsopps and their descendants.

John Allsopp-Brampton, England
(continued from Alsop's Tables, Vol. II, Chapter II, page 52)

Now for the breakfast. The company had been seated for about ten minutes, when my dignified mother waved her hand and instantaneously did the massive folding doors fly open, presenting to the gazing gaping multitude a picture at once grand and magnificent, not fictitious but real. I allude delicately to the Breakfast Tables. The boards did groan and crack under the weight of the sumptuous viands. In the centre stood a broad round solid tower, pointing its snowcapped battlements towards the ceiling of the room conspicuously ornamented with a hundred weather cocks, in the shape of sugar baked pigeons. Mr. David Evans Senior, our paternal fount, was the first to perpetuate a wide mouthed breach, putting the rich inhabitants to the knife, many of whom were transported into foreign regions, many massacred on the spot. And here I must state that in this noble edifice, the plums were not few and far between; for suffice it to say that it was a glory to Shrewsbury and an honour to Mrs. Davis, though in both cases somewhat transient and let me add that in plum cake and poultry the county of Salop has from my own experience been seldom equaled, never excelled. This remark I beg you will repeat to my talented Aunt Mary with whom in contention of words, O'Connell can have no more contentions to compete than a rat with our dog Blucher. To enumerate the decoration of the dishes and the "Viandes Creuses" would be a vain attempt to increase in the first place the well-known judgment of my mother and in the second place the culinary fame of Miss Leach, the first showing mental, and the second, manual skill......

The Breakfast proceeded admirably, Mr. and Mrs. Alsop sitting together now, for the first time, man and wife. .... The substantials being removed, the most costly fruit suddenly and as if it were by magic, adorned the tables. Champagne flowed around, conversation grew brisk, spirits waxed. The scene became animated, every eye twinkling, every chin dimpling, every mouth uttering witty sayings, except when masticating bridal cake. While ever and anon was heard at the distance the merry shouts of the gladsome servants unanimously singing the wedding Hymn. ...... In the midst of this prolific flow of animal spirits, a smart but significant tap on the table declared itself the offspring of an important set of knuckles. An awful pause ensued. I cast my eyes around and I saw my hoary locked grandsire standing on his venerable legs. His speech was this verbatim: "Ladies and Gentlemen. As Patriarch of this happy family, will you allow me to propose a toast: May Heaven grant Health, Happiness and a prosperous longevity to the Bride and Bridegroom and to every member of their respective families. In some twenty five years, when I am no more, may the fathers and mothers of these united families live to propose a similar health to their descendants of the succeeding generations, and may all obtain Heaven at last."

The health of the happy two in hand were drunk with the most sincere delight, though as a faithful historian I feel it my duty to remark, that in my opinion they were not drunk with that loudness and distinction of voice which ought to characterize the reception of a wedding toast. Tom Alsop was the first to pronounce with a voice once sonorous and clear: - "Mrs. Alsop your very good health and happiness".

The scene now waxed highly animating, jokes a ratifiers, maccaroons and pears flying about as thick as pills when David is working the brazen machine at the rate of 500 boli per hour. ...... A decent interval of time having elapsed, the gaily apparelled bridegroom rose to return thanks and spoke nearly as follows: - "I thank you from the bottom of my heart for the honour you have done my dear wife and myself. Since you may perceive that my feelings will not allow me to make a speech, I must again assure you that we thank you most heartily and most sincerely". During this excellent and appropriate speech, the feelings of the speaker were deeply agitated. The remainder of the speeches went off equally well....... So much for the breakfast, which as it has occupied a long chapter it ought to give an impression of the exquisite handicraft of Miss Bessy Slack. In singing her praise, I must not act up to her name, for she proved herself as tight a body as the renowned Benjamin, Mr. Alsop's faithful servant, who on this memorable occasion, did in the roasting line, acquire immortal glory. I leave this subject with reluctance. However, I feel it my bounden duty to remark that the guests were worthy of the breakfast and the breakfast of the guests, for they did it ample justice, and by this observation I mean nothing more or less than both the guests and the breakfast were made of real, good stuff, though the former were of better stuff at their departure than at their arrival.

At half past one, the travelling carriage drew up at the gate. We bade them farewell in the hall, all of us tear-distilling. When I had seen the happy couple comfortably seated in the snug conveyance and had heard "All right!" accompanied by an important smack of the whip from the white-gloved post boy, then in due form, I took my worthy father's ancient slipper and raising it aloft over my head and exclaiming aloud with a stentorian voice "even as I throw this slipper over your devoted heads, so may happiness attend all your actions " projected it over the roof of the carriage. Immediately the nuptial pair drove off at a slashing rate drawn by a pair of slashing greys. The difference between the two gallant pairs being thus, that the yoke of leather took precedence of the yoke of matrimony, and the horse-groom of the Bridegroom. Now if my sentiments are of any value, I sum up the general opinion of the wedding thus: In grandeur of appearance it may have been surpassed often: in testiness of style, never: in good feeling, never. In conclusion, I must tell you, I am heartily proud and happy in my new relations, having eight brothers and ten sisters to rejoice in. And I request, you will, all of you join me in wishing Mr. and Mrs. Alsop an uninterrupted flow of good health and that unsullied happiness which alone is built on foundations of social concord and domestic harmony. .....

And now I come to the final conclusion of this now tiresome history, heartily wishing that you and your worthy husband had been present thereat, that you might have seen with eyes of reality what now you must see with the eye of fancy, a scene so charming, so captivating, and I request that having accepted my best affections, you will impart the same to my dear uncle. ..... Be assured that I remain what I was the moment after the matrimonial riband between you and your spouse had been tied.

Your ever affectionate and loving nephew,

(Thomas Sanders Evans)

(The Australian families will be continued in Alsop's Tables, Vol. IV.)

CHAPTER III

England to America

(continued from Alsop's Tables, Vol. II, page 74)

This led Othniel into a digression on the wickedness of foreign governments in allowing thousands to be slaughtered to gratify the avarice and ambition of a few, and so back to the more virtuous American government: "Tho' the Legislature endeavoured by the gentlest means to Convince these People of their egregious folly, yet when they found mild measures tended but to add Insolence to Delinquency, a number of Volunteers stepped forth in defence of the insulted Laws of their Country, and marched back to quell these mighty Champions of Sedition, who are now slinking away - as many as can." To another correspondent he explained that the rebellious folk in the neighborhood of Pittsburgh were "great folk for Whiskey, being principally Irish Settlers of the Lower Class, hence used more Whiskey than their neighbours."

Othniel admired the way Philadelphians turned out to fight a fire. He described the burning of the German Lutheran Church on Fourth Street, which he called the most elegant in the city. "As soon as the alarm is spread," he wrote, "all the bells are set to work, and the men turn out from all parts of the Town, with their Buckets, of which there are several in most Houses, and form themselves into double Rows from the Pumps to the engines, one Row passing along the full Buckets, which are then emptied and handed back by the other; as they are careful to keep their Ranks unbroken the Engines are supplied by this means in a very expeditious manner, but not so well as from the Fire Plugs of London." This was the second time he had acknowledged that London had something superior to Philadelphia. The first was just after his arrival, when he wrote that the country round about was not so pretty as in England.

But neither John nor Othniel ever had a moment's regret about leaving the old country. The summer's heat was not too hot, nor the winter's storms too cold; both men had better health than in England. In less than two years Othniel was investing money to import goods and making mild speculations in land, not to farm, but only to sell. The idea of farming in America had originally occurred to him, he explained to his friend William Marsden in 1795, because of a chance meeting in England with a couple going out to farm. As his business of staymaking was not very profitable, he and John had decided to go along. The farm scheme had fallen through on the ship, however, the couple proving disagreeable, and the woman, who was supposed to cook for them on board, being so useless that they had to cook for her. "Let me tell thee," he added, "I was egregiously deceived respecting Stay-making, which is a miserable poor business here - the Women having mostly left off the use of them. I think a Woman never looks so well as when fitted with Stays, yet I cannot but commend the disuse of them certainly they are very injurious to Health. I know I have frequently laced them up till the wearers could hardly move or breathe, yet still they must be made a little less to allow for stretching. "

Manners and customs in Pennsylvania he found much like those at home, yet some were queer to a stranger. "To see everybody Barefoot has a strange appearance...in the country shoes and stockings were only worn in the winter, even in Philadelphia boys and girls went barefoot and the girls without caps. " Those who came over, he wrote, must learn to go without supper. He recalled their very first invitation to tea. They ate sparingly, English-fashion, only to find later that this was also the evening meal, and they went hungry to bed. So they had learned to take cheese or hung-beef or fish with their tea, even though they didn't like it. But Othniel liked the shad, which were running up the Delaware even as he was writing and being caught by the thousands in the nets. "The use of Spirituous Liquors, formerly very prevalent, is on the Decline," he observed with approval. "The diabolic traffic in our fellow creatures the Africans is also much on the Decline," and societieswere being formed to help these unfortunates. But one American custom he could not approve. If a young man went calling at a house where there were girls, he noted, the old people presently went off to bed. The young man then moved over beside one of the girls and "the other girls, taking the hint, decamp." This was known as "sparking," and it was very popular.

Othniel's insistence on the superiority of everything American evidently cause some friends from the other side to tease him. So in the latter part of 1795, when he had been in America just two years, he admitted that there was some political trouble, though, as in the Whiskey Rebellion, he blamed it on the vulgar and the jealous. John Jay had just returned with the English Treaty. "The Sons of Anarchy began to predispose the public mind for what was to follow," he wrote. What followed was near-riots and the hanging of Jay in effigy with the Treaty round his neck. The rabble had objected to sending an envoy at all: after all, we had won the war; we should have demanded war damages from Great Britain, which was in no state to refuse. "Don't we talk big!" Othniel commented. The Senate deliberated the unpopular treaty in private. This, he remarked ironically, annoyed the "Sovereign People," who said that republics should have no secrets, that they should be able to follow every step of a debate and to protest, if they wanted, while it was in progress. At which point "a Senator, a furious Democrat, let the Cat out of the Bag, by furnishing a Printer with a copy" of the discussions, and the excitement became even more intense. This whole affair has a modern ring to it. But Othniel added that sane men thought the Treaty good on the whole; and then, as if afraid of showing his more conservative attitude, he went back to the European nations that were tearing each other to pieces.

There were few letters in 1796. Othniel spent part of that year on the road. At one time he traveled more than two hundred miles back into Pennsylvania, and in the winter he rode south on horseback as far as the new Federal City a building on the Potomac, and back through York and

Lancaster, "a tour of about 550 miles." He thus missed an intensely cold Philadelphia winter. "The Delaware was open the 22nd [of December]," he wrote, "but next morning people walked over the ice to the opposite City - loaded teams passed over and it had every appearance of a highroad . . . There were several taverns built on the ice." The ice had broken just before his return from the south.

He did not mention the specific reason for either trip, but it was undoubtedly business. John had become a "flour factor," and he himself was a partner in a firm importing dry goods and hardware. It was not the best time, he admitted, to go into trade, the French in retaliation for Jay's Treaty, "having come to the shameful resolution to seize all Vessels bound to or from English ports, in consequence of which many Americans have been already captured." If the French, he added, "make enemies of the Americans, they may do themselves more harm than they are aware of. . . it looks as if a rupture with France was highly probable." He would have more to say about the war the United States nearly got itself into with its late ally.

The same letter, dated March "1797, told of the retirement of George Washington as President, to be succeeded by John Adams. He was greatly moved to "observe the President of a great Nation, after holding the helm of Administration from the time when she first rose to Independence to her great prosperity, voluntarily to resign that honorable Post to return to private life"- which led him back to his favorite theme of wicked monarchs grasping after power and to "England, where even an Election for Representative of a petty Borough is attended with bloody noses and broken bones."

"When I contemplate this great Character [Washington] I cannot but wonder at the contrarieties which exist in Man. . . Is it not almost incredible that a Man whose general conduct has created universal admiration - who has firmly stood the undoubted Champion of Civil Liberty . whose prudent, humane, benevolent disposition has almost invariably been displayed . . . is it not astonishing that such a Man should nevertheless hold in abject slavery several hundreds of his fellow creatures? Yet such is the fact. . . . When I look at this, I am astonished indeed that Slavery should exist in such a country as this when the Constitution declares every Man free. . . The introduction of the Africans into this country has been - humanity aside – a highly impolitic measure, for besides the miserable condition to which this class of our fellow-men have been thereby reduced, the whites, living on the fruits of their labour have become habituated to idleness, thinking industry disgraceful since it puts them on a level with Negroes, thus they waste their time in gaming and reveling."

The Yellow Fever had broken out again, though far less virulently than in '93. Othniel remained in an almost deserted town; John took his young wife away, and his brother reported to him by letter, telling him about the closed shops, the scarcity of flour, the deaths of various friends. Most deaths occurred along Front Street or Water Street, or the mosquito-ridden, swampy southern districts, but it was to be a long time before any doctor suspected a connection.

By 1798 Othniel was certain there would be a war with France. "Ports and harbours are to be more strongly fortified, a number of Cannon founderies are now at work. . . the president to raise a standing army of 20,000. . voluntary associations forming with enthusiastic ardour . . . The old Veteran patriot Washington again steps from his solitude and accepts the command of the Armies of America. . . a number of Armed Vessels have been put in commission to protect our Coast" - and more to this effect in a most un-Quakerlike tone. "Thus France will find that instead of being able to divide and destroy here, as in most places where her arms have been carried, the great mass of people seeing thro' her. . . are ready to join in a great phalanx against her."

The Yellow Fever returned again this summer of '98. Othniel's letters are full of lists of the friends who died, the worst cases, as usual, around the docks. He himself came down with what was obviously a light attack. He almost gave up and sent for a physician, but fortunately did not, and so escaped the blistering, bloodletting, and physicking which were standard remedies for everything. He left for the country, taking the cat with him. In town the deaths ran from eighty to a hundred a day, and some enterprising burglar, taking advantage of the distracted state of things, broke into the Bank of Pennsylvania and stole $100,000. When the plague returned the following year, Othniel made no attempt to stay in town, but, taking all the yards goods out of his store, moved it and himself to Woodbury, New Jersey. He did not mention the cat.

In 1800 he described the building of the Water Works in Philadelphia: "Among other improvements going forward here at this time, a plan long since agitated for supplying the City generally with wholesome water, is carrying into effect with great spirit.

On an elevated spot near the banks of the Schuylkill, a steam engine is building, which is to throw water from a Basin so constructed at its entrance as to admit none of the tide water, into a brick culvert brought a considerable depth underground to a public square about half way between Schuylkill and Delaware, in the centre of which a handsome edifice is raised tho' not completed. This is intended to contain another steam engine to raise the water from the culvert to a Reservoir in the upper part of the Building, of sufficient elevation to force water through Pipes - constructed on the same principles and laid in the same manner as those in London - to all parts of the City, and to the tops of the Houses if wanted."

For the next four years Othniel's book contains more business than family letters - the finest flour was $5.75 a barrel; middlings and scrapings, $5.25; Russian sheeting, $18.00 a pair. Late in 1803 he came down with the Yellow Fever. But it was not so severe that year, and he was no doubt a little immunized by his previous illness. He recovered and gave the doctors the credit.

In 1806 Othniel married Hannah Brown; he was then in his mid-thirties. "Give me leave to introduce to you a new sister-in-law, even my Hannah," he wrote. "I would describe her but don't know how. Let me consider - just my own height – of perfect shape - handsome countenance - darkish Hair and Eyes - Disposition amiable - a careful, prudent housewife - and one of whom everybody speaks well. Her age, twenty-eight." Two years later he wrote: "I have found one whose value is above Rubies. We had a son about 12 months ago but he died without a Name. Many heavy losses in the mercantile firm. . . determined me to quit. I now keep a vinegar, wine and tea warehouse. My principal business is vinegar making; having a considerable business in that line and the prospect is flattering."

But the "flattering" prospect was illusory. There was a long gap in the correspondence. Finally, in 1809, Othniel explained it to his favorite sister Judith: "I daresay my beloved sister will readily recollect that I never was apt to trouble my friends with my complaints . . . when therefore I tell thee that by placing too much confidence in faithless men I became involved in losses . .but, thank God, the business I am now engaged in . . . is one I have not much doubt I shall get along [in] with Safety and Satisfaction." But Othniel was still not entirely out of trouble. It was the period of the Embargo and Non-Intercourse Acts. Foreign trade was suspended; there was no contact with England except by infrequent packet boats from New York. But in January 1812, "my children being put to bed," he settled down to renew the correspondence. Business had been so bad that he had called his creditors together and laid everything before them, expecting them to take over everything he owned. Instead, they accepted fifteen percent on the pound, payable in installments, taking his note and no security. Confining his business entirely to vinegar, he had met these and already had paid over $1000 on the balance.

By now he had three children, Rebecca, Robert, and George. "The name of my youngest I wish to be a memento to a man to whom I owe more than to any man on earth - George Morris, merchant of this city. He stepped forward as my friend when those I considered my best friends had withdrawn themselves. . . his purse and his credit have at all times been at my service. He is a Scotch man and a Presbyterian, I am an English man and a Quaker. Some would think two such characters would hardly come in contact . . . thou wishest to know how to direct thy future letters; Othniel Alsop, Philadelphia, is quite sufficient. I am well enough known to render any addition altogether superfluous." Business was apparently looking up.

Later in 1812 he wrote his brother Robert: "Our country and yours being now at war, conveyance for letters will no doubt become difficult." He went on to deplore the war, but this time for economic, not religious, reasons: "It was a maxim of the great Chatham that England ought to make it to the interest of America not to manufacture even a Horse Shoe Nail. How her statesmen could be induced to pursue a line of conduct so diametrically opposite is astonishing. . .it has been admitted in Parliament that in cottons we might possibly succeed to a certain extent, but as to woolens, it was utterly out of the question. .I shall mention some returns, under our Third Census. In- complete as they naturally are, it appears that Vermont contains 450,000 sheep, Massachusetts 399,182; Connecticut 400,000, Pennsylvania 466,918; to say nothing of other states."

So much was thought of the wool trade, he went on, that even when a man's goods were seized for debts, he was allowed to keep six sheep. "One man from Connecticut, Thomas Rotch, removed last summer to the state of Ohio with a flock of 300 merino sheep, intending to turn his attention exclusively to the raising of them." The war was obviously having a stimulating effect on American economic life. There were 530 cotton mills, he wrote, working 100,000 spindles, on an average spinning 400,000 to 500,000 pounds of yarn, enough to weave 18,000,000 yards of cotton cloth, three quarters of a yard wide - and this was independent of the cotton spun and woven in the homes! Othniel must have had a book of statistics before him. He went on: fulling mills, carding machines, gunpowder mills, forges, furnaces, saltpetre. He even had the figures on the number of straw bonnets. From Ohio alone 3,000,000 pounds of maple sugar, and of "ardent spirits" the prodigious quantity of 23,720,000 gallons yearly. America, he said, was amply able to provide for herself throughout any war.

He managed to get a few letters to England during the fighting; they went by way of New York and Lisbon. In the winter of 1813 he described a new type of epidemic, at first called spotted fever and later typhus, which struck suddenly, violently, and usually fatally. "Our physicians prescribe as much wine and ardent spirits as the patient can bear," he wrote Ann; "bleeding they esteem fatal" - which was the first ray of medical common sense. The epidemic at first left the towns alone and spread only in the country, but the following year Othniel caught it and was many months recovering.

For some months family news crowded out all other items- brother John's eight children and his own five; then, fairly quickly, the deaths of John's wife and his own beloved Hannah. Then John's death from dysentery, which also carried off his two youngest sons and very nearly killed two of his daughters. A more cheerful note appeared some years later when he made a sensible re-marriage with a widow, Sarah Waring, nee Coleman, who had come over from England in 1795 and belonged to Abington Meeting. This marriage, on March 14, 1824, came in time for her to help nurse his son Thomas through a long, mysterious illness with high fever and a swollen leg. Othniel wrote sadly that not all the bleeding, blistering, purging, and leeching had helped - evidence that the doctors were at it again!

In 1824 he noted the beginnings of the controversy which was to divide Philadelphia Quakerism for a century and a quarter. "Two years ago," he wrote sister Ann, Elias Hicks, preaching in Philadelphia, had "sowed the seeds of Briars and Thorns which have been producing a plentiful crop." To Othniel it was "notorious" that the Long Island minister had "long been labouring cunningly to undermine the foundations of Christian Faith . . . yet such is the infatuated attachment of a large number of members of our Society that the evidence of his unsoundness went for nothing." As the controversy went on to its sad and bitter climax, he could note with satisfaction that Philadelphia itself was "preserved for the Truth," but he had to record sorrowfully that the Hicksites claimed seven of the eleven Quarterly Meetings around the city. Abington in particular was a somewhat rowdy Hicksite stronghold: on one occasion the regular members were locked out of the meeting house and had to hold their meeting sitting on the grass under the trees. It was small consolation to Othniel to report in 1830 that Hicks had died after a stroke, for he had many disciples to carry on his teachings. Moreover, "an Italian Statuary" had actually exhumed the body and made a plaster cast of the face. Now, said Othniel bitterly, he supposed his image would be for sale.

Othniel had six more years to live, and they were peaceful ones. He rejoiced when brother Robert became a minister. The three sisters, who had never married, died, and he was sad as though he had seen them only the week before, though it was forty years since he had left England. Letters went regularly to Robert and to Robert's son and daughter, now married. They were quiet letters, those of an elderly man withdrawing more and more into his family, watching the children grow up, learn a business, marry, and start a new generation.

Life was orderly now, peaceful, and at last secure.

(Thus ends the review of Othniel's Letter Book.)

Othniel became a naturalized citizen of the United States on 22 June 1798, and his brother Ruhamah John on 17 June 1799. Othniel married Hannah Brown, daughter of Samuel and Rebecca Brown of Philadelphia on 9 January 1806, and their children wereRebecca, born 1808; Robert, born 1809; George Morris, born 1810; Samuel, born 1813; and Thomas, born 1815.

Ruhamah John Alsop married Elizabeth (maiden name unknown) in 1797, and their issue were Leah, Rachel, Mary, William Jeanes, Jacob, John, and Elizabeth. Elizabeth, wife of John died 25 October 1818, age 47, and their son, John Jr., died 2 August 1821, age 8. Another son, Jacob, died the same week, while Ruhamah John died 19 August 1821, the last three of dysentery. Elizabeth, daughter of Ruhamah John and Elizabeth Alsop, married on 6 June 1839, Samuel Allinson, Jr., son of James and Bernice, of Mercer Co., New Jersey at Mulberry St. Meeting, Philadelphia. Her brother (the only son of Ruhamah John and Elizabeth who lived to adulthood) William J., married Amy Eastlock on 20 August 1846 at Haddonfield, Gloucester County, New Jersey. Othniel Alsop died in 1836, and his will is recorded in the Wills and Administrative Records of Philadelphia, File 218, Will Book 12, Page 306.

(The next five pages will contain an exact reproduction of the will of Othniel Alsop as copied from the Wills and Administrative Records of Philadelphia).

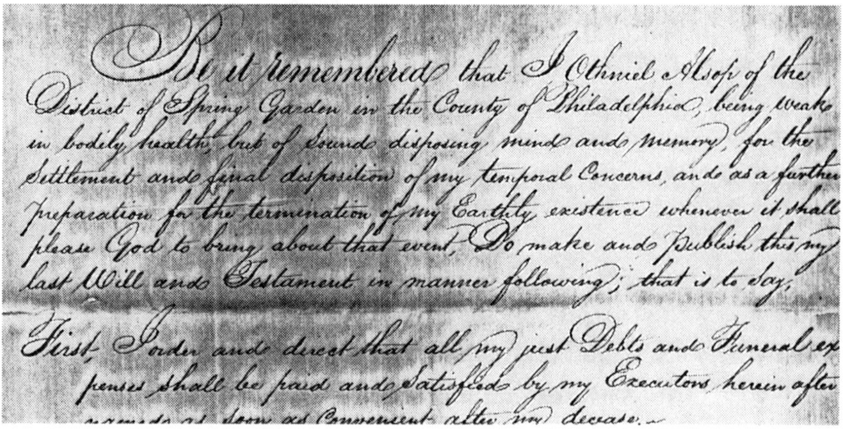

Be it remembered that I Othniel Alsop of the District of Spring Garden in the County of Philadelphia, being weak in bodily health, but of sound disposing mind and memory, for the Settlement and final disposition of my temporal Concerns, and as a further preparation for the termination of my Earthly existence whenever it shall please God to bring about that event, Do make and publish this my last Will and Testament in manner following; that is to say,

First, I order and direct that all my just Debts and Funeral expenses shall be paid and Satisfied by my Executors herein after named as soon as Convenient after my decease.—

Whereas my beloved Wife Sarah (whose Estate at the time of our marriage was principally conveyed to Certain Trustees in Trust for her sole and separate Use and Benefit,) did sell and dispose of her Household and Kitchen Furniture and Utensils, Beds, Bedding &c. the Proceeds whereof were received by me and appropriated to the general Uses of myself and family; Therefore

Item, I give and bequeath to my said beloved Wife all my Beds, Bedding, Household and Kitchen furniture and Utensils of every description now in my Dwelling House, not herein otherwise particularly bequeathed and disposed of. — It is also my will and desire that she my said Wife shall have the Use of the few Articles of Silver ware and plate herein after bequeathed to my daughter Hannah, so long as she, for her own Convenience, may desire. —

Item, I give and bequeath to my Son George M. Alsop my Silver Watch. —

Item, I give and bequeath to my Daughter Hannah Alsop all my Silver Ware and Plate, Subject nevertheless to the Use thereof by my beloved wife as above expressed. —

Such of my Books, Papers and Personal effects other than the Household Furniture &c. herein before bequeathed, which my Children may desire to keep, it is my Will that they shall be permitted to do so by making such equitable division and distribution thereof among themselves as may be mutually satisfactory and agreeable to them. —

All my Real Estate and all the Residue of my personal Estate not

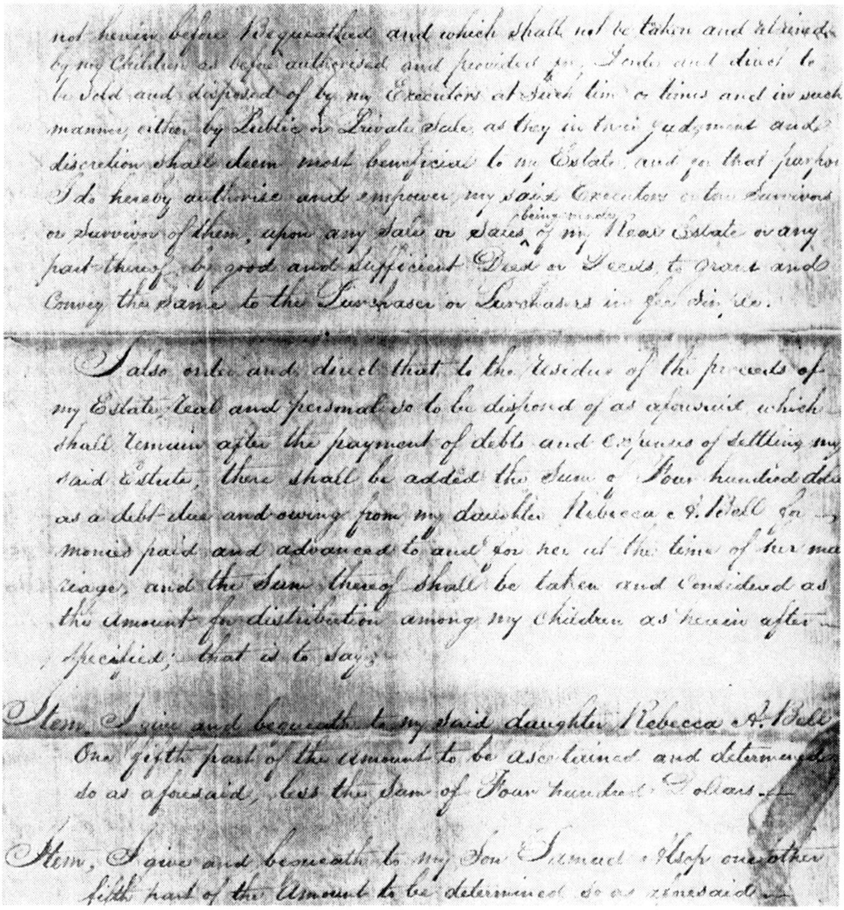
not herein before bequeathed and which shall not be taken and received by my Children as before authorised and provided for, I order and direct to be sold and disposed of by my Executors at such time or times and in such manner, either by Public or Private Sale as they in their judgment and discretion shall deem most beneficial to my Estate, and for that purpose I do hereby authorise and empower my said Executors or the Survivors or Survivor of them, upon any Sale or Sales being made of my Real Estate or any part thereof, by good and sufficient Deed or Deeds to grant and Convey the same to the Purchaser or Purchasers in fee sim, &c.

I also order and direct that to the residue of the proceeds of my Estate real and personal so to be disposed of as aforesaid which shall remain after the payment of debts and expenses of settling my said Estate, there shall be added the sum of Four hundred Dollars as a debt due and owing from my daughter Rebecca A. Bell for monies paid and advanced to and for her at the time of her marriage, and the sum thereof shall be taken and considered as the amount for distribution among my Children as herein after specified, that is to say;

Item. I give and bequeath to my said daughter Rebecca A. Bell One fifth part of the amount to be ascertained and determined so as aforesaid, less the sum of Four hundred Dollars.

Item, I give and bequeath to my Son Samuel Alsop one other fifth part of the amount to be determined so as aforesaid.

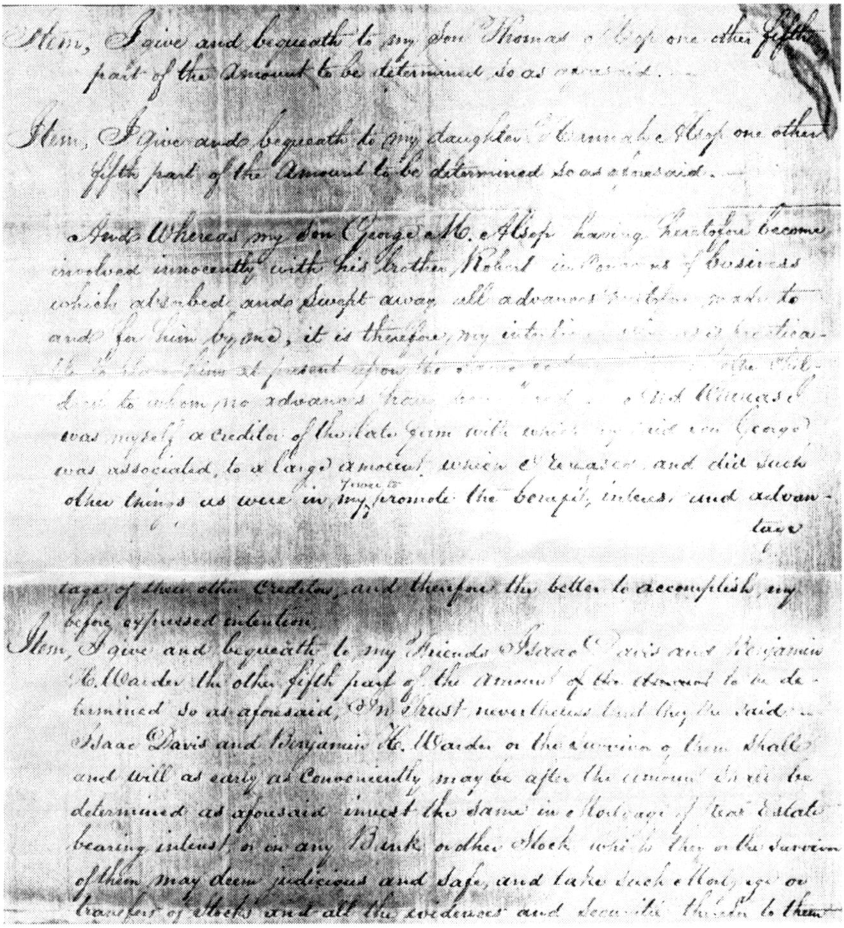

Item, I give and bequeath to my Son Thomas Alsop one other fifth part of the Amount to be determined so as aforesaid. —

Item, I give and bequeath to my daughter [illegible] Alsop one other fifth part of the Amount to be determined so as aforesaid. —

And Whereas my Son George M. Alsop having heretofore become involved innocently with his brother, Robert in [illegible] of Business which absorbed and swept away all advances [illegible] made to and for him by me, it is therefore my intention [illegible] practicable to [illegible] him at present upon the [illegible] the Children to whom no advances have been [illegible] I was myself a Creditor of the late firm with which my said son George was associated, to a large amount, which I [illegible] and did such other things as were in my power to promote the benefit, interest and advantage

tage of their other Creditors, and therefore the better to accomplish my before expressed intention

Item, I give and bequeath to my Friends Isaac Davis and Benjamin H. Warder the other fifth part of the Amount of the Amount to be determined so as aforesaid, In Trust nevertheless that they the said Isaac Davis and Benjamin H. Warder or the survivor of them shall and will as early as Conveniently may be after the amount [illegible] be determined as aforesaid invest the same in Mortgage of Real Estate bearing interest or in any Bank or other Stock which they or the survivor of them may deem judicious and safe, and take such Mortgage or transfer of Stocks and all the evidences and securities thereof to them

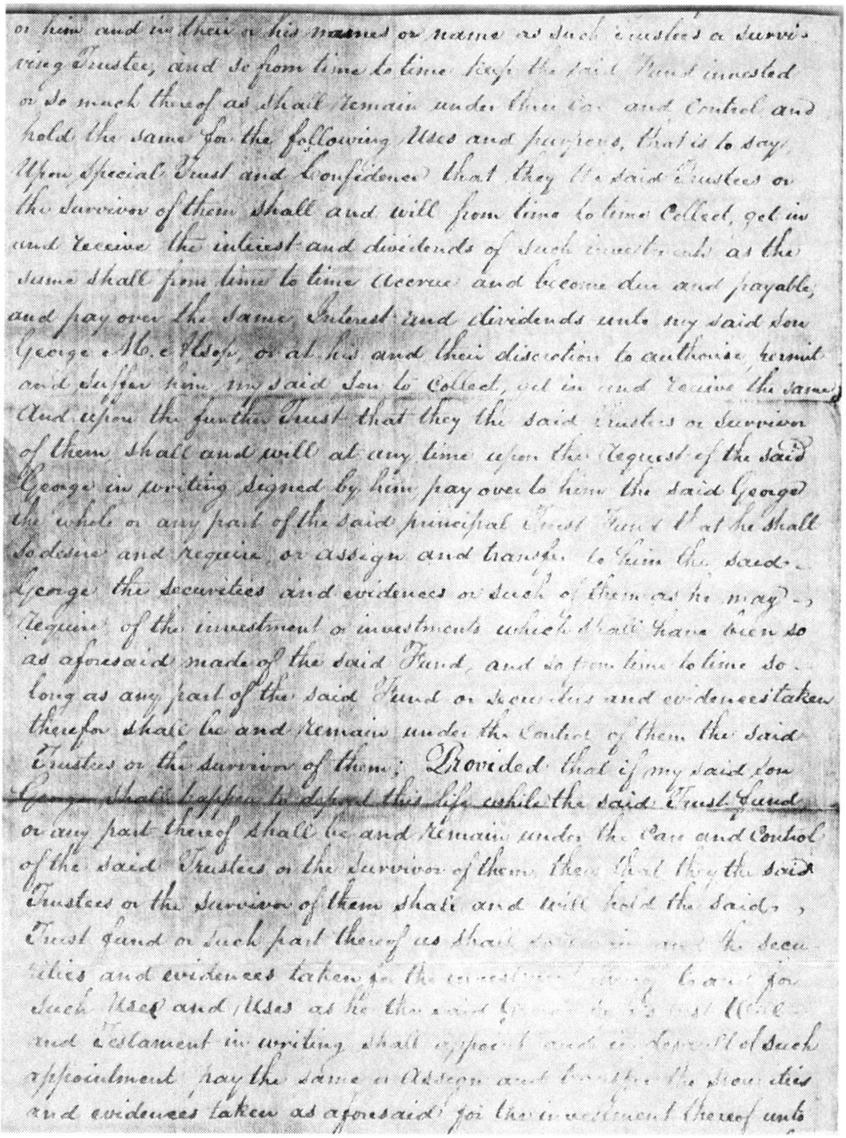

or him and in their or his names or name as such Trustees or Survi-
ving Trustee, and so from time to time keep the said Fund invested
or so much thereof as shall remain under their Care and Control and
hold the same for the following Uses and purposes, that is to say,
Upon Special Trust and Confidence that they the said Trustees or
the Survivor of them shall and will from time to time Collect, get in
and receive the interest and dividends of such investments as the
same shall from time to time accrue and become due and payable,
and pay over the same Interest and dividends unto my said Son
George M. Alsop, or at his and their discretion to authorise, permit
and suffer him my said Son to Collect, get in and receive the same
And upon the further Trust that they the said Trustees or Survivor
of them shall and will at any time upon the request of the said
George in writing signed by him pay over to him the said George
the whole or any part of the said principal Trust Fund that he shall
so desire and require, or assign and transfer to him the said
George the securities and evidences or such of them as he may
require of the investment or investments which shall have been so
as aforesaid made of the said Fund, and so from time to time so
long as any part of the said Fund or securities and evidences taken
therefor shall be and remain under the Control of them the said
Trustees or the survivor of them; Provided that if my said Son
George shall happen to depart this life while the said Trust Fund
or any part thereof shall be and remain under the Care and Control
of the said Trustees or the Survivor of them then that they the said
Trustees or the Survivor of them shall and will hold the said
Trust Fund or such part thereof as shall remain and the secu-
rities and evidences taken for the investment thereof to and for
such Uses and Uses as he the said George by his last Will
and testament in writing shall appoint and in default of such
appointment pay the same or assign and transfer the securities
and evidences taken as aforesaid for the investment thereof unto

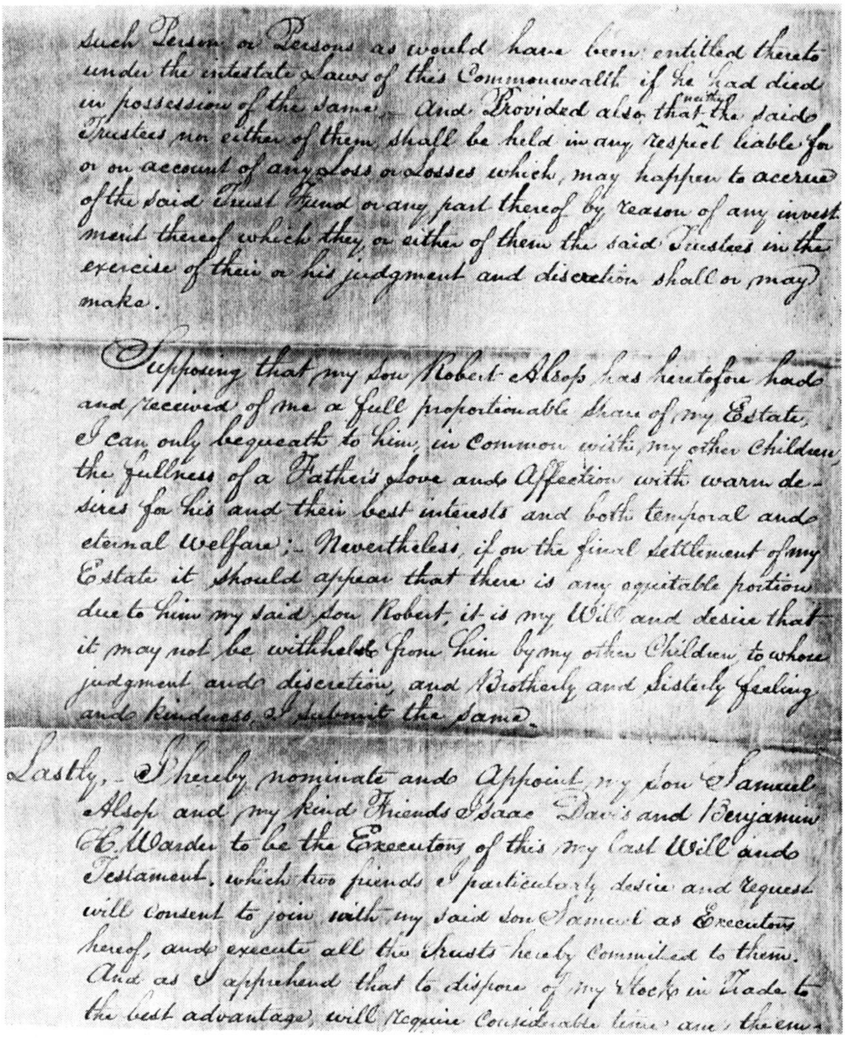

such Person or Persons as would have been entitled thereto under the intestate Laws of this Commonwealth if he had died in possession of the same. - And Provided also that neither the said Trustees nor either of them shall be held in any respect liable for or on account of any Loss or Losses which may happen to accrue of the said Trust Fund or any part thereof by reason of any investment thereof which they or either of them the said Trustees in the exercise of their or his judgment and discretion shall or may make.

Supposing that my Son Robert Alsop has heretofore had and received of me a full proportionable Share of my Estate, I can only bequeath to him, in Common with my other Children, the fullness of a Father's Love and Affection with warm desires for his and their best interests and both temporal and eternal Welfare; - Nevertheless, if on the final Settlement of my Estate it should appear that there is any equitable portion due to him my said Son Robert, it is my Will and desire that it may not be withheld from him by my other Children, to whose judgment and discretion, and Brotherly and Sisterly feeling and kindness, I submit the same.

Lastly, - I hereby nominate and Appoint my Son Samuel Alsop and my kind Friends Isaac Davis and Benjamin H. Warder to be the Executors of this my last Will and Testament, which two friends I particularly desire and request will consent to join with my said Son Samuel as Executors hereof, and execute all the trusts hereby committed to them. And as I apprehend that to dispose of my Stocks in Trade to the best advantage, will require considerable time and the employment of some Competent Person as an agent to attend to the same, if my said Executors shall be of the like judgment I hereby recommend their appointment of my aforesaid Son George M. Alsop for that purpose, who I believe is well acquainted with my business and is altogether Competent for the purpose; — And if they my said Executors shall see proper so to appoint and employ my said Son George as their agent it is my Will that they the said Executors shall not be held liable personally or otherwise for any act of him my said Son with respect to said business or the disposal of said Property, not authorized by them. —

In Witness whereof I, Othniel Alsop the Testator aforesaid

aforesaid have hereunto set my Hand and Seal this Sixth day of the Twelfth Month in the Year of Our Lord one thousand eight hundred and thirty six..

Signed, Sealed, pronounced and declared by the said Testator as and for last Will and Testament in the presence of Us who at his request and in his presence have respectively subscribed our names as Witnesses thereto — there being two interlineations first made upon the 2d page thereof, and one interlineation upon the fourth page. —

Othniel Alsop

Thomas Williamson

Elihu Pickering

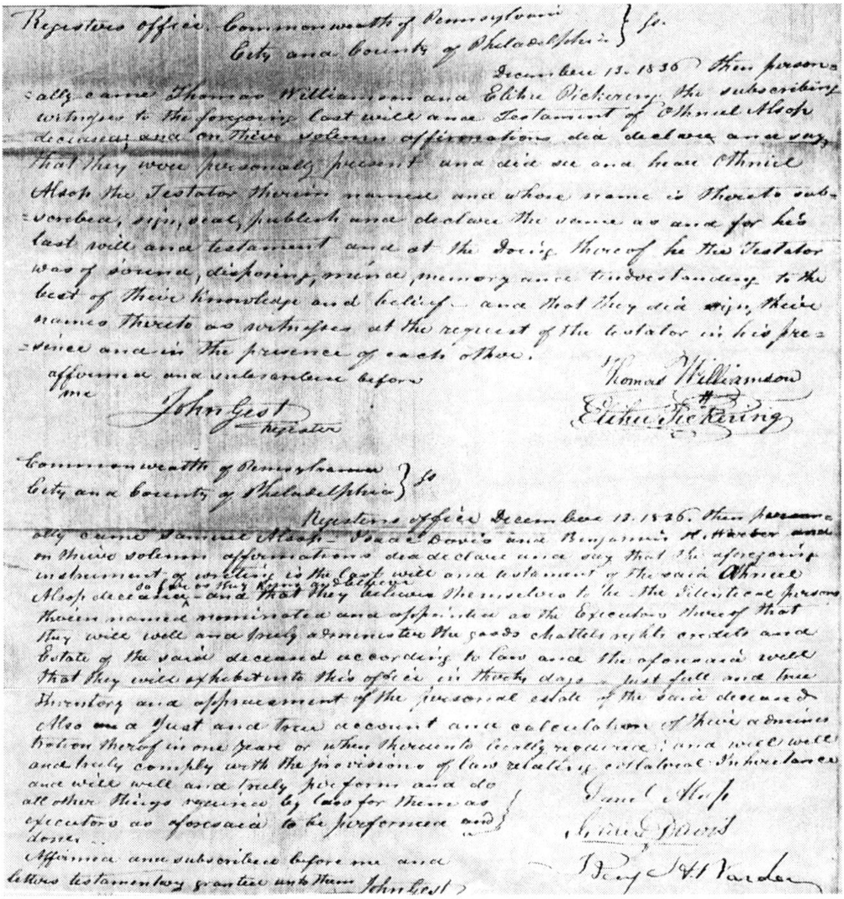

Registers office. Commonwealth of Pennsylvania } ss.
City and County of Philadelphia
December 13. 1836 Then personally came Thomas Williamson and Elihu Pickering the subscribing witnesses to the foregoing last will and Testament of Othniel Alsop deceased and on their solemn affirmation did declare and say that they were personally present and did see and hear Othniel Alsop the Testator therein named and whose name is thereto subscribed, sign, seal, publish and declare the same as and for his last will and testament and at the doing thereof he the Testator was of sound, disposing mind, memory and understanding to the best of their knowledge and belief and that they did sign their names thereto as witnesses at the request of the testator in his presence and in the presence of each other.
affirmed and subscribed before me
John Gest Register
Thomas Williamson
Elihu Pickering

Commonwealth of Pennsylvania } ss
City and County of Philadelphia
Registers office December 13. 1836. Then personally came Samuel Alsop Isaac Davis and Benjamin H. Warder and on their solemn affirmations did declare and say that the aforegoing instrument of writing is the last will and testament of the said Othniel Alsop deceased so far as they know and believe and that they believe themselves to be the Identical persons therein named nominated and appointed as the Executors thereof that they will well and truly administer the goods chattels rights credits and Estate of the said deceased according to law and the aforesaid will that they will exhibit into this office in thirty days a just full and true Inventory and appraisement of the personal estate of the said deceased Also a just and true account and calculation of their administration thereof in one year or when thereunto lawfully required; and will well and truly comply with the provisions of law relating to collateral Inheritances and will well and truly perform and do all other things required by law for them as executors as aforesaid to be performed and done.
Affirmed and subscribed before me and letters testamentary granted unto them John Gest
Saml Alsop
Isaac Davis
Benj H Warder

George Morris Alsop, son of Othniel and Hannah Brown Alsop, grew up in Philadelphia where he was active in the Society of Friends (Quakers), as he was a member of the Philadelphia Monthly Meeting, Northern District, for many years, and he was a member of Burlington Monthly Meeting of New Jersey from 1827 to 1832. In 1850, George was living with his wife, Elizabeth, in the South Mulberry Ward of Philadelphia,and his occupation was that of a manufacturer. He is not known to have had issue, and he died 11 January 1877 at the age of 66.

Thomas, the youngest son of Othniel and Hannah, lived his earlier years in Philadelphia, where he learned the trade of watchmaking. He married his first wife ca. 1839, and their two sons, Edwin and Henry were born in 1841 and 1843 respectively. Thomas' wife, (name probably Margaret), died not long after the birth of their second son, Henry, who was born in Illinois. In 1850, Thomas and family were back living in Philadelphia before moving to Springfield, Ill. some time prior to 1860. There he met and married on 9 February 1860, Jane Hopkins, who was born in Ireland ca. 1830, and who after emigrating to the U.S. earned her livelihood as a milliner.

Edwin, the eldest son, was living near his father and stepmother in the home of a Springfield merchant who had employed him as a clerk in his store during the year of 1860. Edwin Alsop joined the 72nd Infantry, Co. F., from Sangamon Co., Ill., as a Union soldier and died during the war. In 1881, a Soldier's Monument was erected in the north west corner of Oak Ridge Cemetery to honor the 40 Union soldiers who were killed in the Civil War. Edwin Alsop is one of the names inscribed on the monument dedicated to those brave men from Sangamon County.

Thomas and his wife, Jane Hopkins Alsop, moved during the early 1860's from Springfield to Elkhart, Ill. located in Logan Co. about 20 miles northwest of their Sangamon Co. residence. On 18 October 1860, Logan Co. Deed Book MSS 1, pages 108-9, William and Thomas Allsop sold property to W.G. Whitney. William was probably the first cousin of Thomas and son of Ruhamah John, brother of Othniel. The court records also show that William Allsup obtained property from W.F. Enders and Co. on 39 June 1860, (Book "W", page 511); from Jabez Capp on 5 July 1860, (MSS 1, page 108); and from Jabez Capp on 26 December 1860, (Book "Y", page 48). Book "G", page 496 contains the sale of property from Thomas Alsop to Charles Elwood in Logan Co., dated 17 May 1860, and on 6 December 1864 in Book "J", page 112, Thomas is recorded as selling property to Edward Rigney. During this same year, Thomas Alsop held a warranty deed from Edward Rigney as found in Book 32, page 289, of the Logan County Court Records. Gilbert Updyke and Co. authorized Thomas Alsop the power of attorney on 30 July 1867, and it was duly recorded in the county records in Book "L", page 53. Thomas also held a warranty deed from Addison Hickox, 17 October 1875, Book 32, Page 288.

Thomas was living in Logan Co., Ill. in January 1863, as proven by the fact that he was chosen Captain of a company of soldiers in Logan Co. called Middletown Company or Captain Alsop's Company. Thomas, obviously from an educated background, became a township supervisor in Hurlburt Township, Elkhart, Logan Co., Ill., as he was elected a justice in 1867, 1869, 1870, 1874, and 1877; in 1869, a collector; and in 1875, 1878, and 1879, a clerk.

The census report of 1870 for Logan Co. Ill. locates Thomas and Jane in Elkhart City with his occupation listed as owner of a mill. His real estate was valued at $16,000 and his personal wealth was given as $1,000. Thomas died in 1896, and is buried at Elkhart Cemetery which is located in the south west corner of Logan Co. In 1900, Jane, wife of Thomas, was boarding in Lincoln, Ill. in the house of Julia Hanger. She was living in Lincoln in 1910 in the household of Charlotte Bockhams, but the date of her death has yet to be determined.

Henry Alsop, the younger son of Thomas, enrolled at Springfield, Ill. on the 25th day of April 1861 in the Union Army as a private in Company "I", 7th Regt. Volunteer Infantry, and was honorably discharged at Mound City, Ill. on 25 July of that same year. He had been born on 2 October 1843 in Springfield. He rejoined the Union Army for the duration of the war, this time enrolling on 25 November 1861 in Co. "G", l0th Ill. Regt. Volunteer Infantry where he served as a clerk while attaining the rank of sergeant before being discharged on 13 January 1863. At time of his enlistment, Henry's personal description was given as follows: age 18, height 5' 7-1/2", complexion dark, hair black, and eyes brown.

In October 1862, while on duty at Old Town Landing, near Helena, Arkansas, Henry contracted swamp or malarial fever which resulted in malarial poisoning, and he was nearly dead when discharged. He was placed in a temporary hospital during October and November of 1862 in Helena and then transferred to Jefferson Barracks at St. Louis, Mo. in December where he remained until his release from military service.

On 18 July 1864, Louise Maria Fowler and Henry Alsop were married in Springfield, the ceremony being performed by Rev. H. C. Hubbard, M.G., in the Baptist parsonage. Louise was born on 28 October 1847 at Yellowbud, Ohio.

Prior to his entry into the service, Henry was employed as a railroad brakeman. After the war, he moved to Elkhart City, Ill. in Logan Co. to work with his father, Thomas, who owned and operated a mill for grinding grain into flour. Their first child, Eddie, was born 23 October 1865, and died the next year of spinal meningitis at the age of eight months and twenty days (20 July 1866). Bertha May, born 22 September 1868, was the only other child born to this union.

Henry, Louise and Bertha lived in the Elkhart City community near the mill until they bought their own property from J.G. Taylor on 14 July 1873, as recorded in Deed Book 29, page 256 of Logan County records. He sold this property on 24 April 1875 to Samuel B. Hunter and purchased other real estate from Augusta Taylor as found in Deed Book 32, page 416.

Later that year, Henry for reasons unknown, parted company from his father and the milling business and moved to Chicago in Cook County. He was employed there by the Union Stockyards as a salesman and stockbroker. On 11 March 1897, Henry applied for an invalid pension claiming that he was partially disabled due to the health problems which occurred while he was in the military service. He described his health problems as piles, total loss of teeth, malaria, bronchitis, chronically sprained ankles, pleurisy and other throat and lung complications. On 8 June 1912, Henry applied for a full pension under the provisions of the Pension Act of May 11, 1912. He gave his address at 4137 Racine Ave. in Chicago and gave his pension number as 1055518. He was approved for the full pension of $38.00 per month until his death on 4 October 1919. Henry was living with his wife and widowed daughter at 4403 Indiana St. when a cerebral hemorrhage ended his life with arterio schlorosis as a contributory cause. He died at 9:45 P.M. with Dr. William C. Lepold in attendance and was buried in Oakwood Cemetery on 7 October 1919.

Louise applied for a widow's pension on 10 October 1919, and received $40.00 per month, pension 880556, until her death which occurred on

23 October 1929 at her home at 4063 Ellis Ave. in Chicago where she lived with her daughter Bertha Alsop Hilbourne. Death was attributed to pneumonia, nephritis, and myocarditis, and her physician, Dr. Thomas E. Griffiths, attended her during the final twenty days of her illness.

Bertha applied for reimbursement of expenses relating to the terminal illness and burial of her mother. She received funds from the Department of the Interior, Bureau of Pensions, which included the following:

Dr. Griffiths $35.00
Undertaker (O'San) $220.90
Chicago Nurses Assn. $ 5.00
Rev. George Drake $ 15.00
(For funeral services)
Medicine $10.00
Burial Clothes $ 10.00
Total $295.90

Samuel Alsop, born 1813, son of Othniel and Hannah Brown Alsop, married ca. 1839, Rachel Stewart Grissom, widow of David Grissom of Chester Co., Pa. She was born 1818 in New Jersey and lived in Philadelphia, Pa. with Samuel when their first two children, Samuel, Jr., and Rachel, were born. In 1850, Samuel and his family were living in New Castle Co., Delaware with the children's ages given as Samuel, 9, and Rachel, 5.

Samuel Alsop followed the profession of a school teacher, however, little else is known about him. Samuel, Jr., son of Samuel and Rachel was living in Chaffee Co., Buena Vista, Colorado on Cottonwood Avenue in 1880. He had relocated to Colorado after 1876 in order to participate in a mining operation as a mining superintendent. Living with him were his wife, Esther Kite, age 41, and his children, Mary Foster, 15, Susan K., 12, Rachel G., 12, Edmund S., 10, William Kite, 7, and Esther, 4. Samuel, Jr., also taught in college as a professor of engineering.

By 1900, Esther Kite Alsop was living in Manhattan, New York, at 405 W. 123rd. Street with her twin daughters, Rachel G. and Susan K., and her son, William Kite Alsop. Samuel, Jr., was probably dead by this time as he is missing from the family situation. Mary Foster, eldest daughter, married in 1886, Lloyd Balderston, PH.D., born Wilmington, Delaware, a leather chemist (professor of physics), and they were the parents of John L. Balderston, husband of Marion Balderston who wrote the article on Othniel Alsop. Esther, the youngest daughter of Samuel, Jr. and wife Esther Kite, married 1901, Channing Page Harris of Bridgeport, Connecticut. Susan Kite Alsop, one of the twin daughters married William Brown Bell in 1903. Edmund S.Alsop was found in Philadelphia, Pa. in 1900, living at 905 N. 41st St. with wife Bertha S., age 26 years, and a son Samuel, age 4 years. He was living in Porterville, Tulare Co., California in 1910, as a boarder in the home of Voluma Divinell.

William Kite Alsop, the youngest son of Samuel Alsop, Jr., and Esther K., was born in 1873 in Philadelphia, Pa. and lived in Colorado, New York, and Connecticut prior to establishing residence at Ridgeway, Pa. in 1910. He had married Jane M. (maiden name unknown) ca. 1901 in New York City, and their children were Elizabeth Billings, born 24 Nov. 1902 in New York, and William K., Jr., born 12 January 1907 in Connecticut. Also living with them were Lloyd Balderston, William's brother-in-law, and Lloyd's two daughters, Esther, 19, and Catherine C., 17. Additional information on this particular line of Alsops can be found in the "Encyclopedia of American Quaker Genealogy" by Hinshaw.

Robert, eldest son of Othniel and Hannah Brown Alsop, was born in Philadelphia in 1809, and chose the legal profession as his chief pursuit in life. He and Maria Fell were married in Philadelphia ca. 1830 and their children were Caroline, born 1830, Edward Brown, born 1835, and Reese Fell, born 1837. The death dates of Robert and his wife, Maria Fell Alsop, are not known. Also, no information has yet been found concerning the daughter Caroline.

Edward Brown Alsop, the first son of Robert and Maria Fell Alsop, was born in Philadelphia in May 1835, and decided as a very young man to make his permanent home in Pittsburgh. He went into business in association with C.G. Hussey who had established the firm of C.G. Hussey and Co., copper manufacturers. Alsop became the vice-president upon the organization of the Hussey-Burns Shovel Company. He later became a Director of the Exchange National Bank. Edward courted the daughter of his employer, C.G. Hussey, and he and Emma Hussey, born Feb. 1856, were married in Pittsburgh ca. 1885. In 1900, Edward and Emma were living at 5200 Central Ave. in Pittsburgh with their two sons, Harold P., born February 1889, and Edward H., born January 1892.

After the death of his wife, Edward moved to Washington, D. C. about 1907, and lived at 1502 Twentieth Street. Here the retired capitalist met and married on 15 Feb.1912, as his second wife, Effie Pope Hill, a telephone operator. The aged millionaire escorted the 20 year old Miss Hill for several months prior to their matrimonial union. They lived together only until April of that same year at which time he transferred practically all of his Pittsburgh property, valued at more than $3,000,000, to his two sons, Harold P. and Edward H. Alsop, then students at Harvard. This transfer was accomplished by a deed of trust which clearly stated that Mrs. Alsop was not to share in any of the estate.

In October, 1913, although they were not living together, Alsop went to her rescue when Effie was arrested because she did not have enough money to pay her taxi fare. They were divorced in 1915, Edward Alsop having initiated the divorce which charged desertion. In October, 1922, Effie Pope Alsop was taken to Bellevue Hospital in Washington, D.C. from her home at 51 West Forty-Seventh Street, suffering from acute alcoholism, and she remained there for several days. On 12 November 1922, Edward Brown Alsop, age 87, died in his residence on Twentieth St. His son, Edward H., died in 1966.

Reese Fell Alsop, youngest son of Robert and Maria Fell Alsop, was born in Richmond, Indiana on 17 November 1837. His parents, who were evidently living in this Indiana town temporarily while on a business trip, were born in Philadelphia, Pa. and lived most of their lives in this Pennsylvania metropolis. They moved back to Philadelphia by 1840, as proven by the Federal census record of that same year. Reese F. graduated from Philadelphia High School in 1855; he received his M.A. from Divinity School of Philadelphia in 1858; and Rev. Alsop obtained his D.D. from Kenyon College in 1860. He became an Episcopal clergyman by being appointed deacon in 1858, priest in 1861, and assistant at St. Phillip's

Church in Philadelphia from 1861-64. He was made rector of St. John's Church in Framingham, Mass. from 1864-66.

Mary Lee Spring and Reese F. Alsop were married in Pittsburgh, Pa. in 1866, she being a descendant of the Rev. Gardiner Spring, for whom Spring Street in Manhattan was named. Rev. Reese F. and his wife accepted the call to Christ Church in Rye, N. Y. in 1866, and remained there until 1875. The Bible of Peter Augustus Jay (1776-1843), son of the first chief justice of the United States, John Jay, now in the possession of Dr. John C. Jay of New York, lists the marriage of Peter Jay and Julia Post on 30 March 1869, as performed by Rev. R. F. Alsop. Their first son, Pierce Jay, born in Warwick, N. Y. on 4 May 1870, was baptized by Dr. Reese F. Alsop at Rye on 1 September 1870.

Reese F. Alsop served as rector at St. Andrew's Church, Pittsburgh from 1875-83 and at Grace Church, Philadelphia from 1884-86. He then accepted the position of rector at St.Ann's Church in Brooklyn, N.Y. where he remained from 1886-1909.

He and his wife Mary Lee Spring Alsop had a family of three daughters and a son, who were Gulielma Fell, born 1881; Reese Denny, born 1884; Mary O'Hara, born 1885; and E.T., born 1889. Mary Spring Alsop died in New York in 1897, and the following year on 26 April 1898, Dr. Alsop married Florence Righter, born May 1856 in Newark, N.J. In 1900, R.F. Alsop, his second wife and their four children were living at 127 Remsen St., Brooklyn, N. Y.

From 1890 to 1898, Dr. Alsop was named archdeacon of Brooklyn, and after he resigned as rector of St. Ann's in 1909 to make a trip around the world visiting missions in behalf of the Board of Missions, he was designated Rector Emeritus of St. Ann's Church and canon of Cathedral Garden City, L.I. He wrote Series I & II of the Episcopal Sunday School Lessons at his home at 96 Remsen St., Brooklyn, N. Y. Rev. R.F. Alsop was a member of the Republican party, belonged to the Hamilton Club of Brooklyn and was a Mason (KT). He died in New York on 17 October 1922, and his widow, Florence Righter Alsop died on the morning of 9 May 1930 at her home, 161 Henry Street, New York, age 74 years. No information is presently available on the youngest daughter E.T.

The first child of Dr. and Mrs. R. F. Alsop, Gulielma Fell Alsop, was born in Pittsburgh, Pa. where her father was an Episcopal clergyman. She attended Woman's Medical College in Philadelphia which was the first U.S. medical school for women, being established in 1850. After graduating from medical school, Gulielma served as a medical missionary in China from 1908-1917. She then returned to the United States and joined the faculty of Barnard College of New York, where she founded the medical department and headed it for 35 years.

From the book "A History of Barnard College" by Marian Churchhill White, graciously made available to me by Melissa Fisher, Admissions Associate at Barnard, are several paragraphs which detail Dr. Alsop's involvement in the school in which she devoted most of her life.

(Excerpts from "A History of Barnard College")

In 1915, however, the new building looked ample. In addition to the services already mentioned, it provided headquarters for the College's own doctor, whose appointment was a major step forward in a health program. From her little office on the second floor, Doctor Gulielma Alsop, herself an alumna, began to conduct a strong campaign against illness and ignorance. Her dark eyes snapped and her braids, pinned tightly around her small head, fairly quivered when she charged one of those twin enemies. She saw to it that her girls were aware, long before the general public, of vitamins and hormones. She had the brisk common sense to recognize psychiatry as a weapon, too, before it swept the country. For thirty years she worked with the physical education department, taught a hygiene course, doctored minor ailments, advised on major ones, and dispensed a world of humorous kindness along with her prescriptions of nasal sprays. The actual nasal spraying was, for fifteen of those years, in the competent Scottish hands of Nurse Jean Leischman, who was very fond of all her girls but who took no nonsense from them. (Pages 80-81)

Two of the required courses were physical education and hygiene. The need for good health never loomed larger than when both faculty and student body were exhausted by the epidemic of influenza which terrified the country in 1918. There were no deaths in the College family, but many showed the after effects for a long time. Both Doctor Alsop and Professor

Wayman hammered away at their doctrines of the necessity for sound routines of food and exercise. Gradually the students were trained to call at the doctor's office for what amounted to preventative medicine - the "safety first" calls. After 1926 Doctor Alsop gave up her private practice and devoted her full attention to the College. (Page 115)

Miss Weeks, Assistant to the Dean in charge of Social Affairs, was often consulted by students about problems which were not strictly academic, and so was Doctor Alsop, the College physician, who listened and advised on "all sorts of human perplexities and tragedies." (Page 130)

The administrative staff underwent a reorganization much more far-reaching than that of the Faculty or Trustees. In 1946 four important officers reached retirement age: one being Doctor Gulielma F. Alsop, '03, College Physician; (Page 172)

Dr. Alsop was the author of seven books which included a history of Woman's Medical College of Pennsylvania and an autobiography of her childhood in Pennsylvania. She died 26 January 1978 in White River Junction, Vermont.

(This family will be continued in Volume IV)

Chapter IV

Richard Alsop the Immigrant and His Descendants

(continued from Alsop's Tables, Vol. II, page 75)

Richard Alsop again met with the General Assembly on the 11th and 16th of October 1771. He was appointed by the General Assembly of Connecticut as one of the managers of the New Haven Lottery on 25 December 1772. Richard was elected to the Connecticut House of Representatives on 13 May 1773. He also met on 14 October 1773 with the General Assembly in New Haven.

Already known as Captain Alsop when he moved to Middletown in 1750, Richard helped to plan Christ Church. He and his future father-in-law, Joseph Wright, who came from Colchester, Connecticut and was from the same family as Orville and Wilbur Wright, recommended some swampy land on Green St. and served on the church committee which was responsible for having the land drained and surveyed in preparation for the building of the new church. Alsop, Wright, and other members of the building committee signed final papers in December 1754 to build the building.

Captain Richard Alsop became wealthy and successful due to his willingness to try new and innovative practices and adapt when the situation required it. His West Indies trade was very successful as well as his marine insurance program which insured the vessels of others.

Not only was Alsop a successful merchant, but he was very active in civic and patriotic affairs in his state. He was a charter member of St. John's Lodge # 2, A. F. and A. M. established February 1754. This was one of the earliest Masonic Lodges in the country.

About the time of his marriage in 1760, Captain Alsop donated an organ to Christ Episcopal Church which was the first known gift to the parish. The organ stayed in the church until about 1830 even though it had an engraving of the British Crown intertwined with a bishop's mitre on the front panel.

On 6 May 1768, Richard and his wife Mary pledged twenty pounds and ten pounds respectively toward the purchase of a glebe. Captain Alsop also served on a committee to help raise money to provide navigational aids on the Connecticut River.

He was named warden 11 April 1757, serving with Daniel Johonnot, and fulfilled this position until his death about twenty years later.

Richard Alsop and Mary Wright were married in Christ Episcopal Church by the Reverend Ichabod Camp. Years later, about 1785, Sarah Camp Thompson wrote a letter to her father, Ichabod, who was then at Kaskaskia, Illinois and mentioned that Mrs. Alsop, widow of Captain Alsop, had never remarried.

Both Captain and Mrs. Alsop were frequent benefactors of Berkeley Divinity School. Money became very scarce at Christ Church toward the end of the Revolutionary War and various methods were used to secure operating funds. In 1784 pews were rented and Mary Alsop obtained number two for her family and retained the same one for many years. The following year she donated an acre of land to help pay some debts incurred by the church.

John Alsop, brother of Richard, lived in Middletown during the Revolutionary War and was a firsthand witness to the partial destruction of the church bell by a group of ruffians. When he returned to New York, he had a new bell delivered to the church which was installed in 1786. This bell remained in Christ Church until a new church was built. Then the bell was removed and hung in the tower of the Church of the Holy Trinity where it rings today.

Richard and Mary Alsop's eldest daughter, Mary, was betrothed to Ichabod Wetmore, Jr., a fine young man of one of the affluent families of Middletown. Their wedding, which was to have taken place in the fall of 1785, was tragically interrupted by the unexpected death of young Wetmore in August of that year. The grief stricken Mary was compelled by the unforeseen circumstances to attend the burial services of her intended bridegroom. The young man was laid to rest in a burial site next to that of his mother, but when the Airline Railroad moved through the cemetery years later, the graves had to be relocated to the Indian Hill Cemetery.

Mary lived to be ninety-four years of age serving as an active member of the Ladies Missionary Society, and chose never to marry. She is buried, by personal request, next to Ichabod who had been interred the second time just west of the Alsop tomb, it being enclosed by and iron rod fence.

Mary, widow of Captain Richard Alsop, turned the family shipping and mercantile business over to her son, Joseph Wright Alsop, about 1790 and concentrated on civic, patriotic, and church interests. She was the first president of the Middletown Female Charitable Society, which met in the Dekoven House on lower Washington St. It was only the second organization of this type in the United States in the early 1800's. Mary's two unmarried daughters, Mary and Fanny, lived with her in the family home until her death at the age of 90 years. Her obituary described her as the mother-in-law of the editor of the New York Daily Advertiser.

The church of Holy Trinity of Middletown was the new church built to replace the Christ Episcopal Church in June 1843. Frances "Miss Fanny" Alsop, daughter of Captain Richard and Mary, remained active in the parish and at her death in 1845, a gift of eight hundred dollars was left to the church (Dr. Goodwin was the rector at the time).

Richard Alsop, Jr., the first child born to Captain and Mary Wright Alsop, spent most of his life in the pursuit of literary achievements, although he was a very capable businessman. He wrote a forty-eight page book entitled "A Journal Kept at Nootka Sound" from interviews with John Rodgers Jewitt who was the only survivor of the ship "Boston" which was captured by the Nootka Indians and held from 1803-1805. After the death of Richard, Jr., his widow Mary "Maria" married S. W. Dana, the mayor of Middletown. Maria Alsop Dana's second husband died, and she lived with her unmarried daughter, Frances Maria, until her death.

In the church records of Christ Episcopal of Middletown dated 27 November 1812, John and Joseph Wright Alsop, sons of Captain Richard and Mary, were mentioned as being vestrymen. Joseph and his wife, Lucy Whittlesey Alsop, have memorial windows located beneath the rose window on the east wall of the church of Holy Trinity.

Their son, Charles Richard, was an outstanding businessman who was also a church and civic leader. He was on the committee of Wardens and Parishioners of 6 April 1842, that accepted the resignation of the rector, Dr. Jarvis. He was also a vestryman for many years.

Charles and his family lived on Washington St. during the time that Charles was the mayor of Middletown, 1843-46. He was an active leader in the movement to bring the New Haven Railroad through Middletown by seeing that a number of bills were presented to the state assembly which paved the way for his dream to become a reality. The Airline Railroad was completed in 1862, three years before Charles died.

Joseph Wright Alsop, III, grandson of Joseph W. and Lucy Whittlesey Alsop, and son of J. W. Alsop, II, and wife Mary Oliver, was a veterinarian and served on several agricultural committees in the Connecticut State Legislature.

Dr. Alsop was elected a warden in 1873, but as he had been asked by the rector, Dr. Goodwin, to raise money for the building fund in 1870, he resigned in order to devote adequate time to the first project. He did more for the church in the areas of service and financial aid than probably any other member. Dr. Alsop was living with his wife and children at the corner of 81 Broad St. and College in 1875 when he declined election as a vestryman.

In 1877, Joseph W. Alsop, III, was due $ 540 in interest money which he generously donated to the church. Mary Oliver Alsop, wife of Dr. J. W., gave a gift of $1,000 to the church about the same time to pay off a rectory debt. On 2 April 1890, Dr. Alsop was elected junior warden but died unexpectedly a year later at the age of 53 years.

Miss Lucy C. Alsop, daughter of Charles Richard and Margaret Eleanor Armstrong Alsop, was also active in the Church of the Holy Trinity of Middletown, and records of 1897 show that the Helping Hand, a ladies church group met every Friday afternoon. The minutes of one particular meeting held at Miss Lucy C. Alsop's house on Lincoln St. indicated that: sewing plans were made for the following week; officers were elected; work was done on three napkins and some pillow cases; and a program was presented which included piano solos and duets, a piano and violin duet, readings, recitations, and a ghost story by Helen Russell.

The fourth Joseph Wright Alsop bought 600 acres of farm land about twenty-five miles northwest of Middletown in 1902 at the age of twenty-six, and seven years later made it a permanent home. He brought with him, his new bride, Corrine Roosevelt Douglas Robinson, the niece of Theodore Roosevelt. The house was a rambling, two-story, clapboard farmhouse on a muddy back road near the small town of Avon.

The Alsops started their family; made efforts to fit into the community of rather cautious, uncommunicative townsfolk; filled the long, long days with farming duties and domestic needs; and attempted to adapt their mental attitudes to find fulfillment in the various avenues provided by the encompassing environment.

Corrine and Joseph were both active in politics with Corrine serving in the State Legislature in 1924 and again in 1930 brought about by her promise to the farmers in her area to get them out of the mud. Joseph was an active participant in the Republican party and was a possible future gubernatorial candidate in 1912 until he broke away from the party with Teddy Roosevelt who had formed his own "Progressive Party." Joseph Alsop never became governor and his wife, Corrine, never returned on a regular basis to New York Society or the evenings at the theater, but they did find another kind of contentment in the home environment they provided for their children and grandchildren.

In Connecticut Mrs. Alsop reigned supreme for many years prior to her death as the perennial first lady in society and politics. She always wore a hat, even in her own home, and carried a reticule (a kind of portable pocket) across her arm as she moved about, the last of an authentic age of aristocracy. Joseph saw two of his sons, Joseph and Stewart, become the best political writers in the world and, although he did not live to see it, his third son, John, was the Connecticut candidate for governor in 1962.

(This family will be continued in Volume IV)

Chapter V

George Alsop,

Author of the Book
"A Character Of The Province Of Maryland"

(This information continued from Volume II, pages 87 and 88)

George Alsop in his early history reflected upon the glaring inequities of the European social structure with its prison sentences for minor thefts, debts, or lustful thoughts, and compared them with the opportunistic possibilities of America which had none of these penalties. He presented this new world with its different concept of controlling its inhabitants as an exciting alternative. The author concludes his book by denouncing Cromwellian-Puritan beliefs through his letters to his family and friends in which he confesses his conviction of sin and his intention to dedicate the rest of his life to "the love of God."

(George Alsop spent his time in America in the Maryland Colony as an indentured servant to Captain Thomas Stockett of "Bourne." Captain Stockett was one of the founders of Ann Arundel County and served in the Assembly of Delegates at St. Mary's from 1661 to 1666. Thomas was also the sheriff and judge of the County Court of Ann Arundel County beginning in 1668 and continuing for many years. George Alsop lived at Stockett's Run, Birdville in Ann Arundel County on the 664 acre farm named "Obligation" by Captain Stockett who had come to the new world from Kent in England.)

Chapter VI

Alsops from Montgomeryshire, Wales and Shropshire, England

(This family is continued from Alsop's Tables, Volume II, page 105)

In 1880, Richard, Ellen and their children were living in Wakefield along with James Henry Alsop, the twenty year old nephew of Richard and son of his late brother William. James Henry returned to Wakefield from Fort Leavenworth, Kansas, and there he made his home with his uncle until his mother and her younger children returned to the area.

Elizabeth Bayliss Alsop, widow of William, went back to the Wakefield area after her husband's death accompanied by the children who had neither married nor left home. Her oldest daughter, Lizzie, married William Carr and their children were: Nellie who married Mr. Chapman; Will, a miner, married Julia and lived at W. 1926 Riverside Ave., Spokane, Washington; Alfred, a contractor, married (1) Elizabeth, (2) Mildred and lived at W. 1001 20th Ave., Spokane, Washington; Harry, involved in the manufacture of farm implements, married Mammie and lived at 33 Bedford Rd., Battle Creek, Michigan; Wallace who was in advertising in Los Angeles; and Herbert, a printer, who lived with his wife Mable, in Spokane, Washington.

Mary Jane "Polly" Alsop married William Eustace on 19 June 1873 before her parents, William and Elizabeth moved from Wakefield to Fort Leavenworth. Her husband served as the postmaster at Bellaire, Kansas where their nine children were born. They were: James Percival who married Margaret and operated a farm in Carter, South Dakota; Ethyl Elizabeth who married 18 September 1901, Robert Crosswhite and lived at 62 South 23rd St., Kansas City, Kansas where they were the parents of Vivian, Alfred S., and Edith who married Basil B. Baker; Maurice L., born 1878 and died 1903; Mabelle A., the wife of Charles E. Jobes who farmed at Sedan, Kansas, where their son, Kenneth, was born in 1906; Maude L. who married Fred Hutchinson, a rancher of White River, South Dakota, and their issue consisted of Willis, Hobert, Edwin, and Lucile; Richard R., the husband of Anna Hubbard, who worked from his home in Reynolds, Nebraska as the Burlington Road Master; Edith Myra, the wife of Guy Hutchinson, a rancher of White River, South Dakota, whose children were Geraldine, Mildred, and Irene; William C., who worked for the Burlington Railroad as a pumper; and Kenneth W., a foreman for Burlington Railroad, who wed Florence Carpenter and resided at Endecott, Nebraska. Mary Alsop Eustace was once invited to spend the summer with Alsop relatives in Wolverhampton, England.

On 8 August 1876, Sarah A. Alsop was united in wedlock to Edwin "Ted" Eustace, born 1851, who had worked in the government meat market at Fort Leavenworth managed by his father-in-law, William. After the grasshoppers wiped out the 1874 crops, Ted accompanied his neighbors, the Alsops, from Wakefield to Fort Leavenworth, but after the death of William Alsop, he returned with Sarah to the family homestead and secured employment as a bank cashier for the Bank of Wakefield and later the Farmers and Merchants Bank. He held this job until his death in 1929. Sarah died in Lawrence, Kansas on 21 October 1945, and she and her husband are buried at Highland Cemetery. Eight children were born to this couple, all at Wakefield: Eveline, died young; Harry E., born 18 November 1879, died 19 August 1967, Portland, Oregon, married April 1905, Ethel J. Eustace, daughter of William and Catherine (Cliff) Eustace; Beatrice E., born November 1881, died December 1967, Junction City, married October 1904, George Henry Lumb, son of Edward W. and Mary A. (Hallowell) Lumb; Dora Y., born December 1883, died July 1791, Yakima, Washington, married 1913, Jeffrey Eustace, son of William and Catherine

(Cliff) Eustace; Phillip J., born March 1886, died March 1974, Yakima, Washington, married (1) 1910, Esther Peterson, (2) 1935, Vella; Everett W., born January 1888, died May 1971, Lebanon, married June 1943, Ruby E. Malsbury; Alan L., born December 1891, died May 1972, married (1) Ruth Cornell, daughter of Fred and Rosaline (Mate) Cornell, (2) in Bartow, Florida to Marie Poore, daughter of William Hannan and Anna (Nicholson) Poore; Lawrence B., born February 1896, married October 1934 at Hill City to Iva Lee, daughter of Joseph and Ida(Garrit) Lee.

Lucy Hannah "Anna" Alsop, another daughter of William and Elizabeth Bayliss Alsop, was married in 1881 to Edward Southwick, and they made their home on the Southwick farm located a mile and half south of Wakefield. Their children were Daniel, Clarence, Lucy and Helen. Anna Alsop Southwick died of pneumonia at age 65 at the home of her daughter, Mrs. Lucy Weaver, in Kansas City. She was loved and respected by all who knew her, and she was one of the untiring and faithful workers in the Congregational Church in Wakefield. Anna's funeral services were conducted by Rev. C.C. Green, and she was buried in Highland Cemetery. Edward Southwick, her husband, died on 26 December 1918.

Agnes Myra Alsop, the youngest daughter of William and Elizabeth, received her education in the public schools of Clay County and began her teaching career at the age of 16. She taught school 30 years in Kansas (most of those schools were in and around Wakefield) then moved to Nebraska where she continued teaching until her retirement.

For 50 years she and a close friend, Mrs. Nell Flanders, had made their home together. At the time of her death, they were living in Beatrice, Nebraska.

Myra died at 9:30 p.m. on 7 June 1962, aged 99 years, 5 months, and 27 days. She was the last surviving person who had migrated to the Wakefield community with the original English Colony from the Montgomeryshire-Shropshire area, and she was the oldest person on the Kansas Teachers Retirement plan. Myra helped compile much of the family history by recording remembrances in correspondence with Gwen Alsop Kincaid. She was buried in the Madura Cemetery in Wakefield following funeral services by Rev. J. Orville Bookless at the Mercer Chapel.

Frederick William and Basil Bayliss Alsop were the two youngest sons of William and Elizabeth Alsop. Fred was a farmer around the Wakefield area who never married and died in 1900. His brother, Basil, was also a farmer who lived in Billings, Oklahoma with his wife, Nelle, and daughter Doris Alsop Guice, who taught school in Dillsworth, Oklahoma.

James Henry Alsop lived in Wakefield with his mother and brothers and sisters after their return from Fort Leavenworth. He helped operate the Caine's Creek farm until the youngest members of the family were able to fend for themselves. This farm was located half a mile east of the farm of William and Delilah (Harsh) Dunn who had settled in Wakefield from Pennsylvania and Ohio respectively. James had grown up with the Dunn children, and in 1888, he and Effie M. Dunn, born 1861 in Ohio, became engaged. Following is an actual copy of Effie's wedding invitation in her own handwriting. It was the custom in the 1880's in the rural areas of Kansas for brides to write out their own invitations.

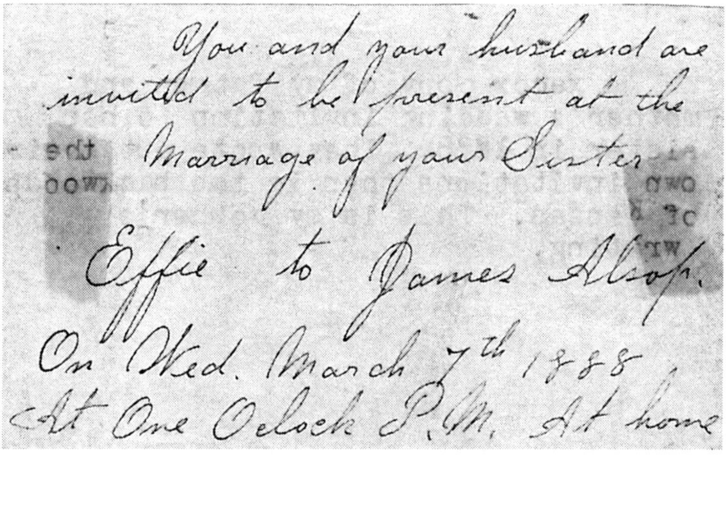
You and your husband are invited to be present at the Marriage of your Sister Effie to James Alsop. On Wed. March 7th 1888 At One Oclock P.M. At home

James and Effie first rented a farm located two miles southwest of Wakefield and later bought a farm three miles north of town which was to be the place where all of their children were born and grew to adulthood. The "old home place" as it was fondly remembered by their children who experienced the formative years of their lives there, contained a section of good bottom land with a railroad running through it. The farmhouse has been removed and part of the land is now under Milford Lake.

The Winter of 1908 at the Alsop family farm near Wakefield.

The children of James and Effie were: James E., born January 1889; Florence M., born November 1890; Inez G., born May 1892; Edith L., born September 1893; Malcolm L., born December 1894; Ethlyn M., born January 1896; Delilah, born April 1900; and Bryan, born in 1903 and died that same year. A family reunion was held prior to the birth of the last two children and a picture taken at that time has preserved for posterity a likeness of many of the members of this lineage.

ALSOP-EUSTACE REUNION 1898--The reunion was held in 1898 with the following present: back row, left to right, Dan Southwick, Harry Eustace, Frank Swezey and (?) and Dora Eustace; next row, left to right, Fannie Alsop Guy, Emily Alsop Swezey, Nellie Alsop Dalton, Anna Alsop Southwick Jevons Alsop holding Mildred; next row: left to right, ?, Beatrice Eustace Lumb, Myra Alsop, Sarah Alsop Eustace, Mary (Polly) Alsop Eustace, Mary Boise and husband from Junction City, Effie Alsop holding Ethlyn, Fred Alsop, Next row: Richard Alsop holding Francis Guy and Malcolm Alsop, Ellen Brown Alsop (Richard Alsop's wife), Elizabeth Bayliss Alsop (Grandma Alsop holding Kenneth Eustace), Eliz. Alsop Carr holding Lawrence Eustace, Sarah Alsop Boise, Donald Swezey, Robert Boise, James Henry Alsop and Old Skip the dog, and Clarence Southwick; front row, left to right, Edith Alsop Noakes, Inez Alsop, Florence Alsop, James Alsop Jr., Herbert Carr, Allen Eustace, Carrie Swezey, Everett Eustace, Phil Eustace, Harold Swezey, Helen Southwick and Lucy Southwick Weaver Amos.

Alsop - Eustace Reunion – 1898

After the loss of her infant son, Bryan, in 1903, Effie Dunn Alsop was shocked and overwhelmed by the death of her husband in 1904. She was left with seven children still living at home whose ages ranged from 15 to 4 years. With the help of kind, concerned relatives and neighbors, but mostly from their own hard work and perseverance, the Alsop family survived. However, they didn't just survive, but grew up to be successful,contributing citizens who gave back more than life required of them.

The seven Alsop children attended college and each one left with a degree. They all became school teachers and two, Inez and Malcolm, taught at Kansas State University in the history and physics departments, respectively. All the rest were high school teachers, except Lila, who taught in the elementary grades. Though they taught in a number of different states,

This picture was taken in 1914 with Inez and Malcolm seated in front, and James, Florence, Edith, Lila and Ethlyn on the back row.

the brothers and sisters kept close contact during the passing years and even had a tape recorder round robin going during the latter part of their careers. They met each Christmas at their mother's home for as long as she lived and then planned to meet annually at one of the various homes of the brothers and sisters. A family reunion was held in 1926, and family members took photographs, some of which still survive.

James "Jim" Alsop, the oldest brother, now deceased, married Eudora Lila Thoren, and there was no issue. Florence, who never married, died in Berkeley, California in 1969. Inez, who also never married, is now deceased. Edith married Ray Noakes and lived for many years in Filley, Nebraska. They had no children. She lived to be past 100 years of age and resided on Laramie street in Manhattan, Kansas during her final years. Edith, at the time of the writing of this book, is the only one of her brothers or sisters still living. Malcolm married Jean Baker and their children were Loueva, Robert, and Carolyn. Ethlyn was wed to Louis Pastrone in San Francisco, California, but no children were born to this union. Lila attended college at the Art University in Austin, Texas where she met and married Frank Bengard after teaching school for one year. Their only daughter, Bonnie, was the mother of Sherry, Roy, Hal, and Shawn. Loueva, daughter of Malcolm, had two children, Ted and Janice. Malcolm's son, Robert, was the father of Alison, while Malcolm's daughter, Caroline, had children Steven and Julie.

After retiring from teaching, the five surviving siblings assembled in Manhattan, Kansas to enjoy their "golden" years. Ethlyn and Inez lived at 1646 Laramie St. in a house which they purchased. Malcolm Alsop and Jean lived in their house across the street, and Lila and Edith lived in their own apartment in the same block. The sisters all became active in a wide variety of activities which included participation in writing clubs, poetry clubs, university woman's club, and church clubs. They ate out together two or three times a week and celebrated all birthdays and holidays together. They also wrote articles and poems for magazines and book reviews, essays, and poetry for the various newspapers in the area. In 1987, Ethlyn Alsop Pastrone sent me several sample pressed flower all-occasion cards that she and her sister made together as a hobby. She mentioned that life still had sparkle for them though they were all in their nineties or very close.

Ethlyn Alsop taught high school English for 15 years in Kansas after earning her first degree. She received her master's degree at this time and moved to California where she taught English in South San Francisco High School for the next twenty years. As she was contemplating retirement after 40 years of teaching and wondering if she would ever see another spring on a farm instead of in a large urban area, she composed the following poems.

APRIL IN KANSAS

O, say, have you seen April,
A friend I used to know
Away back there in Kansas land
Some forty years ago?
And does she still have temper
And storm by flash and roar,
Then peek around a cloud and smile
As pleasant as before?

Does earth turn green in pastures,
And blue white daisies grow?
Are violets still by railroad tracks,
Where sorrel and snake flowers show?

And do the lilacs glisten
After every rain,
And does the earth smell sweet when rolled
By plows for crops again?

And do the dripping willows
Still reflect in swollen streams?
Do new born colts and lambs still play
As they do in my dreams?

It is years since I saw April
Out on a Kansas plain
And heard the birds by river banks
Sing their spring refrain.

But since I once knew April,
She is part of me it seems,
For every year at springtime
I see her in my dreams.

ALSOP FARM LIFE SOME SEVENTY-FIVE YEARS AGO - 1908

By Ethtyn Alsop Pastrone

We were five girls and two boys;
We had struggles; we had joys,
Grew up on a Kansas farm
With lots of work mid lots of charm.
Up at five, retire by ten
That is how we lived it then;
We thawed the pump on winter morn,
Fed the chickens daily corn;
Milked the cows and slopped the hogs;
Brought in cobs and hauled in logs;
Broke the ice for stock to drink
Down by our winter skating rink.
We cooked the breakfast, but alas
Not on electric stove or gas,
But cobs and dry wood made it glow,
And what a breakfast long ago:
Pancakes heaped away up there,
Fried potatoes, beefsteaks rare,
Fruit, eggs, jelly, all home grown ;
O, those years, how fast they've flown:

Years of canning, raking hay,
Sorting eggs from day to day,
Butchering and salting down
Better meat than found in town;
Washing clothes, yea many lots
Every week by hand, no stops;
Cleaning each week room by room,
Beating rugs with sticks and broom;
Cooking for the threshers when
Thermometers showed hundred ten.
Painting, churning, baking bread;
Keeping mortgage paid ahead;
Walking home when evening comes
With wild gooseberries, grapes, or plums.
From soot of stove lid, pair by pair
We blacked our shoes for Sunday wear;
And when we slept, each slept like lead
On strawtick and a feather bed.
We walked to school, no use to moan
Two miles there and two miles home;
Zero weather way below,
Rain or snow we had to go.
When sleeping out on summer nights
One wakened to the awesome sights
Of falling stars and fireflies,
Of endless space and open skies,
One reached with all one's might to know
The hidden stranger, God, and lo
The substance of all hopes drew near
And unseen evidence was clear.
Times throws pictures on life's screen;
The pictures change from scene to scene.
Time takes a hand and now and then
Wipes the slate and starts again.

****

Emily Jane Alsop, the first daughter of Richard and Jane Pryce Alsop, married on 2 February 1887, Frank Swezey, a farmer who lived in the Wakefield area. Their five children were: Carrie Frances, born 29 April 1885 - died 20 January 1920, married 9 January 1907 at Gladstone, Colorado, George I. Camp and their children were Emily, Elinor, and Sylvia; Donald Horace, born 25 February 1890, married Ermah Carolyn Beck on 13 July 1921 at Junction City, and their two children Elizabeth and Donna were born in Wakefield in 1924 and 1929 respectively; Harold Richard, born 24 July 1891, married Flora Shepherd on 15 April 1915, and their only child was Elinor, born in 1817; Elinor Emily, born 13 April 1899 - died 5 January 1901, buried in Wakefield at Madura Cemetery (Congregational Church); and Jeanette Cooper, born 1 May 1902, married 1924, Samuel J. Kiggins, and their one child was Harold.

The eldest son of Richard and Jane Alsop was John Richard,born in England but raised in the Wakefield, Kansas area. He and Emily Joanna Jevons were married on 26 December 1895. After living on a ranch outside of Wakefield for a while, they moved into town where John was a mail carrier from 1902-1934. John and Emily were faithful members of the Methodist Church and were also active in school and other community affairs. They were the parents of daughters Mildred, Gwendolyn, and Helen. John was a tribute to his community, as he always displayed a friendly, helpful attitude; he was an inspiration to all who knew him. He died 15 April 1947 of a cerebral hemorrhage after suffering a paralytic stroke five years earlier. John Richard Alsop was buried in Highland Cemetery as was his wife who died 4 March 1949, while visiting her daughter in Pearl City, Hawaii.

John Richard Alsop and a friend he dated prior to his marriage.

John Richard Alsop of Wakefield, Kansas in later life.

Mildred Agnes Alsop, the eldest daughter of John and Emily J., was born 11 December 1896 in Wakefield and married Francis Reid Williams on 27 October 1921. Their children were Robert, Majel, and John Benjamin. Her sister, Gwendolyn, was born 13 October 1899 - died 11 February 1968, married Calvin Kincaid, and they were the parents of William, Mary, and John. Gwen helped preserve much of the Alsop family history. The third child of John and Emily Jevons Alsop was Helen M. Alsop, born 15 June 1905, married Ross B. Schaulis 8 April 1921, and their family consisted of Audrey, Ross, and Ruby Elaine. Audrey Schaulis who married Bill Keeling has provided much of the information on Richard Alsop and his descendants.

This picture of Gwendolyn Maxine Alsop, age 13, Helen Mary Alsop, age7, and Mildred Agnes Alsop, age 16, was taken in 1912 at the Alsop residence in Clay Co., Kansas.

Frances "Fannie" Anne Alsop, the first child born to Richard and Jane Pryce Alsop in the United States, was born 15 July 1871. She wed Arthur Leonard Guy on 15 December 1892, and their children were born as follows: Francis A., born 16 September 1894; Richard W., born 4 February 1900; and Eleanor Selina, born 7 March 1902. Mr. Guy, a very successful merchant in Wakefield, succeeded to this business established by his father and was able to provide excellent educational opportunities for his children.

Edward "Ted" Henry Alsop was the last child born to Richard and Jane Pryce, as Jane died the year following Ted's birth. Ted lived in the home of his father and stepmother until her death in 1899, and then moved in with his brother, John Richard. The following year on 25 September 1901, he and Matilda "Mattie" Male, born 15 April 1877 in Kings County, Ireland, were married and their issue consisted of six sons and one daughter as follows: Pryce who died in infancy; Lt. William G. Alsop, missing in action in W.W. II; the only daughter, Jane, who died in 1947; Richard N.; Samuel E.; John H.; and Everett. Ted was a substantial farmer and stockman in Clay County where he took a lively interest in the promotion of better agricultural methods and improved livestock. He was also very active in both local and national political functions. As he and his wife advanced in years, they retired from the farm and lived in Wakefield. Ted's death occurred about 1 p.m., Sunday, November 9, 1952 in a nursing home in Topeka where he had recently been taken due to failing health. Mattie died 20 February 1963 in the Junction City Hospital near her home. She was a loyal and active member of the Episcopal Church of Wakefield. They were both buried in the Highland Cemetery.

Richard N. Alsop was the first child born to Ted and Mattie. He was reared in the Wakefield area and was associated with Reed and Wheelock Construction Company in Clay Center, Kansas. He later lived and worked in Phillipsburg where he died on 4 January 1968, and his burial site is located there. Richard and his wife, Alma Kady, were married 24 December 1927, and they had no children.

On 25 October 1904, in Wakefield, John Henry was born to E.H. "Ted" and Matilda Male Alsop. Known as "Jack," our subject married Gladys Van Der Stelt on 4 March 1931, and for the next twenty years he was active as a Kansas highway contractor. He owned and operated sand plants in a number of counties, as well as serving as a city councilman in Wakefield. He was a member of the Masonic Lodge and also a member of the Methodist Church. Jack and Gladys were the parents of two daughters, Mary Jo and Lila. Mr. Alsop died of a heart attack while driving to one of his gravel plants in Belleville, Kansas. He was buried in Highland Cemetery on 30 August 1953, after funeral services at the Mercer Chapel. His wife died 9 August 1969 at the Republic County Hospital in Belleville. She was buried next to her husband.

Edward H. "Ted" Alsop

Everett "Buck" Alsop

Sam Alsop, born 3 December 1906 in Wakefield, was another son of Ted and Matilda Alsop. He married Madge Wright of Sublette, Kansas in 1943, and their two sons were Samuel Edward, born 27 April 1946, and William Richard, born 6 January 1952. Sam lived most of his life in Garden City where one of his sons "Bill" grew up and became a physician. He now lives at 484 Upper Mill Heights Dr., Salina, Kansas, with his wife Jane B. Alsop.

The birth date of Everett "Buck" Alsop, offspring of Ted and Mattie, was 15 March 1910 in Wakefield. He and Filomena Flora Milani were married on 27 December 1944 in Bari, Italy. She was born 13 April 1925. Their children were Anna Maria, born 21 February 1947; Edward Henry, born 29 April 1948, married 1981 Anita; Delores Jane, born 14 February 1950, married 1970, Ed Minnock, and lives in Topeka where she is a teacher; and Frances Sophia, born 24 November 1952, married John Mallon.

In 1900, the Federal census reported that Richard Alsop was a widower living with his two youngest children, Ellen C. and Alfred C. in their Wakefield family home. After his last son and daughter had married and started their own families, Richard lived with his son John Richard in their home near Wakefield. On 2 October 1904, Richard took the time to record much of his family history in his own personal Bible. He took part in building the First Methodist Church building and the parsonage. His joy and delight was in his Savior and the Lord's organization on earth, the church. Richard was a musician of considerable degree, having had some education in that art as well as having perfect pitch. He was the organist and song leader for many years in his church and was also instrumental in securing their first organ.

He served in various public offices such as justice of the peace, police judge, township trustee, and he was elected to two terms as the Clerk of the District Court of Clay County. He served the public with fidelity and effectiveness. Amidst the love, esteem, and honor of his fellowmen, he remained modest, quiet, humble, but earnest and resolute, ever trodding the path of duty as he saw it without ostentation or pride. He died on 4 May 1926 in his residence which had been his home for many years.

Relatives and friends gathered at 10:00 a.m. on Monday morning at the home of his daughter, Fannie Alsop Guy, for a brief service, and final rites were held at the Methodist Church. His body was laid to rest in the Madura Cemetery next to his two wives.

Ellen "Nell" Charlotte Alsop, the last daughter of Richard and second wife Ellen Brown, married William B. Dalton on 25 June 1902 in Wakefield, and their first child, William Alsop Dalton was born 1 July 1903 at St. George, Kansas and married Dorothy S. Roop, 31 March 1929 at Topeka, Kansas. They had no descendants. Elinor Marian, only daughter of Nell and Bill Dalton, was born 9 March 1906 at St. George and married Willie Clyde Epperson on 8 August 1931 at Topeka. Their only child was Elinor Sue Epperson, who married Roger Michael McCoy, and their two children were Michael and Leah Beth.

Alfred Charles Alsop 1879-1943

The last child of Richard and Ellen Brown Alsop was Alfred Charles, who was married on 26 December 1915 in Manhattan, Kansas to Anne Adele Fairman, born 12 December 1878. They were the parents of three daughters, Annette, born 24 August 1917; Margaret Ellen, born 25

November 1920; and Marian Louise, born 15 October 1924. Alfred C. died 28 July 1943 at Bradenton, Florida and is buried there. His occupation during his lifetime was that of a building contractor.

(This family will be continued in Volume IV - Alsop's Tables)

CHAPTER VII

Jacob Allsip (Alsip, etc.)

Emigrant from Prussia?

(This family is continued from page 122, Vol. II, Alsop's Tables)

In the previous volume of this family history Jacob Allsop (Allsip, etc.) was described as possibly being the emigrant ancestor from Prussia. However, a Maryland court record discovered by Jim Artherton reveals that John Alsop-Alsip indentured his son Jacob in 1790. This is a very strong indication that the Jacob Alsip who was born about 1774 was a son of John. A Joseph Alsip, born about 1794, was very likely the brother of Jacob or his son. Either Jacob or Joseph Alsip was the father of Jacob Alsip who was born in 1815. The theory about Jacob Alsip arriving in this country from Prussia has just about been eliminated from consideration by the record listing Jacob as a son of John. John left official records proving that he came to America from Surry Co., England.

Susanna M. Norris, daughter of George Norris and wife Catherine Kefauver, was the wife of Jacob Alsip.

Jacob Alsup married Susannah Norris and moved from Maryland to Kansas. Two of his sons set up residence in Oklahoma while one son remained in Kansas. The daughters married and had children who grew up in either Kansas or Oklahoma. The descendants of these sons and daughters will now be described as fully as available records will permit.

Amanda Kate Alsip and husband Joseph Stone, along with the Jacob Alsip family, relocated to Louisville, Kansas in 1870. Amanda and Joseph were the parents of Luther Stone, born 1865, Anna Stone, born 1867, William Stone, born 1870, Joseph Stone and Susan Stone, born in the early 1870's, Florence Stone, born 1877, and Lula Stone, born 1879. Joseph and Susan Stone were adopted by M. D. Terry and wife on 25 May 1878. At least one child, Anna, died in a fire when her parents' house burned during the 1880's.

Joseph Stone signed a statement concerning a Civil War pension for Josephus Alsip in 1890 in which he states that he had known Josephus for forty years, had gone to school with him in Maryland, and worked with him on the same farm before and after the War Between the States. Amanda was already deceased when her mother Susan Norris Alsip died in April 1904. Family tradition indicates that Milburn Stone who performed the role of "Doc" on the television program Gunsmoke was a relative of this Stone family. Joseph Stone died 27 April 1920, in Pottawatomie Co. and is buried there next to his wife.

Amanda Kate Alsip Stone and husband Joseph Stone

Mary Alsip married John Long and moved with her parents to Kansas. Later in life, she and her husband and family relocated to Illinois. Her sisters Emily "Emma" and Alice also married and had families of their own who established permanent residence in Kansas near Jacob and Susannah Alsip. Elizabeth Alsip, the youngest sister died at about the age of six years.

William A. Koontz and wife Emma J. Alsip Koontz

Milton Jacob Benedict, wife Alice Matilda Alsip, and children George Frederick Benedict and Mary Magdalene Benedict.

Emma Alsip Koontz died 19 Nov. 1917, and her husband William died 2 Feb. 1918. They are both buried in the Fairview-Alsip Cemetery, Union Twp., Pottawatomie Co., Kansas. Alice Alsip Benedict was born in Hagerstown, Maryland on 10 Nov. 1852, and married Milton Benedict on 21 Nov. 1878, in Kansas. They lived in Salina, Kansas where she died 28 Dec. 1912, and her husband on 17 July 1922. They are both buried in Gypsum Hills Cemetery in Salina.

The above photo was made in Wamego, Kansas about 1890. From the left are Edith M., born 1884; Jacob E. Alsip, born 20 Feb. 1856, in Washington Co., Maryland and died 16 Jan. 1913 in Wamego; Effie J., born 1886; and Florence Sherman, born 19 Feb. 1860 in Iowa and died 3 March 1949.

Jacob and Florence were married on 21 April 1878. They were buried in the Wamego City Cemetery.

Jacob E. Alsip, Jr., youngest son of Jacob and Susanna Alsip, and his wife Florence were living in Pottawatomie Co., Kansas in 1900 when the Federal census was completed. Living with them were their three children Edith M., age 16, Effie J., age 14, and Kenneth, age 5. In 1920, Florence

Alsip, widow of Jacob, Jr., was still living in Wamego, Kansas at 714 Lincoln St. in Pottawatomie Co. Living with her were her daughter Effie, her son-in-law Frank Laughlin, and her two grandsons Truman and Claud. Kenneth Alsip and wife Effie were living nearby, but had no children yet, as they had just recently been married.

The Federal census of 1930 for Wabaunsee Co., Kansas reports Kenneth Alsip as living in household 51-51 in Wabaunsee Twp. His new residence was just a few miles south of Wamego where he had formerly lived. Living with him were his two children Joetta, age 10, and Howard, age. 8. Also living in his home was his widowed mother Florence, age 70. Kenneth Alsip's wife Effie who was born 1 May 1899, and died 26 Feb. 1924, was buried in the Louisville Cemetery in Pottawatomie Co. Kenneth and his mother were left to care for the two small children. Kenneth born 8 Jan. 1895-died 3 Jan. 1969, was buried next to his wife. Howard L. Alsip, son of Kenneth and Effie, born 26Feb. 1922-died l8 June 1977, was also buried in the Louisville Cemetery near his parents.

Horatio T. Alsip, born in Washington Co., Maryland on 28 Sept. 1854, married Maggie Belle Witter, and they were the parents of three sons and two daughters. After the unexpected death of "Rash" Alsip, his widow Maggie, born 9 July 1862, in Fulton Co., Pennsylvania, remarried, but she also died at an early age on 18 Aug. 1903, and both are buried near Jennings, Oklahoma in what is now Pawnee Co.

The above photo was taken in the 1890's in Indian Territory Creek Nation (l. to r.) Roy Lee Alsip, Arthur Lee Alsip, and George R. Alsip.

The children of Horatio "Rash" and wife Maggie Belle Alsip grew up in Oklahoma, although all of them were born in Kansas except Roy, the youngest one, who was born in Oklahoma Territory. The census of 1910 lists George R. Alsip, age 26, as living in Creek Co., Oklahoma with his wife Lillie, age 24, and son Arvis, born 1909, died 1998 in Beaumont, Texas. They were also the parents of a daughter Helen who is now deceased. George R. Alsip moved to Beaumont, Texas and died there on 3 Sept. 1959. Another son of Horatio and Maggie Belle was Roy Lee Alsip who married Edna Kitterman, and they were reported in the 1920 census as living in Payne Co., Oklahoma with their two children George, age 5, and Hazel, age 3. Roy died in Oklahoma in 1934. The two girls of Rash and Maggie were Ada Myrtle and Bessie. Ada was born 19 Sept. 1885, and is shown with her sister in the following photograph. Ada died in May 1957.

Arthur Lee Alsip was born in October 1882 in Pottawatomie Co., Kansas and moved with his family to Oklahoma while still a young boy. He married Ollie Sarah Barnes, born 1886, and they were the parents of Roy Lee, an oil field worker who was born in 1907 in Indian Territory near Jennings which was the same year that Oklahoma became a state; William "Willie" Arlando, born 1908; Faye Belle, born 1910; George Ross, born 1912; Glen Jacob, born 1914; and Herbert James, born 1920. Herbert

James Alsip was still living in 1991, the only surviving child of Arthur and Ollie Alsip, when he celebrated his 50th wedding anniversary with his wife Lena Rosalee Ford, the wedding having been performed on 18 Jan. 1941, in Drumright, Oklahoma. Herbert and Lena had two children, Jimmy Alsip and Cherry Alsip Runnels, both of Odessa, Texas. Herbert was the owner and operator of the Permian Contracting Co. during his working years.

Photo made Jennings, Okla. 14 Nov. 1935-Bessie C. Alsip White, Arthur Lee Alsip, George R. Alsip, and Ada Myrtle Alsip Cotton.

Roy Lee Alsip, first born son of Arthur Lee and Ollie, was married to Leona Pauline Rice, who was a daughter of Rosella Baker Rice. He worked most of his life in the oil fields of Oklahoma with some farming in the early years.

Ollie Sarah Barnes Alsip-Wife of Arthur Lee Alsip

Leona Pauline Rice-Wife of Roy Lee Alsip Born 10 Oct. 1913- Age 16 when photo made.

(l. to r.) Louis Barnes, Stanley Meyers, Frank Jenkins and Roy Lee Alsip. All married daughters of Rosella Baker Rice.

Roy Lee Alsip and Leona had four children as follows: Wanda Lee Alsip Byrom, Billy Ray Alsip, Linda Roseann Alsip and David Leroy Alsip. Billy Ray and Linda Roseann have lived their entire lives in the Mannford, Oklahoma area.

Roy Lee Alsip, wife Leona, dau. Wanda Lee, age 5,and son Billy Ray, age 2. Photo made 1938.

Sept. 3, 1967-David LeRoy Alsip on Wedding Day. (l. to r.) Wanda, Linda Rosanne,David, Leona, and Billy Ray.

Roy Lee died in 1966, and his widow Leona continued to live in the Mannford, Oklahoma area in her own home until she had several health problems. In October 1998 she and her children decided that she needed the care of a nursing home with her medicine even though she was still active. In 2000, she was still doing well for 87 years of bountiful living.

Wanda Lee Alsip married Harold Byrom, and they acquired a farm located a few miles outside of Mannford. Harold died of cancer about three years ago, and Wanda continues to live on the family farm. Wanda has contributed significant information for the last two volumes and wrote an excellent article for Volume II of Alsop's Tables. She has a strong interest in her family history and has worked on her specific lineage for many years. I visited Wanda and Harold at their farm a few years ago, and the trip proved to be truly rewarding as relates to meeting my kin and enjoying their hospitality and sharing the love of genealogical pursuits.

David and Marilyn Alsip-1995

Wanda Alsip Byrom

David L. Alsip, one of the sons of Roy Lee and Leona Alsip and grandson of Arthur Lee Alsip, is an architect who, among many other projects in the past few years, has designed a shopping center in Edmund, Oklahoma and a 110 acre housing development nearby. He lives with his wife Marilyn on Poplar Lane in Midwest City. Recently, David has become associated with Cooper Medical which is a company that builds medical facilities all around the country. He is presently involved in building a large hospital near Biloxi, MS, spending the night there and returning home the next evening. Marilyn is interested and active in family history and has provided valuable genealogical materials on the Alsip family. David and Marilyn have contributed to the Alsip family history through their progeny which consist of Lisa, Tony, and grandson Brent.

Josephus Alsip oldest child of Jacob and Susannah Norris Alsip was born 6 Feb. 1842 in Rohrersville, Washington Co., Maryland and from 28 March 1864, until 29 May 1865, served in the Union Army in Company E, 3rd Regiment, Md Vols., PHB Infantry. After his return from military duty in the Civil War, he married on 25 Jan. 1866, Anna Maria Poffenberger who was born in Washington Co., Maryland on 5 Aug. 1845. The marriage took place in Hagerstown, Md. and was conducted by Joseph S. Grigg, Vicar, of Rohrersville, Md. Anna Maria was the daughter of Thomas and Mary Ann Thomas Poffenberger.

This photo of the Josephus Alsip family was made ca. 1893. From l. to r. Daniel Rose, Tausie Sybil, Anna Maria, Lillie May, George Washington, Josephus, John Jacob, Ray Thomas, Laura Kate, and Susan Alice.

Josephus moved with his wife and family in 1890 from Pottawatomie Co., Kansas where he had been living since 1870 to Cowley Co., Kansas and acquired a farm south of Arkansas City. Accompanied by his seventeen year old daughter Laura Kate (he needed a cook) and thirteen year old son Daniel Rose, he participated in the Cherokee Strip Run of 1893. Although he was not able to claim any land, he liked the area and in 1898 bought land and settled about one mile west of the town of Silverdale. He and wife Anna Maria were on the 1920 census record for Cowley Co., Kansas. The only child still living at home was Tossie (Tausie?) Sybil who was age 41. The 1930 census lists "Toss" as age 51 and living with her widowed mother

Anna Maria. To the surprise of most of the family, Tausie, born 21 Dec. 1877, married on 26 July 1953, Ferry Aaron Turner. She was fondly known as "Aunt Toss" by her nieces and nephews. Tausie died 21 Mar. 1962, and her husband died 23 July 1957. They were interred in the Silverdale Cem. Josephus and Anna lived out their lives in this area where he was a farmer and J. P. He died 23 Feb. 1927, and she died 24 Nov. 1930. They are both buried in the Silverdale Cemetery.

John Jacob Alsip oldest son of Josephus and Anna was born in Wamego, Kansas on 21 Sept. 1872. He moved to Silverdale, Kansas with his parents, and on 17 May 1896, married Rosa Belle Nelson, born 19 Oct. 1876, in Olney, Richland Co., Illinois, and they had two children Robert Josephus, age 3, and Alberta "Bertie" M., age l, as reported on the 1900 census for Cowley Co., Kansas.

John and Rosa had a large family of children, and from time to time some of the children lived with her mother Frances N. Nelson. In 1910 Robert J. was living with his grandmother and in 1920 Alberta "Bertie" age 20, was listed as living at 316 N. 16th Street. in Arkansas City in the home of Frances N. Nelson. John J. and Rosa were still living in Cowley Co. in 1920, and the census reported that the children still living at the Alsip residence during this count were Frank Monroe, 17, Jess Calvary, 13, Nellie Gladys, 12, Rosetta "Etta" Pearl, 8, Anna Mae, 6, and Carl H., 2. Bertie married and had a family and lived in Arkansas City where she died in 1976. John J. and wife Rosa lived out their lives in Cowley Co. where he died of cancer on 23 April 1929, and was buried in Riverview Cemetery in Arkansas City. In 1930 Rosa was living with her mother Frances in Arkansas City and four of the children were still single and living at home. Rosa passed away in Arkansas City on 23 Aug. 1938. Frank died in 1968, Jess in 1974, Carl in 1980, and Nellie in 1981. Anna Mae established residence in Washington state and died there in 2001. Rosetta moved to Parsons, Kansas and was the only child still living at last report.

Robert Josephus Alsip, oldest son of John J. and Rosa, was born in Cowley Co., Kansas in 1897 and moved to Texas where he married Elizabeth Waller in December 1931. Elizabeth taught school from 1928 until 1932. On 13 Nov. 1937, at Fort Sam Houston, Texas, Robert J. and wife Elizabeth became the parents of a son named James Barney Alsip. Robert's middle name was actually Josephus, but he didn't like the name and changed it to James. During the World War, Robert served in the armed forces and was stationed in France. He worked as a telegrapher for the railroad after returning to civilian life, and he and his wife lived nearly all of their married life in San Antonio. He worked for fifteen years at the International Airport in San Antonio. Robert J. Alsip died in San Antonio, Texas in 1964 of a heart attack. On 18 Nov. 1996, Robert's wife Elizabeth wrote a letter to Fay and May Alsip, twin daughters of Daniel Rose Alsip, and in this letter gave them a brief review of the Alsip family history as she knew it. Elizabeth lived at 131 Irvington Dr. in San Antonio, Texas until her death in 1999.

James Barney son of Robert and Elizabeth obtained his master's degrees in history at TCU in Fort Worth and in librarianship from Emory University. He married Barbara Kathryn Wittman (descended from German immigrants who arrived in the U. S. in the 1870's) in Fort Worth, Texas on 8 May 1959. (She has a doctorate in Romance Languages from Emory University.) James and Barbara moved to Annandale, Virginia in October, 1979 with their two sons William Clinton, born 21 May 1962, in Fort Worth, and Brian James, born 13 Feb. 1968, in Atlanta, Georgia. William Clinton received his degree with a major in business administration from George Washington University in Washington, D. C. and then became the International Business Manager at Gannett (U. S. A. Today) in New York City. Brian James obtained a degree in neurobiology from Cornell University in 1990 and then attended medical school at Georgetown University, Washington, D. C. His grandmother Elizabeth Waller Alsip noted in her letter of 1996 that Brian was a doctor in the army near Washington, D. C. She also informed her twin first cousins (by marriage) that she and Robert had had a daughter named Carolyn Beth. Carolyn married and her son is Todd Alan Varian. Elizabeth also mentioned a nephew who lives in Iola, Kansas and is a retired college teacher. James B. and wife Barbara K. Alsip were still living in Annandale, Virginia at last report.

One of the other children of Josephus and Anna Maria was Susan Alice, born 28 Nov. 1870, who married on 20 May 1891, Joseph Frank Lenhart who was born 22 Aug. 1863, at Madison Co., Ohio. She and her family lived their entire lives in Ponca City, Oklahoma where Susan died 2 July 1956, and Frank died there on 12 May 1932.

Laura Kate daughter of Josephus and Anna Maria was born 27 Feb. 1876, and married William Frederick Lenhart who was born in Ohio on 17 Nov. 1872. He was the brother of her sister's husband. The date of the wedding was 23 May 1894. Laura Kate lived near the area of her birth and died in Wamego, Kansas on 8 Dec. 1961. Her husband had died there on 13 May 1929.

Lillie May, born 4 Oct. 1882, near Westmoreland, Kansas and Ray Thomas, born 31 Dec. 1884, at the same location were the two youngest children of Josephus and Anna Maria Alsip. Lillie May married on 11 March 1905, John Tousley who had been born in Rock, Kansas on 3 March 1880. She died in New Kirk, Kay Co., Oklahoma on 4 June 1946, and her husband died in Blackwell, Oklahoma on 10 April 1950. Both are buried in the New Kirk Cemetery. Lillie's brother Ray married on 12 Jan. 1910, Ethel May Campbell who was born in Osceola, Iowa on 10 Oct. 1891. In 1920, Ray was living with his wife in Kay Co., Oklahoma and living with them were his father-in-law Fred Campbell and his two children Fred and Gladys Campbell. Both Ray and wife Ethel are buried in Silverdale with their dates of death being 12 Jan. 1979, and 13 Nov. 1961, respectively.

Daniel Rose Alsip son of Josephus and Anna Alsip was born near Westmoreland, Kansas on 4 July 1880, and came to Cowley Co., Kansas when his father bought land near Silverdale in 1898. He lived at home until his marriage on 2 Sept. 1911, to Mary Elizabeth Bauer (Bower) at Ponca City, Oklahoma in Kay Co. Mary Elizabeth was born in Pueblo, Colorado on 29 Aug. 1892. They were the parents of twins Lisna May and Linna Fay, born 1915, Robert Kenneth, born 1918, Richard Dale, born 1921, and Dorothy Gertrude, born 1923. Mary Elizabeth died on 9 Dec. 1923, of childbirth complications when Dorothy was born. She had also lost three other children in their infancy; two of them were twins named Nora and Dora. Daniel Rose died 24 July 1965, in Silverdale and was buried next to his wife in the local cemetery. One of the twins Fay died in 2002, and the other twin May is still living in Arkansas City.

Robert Kenneth Alsip married Louise Benshoof, and they are still living in Arkansas City at 1201 W. Oklahoma Ave. They have four children who are Roberta K., Daniel K., Barbara, and Sharon. Bob and Louise are very interested in their family history and have accumulated quite a bit of family information and historical photos from years of genealogical research. They have been very generous and considerate in providing information and photos for the last two volumes of Alsop's Tables.

George Washington Alsip son of Josephus and Anna Poffenberger Alsip was born near Westmoreland, Kansas on 29 March 1874. He married on 3 July 1896, Ella Elizabeth Thompson, born in Dexter, Cowley Co., Kansas on 24 June 1878, and by 1900 they were living in Lincoln County, Oklahoma in North Wichita Township with their first two children Golda Blaylock and Raymond. In 1910 George, Ella, and four children Goldie, Russia, Jesse, and Laura were recorded by the census in Oklahoma County, Oklahoma. They had moved back to Lincoln Co., near Chandler, Oklahoma where they were living in 1920. Children in the household were Russia, 16, Jesse, 14, Evelyn, 11, Nancy, 9, Oliver, 6, and Joe Theodore, 4. Other children born to George and Ella were Alma Mae and Etta Belle. George and his wife Ella lived the remainder of their lives in or near Chandler, Oklahoma. Laura Evelyn Alsip married an Owens; Nancy Alsip married a Williams; and Russia Alsip married a Becker. George died in Chandler, Oklahoma on 22 Sept. 1957, and his wife Ella died there in 1949. They are both buried in Chandler at the Oak Park Cemetery.

George Washington Alsip-1954

Jesse Marion Alsip, known as J.M. by most people, was born in Luther, Oklahoma on 18 December 1905, and then returned with his family to Chandler where he lived his teen age years. He married Zelda Saulsberry on 5 April 1934, in Wewoka, Oklahoma which is the county seat of Seminole Co. It joins Lincoln Co. on the south east. Zelda was born in Louisa, Kentucky on 8 August 1912, and later moved to Oklahoma. Jesse and Zelda owned and operated the "Alsip Lumber Yard and Redi-Mix Concrete Co." in Chandler for more than 50 years. Jesse was also a home builder and built many new homes in Chandler and surrounding towns. J.M. and Zelda were the parents of five children who will be covered in detail in the next few paragraphs. Jesse died in Chandler on 21 June 1995, and his wife Zelda died there on 11 May 1994. They were interred at the Oak Park Cemetery where his parents were buried.

Jesse and Zelda Alsip and their children Danny, David, Joan, Tommy, and Dale

Jesse and Zelda lived in Chandler most of their lives and maintained a very close personal relationship with their children and grandchildren. At Christmas and Thanksgiving and other appropriate holidays, the families would gather for a reunion. The previous photo was taken at one of those meetings. The next photo was taken on the 4th of July 1999, at another of the Alsip family gatherings.

(Back row l. to r.) Danny Ray, David Marion, Dale Lee, Joan Alsip Birkes, Tommy Gerald, Kim Alsip; (Front row l. to r.) Bradley M., Steve Neu and his daughters Stevee and Brittany.

Thomas Gerald Alsip eldest child of J. M. and Zelda was born in Chandler on 27 June 1935. Tommy married Joyce Burchette, and they have lived for many years in the Oklahoma City and Edmond areas. In 1991 Tommy was appointed by the Oklahoma governor as adjutant general in charge of the Oklahoma Army and Air National Guard with a rank of Maj. General. He is presently the manager of "The Links Apartments and Golf Course" in Oklahoma City. His wife Joyce works for a bank in this same city where they are now living. To this union have been born three children as follows: Thomas, Mark, and Kimberly Kay.

Joan Alsip only daughter of Jesse and Zelda Alsip was born in Chandler on 18 Sept. 1936. She had one son Stephen R. Neu by her first marriage. She then married Jim Birkes, and they now live in Chandler. Joan and Jim are retired from construction building.

Dale Lee Alsip another son of Jesse and Zelda was born in Chandler on 27 July 1938. He married Sheridan "Sheri" Hamilton in 1960, and they have established their residence in Webbers Falls, Oklahoma. Dale works for the National American Insurance Company. Dale and Sheri have one child, a daughter named Melanie who is the mother of Shawna and Dustin James.

David Marion Alsip third born son of Jesse and Zelda became a member of the Alsip family on 10 May 1946, which was the year following the end of the second world war. Jesse and Zelda were living in Chandler when David was born. He married Denise Pozzuolo and they now live in Chandler. In January of 1984, David assumed the operation of his father's ready mix concrete business and ran this company until it was sold in February 1995. David is also retired from the government, and as does his brother Dale, works for the National American Insurance Company. Denise works for the Policy Management Services Corporation out of South Carolina. David and Denise have three children. They are David Andrew, Bradley Marion, and Jennifer Jean. David Andrew and wife Kathy are expecting their first child in October 2003. Bradley Marion and wife Crissy have two children, Alexandra Nicole and Cason Bradley. David Marion's stepchildren are Peter and Andrea Marie Calvanese.

Danny Ray the last child of Jesse Marion and Zelda was born to them in Chandler on 20 March 1948. Danny married Rinda Starr, and they maintain their present residence in Stillwater, Oklahoma. However, Danny works in Chandler where he is vice president of the Union National Bank. Rinda is employed by Oklahoma State University in Stillwater. Their children are Jessica, Marshall, and Benjamin.

The tradition that Jesse Marion Alsip and his wife Zelda left behind of helping many individuals in the town of Chandler, both financially and spiritually, is a family heritage treasured by his present day descendants.

They were quick to lend a helping hand to anyone in need. Dale and David Alsip also remember the hunting trips that their father Jesse took them on when they were boys. David and Dale continue this family honored pastime to this day with the memory of Jesse accompanying them.

Chapter VIII

John Alsop of Surry Co., England

(This family is continued from page 132, Vol. II, Alsop's Tables)

John Alsop came to this country after being sentenced for a crime in England. He served in the Revolutionary War and the History of Western Maryland reports that John Alsop of Frederick Co., Maryland, 2nd Regiment, was wounded at the battle of Cowpens in 1781. He was wounded again in 1783 and used the act of General Assembly of 1778 of Maryland to receive half-pay for his wife and annuities for his children after the war. John, according to his military records, died on 2 May 1805. He left descendants, one believed to have been a son named Jacob, as a court record of Maryland has been discovered which states that John indentured his son Jacob in 1790. This Jacob was either the brother or father of Joseph Alsop who married Mary McKim in 1814. Joseph Alsop (Alsip) lived first in Frederick Co. and then in Washington Co. where he died and left descendants who have already been covered or will be in the following paragraphs.

Children of Joseph and Mary McKim Alsip were determined by available information and the final conclusion cannot be considered absolutely accurate. They are believed to have been Jacob, Joseph, John, Hezekiah, Elizabeth, Mary, and Julian (n) who was either a sister of Joseph, Sr., or his daughter. Accounts of the life of Jacob and his descendants were given in the preceding chapter.

Hezekiah Alsip was reported in Alsop's Tables, Vol. II, page 127, as living with his wife, a child named Susan C., and his brother John. The census record was approximately as follows:

Alsip (Allsup), Hezekiah -Age 21-Male-Born Maryland-Occupation Laborer
Alsip, Hannah -Age 20-Female-Born Maryland
Alsip, Susan C. -Age 3 Months-Female-Born Maryland
Alsip, John -Age 35-Male-Born Maryland

A summary of the census record ten years later for the 1860 enumeration for Washington Co., Maryland, Hagerstown follows:

Alsip(Allsup), Hezekiah -Age 30- Male-Born Maryland-Occupation Laborer
Alsip, Elizabeth -Age 35- Female-Born Maryland
Alsip, John -Age 14- Male- Born Maryland
Alsip, Norman- Age 5- Male- Born Maryland
Alsip, Elizabeth- Age 3-Female- Born Maryland
Alsip, infant (William H.)-Age 1 Month-Male-Born Maryland

Next is the 1860 census for Allegheny Co., Maryland- District 9- Flintstone, Maryland:

Alsip(Alsupe), John -Age 47- Male- Born Maryland- Occupation Laborer
Alsip, Hannah- Age 30- Female- Born Maryland
Alsip, Susan C.-Age 11- Female- Born Maryland
Alsip, William C.-Age 7- Male- Born Maryland
Alsip, John F. - Age 5- Male- Born Maryland
Alsip, James H.-Age 2- Male- Born Maryland

From the above census records, either the census taker put the wrong husband with the wrong wife in the 1850 census or John ran off with

Hezekiah's wife by the next census in 1860. Since John and Hezekiah moved to Ogle Co., Illinois in the late 1860's, circumstantial evidence indicates that the enumerator made the mistake and should have placed John with Hannah as man and wife. On page 128 of Alsop's Tables, Volume II, Hezekiah was reported as being in Monongalia Co., West Virginia. He was also reported in Ogle Co., Illinois for this same 1880 census living with the F. Dorsey Fouke family and his age was 52.

Dorsey Fouke and wife Elizabeth Ellen Alsip Fouke-
Taken 1913 on 40th wedding anniversary

On page 128 is a statement that Sarah Elizabeth Alsip, daughter of Hezekiah, returned to Maryland. Supplementary information has proven that she is not the Elizabeth Alsip who married David Powell. Elizabeth "Eliza" Ellen Alsip, born 5 Nov. 1857-died 7 April 1938, the daughter of Hezekiah remained in Ogle Co., Illinois and married in 1873 Fredrick Dorsey Fouke, born 20 March 1837-died February 1917.

The children of Dorsey and Ellen Fouke were Flora Norene "Nora", born 4 Feb. 1875, Fredrick Scott, born 21 Nov. 1877, William Hezekiah, born 6 May 1880, and Robert Hitt, born 21 July 1885.

On a genealogy research trip in September 1992, I traveled to Ogle Co., Illinois and determined that Hezekiah Alsip had died in 1893 and was buried in the Plainview Cemetery in Mt. Morris. I had a most enjoyable visit with his great-granddaughter Mrs. Lela Mae Stromberg who is the one who provided the photo of her grandparents. She lived in Oregon, Illinois which is the county seat of Ogle Co. She said that her grandmother told her that her father Hezekiah Alsip worked for the Chicago and Iowa Railroad, and while at work always had a pencil behind his ear. A workman came up to him one day and said, "If that pencil on your ear was as heavy as these railroad ties that I carry around, your ear would be hanging way down." Her grandmother Elizabeth "Eliza" Alsip Fouke also told her that her mother Elizabeth, wife of Hezekiah, had died when Eliza was eight years old. The cemetery records of Hagerstown, Maryland indicate that Elizabeth Alsip, wife of Hezekiah, died on 25 April 1867, which proves that Eliza had a good memory but not a perfect one. Eliza also told her granddaughter that her mother Elizabeth had died in a mental institution. Eliza said that Hezekiah Alsip, her father took them to Daysville when they first arrived in Ogle Co. which was a small town about four or five miles south of Oregon, Illinois. Several years later they moved to Mt. Morris where they established permanent residence.

Hezekiah Alsip bought two acres for 70 dollars from Jacob Hilger on 8 August 1879, and sold this same lot in Mt. Morris to Frederick Brayton in 1881 for 60 dollars. He also bought Lot 14, Block 6 in Mt. Morris from Joseph Waggoner and wife for 110 dollars in 1881. He also bought Lots 5-10, Block 17 from Charles Newcomer in 1883 for 150 dollars. He sold most of this property to his daughter Elizabeth E. Fouke and her husband in 1886. The court records show that Hezekiah Alsip and George Windle were involved in a court suite dated 14 Aug. 1886, which probably accounted for Hezekiah disposing of all of his property.

I visited the Plainview Cemetery located on the southwest edge of Mt. Morris off Brayton Rd. behind the high school. Hezekiah's tombstone is located in the circle, and next to his marker is the grave stone of his son Norman who died on 3 Nov. 1877, at the age of 22. Also buried nearby are Hezekiah's daughter Eliza, her husband Dorsey, and two of her sons Fred S. and William H. Mrs. Lela Mae Stromberg was the daughter of Flora Norene Fouke. Jeff Wilken, a grandson of Mrs. Stromberg, has corresponded with me and is doing research on the Hezekiah Alsip lineage.

John Alsip, brother of Hezekiah, moved to Ogle Co. at the same time that his brother did. His wife Hannah is replaced in the 1870 census by Julia A. Alsip whose maiden name is believed to have been White. It is unknown what happened to Hannah or John's oldest daughter Susan C. The rest of his family moved with him to Ogle Co. There is a marriage record in the Ogle Co. Courthouse for a John H. (F. or T.?) Alsip to Julia A. Hagerman in 1873 as recorded in Marriage Book "C", page 139. This is probably the son of John and Julia A. White Alsip who was born about 1855 in Maryland This son John is not living in Ogle County in 1880, but the census reports him in 1900 as age 44 and living in the household of Levi Shambow in Madison Co., Montana where he was a hired hand. Another marriage record was found in this same county as William C. Alsip, another son of John and Julia A. White Alsip, married Martha Harmon in 1882, as recorded in M. B. I, page 62. Their move to Missouri was detailed in Alsop's Tables, Vol. II.

John and his wife Julia White Alsip bought and sold numerous pieces of property during his residence in Ogle Co. He moved from Polo to Grand Detour after a few years and lived there until at least 1886, which was the last year that the records list property bought or sold by John. In 1882, John sold 38 acres to James Creed, and he was reported on the deed as a widower. It is unknown if John died in Ogle Co., but none of his male children were living in Ogle Co. when the 1900 census was completed.

Joseph Alsip, son of Joseph Alsip and wife Mary McKim, died prior to Aug. 1851, and his widow Eliza Yowler had a daughter Alice, born ca. 1853, a son Franklin P., born 1855 or 1856, and another daughter Amelia, born ca. 1857. When Eliza married as her second husband Samuel Gouker in 1860, her last three children kept the Alsip surname. They were also listed as step-children of the head of the household on the 1870 census which would have been Samuel Gouker, thus he was evidently not their father. It is unknown who the father of these last three children was, but Joseph Alsip could not have been their father.

In the History of Western Maryland, Volume II, page 1268, John Henry and brother Silas D. Alsip were reported as living in Cavetown Dist. 7, on the extreme eastern border of Washington Co. near the Pennsylvania State Line. Their homes were located in Election District 18, School District 1, and Silas was elected a trustee in May 1882.

Millard S. and Charles Travice Alsip, sons of John Henry and Mary Grove Alsip, joined their sister Edith F. Alsip Wine, who had married Edward S. Wine in Carroll Co., Illinois on 16 Oct. 1891, and established residence in Milledgeville, Illinois. On 17 Oct. 1895, Edith Wine and husband sold their home to her brother Charles T. and wife Mary Emma Brown Alsip and moved away. Charles and Emma lived the remainder of their life in Carroll Co. When Emma died on 2 Aug. 1943, at Milledgeville, Charles was already dead. He died sometime after 15 Nov. 1941, as on that date he and wife Emma sold property to Carl and Dorothy Merchant. Emma left an estate valued at $ 7, 493.23 which was divided among her sisters Louise Merchant and Alice Plock after gifts of $ 500 each were given to her nephews Harold and John Alsip, sons of Millard and Francis Secelia Bentley Alsip and $ 1,000 to her niece Louisa Merchant, daughter of her sister Louise Brown Merchant.

Francis Alsip, wife of Millard, died in Milledgeville on 28 Jan. 1905, leaving her husband and two minor children to share her estate. Harold Alsip was 9 years of age on 7 Feb. 1905, and John was 6 years of age on 6 Oct. 1904. On 12 July 1912, Harold and John each received money from the John Bentley estate (their maternal grandfather), and they each received an amount from their mother's estate of $ 1,632.49 on 23 April 1917.

By 1920, Millard had moved to Dakota Co., Minnesota and was living on Spring Park Hill Street in St. Paul with his second wife Ella, age 39, born in Denmark, and their children Charlie, 8, Harry, 6, Clarence, 5, Kenneth, 3, and Allen, 1. Living with them was Harold Leroy Alsip, 23, son of Millard and his first wife. In 1943, both Harold and his brother John were living in Oelwein, Iowa.

Harry W. Alsip, son of John Henry and Mary Grove Alsip, had a daughter Hulda, born 1903, who was still living at home with her widowed mother Martha and her brother Ferdinand, age 22, when the 1920 census was enumerated. Also living in the household located at 312 S. Mulberry St. in Hagerstown was a granddaughter Martha A. Oubert, age 2. It has not yet been determined which of Martha's daughters was the mother of this grandchild.

Joseph Ragan Alsip, son of John Henry Alsip and second wife Sarah Reynolds Alsip, and his wife Nora Emily Bidle were the parents of seven children with a set of twins among the group. The census of 1920 lists Joseph R., age 28, wife Nora, age 29, Ruth, age 6, Joseph, age 4, John, age 3, and Silas, age 3. The other three children were born after this census. Lawrence Nathan Alsip, the last child born in this family grew up and married Ida Bernice Mowen and has lived his life in the Hagerstown, Md. area. He was the father of Lawrence Nathan, Jr., and Susan Marie Alsip.

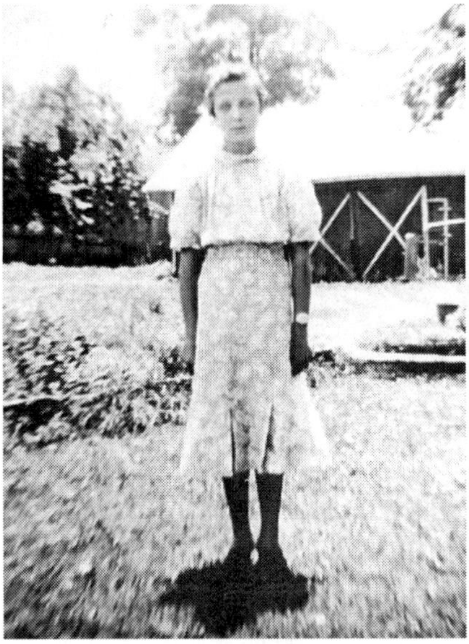

Louise Alsip Tracy

Joseph Daniel Alsip

Ruth Elizabeth Alsip South

Joseph Daniel, John Edward, Silas Raymond and Ruth E. Alsip

I visited Lawrence Nathan Alsip, Jr., ca. 1985 at State Line, Pennsylvania where he operated a barber shop. He was very helpful with family information and interested in the family history. He has a son Lawrence Nathan, III, who still lives in the area.

Franklin Pierce Alsip

Franklin Pierce Alsip and his wife Annie "Anna" Robinson Alsip were living in their home in Hagerstown, Maryland in Washington Co., 27th Election District, 5th Ward when the census of 1930 was compiled. Frank was 73 and his wife was 71. He listed his occupation as the Superintendent of Washington County Farm-Bellvue Asylum.

Franklin P. Alsip, son of Joseph and Eliza Yowler Alsip, was living at 680 Pennsylvania Ave., Hagerstown, Md. with his wife Anna when the census of 1920 was recorded. Their children had all left home and were starting families of their own. Franklin died in 1933, and his wife

Anna died in 1932 with both being buried at the Rose Hill Cemetery in Hagerstown. Buried in the Smithburg Cemetery is Sarah E. Alsip, wife of David H. Powell, who was born 11 Oct. 1856, and died 8 Aug. 1933. She is believed to have been a sister of John Henry, Silas D., and Franklin P.

George E. Alsip, son of Franklin Pierce Alsip and wife Anna, lived in Hagerstown where he and Armetta had four children. They were Kathryn R., born ca. 1905, Dorothy L., born ca. 1907, Mary B., born ca. 1911, and William F., born ca. 1911. I visited Kathryn in the 1980's at her home at 340 Belview in Hagerstown, and she told me that her mother had died in 1918. After their mother's death, the children went to live with their grandmother Martha Shrader at 729 Potomac Ave. in Hagerstown where they were in 1920. That same year their father George E. Alsip was boarding with the Deffendall family at 328 W. Washington St. George married as his second wife on 2 Jan. 1925, Clara B. Cain, a divorcee who was aged 29. Data R., a daughter of Franklin and Anna, married a man named Bockman, but nothing else has been learned about her. Data's brother Harry P. Alsip had a serious argument with his father Franklin P. and ran away from home never to return.

Edith Elmire Alsip, daughter of Franklin Pierce Alsip and wife Anna Isadore Robinson Alsip, was born in Hagerstown on 2 May 1900, and married twenty year old Burton Taylor Shaffer on 22 Sept. 1914, at the tender age of 14. He operated a blacksmith business in Hagerstown until he went to work for the Posey Iron Works and stayed with them until his retirement. He worked in Glens Falls, N. Y. and ca. 1926 moved permanently to Lancaster, Pa. where he and Edith established their residence at 2828 Columbia Avenue in Lancaster. They were the parents of Stanley, June, and Burton, Jr. Edith was a member of the Lancaster Chapter 501 Order of the Eastern Star while Burton was a Mason. Paul R. Cogley, a grandson of Edith and son of her daughter June, remembers her as a typical, loving grandmother, a great cook, and someone with whom he spent a lot of time. Burton died 6 Oct. 1974, and Edith died 14 June 1993 at Rheems Nursing Home.

Living at 134 W. Washington St. in 1920 were Edwin B. and wife Clara V. Kelly Alsip. This son of Franklin and Anna was married to

Clara at the Christ Reformed Church on 27 Oct. 1919, and their progeny consisted of three daughters.

Wanda Lee, first child of Edwin and Clara, was born in Hagerstown on 24 Feb. 1922, and married on 20 Oct. 1939, Carroll Walter "Mac" McPherson, Sr., born 13 May 1917. Their children were Walter, Douglas, Carolyn Brinkman, Connie Miller, Patricia Johnson, Brenda Earnest, and Sheryl Stout.

In 1946, Carroll and Wanda left Hagerstown and moved to Florida. Their son Carroll Walter McPherson, Jr., was born 3 July 1944, and was two years old when his family relocated to Orlando. Carroll, Sr., was in the trucking business there and was semi-retired in 1989. Wanda was a full time homemaker and mother. Carroll Walter, Jr., has a daughter Stephanie McPherson who married Joe Grohol and they live in Pennsylvania. She is very interested in her family history and has supplied very helpful information on her specific lineage.

. On Sunday 22 October 1989, the following photo appeared in the Colorado Springs, Colorado newspaper announcing the 50th wedding anniversary of Wanda and her husband.

Carroll and Wanda McPherson

The second daughter of Edwin and wife was Ellen who was born 19 April 1926, in Hagerstown. She married first a Miller and then a Demsey and had four children. Her oldest was Ronnie Miller who was born 24 June 1946; then Robert, born 13 Sept. 1949; Dennis, born 6 Nov. 1956; and Sherri, born 30 April 1962. Ellen now lives in Grand Prairie, Texas to be near her son Ronnie.

The last child born to Edwin and Clara Alsip was Emily, born in Hagerstown 2 Nov. 1931, who married Charles Daymude. She and her husband lived in the Hagerstown area with most of that time spent residing in Smithsburg, a suburb of Hagerstown. Emily and Charles were the parents of three children: Charles, Jr., born 22 May 1949, Raymond, born 17 July 1950, and Vickie, born 25 Dec. 1952. Charles, Sr., is now deceased, and Emily was still living in Smithsburg in 2003.

Chapter IX

Joseph Alsop of Surry Co., England and His Descendants

(This family is continued from page 136, Vol. II, Alsop's Tables)

Joseph Alsop, along with his brother John, was exiled to America as a convicted criminal from his native country of England. He fought and died for his new country in the Revolutionary War, but left two sons to carry on the family name. These two sons left descendants who were described, as well as extant records would allow, in the previous volume of this family genealogy. We now continue with Joseph's descendants.

Joseph and Sarah Alsip had one more child, a son, Reamer, born in 1861, in Bedford Co., Pa. Sarah died in September 1864, leaving Elizabeth the task of helping her father raise the two youngest children. The census of 1870 records Joseph as having personal property worth $500 and owning no real estate. Nothing more is known about Joseph or any of his children except Nelson and Reamer.

By 1900, Reamer Alsip, born July 1861, his wife Kate M., born December 1865, and his children were living in their home at 88 Commercial St., District #22 Union, Alleghany Co., Cumberland, Maryland. Living nearby at 158 S. Mechanics St., District #4, Cumberland Canal, was his brother, Nelson. He was the guest in the household of Canda Wilson. Cumberland, Maryland is located only about 30 miles directly south of

Bedford, Pennsylvania. Additional research should determine present day descendants.

The census report of 1870 for Bedford, Pennsylvania discloses that John and Mary Metzger Alsip were living in Bedford Twp. near Bedford, where John had a large farming operation. His real property was evaluated at 14,000 dollars and his personal property at 600 dollars. Living with him were his children Elwood, 22, Charles E., 19, Emma, 17, Frank, 15, Wandal,12, and Addell, 9.

Joseph Taylor Alsip, son of John and Mary, was living near his parents in the home of his mother-in-law, Mary Smith, in 1870. He had married Delilah Smith, born 1846, two years earlier in Bedford. Joseph was employed in farming and claimed real estate evaluated at 15,000 dollars which was probably the property of his wife's mother.

In Waterman's History of Bedford, Somerset, and Fulton Counties, pages 488 and 489, is found the following biographical account of Joseph Taylor Alsip.

HON. JOSEPH TAYLOR ALSIP

Joseph Taylor Alsip, whose name heads this sketch, the genial and well known hotel proprietor, and who has for many years represented the interests of his county in a worthy and masterly manner, owes the greater part of his success in his various undertakings to his own indomitable energy and perseverance.

He was born in Shellsburg, Bedford County, Pennsylvania, March 11, 1845, and at the age of six years removed with his parents to Bedford, in the same county, his father having been appointed sheriff of Bedford County. There he has since had his residence. He was educated in the public schools of Bedford, in the Bedford Academy and at Duff's Commercial College, in Pittsburg, Pennsylvania. He was thus practically and well equipped for the burdens and responsibilities placed upon his shoulders, and he has borne the burden nobly. He served one year in the office of the Pennsylvania Railroad office as clerk at Middletown, and later became the proprietor of the Arandale Hotel, which he conducted very successfully for thirty years. He was also manager of the Bedford Springs Hotel for five years.

His interest in the public affairs of the county was always of the keenest description, and he devoted much time and attention to the conduct of public matters, investigating every subject thoroughly and deliberately. He was elected a member of the house of representatives in 1902, and so satisfactory with conscientious and efficient discharge of the duties of his office that he was re-elected in November, 1904. He is possessed of the confidence and respect of the entire community, who feel that he is conducting the affairs of the county in a most competent manner.

This same history of Bedford Co. also has other entries for members of the Alsip family. On page 206 is found the listing of the Members of the Bar for Bedford Co. They were J. Nelson Alsip, 22 Nov. 1882; Espy N. Alsip, 6 May 1863; and John Alsip, 13 Feb. 1868. On page 217 J. Nelson Alsip was reported as born in McConnellsburg, Fulton Co., Pennsylvania on 25 Aug. 1850. Page 225 lists an Alsip as a Justice of the Peace for Bedford Co. between the years of 1864 and 1878. Page 252 records John Alsip as being an attorney in Bedford in 1860. Page 253 also notes that John Alsip was a retired farmer in 1860. John Alsip was described on page 268 as owning an old grist mill in Wolfsburg, Bedford Twp., in 1860. John Alsip was also reported to have had another grist mill in the town of Buffalo Mills, Harrison Twp., from 1850-1860 as found on page 365. On page 369 John Alsip was credited with being one of the founders of the Dry Ridge Reformed and Lutheran Church which was built in 1842. This was the first church in Juniata Twp. in Bedford Co.

John Alsip, Jr., was involved in numerous avocations and pursuits during his lifetime and seems to have been successful in all of them. He died in Bedford in 1885, a highly respected member of the community. His wife, Mary Metzger, was living in the home of her son-in-law, George W. Purcell, in 1900, and died there the following year.

Always considerate and accommodating individuals, Joseph Taylor and his wife, Delila Smith Alsip, looked after her mother and sisters in their own home, as none of the four sisters ever married. The sisters were Willa, born 1825, Malvina, born 1829, Eliza, born 1837, and Amanda, born 1843.

In December, 1872, Joseph and Delila's only child, Gussie F., was born. She was still living at home with her parents and aunts when the

1900 census enumeration was enacted. Gussie married Alvin L. Little sometime in the early 1900's and became a member of the DAR through her ancestor, Joseph Alsop, of Frederick County, Maryland, who was killed in the Revolutionary War.

The death of Joseph Taylor Alsip occurred in 1914, in Bedford, Pa. It is unknown when his wife died. No date of death is yet available for their only daughter, Gussie.

Several daughters of John and Mary Metzger Alsip remained in Bedford where they married and had families of their own. Espy M. Alsip, the only other son of John and Mary to stay in Bedford, was living on Juliana Street in 1880 with his wife, Mary E. Hafner, age 33, and their two children Rena E., 10, and Cora E., 8.

Espy was probably dead by 1900, as the census of that year lists his wife, Mary and daughter, Rena W. Alsip as living in the home of her mother, Caroline Hafner, in Bedford County near the town of Bedford. In the next census Mary had inherited the home of her deceased mother and was living there as head of the household. Living with her were her daughter, Rena, and her brother, Harry O. Hafner, who was a boarder.

The Pennsylvania Magazine of History and Biography, Vol. XXXIV, No. 2, published in 1915, says, "The Bedford House, a stone structure now owned by Mrs. Mary E. Alsip (widow of Espy Alsip), was built in 1771 by Rev. William Smith, D. D., first provost of the University of Pennsylvania." In 1920, Mary E. Hafner Alsip, age 72, was living at 125 W. Pitts St. in the town of Bedford, Pa., and her unmarried daughter, Rena, age 50, was living with her. Mary's brother, Harry, was also still living with her. The 1930 census reports Rena Alsip as age 60, single, and living alone in Bedford Borough, Bedford Co., Pa. in household 162-184. This tends to indicate that her mother Mary E. Hafner Alsip was deceased by this time.

Reamer Alsip, age 39, and his wife Katherine Lottig Alsip, age 34, according to the 1900 census, had the following children living in their household: Russell H., age 12, Louisa S., age 10, Albert W., age 9, Ralph C., age 6, Herman L., age 3, and Margarett E., age 1. Reamer Alsip was the son of Joseph and Sarah Cromwell Alsip. Twenty years later when the 1920 census was reported, Reamer was still living in Allegheny Co., Maryland with his wife Katherine and the children still at home who were Herman, Margurite, Clarence, and Mildred. Their address was 34 South Smallwood Ave. in Cumberland, Maryland. One of their children Albert W. Alsip was living in Fayette Co., Connellsville, Pennsylvania at 217 Cedar Ave. where he was boarding with a Mrs. Lydia McManis.

The census of 1930 listed three families of Alsips living in Cumberland, Maryland which is in Alleghany Co. Reamer H. Alsip was living in the lst Ward with his wife Katherine, age 66, and his son-in-law William E. Green who had married his daughter Mildred V., age 24. William and Mildred had one child, a daughter named Shirley who was two years of age. Clarence F. Alsip, age 28, son of Reamer and Katherine, was living with his wife Anna N., age 24, in the 4th Ward. The other family was that of Herman L. Alsip, another son of Reamer and Katherine. He was age 34, and was living with his wife Marie C., age 31, and their two children Catherine, age 9, and Mary L., age 6.

Blair Alsip who lives at 467 S. Washington St. in Tiffin, Ohio is a grandson of Reamer through his father Russell Alsip. He is interested in the family history and is researching his specific branch of the family tree.

Chapter X

John Allsop of St. Mary's Parish, Nottingham, England

(This family is continued from page 156, Vol. II, Alsop's Tables)

Most of the material in this chapter is being presented just as I received it from descendants of John Allsop who came to the United States in 1854 from England. My appreciation and admiration are extended to those members of this branch of the family tree who had enough interest and forethought to document their family happenings, though they may have thought them very ordinary at the time. Special thanks are due Elaine Allsop Andersen who collected many of these family stories and historical records and sent them to me so that they could be preserved for posterity in this third volume of our family genealogy.

(Elizabeth Allsop Hamp daughter of John and Mary Ellen Wood Allsop wrote a short summary of the lives of her parents, a portion of which is now presented.)

John Allsop was born in England and there joined the Mormon Church. (Records indicate that his brother Richard was the only other member of his family to be baptized by this church.) John immigrated to Utah, bringing with him his wife Susannah Robbins who was in poor health. Susannah died at the first camp ground and was buried there. Mary Ellen Wood was in the company and married John Allsop, my father, on 12 Sept. 1854.

They first made their home in Bountiful, Utah, where they had four children: John Ira Allsop, Mary Ellen, Susannah, and Charles. They moved to Richmond, Utah in the spring of 1860, and built a log house with three rooms. Times were hard, and they endured all the hardships of pioneer life. My father was a carpenter by trade, and he had a lathe and made furniture for all the people around. He took anything they could eat or wear for pay. In this way, they got along.

Father took a third wife in Salt Lake City, Utah on 15 March 1867. (She was actually his fourth wife. Caroline Moore was his first wife, Susannah Robbins, his second.) Mother divided all the household goods to start a new home for Aunt Hannah Eskelson Allsop. They built a log home for her, and they were all very happy.

Father was a very faithful latter-day saint, and always tried to do right. He was a counselor to Brother Merrill in the bishopric. I remember when he took us four little girls to Sunday School on a hand sled so we would not get our feet wet.

Father died 25 October 1876, at Richmond, Utah leaving mother a widow with nine children. It was sixteen years from the time he came to Bountiful until his death at Richmond.

(Effie Allsop Greene, granddaughter of John and Mary Ellen Wood Allsop, left a brief, but very descriptive treatise of her grandmother which grew out of her childhood reminiscences.)

I remember grandmother first as a Primary president, when she lived at Richmond, Utah. I loved to go to her home; she had so many pretty ornaments, vases, dishes of a novelty nature and one especially, a beautiful Madonna which stood one and a half feet high. I used to love to look at this and dream of Mary, the mother of Christ, and her child.

Grandmother was Primary president of the Richmond Ward for about 15 years. She must have been exceptionally good at the work, for many times during my church work as stake president of the Relief Society in Benson Stake, I was told by men and women who were once her primary children, that she was indeed an influence for good in their lives. Sometimes I felt as though I were riding along on her fame.

In her later years she left Utah and moved to Gentile Valley, Idaho, where her children lived. She died at Turner, Idaho, 18th of April 1911, and was buried at Richmond, Utah beside her husband on the 21st of the same month.

She left her home in England as a young girl, 18 years of age, to join the Latter-day Saints.

She lived at one time with us, or in an apartment in our house, at Thatcher, Idaho. She loved to go to church, and I can remember her so well, when she used to bear her testimony in fast meetings.

I used to love to go into her room sometimes when she would tell me a story or about some book she had read.

One day she told me this story about herself. It was a cold, snowy, frosty day. She was president of the primary. There was no janitor to care for the church house, so when it came time for primary, she had to gather kindling wood from her own meager pile and carry it to the church, which was about three blocks, and start a fire to warm the house for primary. Being terribly discouraged because of her duties at home, being a widow, and having to take the part of father as well as mother to her family, she deemed it all a task which was too big for her to carry.

Just as she was breaking the wood to start the fire, a window from across the room was raised and the head and shoulders of a man appeared in the window. He called her to him and told her how much good she was doing among the children in the ward, and promised her that she should be blessed with the necessities of life and health and strength to perform her duties. She said that she did not stop to consider whom she was talking to at the time, but after the fire was burning and she had time to pause, she was really bewildered. She went outside to see if she could see anyone nearby, and she noted that there were not even foot-prints in the new-fallen snow anywhere leading to the window. To grandmother, it was definitely one of the three nephites who had paid her a visit, and left with her an influence that was most consoling and uplifting.

As I remember her she was spiritual minded, and faithful to her convictions. She loved a party, and she loved a joke, and she lived to laugh, and like Santa Claus, she had a little round belly that shook when she laughed like a bowl full of jelly.

(The following information about Johannah Marie Eskelson, the fourth wife of John Allsop, was compiled by Sharlene Turner from material left by Vetris Adams Barnes. Vetris was the daughter of Johannah by her second husband Samuel Ferry Adams. It has been edited to reflect the portions of her life that related to the Allsop family.)

JOHANNAH MARIE ESKELSON ALLSOP ADAMS

Johannah Marie Eskelson was born January 29, 1849, near Copenhagen in Urland, Denmark, the daughter of Niels Christian Eskelson and Mette Marie Larsen. With her parents she embraced the Gospel of the Church of Jesus Christ of Latter-day Saints, was baptized March 20, 1858, and at the age of 15 she and her parents came to America for the sake of her religion. The following year she and her family came across the plains with the Mormon pioneers with the Napika Handcart Company. She pushed a cart until they reached the Rocky Mountains when she was taken ill with mountain fever and had to be confined to a covered wagon the rest of the way. She and her family settled in Richmond, Cache County, Utah, where she grew to womanhood.

On March 16, 1867, she was married to John Allsop of Richmond in polygamy and was his second wife. To this union were born four children - Sarah, born March 17, 1868 (married Edward E. Thompson on March 18, 1883), and died May 6, 1928; Josephine, born July 12, 1870 (married to William Fresh September 1, 1888) and died April 3, 1957; Ezra, born March 10, 1873 (who had three marriages), and died January 20, 1963;

Parley, born September 25, 1875, and died October 25, 1876. While the children were young her husband passed away.

She has been a faithful and willing church worker and has always been of great assistance in times of sickness and trouble in the community. "Aunt Hannaher" brought the babies (Mormon and non-Mormon) into the world. She nursed the sick and washed and prepared the dead for burial. Her heart was as big as her territory. Eliza E. Wilson, going with her, became as skilled as she.

She was tall and strong, had a great sense of humor, worked hard all her life, and was blessed with good health. She loved everyone, especially her Father in Heaven, and had a devout testimony of the Gospel. She helped everyone she could and was very independent to the day of her death. She passed away in June 1936 at the age of 87 in the home she loved so much and helped to build. She is buried in the Thomas-Riverside Cemetery.

At the time of her death she was survived by three sons and two daughters: Ezra Allsop, Josephine Fresh, John Adams, Roy Adams, and Vetris Barnes. She also had three stepchildren: Mrs. Thomas Clark, Mrs. Joseph Clark and Herbert Adams. Other living relatives were two brothers, John and Nils Eskelson plus 59 grandchildren and 94 great-grandchildren.

(The next genealogical sketch was written by Evelyn Allsop Sessions, daughter of John Ira Allsop)

A BIT OF IDAHO PIONEERING

John Ira Allsop was born at Bountiful, Davis County, Utah, on July 2, 1855 son of John and Mary Ellen (Wood) Allsop. Bountiful was then called "Sessions Settlement" and was considered a part of Salt Lake City.

He was between 7 and 8 years of age when his parents were called to settle Richmond, Cache County, Utah. There he experienced the trials of early pioneer life.

His father was a carpenter and brought his tools with him from Cross Irk Street, Manchester, Lancaster County, England. Among them was a turning lathe, with which he made most of the furniture used by the early settlers of Cache Valley. John Ira learned the carpenter trade from his father.

As a young man, John Ira was tall and slender with medium brown hair and blue eyes, and a happy cheerful disposition. He gained weight in later life to 250 lbs.

His wife Mary Elizabeth (Tanner) Allsop, daughter of George and Martha (Craner) Tanner, was born November 5, 1862 at Tooele, Tooele County, Utah. Her father died when she was 10 years of age. The family lived several miles from Tooele City, and the children had to go to school on horse back. Her mother thought it was too dangerous to send her so far in the cold weather, consequently she received very little education.

After her family was raised and her husband had died, she taught herself to read, and kept quite well posted on current events.

Mary Elizabeth's mother later married Alexander Harries, Jr., and moved into Gentile Valley, Idaho. They lived on the place owned at present by her son John Alma Tanner.

Mary Elizabeth went to Richmond to work in the home of Sam Orsen. While there she met her future husband, who was doing a job of carpenter work on the same home. About two and one half years later, she again went to Richmond to work for Lib Bullen. On May 8, 1879 she and John Ira were married in the Endowment house in Salt Lake City, Utah by Daniel H. Wells.

They made their first home at Richmond at which place their oldest child John Ira, Jr., was born April 12, 1880. He died of pneumonia January 20, 1889 at Gentile Valley.

John Ira worked at the carpenter trade for a while, and then went into the butcher shop business.

On June 26, 1882, their second child Evelyn was born. She married Kepler Sessions, Jr. He died February 4, 1956 at Salt Lake City, Utah, and was buried February 7, 1956 at Chesterfield, Idaho.

When Evelyn was one year old, they moved into Gentile Valley. He paid $300.00 for 160 acres of land on the hill east of the James McGregor place, and south of the Henry Perry place, which was east of the Bear River Bridge and on the place at present owned by Frank Harris.

While living there, Johnny Perry, James McGregor, John Ira, and his brother Charles needed some recreation. One afternoon in mid-winter they took a pair of skis and fastened a barn door on top of them. They took it even higher on a hill than the house, which gave them about 3/4 of a mile run before they reached the river. They went down the first slope and across the level portion where the buildings were and headed for the river, gaining momentum every yard it traveled.

There was snow enough to take it over the rocks and the stiffest of the shrubs, then they came to a sudden drop and their humble little barn door arrangement immediately took on the dignity of a great air liner. Headed downward, it maintained this angle until it landed in the middle of Bear River. The impact broke the ice, and the whole passenger list was thrown into the river. Fortunately the water was shallow enough for them all to get their footing, and they took time out to drag their precious craft to safety. Then all set out for home sincerely hoping they would find a nice warm fire and some clothes that were not so stiff.

One can easily imagine the words of the old Sunday School song "Who Can Think The Winter Dreary," running through their ears, while their clothes were rapidly freezing to their bodies.

About this time reading novels and round dancing were almost considered the unpardonable sin. Never over two round dances were allowed in an evening.

John Ira had a strong musical voice and most always called for the quadrille. He would fairly sing his dancing instructions with the music. If he ever had to stop for a rest, the dance simply was not the same.

Only rarely did he read a novel. He preferred the standard church works; mostly the Book of Mormon.

Mary Elizabeth had a beautiful voice, and their evenings were spent by teaching church and social songs to the children.

This locality was first known as the Mound Valley Ward, and later known as the Perry Post Office.

On March 15, 1885 their third child George Tanner Allsop was born at Perry Bannock County, Idaho. He died 22 March 1950. His wife Eliza

(Christensen) Allsop died at Salt Lake City on January 15, 1957. Both were buried at Grace, Idaho, leaving eight children.

In their new locality in Gentile Valley, John Ira did carpenter work, black-smithing, butchering, and in fact anything that presented itself. He was willing to do any work to earn an honest living for his family.

0n March 13, 1887 Mary Elizabeth (Libbie) was born at Perry Bannock County, Idaho. She married Denzil L. Poulsen and died Aug. 6, 1913 leaving 4 children. John Ira and Mary Elizabeth took Libbie's children at first, but when the husband later remarried, he took the two oldest children. Libbie's parents kept the two younger children until they went for themselves.

Together with the rest of the work John Ira was doing, he was trying to get the water out of his 160 acres of land. However, it was so high above all the surrounding country, that he did not have the means to put over a project so expensive.

So he sold it for $300.00 and bought a team and wagon and went into the Caribou mining district.

He supervised the drilling and giant-powder explosives, and often went home with bursting headaches.

Mary Elizabeth, hard working little lady that she was, took in boarders, did some washing for the men, kept up the little shack and took care of her four children, Johnney, Eva, George and Libbie.

The little shack was near a deep gulch on the opposite side of which was the company boarding house with a negro cook. Johnney and Eva used to go across the gulch and sing negro songs for the cook, and he would always give them pie or cake.

It was difficult for the two older children to take the two little ones across the gulch.

So absorbed were they in their singing episode, that they often neglected the two little children. One day the two opera stars climbed out of the gulch in time to see their precious little sister toddle into the road in front of a four horse team with a wagon load of ore from the mine. The teamster did not see her until one of the lead horses struck her with his knee which threw her into the center of the road, and the entire outfit went over her.

As soon as he could stop that heavy load on the down grade of the canyon road, he ran back and picked up that darling baby and began brushing the dirt off. She rubbed the dust from her own pretty blue eyes, and when she saw the teamsters little dog, she said "Hello Penny." These proved to be two of the most joyful words ever spoken by a baby. She only had a bruise where the horse hit her with his knee.

This most definitely put an end to the afternoon entertainments.

That fall the little family went back to Gentile Valley and lived in the Henry Perry place owned just recently by George Perry. Jan. 20, 1889 the family had the misfortune to lose John Ira, Jr., who died of pneumonia. On January 30, 1889 William Henry, their fifth child, was born at Perry Bannock county, Idaho. He married Lydia Ruth Bonnell and had five children, with the oldest son Ray dying on April 30, 1950. He then married Sarah Alice Fullmer.

At that time Gentile Valley was divided into 4 wards: Lago on the north east; Thatcher on the north west; Mound Valley on the south east; and Cleveland on the south west. Mound Valley was much more beautiful than any of the other localities. It was so peaceful the writer fancies she can see our precious Savior walking leisurely down the road with his long white robe, his sandaled feet, and bare head, looking to the right and the left as if to admire his own handi-work. As he walked he must have pronounced a special blessing on Mound Valley. The country from there to Preston is so like descriptions she has read of the hilly country of Judea.

After a year or so the little family moved into the Snake River country, settling at Milford, and on January 30, 1892 Charles Alma was born at that place.

He married Bessie Whittengton in California while he was a soldier during World War One. They have two children.

John Ira moved into Marysville, Idaho on the North Fork of the Snake River. He and Heber Sharp went in partnership on a saw mill. Mary Elizabeth became ill, and her husband took her to a doctor in St. Anthony. They had to stay all night and when they got back next day, found that the mill had burned down in their absence.

This was the spring of 1893. They went again to Gentile Valley and lived in a part of her mother's house.

By way of recreation and improvement John Ira was always organizing and conducting home dramatic Co.s (this is what the L. D. S. Church wanted the people to do), and he was really gifted in this work. This early fall and winter a lovely company was built up. Among those who took part were Amy and Mana Williams, Arvet Hale and wife, Edgar Hale and wife, John Alma Tanner, Thomas Panter, Emma Perry and Will Williams, 0live and Jonathan Hale, Laura Bennett and others. John Ira painted the scenery.

A brass band was organized under the direction of Edgar and Arvet Tate. Both organizations were a credit to the little community. They traveled from one of the wards to another, and while they were traveling and presenting one play, they were studying the script for another. This was a very enjoyable year, and the best of fellowship was built up in the entire Valley.

Nearly every play had a negro in it, and this was always John Ira's part. He paid little attention to his own lines, only giving the right cue. His players often became so confused at his prattle that they would not recognize their own cue. In one of these plays a family was giving a dinner for some of their aristocratic friends. He the (negro)happened into the kitchen, saw the chicken, picked it up and, (we will let his niece Mrs. Effie Allsop Greene tell the story in her own poetic words).

"Twas the night of the drama and all through the house,
Not a creature was stirring, not even a mouse.
The curtain was closed, behind it the actors
And John Allsop, my uncle, was one of the factors.

I do not remember the sweet leading lady
The hero, to me could have been a doll baby
The villain supposedly must be a scamp
But how well I remember, Uncle John was a tramp.

The curtain ascended, each one played his part
I suppose did it well, and spoke from his heart,
But where's Uncle John? Things to me were not clicking
But Lo: here he comes with a bowl of fried chicken.

He a tramp, just imagine, had been to the cupboard
And left it all empty for poor Mother Hubbard.
He was seized with pure fright, and attempted to hide
So under the table he went with a slide.

The show moved on quickly, but he sat there with ease
And holding the bowl between his two knees,
He gobbled the chicken and flung all the bones
To the folk in the audience, while we dodged and moaned.

That's all I can tell you regarding the show
Just he and the chicken, seems to be all I know,
But the memory lingers with me to this day
He just ate and ate, not a word did he say.

I also remember his eyes how they twinkled
And that chicken I'm sure pushed out all the wrinkles.
Now that's the beginning, an also the end
Of a show, as a child I cried to attend.
To you this poem may sound a bit sappy
To me t'was a pleasure to see Uncle John HAPPY.

It was one thing for a person to eat a whole chicken, quite another for a 250 pound man to get under the table.

On January 13, 1894 their seventh child, Martha Louisa, was born at Perry Bannock County and a beautiful baby she was. She married George Perry and had two daughters. She died January 9, 1929.

In the spring, the family moved up to "The Bench" as it was called then. It is twenty five or thirty miles north of Gentile Valley. It was a large Valley of sage brush with Bear River running through it in a South Western direction.

Uninviting as it was, Mary Elizabeth told her husband the next time he moved her it would be to the grave yard.

"The Bench" greeted them with a frown on his face and half closed eyes, as if to say "If you invade my sacred premises you will have to fight," and fight they did.

He had built a two room log house, but it was not finished. He worked on it for a while, when he was offered a job at Hilliard's Saw Mill. This was in the log's section.

Hilliard was moving his mill in from some other location; they had hewn the brush and under growth off and leveled the ground for the mill yard.

One day John Ira was shoeing a horse, which leaned heavily against him as he knelt on the ground where an evergreen had been hewn off, running a splinter through his clothes and under his knee cap, causing a serious attack of blood poisoning.

The limb became very sore and swollen right from the first. The next day his condition forced him to leave camp and go to his sister, Mrs. Alice Calkins, who lived at Lago. They poulticed the limb and did everything they knew. Mary Elizabeth was ill at Grace, but went down to Lago to do all she could. He had a high fever and the entire limb was swollen and black.

There was no doctor north of Logan, and no way of getting him down there, but by team and wagon.

They were afraid the trip would cost him his life, and to leave him without medical care was equally dangerous.

He had a friend, John Toone, living in Thatcher Ward, who called to offer his help. He said that rattle snake oil was good for blood poison, and he would get the snakes himself, and see to it that they did not bite themselves thus poisoning their own bodies. In about two hours he returned with a quart fruit jar full of oil, still hot from rendering, (had taken the snakes into the home of a neighbor, cut them up in thin slices, and put them in the oven). Mr. Toone went right back to get another supply. The folks took the oil cloth from the table and spread it under John Ira, and with the oil in an improvised double boiler to keep it hot as could be borne, they wrung soft cloths out of the hot oil and wrapped them around the limb, replacing them as often as they cooled. They kept this up for hours and days. In a few hours he grew easier and even silent while they were working over him.

He was terribly weak, but after a few weeks they got some crutches and he was soon able to go home.

With the help of his wife and children he did some more work on the house.

That summer Mary Elizabeth's brother Dan Harris went up to "The Bench," plowed up a piece of ground, and planted some rye which matured enough to furnish hay for the team.

As the fall of 1895 came in, John Ira got to feeling better and did some more work on the house to make it more comfortable.

In December of that year, he was offered a job of carpenter work remodeling a home for Mrs. Anderson at Trout Creek. Included in this project was tearing down a lean-to and building a room in which to put her carpet loom. While pulling the casing from over the door, a can of powdered lye fell out and emptied its contents into his face, some of it going into his right eye. He ran madly out of doors rubbing his hair and face to brush off all he could. Then he began applying snow, but the moisture made the lye cut deeper. Mrs. Anderson took olive oil and applied it on and in his eyes, face, and hair.

Dr. Kackley told them years later that if they had used vinegar, it would have neutralized the eye better than the oil. He wore a mustache because the acid had eaten a hole through his upper lip so that his teeth could be seen. He also had a hole in his eye ball that a small garden pea could have been put in.

Some of the neighbors brought him home with a load of hay for the team. His suffering was intense, again no doctor was available, and what the family did for him, the writer does not know.

The eye lashes grew in causing wild hairs that would scratch the eye ball like sand. Every member of the family learned to extract the wild hairs by rolling the eye lid over a match and pulling them out with a pair of tweezers.

He never could face the sun light or lamp light after that and always wore a black hat drawn down well over his eyes.

This was the winter of 1895-6. On January 7, 1896 Chloe, their youngest daughter, was born on "The Bench," later Grace, Idaho. She married John Milton Goldsberry and had three children.

This was a hard winter with both of the parents ill. Mary Elizabeth soon got up and around the house, but John was sick all winter.

The settlers had to haul water from the Bear River for culinary purposes, and sometimes no teams were available. In that case, all the children would line out with lard or syrup buckets that fit their strength. Each got a bucket full of water, carrying it three fourths of a mile or more.

Mary Elizabeth's brother Frank Harris was working for Barney White who had a little white Shetland pony he wanted to sell. Frank in considering the deal said, "He is just the thing for Sissie's kids." So he bought the pony and gave it to the children.

Shetland was cute as he could be, and the children could do anything with him, but he was just too smart for grownups. He was white as the driven snow with two of the most beautiful black eyes one ever saw. In reality he was a SPOILED little brat, but how the children loved him.

When no teams were available, the children would get on Shetland and ride him up to Brother Fred Burtons and get old Jack, a big grey horse with his harness, and spend the day hauling water for their mother and the neighbors. They used to put a chain on Jack's side of the double tree, so about all Shetland did was to keep the neck yoke from dragging. But did he ever love to travel in double harness with Jack. One could see it in his beautiful eyes that he was having more fun than any one.

One could stand back a few steps from Jack and see Shetland under Jack's body.

In an emergency in the winter time Mary E. would melt snow to do her washing.

Very often in the summer she would load her tubs, boards, dirty clothes, soap and buckets on a drag, then hitch Shetland to it, and drag it to the river where she would heat her wash water and do a big washing. She then would drag her clothes back to the line. This is a hard way to do it, but she always put out a pretty washing.

John Ira Allsop and his wife lived at Richmond in their early married life and then moved to Mound Valley. After a few years they moved into Freemont County, Idaho, and then back to Mound Valley. They then located at Grace where they remained until their deaths.

He and his faithful wife endured all of the hardships of pioneer life at Grace, Idaho (a little less severe than the early pioneers of Utah) trying to establish themselves and build a home.

They raised a family of 9 Children and then a daughter, Mary Elizabeth, died leaving them two of her children Elmina and Earl Poulson to raise. They have both lived an active and busy life and were useful in making the "Desert Blossom as the Rose."

John Ira's health was generally good, but an attack of the 1918 "Flu" so impaired his health that he contracted Bright's disease and died at Logan, Utah on 4 Sept. 1922. Dr. Kackley visited the family just before the funeral, and pronounced him an "empire builder."

Mary Elizabeth toiled on, and six months after her husband's death she lost her grandson, Leland Poulson, who died 11 Feb. 1923. Then another daughter died 9 Jan. 1929. On 22 Mar. 1950, Mary Elizabeth lost her oldest son George, then on 29 Feb. 1952, she departed this life in her 90th year, having been a widow 30 years.

Effie Allsop Greene

Sarah Allsop Thompson

Susannah Allsop Ormond
1858-1883

This next story was taken from Effie Allsop Greene's Book No. 2. She was born 14 June 1889, at Grays Lake, Bingham Co., Idaho, the daughter of Thomas and Sylvia Ann Peart Allsop. Effie and John Platt Greene, born in Escalante, Garfield Co., Utah, on 15 June 1881, were married 24 Nov. 1909, in Salt Lake City. They were the parents of Afton, Erma, Wanda, and John G. Elaine Allsop Andersen describes her Aunt Effie as follows: "Effie, sister to Lew Peart Allsop, was truly a grand lady. Gracious, enjoyed life to the fullest. A happy gentle one. She was a writer, singer, and loved reading and teaching. A great teacher. A gentle soft spoken lady."

"SOME THINGS I HAVE LEARNED AND KNOW ABOUT MY FATHER"

Often times when I ride through the little town of Richmond, Utah, I let my imagination run back to the days of my father's childhood. He was born there on the 21st day of January 1865. His father was John Allsop and his mother was Mary Ellen Wood.

They lived just across the street from Merriner W. Merrill who was an Apostle of our Church. And I am sure that the Merrill family was a real help to Grandmother in her days of widowhood.

Thomas Allsop (my Father) was obliged to go out and find work away from home at a very early age in order to help sustain his Mother and younger brothers and sisters. I have heard him tell of working on the railroad while yet a boy. He was heard to say once, in later years, that he would rather take any child of his to the cemetery than see them pass through such circumstances as he sometimes had to experience in his youth.

As a small boy he was in dire need at times for such things as food and clothing. Pioneer days were hard at best. One thing they used to be in need of were matches to start fires. And often the neighbors would borrow fire from each other.

One morning, he said, when he had no shoes, it was a bitter cold day, and the coals of fire had completely burned out during the night time in their stove, he took a little bucket with a lid, and partly filled it with ashes. In his bare feet he ran through the snow over to Brother Merrills to get some hot coals so his mother could start a fire in her stove.

Father, even as a child, was hard to understand, sometimes. He always stood for correct principles no matter who was concerned, and sometimes his friends were led to think that he was not true to them because he always thought of principle first.

One time when he was a child at Sunday School, he was sitting in front of a smart-alecky boy who kept pulling Father's shirt-tabs out of his pants or sticking a pin in him. He warned the boy to stop, but he paid no heed to the warning, so Father just got up, turned around, climbed over the seat, and proceeded to beat up, in proper style, the annoying child - "beat him until he sqwaked." Well, Father was put out of Sunday School as a bad boy and told to never come back and it was a long time before he did. But it was Father's way always to stand for what seemed to him to be right, and to do a thing when it needed doing. So this time he did not wait until after Sunday School.

I heard him say once that he had tasted tobacco when he was very young, but he knew it was wrong according to his Mother's teachings so he decided to respect her teachings and leave tobacco alone.

Father as a young man was an exceptionally good marksman with a gun. He said that they tied a strap around a big tree and that Father rode a horse, on a gallop, around the tree, and carried a gun, and each time that he fired the gun, he hit the strap on the tree.

Father loved horses; they seemed to understand each other.

Once, so said "Uncle Joe" (Father's brother), Father had a team hitched to a sleigh and was breaking a bronco to drive. He was traveling on the roadway past the old Jenney place near the Folkman ranch in Thatcher, Idaho. A stranger passed him who was traveling southward, and seemingly it was he (the stranger) who had lost a vest from out of his sleigh. About a mile up the road, just after Father passed him, he found the vest. Having a bronco hitched up, and not caring to stop his team, Father just leaned over the vox on his sleigh and picked up the vest.

After he got home, he put his team in the barn and went back to the sleigh to get the vest, and in its pocket he found $1,000 dollars. (One thousand in green backs). He took the vest to the barn, and hung it up under an old leather coat that had hung on the wall for months and maybe years. He never mentioned to anyone of his find. He decided he would wait and see what might happen in a reasonable length of time.

About six months later a man came down through the valley inquiring at each home to see if anyone knew of its whereabouts.

He called at Fathers and Father went and got the vest with the money in it, handed it to the fellow, and told him where he found it.

The man took it in a free careless way and didn't even say thank you. So if Father had ever had any dreams as to what he might do with the money if it were not claimed, they were shattered then and there.

School at Provo

One winter when I was a very small child, Father spent a school year or part of one at the BYU at Provo. When he came back home, he was made Stake President of the Y. M. M. I. A. It seemed at this time that he had a real spiritual awakening come into his life.

He would arise at 4 a.m. every morning and study. I used to love to hear him ask questions to his friends especially Stake President S. S. Pond and our Bishop Ira Hogan. Later in life Father became Bishop Hogan's counselor in the Thatcher Ward, and he dearly loved his Church work.

When I was seven years old, he and Sim Sterrett (his counselor in the Stake M. I. A.) came to Salt Lake City to attend the M. I. A. General Convention, and he let me come with him. We rode on a wagon loaded with big bags of wheat from Thatcher, Idaho, to Richmond, Utah where we took the train for Salt Lake City. All day long they talked about their M. I. A. work and about the principles of the gospel and, young as I was, I simply loved it. I could feel the beautiful spirit, and I knew what they were saying was true. I shall never forget the ride down on the train. The seats were of beautiful red plush, and I would caress it sacredly. I sat on one seat beside Grandmother Allsop who came with us from Richmond and Father and Brother Sterrett sat across the aisle.

Uncle Joe and Aunt Sue met us when we arrived at Salt Lake City and took us in a ludlo buggy out to their home at West Jordan for the night. In the morning we all came into the city for the convention and the big Jubilee celebration. It was 50 years since the Saints came to Utah.

We stopped on the outskirts of town, unhitched the team and fed them hay from the buggy. There was a big stream of water running into a trough from which the horses drank. Uncle Joe has told me since, that the place where we left our team and buggy that day is where the County Building now stands on 4th South and State.

I shall never forget how I felt when Father took my little hand and led me beside him up the long board sidewalks to the tabernacle grounds, and I shall not forget when he sat down on the ledge of that great stone wall surrounding the tabernacle and exclaimed, "This is the only free seat in

Salt Lake City today!" Little did I know then that in just two more months I would come so near losing my Father.

It happened like this. One day he was brought home from work terribly sick. He was working for President L. S. Pond. His sickness was what they called then, inflammation of the bowels or telescoped bowels. Now it is called appendicitis.

In those days it was mostly fatal. Doctors were miles away. Either we had to get one from Richmond 40 miles away or Soda Springs 35 miles away. There were no telephones, no electric lights, no automobiles, but there were hosts and hosts of friends, and that type of friendship scarcely exists today.

It is heartbreaking for me to think of it as I write.

The Doctor came but no hope was given. We children, four of us, were scattered out among the neighbors.

I took Nora and went up to Mrs. Higleys, and Mrs. Toone took Earl and Lulu. Mother had a new baby three weeks old (Burtress).

Weeks went by. Some good friends stayed with her day and night. Occasionally, someone would come for us children to take us home for an hour. As I would approach the home, I would look carefully at mother, and just a glance would tell me if he was better or if this was the tragic moment. It seemed that this happened again and again. He was in a dangerous condition for seven weeks.

The Elders came again and again with no results.

One day the climax came. We children were hurried home to witness the passing of our Father. We all stood at his bed side. Sometimes he seemed gone, then a gasp, another long spell of seeming death, another gasp and finally the flutter of an eye lid. He was coming back. Gradually he raised his eyes, looked at Mother and said, "Why did you bring me back? The longest I can stay is 25 years."

In an hour or so he proceeded to tell them what to do. He was to be treated with hot onion poultice, then a cold pack for so many hours, then discontinue. He called for the Elders and asked for N. D. Thatcher to take charge. They gathered around his bed, and he told them that he had never seen such little faith. He then told them to go out into the woods and ask

God to forgive them of their sins and give them faith in their calling. He finished by telling them that when they felt worthy, they were to come back and administer to him and he would get well.

Just about two years ago, 1956, I went to see this same N. D. Thatcher. He was then 92 years of age and has since passed away. He told me again of this story just as I have written it. He said in telling me, "Effie, never in my life have I witnessed such strength in the face of humility, and never in my life have I prayed so long and as fervently as we did out in the woods that day. When I went back to your father's bed, I knew what it was all about, and I knew he would be healed." He also added, "Now I won't be here much longer myself, and when I get there, I will look him up at once." I wonder now if I had a look of doubt in my eye because he added immediately, "Oh! I'll find him all right, don't you fear, I'll find him."

Well now, strange as it may seem, Father lived just 25 years almost to the day from whence his incident took place. He died at Smithfield, Utah on September 4, 1922 and this happened September 1897.

Afterward he always seemed to live as though every day may be his last one on earth. I remember getting a card from him one time when he was away from home (and it was after I was married). The card read thus "Do not squander time, for time is the thing life is made of." I realize more and more the importance of this quotation. Time is indeed the thing that life is made of and when we leave this world of opportunity, we well know more than ever how fleeting was our time here on this earth.

Family of Lew Peart Allsop and Velva Jamison Allsop. Front Row l. to r.-LuDean, Lew P., Velva, and Richard. Second Row l. to r.-Val J., Afton, Lew Judd, Marvin Sid, and Elaine.

Lew Peart Allsop was born 2 September 1900, at Thatcher, Bannock County, Idaho, the son of Thomas and Sylvia Peart Allsop. His father was a rancher in Grays Lake and then in Thatcher. In 1908, Lew moved with his family to Smithfield, Utah where his father was a merchant and operated his store about three miles west of Smithfield. Lew Peart was a farmer, dairyman, and cattle rancher, but claimed that he was really "raising boys." He married in Logan, Cache Co., Utah on 19 Dec. 1923, to Velva Dean Jamison, born 20 July 1904, in Lewiston, Utah, the daughter of Jefferson D. Jamison and wife Nancy L. Peery. Velva had attended high school at North Cache in Lewiston and Brigham Young College in Logan. She was very talented in the area of music and served her church in this fashion all of her life.

After marriage Lew farmed in Lewiston for about a dozen years and then bought the family farm in Trenton, Utah where he lived until about 1971. He then retired and sold his farm to his son Richard. At that time he and Velva bought a beautiful new home in Smithfield where they loved to have friends and family into their home for visits, meals, programs, and guided tours of their garden and flowers. In addition to their love for flowers and gardening, they were especially fond of their children, grandchildren, and friends. Lew had an exceptional gift for remembering and memorizing that which he read. Lew and Velva really enjoyed people and were gifted with the ability to teach.

Velva Dean died at her home at the age of 78 in Smithfield on 27 Dec. 1982. She was buried in the Smithfield, Utah City Cemetery. Lew P. Allsop married as his second wife Ina Smithson Peterson Johnson on 13 Sept. 1983, in the Logan LDS Temple. He died in Smithfield on Tuesday, 12 April 1988, and was buried in the Smithfield City Cemetery. Funeral services had been held on Saturday at noon at the Smithfield LDS 4th Ward Chapel prior to the burial. Following is a replication of the order of services as conducted by Bishop John A. Merkley.

Services

Family Prayer .... Richard C. Allsop
Prelude & Postlude Music .... Lois Petersen (niece)
Musical Selection .... Grandchildren
Elaine A. Andersen, Acc. - LuDean A. Pond, Dir.
"Oh My Father"
Invocation .... Onzel Smithson (brother-in-law)
Life Sketch .... Val J. Allsop
Obituary-Tribute .... Afton A. Godfrey (daughter)
Musical Selection .... Great Grandchildren
"I Am A Child of God"
Speaker .... Bishop A. George Marchant
Musical Selection .... Grandchildren
"How Great Thou Art"
Speaker .... Judd Allsop
Remarks .... Bishop John A. Merkley
Vocal Duet .... James & LuDean Pond
"In My Fathers House are Many Mansions"
Benediction .... Jay C. Andersen, (son-in-law)

The first child of Lew P. and Velva Allsop was Lew Judd, born 24 Oct. 1924, at Smithfield at the home of his grandmother Sylvia Allsop. He married on 19 Dec. 1949, at Logan, Utah, Kathryn Wight. During his working years Judd was a civil engineer. After his retirement, he and Kathryn purchased and operated orchards in Zillah, Washington. He was also married to Myrna Ballard. Judd is interested in his family history and has achieved excellent results in researching his specific lineage.

Afton Allsop was born on 4 Jan. 1927, at Lewiston in Cache County, Utah. She was the oldest girl in the family and the second child of Lew and Velva Allsop. On 19 Dec. 1946, she and Blaine Benjamin Godfrey were married at Logan, Utah. Blaine taught school at Bonneville High School and then was in school administration for many years. He worked in the insurance business after retirement from the educational field.

Val J. Allsop was born to Lew and Velva Allsop on 26 May 1928, at Lewiston. He married Lou Jean Davis on 22 April 1946, and worked all of his adult life as a chef. Val and Lou Jean were divorced and he then married on 2 July 195l, Geraldine Mohr and they were divorced. Val also married on 9 Feb. 1965, Oline Stratton, and Carlie Nelson Thompson Bunn on 30 June 1973. Val was also divorced from the last two wives.

The fourth child of Lew and Velva Allsop was Marvin Sid Allsop, born 23 Nov. 1930. He earned his degree in civil engineering. Marvin Sid married Louise Erickson on 11 Sept. 1953, at Logan, Utah, but relocated to Santa Rosa, California where he lived until retiring. He is now with FEMA (Federal Emergency Management) and follows hurricanes and tornadoes.

Elaine Allsop, who is mentioned earlier in this chapter, was born in Logan, Utah on 24 September 1935, when her parents Lew and Velva were living in Lewiston. She moved with her family at the age of one and a half years to their new farm in Trenton, Utah. This was the family farm and Elaine grew up in what she describes as "out in the county." On 18 June 1953, she and Jay Clarence Andersen were married at Logan in Cache Co. Her husband became a professor of economics at Utah State University in Logan. Elaine has many interests including music, and she is an accomplished pianist and organist. I have enjoyed my correspondence with her and appreciate her willingness to share her family history.

The last two children of Lew and Velva Allsop were LuDean, born in Logan, Utah on 8 March 1939, and Richard Carl, born in the same location on 17 Feb. 1946. LuDean is a multi-talented person who has a natural gift for music and is involved in many other areas. She married James Marvin Pond on 29 May 1957, in Logan. Richard and Cleone Archibald were married in Idaho Falls, Idaho on 24 Aug. 1967. Richard is a successful farmer and specializes in sod raising. He is active in metal work and has built his own professional forklift. Richard also serves as the mayor of Trenton, Utah.

Thomas Earl Allsop, son of Thomas and Sylvia Peart Allsop, was born 28 Jan. 1893, in Thatcher, Franklin Co., Idaho. He and Bessie Marie Plowman were married 11 March 1914, in Logan. He was a farmer all of his working days. His wife Bessie was born 14 Oct. 1895, at Smithfield, a daughter of John Jacobson and Mary Christine Andersen Plowman. Earl and Bessie were both active in the local Lions Club. They were the parents of Dewey Earl Allsop, born 24 September 1914, in Richmond, Utah; John Darwin Allsop, born in Smithfield on 4 June 1917; Ada June Allsop, born 28 April 1920; Lois, born 2 Feb. 1927, married Roger W. Petersen; and Bessie Jean Allsop, born 24 Sept. 1924. Jean married Boyd T. Jones and was living in Park City, Utah in the 1990's. The following newspaper article is presented because of it's in depth information on Thomas Earl Allsop.

"Idleness prompted me to begin woodworking. It first started as a time killer. Now it is an enjoyable hobby," says Earl Allsop, 86-year-old Smithfield resident.

After retiring as a farmer, Allsop began "tinkering" with wood in his garage and put out his first piece of handwork at age 67. He has made picnic tables, foot stools, children's table and chairs, play house cupboards, doll rocking chairs, canvas covered sand pile boxes, kitchen cabinets and dressers. He helped build a bridge for the city and has paneled two rooms in his basement.

His most prized piece of handiwork is a lamp totally made out of scraps of wood when he was 80 years old. When a lumber yard had a burnout, "a friend found a woodworker's vice that is used for a lathe that was not damaged. He said, 'I'll take it to Earl, he'll make something out of it.' I studied out in my mind what to do with it. I decided that it would make a beautiful stand for a lamp and that's what I made."

The rest of the lamp is also unique as it is made out of wood, shade and all. The shade is made out of two worn-out old double trees that were used to hook up horses to pull the wagons. The sticks were 4 1/2 feet long and 3 inches thick. He cleaned the trees and planed it down until it was smooth with the beauty of the grain showing through. He cut 37 pieces 12 1/4 inches long and 1/8 inch thick (rounded at both edges and formed a circle for the shade. The sticks are held together with leather lace braided in a crisscross design.

Roy Nelson, a long-time friend and father of his daughter-in-law, Phyllis, always "tinkered" and he got Earl interested in doing woodwork. He gave him the pattern for making the doll rocking chairs.

The first experience that Allsop recalls working with his hands and woodwork was with his grandfather. When he was 14 years old, his grandfather went to their home in Thatcher, Idaho where Allsop was born to help his son run the farm.

While there he was hired to build a room onto the existing church and Allsop helped him with sawing and hammering. "I really enjoyed doing it." he beamed.

Later that year, his father's health was not good. He sold the farm and moved his family to Smithfield in November where he sold grave monuments. "You can go through the cemetery and tell which ones he sold and put in as they're still standing," says Allsop.

One wagon was loaded with furniture. His parents, Thomas and Sylvia Allsop, and the family of five brothers and six sisters rode in a large white buggy covered with canvas and bows, both pulled by a team of horses. They started out first. Earl, 15, rode on saddle horse alone driving three milk cows in deep snow. The trip took two days to get to Smithfield.

He attended Summit Elementary School and graduated. After going to Smithfield Jr. High for one year, completing the ninth grade, he quit school and got a job. "My dad told me if I quit school he wouldn't ever pay me a dime. When I quit, he was really disappointed. He's never had to pay me for anything as I worked odd jobs thereafter until I was married."

Bessie Plowman, a girl from Smithfield, became his sweetheart when she was 15 and he 18. "I took another girl to the picture show because her dad owned the show. We were standing on her porch when Bessie walked by. I said, 'There goes Bessie Plowman. I think I'll walk her home.' I've walked by her side ever since."

They were married three years later.

His father-in-law, John Plowman, was called on an LDS mission and asked Allsop to run his farm. He quit his job at Guild Edge Roller Mills in Richmond and had just started working at Smithfield Brick and Tile Company when he took over the farm. They moved into two of the rooms of the family home with her mother, Mary, and three brothers, Jed, Ruel and Rulon and two sisters, Anita and Sidonia.

He again used his expertise in carpentry when they built their first home in 1917, located at 143 E. 4th North. He also built all the out-buildings which are still standing. After being with the mills for another three years, he liked farming so much that after renting a farm, his father-in-law helped him get started on his own place. In the fall of 1934, Allsop purchased 53 acres southwest of Smithfield. When Dewey, their oldest son, was 16 he took him in as an equal.

He farmed until 1960, when he retired and sold everything. He kept one parcel where he built a new brick house located on the corner of Juniper and Main Street. The buyer of the land subdivided into lots for homes. He named it the Earl T. Allsop subdivision.

Even though he was retired, Allsop helped build his new house. He also did some work remodeling for his son. He liked it so well that he and his best friend, Colonel Toolson, became partners in doing remodeling. "Nobody had a better friend than I did in Colonel."

His wife, Bessie, says, "Earl is really handy. I don't know where he gets his ideas. He has always been able to do anything."

Bessie is very talented in her own right. Her specialty is quilts. She has designed and made over 35 bedspreads and quilts in a 17 year span, giving most of them away to her grandchildren. She has entered six quilts and received six blue ribbons at the Cache County Fair. She received two blue ribbons at the State Fair in Salt Lake City. She also crochets afghans and dolls.

Earl pays tribute to his wife: "I have one of the best helpmates the Lord could provide." This year marks their 65th wedding anniversary. Their home, yard and garden reflect the finesse and pride they both possess in everything they touch.

They have five children: Dewey (deceased), Jack (owner of Jack's Market), June Curran, Salt Lake City, Lois Petersen, Benson Ward, Jean Jones, Minneapolis. They have 16 grandchildren and 25 great-grandchildren.

T. Earl and Bessie Allsop

Earl and Bessie celebrated their 65th wedding anniversary on 11 March 1979. This was only about a month after the above article was written. They had been married 72 years when Bessie died at the age of 90 on 18 July 1986, at the Logan Regional Hospital. She had been faithful and active in the LDS Church. Earl died 21 June 1990, at the Sunshine Terrace. He was active in the LDS Church serving as bishop's counselor for eight years and held many other offices. They were both buried in Smithfield City Cemetery.

(This family will be continued in <u>Alsop's Tables</u>, Volume IV)

Chapter XI

Francis Alsop From Belfast, Ireland

(continued from Alsop's Tables, Volume II, page 181)

William Pitt Alsip, III, wrote an annual letter to relatives in his later years to describe his previous years activities. Part of a letter written in 1929 was presented in the previous volume, and the rest of the letter is now shown.

Our next trip was to visit the city of McGregor, Iowa, on the Mississippi River, directly across the river from Prairie du Chien, Wisconsin, an old French Fort and the town of the early times, where I was born July 8th, 1859, and where I have a sister Mary buried, who died when I was three months old. Mother had always wanted a girl baby, but was blessed with six tow-haired, blue-eyed boys, of whom George the third and Roy the fifth have crossed the great divide, and are buried in Winnipeg, Manitoba, beside their Mother and Father. We arrived in McGregor, and drove up on the bench as the level land several hundred feet wide at the foot of a higher and steeper hill, raises to the west. On this bench a road runs west to the foot of the higher hill, and on the south side of the road there stood the white frame house where Uncle Frank and Sam made their homes up to the fall of the Great Chicago Fire in 1871, and here the firm of Alsip Brothers was first started. Their father, William Alsip, Sr., had a brick-yard at Prairie du Chien, which was abandoned when the Alsip Brothers

Company was formed; and all the Alsips as I remember lived out of the same general fund.

The Alsip Brothers transported grain and dressed hogs across the Mississippi River, in fact all the freight the Chicago Milwaukee and St. Paul Railways brought to Prairie du Chien in the wintertime. As soon as navigation shut down and the steam boats were frozen in, great flat boats with sleigh runners under them were made to take their place, and were loaded with wheat, hogs, and merchandise, to which teams were hitched with a long rope. If a soft spell of weather set in and the ice became thin and dangerous, choke ropes were placed around each horse's neck. Then, when the ice would break, the men or an extra team would heave the horses upon more solid ice, and the load in the flat boat which would be floating in the ice and water would have to be transferred to another boat. In the fall and spring the cost of this kind of transportation ran high, as only a few would take the chance. As much as five hundred dollars would be paid for a boat load that ordinarily would cost but twenty dollars. Very few horses were drowned, and few cargoes were lost. It was a cold and dangerous job for the men, as the horses would often get tangled in the harness, of which there was but little; tuggs, collars, bridles, and lines attached so that they could be unfastened with but little trouble. There were times when the drivers would have to go into the broken ice and water to aid the horses who were held in the harness. The conditions made it very dangerous both in the spring and early in the fall, and shippers who must get their wares would bid up until the offers would be so attractive that his goods would be transported in spite of every difficulty.

There was my father William and five brothers, Frank and Sam who made the firm of Alsip Brothers, and the younger brothers Henry and Thomas. Jack was still at school, being about four years older than myself. I believe Samuel and Henry were the most venturesome, and when the bids ran high they would volunteer to make these dangerous trips of wheat and other grain east and merchandise of every kind on the backtrip.

Going back to our auto trip up the hill to the bench, there stood the white frame house, two stories high, in which Frank Alsip and family lived, and attached to the east was a wing story and a half high, where

Samuel Alsip and his family lived. The white picket fence was much the same, although it must have been renewed several times in the fifty-seven years since the Alsip families left it in 1872. We did not drive across the hollow to the site of the old brick-yard and the house of my Grandfather Alsip, as I am quite sure I would have found it difficult to locate either if I had, as it is now all laid out in streets with houses. The old saw-mill and immense pile of lumber are all gone, and there is no water in Bloody Run, and much of the made land of slabs and sawdust have been burned, and the place has the appearance of a deserted village. South McGregor seems to have come to life, but has grown but little in all these years. We drove up to the top of the bluff called Pikes Peak, four miles south on the river bank. Here we had a magnificent view of the Mississippi River, its many channels and islands spread out to the north as far as the eye could search, and then to the south another picture of islands and channels, trees and sand bars. We were so far above the river that our view was much like a view from an aeroplane would be.

After feasting our eyes on this beautiful sight, we started down a very steep ravine, which we crossed and recrossed as we descended until we came to the much talked of Picture Rocks. Here we met many tourists, all in quest of sand from the many coloured sandstone that is found near the foot of the ravine. At McGregor we saw glass bottles, such as Drug Stores place, filled with colored water, in their windows, filled with this sand to represent ships, water and land, with flags and sails on the ships in colored sand, and all made much as a painting would be. It is said only one man had the art of doing this perfectly. We had a large number of paper sacks and filled most of them. We discovered that the brighter sand was very hard and made it slow to get. However, we got enough to make small bottles, with many designs of sand, which, though not so artistic as the professional, was very pretty.

Doris, our four year old adopted daughter was taken to the Isolation Hospital with scarlet fever a week ago. She has had a very light attack, and has been sitting up, and will be there until nearly Christmas. While she has been away, Jack and Bill have worked with the sand and have made a lot of very pretty bottles.

We had the house disinfected, and today their ban is lifted after seven days of quarantine. It has been a hard week for them, but Eva has brought something for them every day, and visited the hospital and taken a letter and a gift to Doris as well.

It was late when we arrived at the Tourist Camp from McGregor, but with our gas stove we soon had sweet corn, potatoes, and a large steak done to a finish, to which we all did justice. Our camp life was wonderful. Eva did the cooking, and we feasted on corn on the cob, potatoes every style, fried chicken, large tomatoes, watermelons, peaches and cream, and beef-steaks and chops. Most of the dishwashing fell to the lot of Eva's cousin Lillian, with my aid at times. We had a folding table, chairs, and a full set of dishes. At times we begrudged the time it took to get meals and clean up, as we had so many places we planned to see in and around Decorah. We learned a lot about tourist camping on this trip. We had a large bag into which all our belongings were put, and at times it became very difficult to find someone's shoes, silk stockings, or whatnots. We made up our mind that next year we would have a different colored bag for each one in the party, where each would keep his own belongings; this would save time and labor. Our icebox was a box with a partition in the centre, set on end and covered with gunny sacking, on top of which was a can of water with a small hole in it to keep the cover damp. This proved to be a great blessing, as our butter was always firm and nice. Our tent was pitched under a spreading hard maple tree, which kept us cooler from the sun, and gave us shade for our table at meal time, as well as being a very pleasant place to lounge.

Fancy the boys surprise when a large truck with one thousand cantaloupe with two men to guard them drove up along side our tent. The owner of the truck and melons, on hearing we were from Winnipeg, Canada, and seeing the boys' eyes bulge out in wonder, called them to the back end of the truck and loaded them down with ten lovely melons. Did we feast on melons? I'll say we did.

The Winneshiek County Fair was held the week we were there, and the truck and melons were there, to sell to the many people visiting the Fair. The owner did not dare put his truck in a garage, as he was afraid his melons would be stolen. While we were at the Fair, Bill got lost, and for what seemed a long time we were unable to find him. We enquired at the Information Center, and they notified the Police, and were just about to have the crier in the grandstand shout through the megaphone for him, when we located Bill in a side show, seeing it over and over again. He was much surprised that we should be worried about him, as he was alright. He had all kinds of eats and drinks, and was thoroughly enjoying himself. Lillian introduced me to quite a number of people who knew me or my father, and after the boys had taken in all the sights, and the midway, and had their stomachs filled, we went back to camp for a rest.

When the cook was getting meals, the boys and I would wander off to some haunt of mine, where I would tell of the things I did when I was their age. We fished off the old mill dam, watched the boys dive in a new swimming hole, and went below the dam and took off our shoes and stockings and waded in the shallow water. We caught minnow under the stones, and saw where the hawks had caught and eaten fresh water crabs, and left the claws and shell part of the bodies in piles on the rocks. We went up the old swimming hole in the mill pond just below the tourist camp, where we used to go to swim and fish. We had our hook and line and we fished for over an hour, but with no luck, so that part of my story about catching fish did not materialize. However, we saw a rabbit and several chipmunks, and Bill was more than pleased, and planned to go back again when we might have better luck.

The tourist camp adjoins the City Park where there is a fountain and swimming pool, where Doris and the boys went every day for a swim. The hollow to the west of the camp is bridged by a rustic bridge, as are all the hollows along the top of the dug road from the dam to Addikin's Brewery. The cliff, and for some little distance back, has all been taken over for a park, and a beautiful path made with little rustic garden houses every little way, with stone fences most of the distance next to the clifts. Every little way there is a rustic bench, and all the garden houses have benches, where one can sit and rest out of the sun or rain. The view from here is most beautiful; the fields of waving corn, the market gardens on the flats next to the river, just beyond the village of West Decorah, with theGrand

Norwegian College towering on the high hill two miles north west across the valley, with the graceful bends of the Aniopa River sweeping through a grove of Poplar, then on to yellow Willow, Elm, ButterNut, Maple, Alder with their different shades of green leaves, with the Birches, Cedars, Pines, and Hemlock lining the north slope of the clifts.

Our first walk the morning after our arrival was along this beautiful walk, up and past the Addikin's Brewery to the Hog's Back. The Hog's Back is a narrow inverted rainbow shaped hill, that divides the valley of Dry Run from the valley of the Aniopa River, and joins the two greater hills at east and west. At the west end of this Hog's Back is a rock fifteen feet wide, twenty feet high that juts out from the hill about twenty feet, with a cave or opening in the face, ten feet high and fifteen feet deep. This we named the Hog's Eye. The stone from which all the steps, walls and fences are made were brought from near Kline's Brewery, and are made of a formation of limestone that resembles petrified sponges, and makes a very pretty as well as unique setting for the Park improvements.

On our trip to the Cave we went up the hollow to Dunnings Springs, which came out of the limestone cliff about one hundred feet above the river. There is enough water to operate a small grist mill with this high head. From Dunnings Springs we went down the river on a one way road to Grear's Mill Dam, above which is the Ice Cave. We had forgotten to take candles or a flashlight, so we could go down only far enough to see, and get a little ice. It was so cold we were glad not to have to go farther, as we were all perspiring freely from climbing the hill, as it was a very hot day.

We left Decorah and drove directly to Minneapolis, where we stayed two nights and one day, during which we were on the go all the time. Eva's cousin had so much to show us that we enjoyed, that the day was both long and short. It was long because we crowded so many things into our stop, and short because we were so well used we wanted more and more. The lakes with boats and swimming, beautiful homes and pleasure resorts, with miles and miles of trees and undulating drives up and down, and around the lakes, made us all want to stay on and on. But with the call of home, and getting the boys rested up and ready for school, we started again on our homeward journey.

We stopped at Birchwood Inn, Detroit Lakes, over-night, and next day made Grand Forks, North Dakota, and put up at Mr. and Mrs. Borden's. We stopped at Maple Lake, where we were told by Burns that Lotta had gone home, so did not call at the Cottage, and were surprised to find she had not gone home as planned, and was still at Maple Lake. We had a very pleasant visit with the Bordens, who entertained us royally and gave us a nice rest on our way home.

Our trip home was without mishap, until we were at the City limits, when our last spare tire blew out, and we phoned my brother Arthur to bring us a spare tire, which he did, so we arrived home safely. Pauline, our maid, had a nice dinner waiting for us, to which we did ample justice. Home looked good, and real beds were again inviting. The boys and their Mother are planning to make the trip again, and want to take Uncle Art and Sid with us, and bring Ruby to see her father's old home. We are all settled down to every day routine, and outside of Doris having to go to the hospital with fever, we are just jogging along and doing about the same each week. We are all well and glad to be alive, and looking forward to the day when we can have Doris back in the home with us. We are all very much wrapped up in her, and she is beloved by everyone who knows her. Her nurses sing her praises, and the doctors make a pet of her at the hospital. Our family doctor goes in to see her every few days, not that she needs doctor's care, but just for love's sweet sake.

Does she love her Mother? You would say she does if you could see Eva and her together. I cannot begin to tell of the many sweet and lovely things she says to and about her Mamma, and Eva's heart has gone out to her, and I am sure if she had her own Baby, she could not love her more.

******

The following letter was written to Mary Ellen Vedder Alsip by her brother from Wisconsin. He was very concerned about diphtheria in the region and was sending a receipt for this dreaded disease.

March 8th 1882

Well Ellie I have no news to write only I Start for jims in the morning, you can guess what for, and I want to write that dipththeria receipt So plain you can read it, if not take it to the drug-Store and they will read it. Io,dide of Po,tassium and
I have marked the syllables
Clo,rid of pot,ash is what you want, now for the Receipt. To gargle the throat, desolve half a tea-Spoonfull of Clo,rid of Pot,ash in a common Size tumbler almost full of water and gargle often. To take inwardly disolve Six grains of Io,dide of Po,tassium in half a tea-cup full of water and give a tea spoon full every two hours. If not very bad once in three hours will do. When a child cannot gargle any thing in their throat you must cut a notch near the end of a Stick or whale bone stick on a soft cloth or sponge of sponge & swab their throat with the stuff you gargle with. turn over

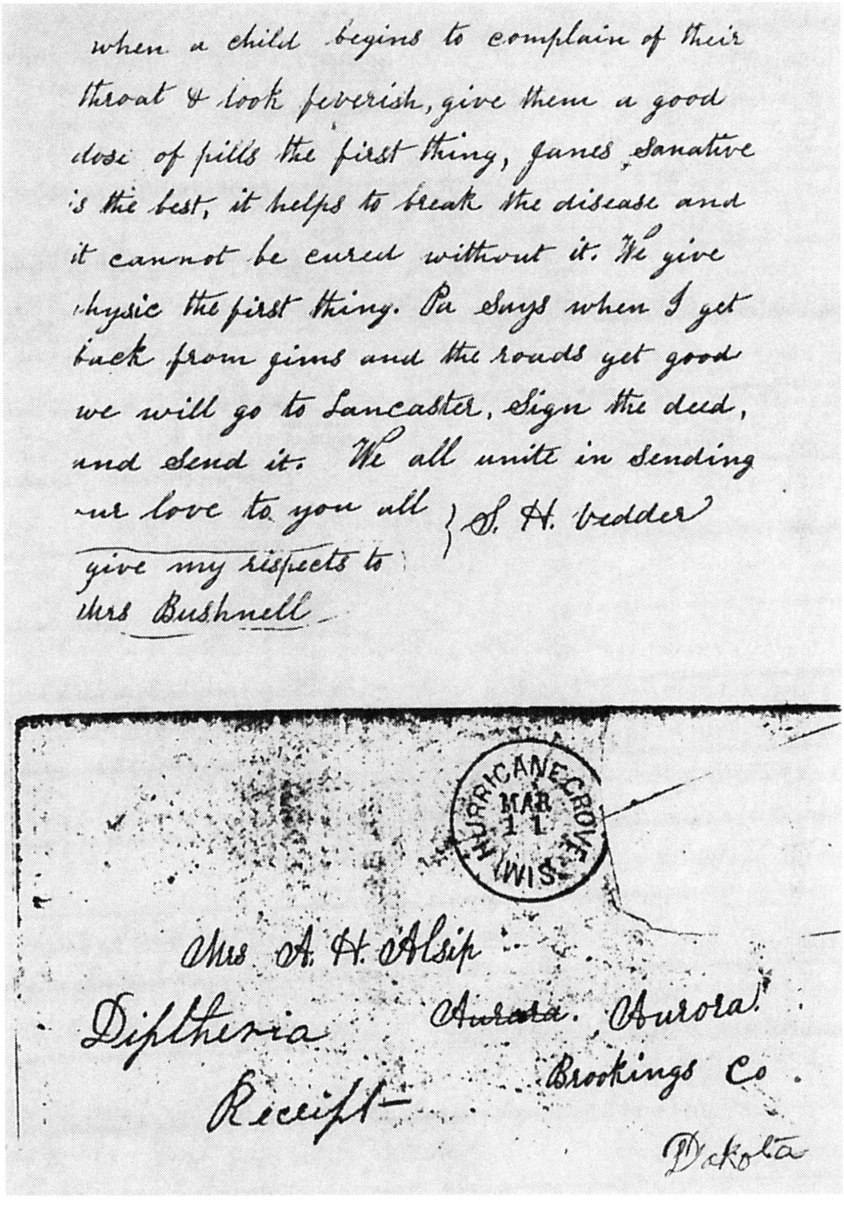
when a child begins to complain of their
throat & look feverish, give them a good
dose of pills the first thing, janes sanative
is the best, it helps to break the disease and
it cannot be cured without it. We give
physic the first thing. Pa says when I get
back from jims and the roads get good
we will go to Lancaster, sign the deed,
and send it. We all unite in sending
our love to you all } S. H. Vedder
give my respects to
Mrs Bushnell

HURRICANE GROVE
MAR
11
WIS.

Mrs A. H. Alsip
Diptheria
Aurora. Aurora
Brookings Co.
Receipt
Dakota

Francis Alsop who immigrated to this country from Ireland had two sons who were the progenitors of all of the known descendants of this specific lineage. His oldest son William Pitt Alsop-Alsip moved from

Pittsburgh, Pennsylvania to Wisconsin, Iowa, and then to Chicago, Illinois. Francis Alsop-Alsip, Jr., stayed in the Pittsburgh area as did some of his descendants. He and wife Elizabeth had sons Francis, John G., and Albert. John G. Alsip died leaving two sons Francis and Albert. Albert, son of Francis Alsip, Jr., and his wife Clara had four children Anna, Albert W., Gertrude, and Lawrence.

Francis "Frank" and Albert, sons of John G. Alsip-Allsip, left Sharpsburg, Pennsylvania, Allegheny Co., after 1910 and were living in Punxsutawney, Jefferson Co., Pennsylvania by 1920. Albert and his wife Frances Mae Hill Allsip were living at 223 Front St. with their two children John William and Ruth E. Frank Allsip and wife Sarah E. and their children Sarah C., Frank W., and Mary G. were living in the family home at 210 S. Elk St. Albert had learned the trade of glass blower in Sharpsburg and continued this occupation after his move to Punxsutawney.

The census of 1930 lists Albert, wife Mae, and daughter Ruth as living in their home in the 3rd ward of Jefferson Co. Living nearby was their son John William Allsip who had married Margaret G. Sutter, born 1898, and they were the parents of John William, age 6, and Mary M., age 3 months. Also in the same neighborhood was Francis Allsip, brother of Albert who was living with his wife Sarah E. and daughter Mary G.

John William Allsip, Jr., son of John William and Margaret Sutter Allsip, became a school teacher and is now retired. He lives in Euclid, Ohio and is a widower. He and his daughter are very interested in family history and have contributed significant genealogical information and photos for this volume.

After Frank and Albert moved to Punxsutawney, the only Allsips found in Allegheny Co. were Lawrence and his wife Bertha, age 22, who were living in Homestead, Pennsylvania when the 1920 census was recorded. In 1930, no members of this family tree were found in the Pittsburgh area that still carried the Allsip name.

Francis Alsop, immigrant ancestor from Belfast, Ireland, had sons Francis, Jr., William Pitt, and Samuel. It is unknown what happened to Samuel. Anne Alsoop (Alsip?), who is believed to have been one of the daughters of Francis and Elizabeth, married James Varner on 1 July 1828, at Trinity Episcopal Church in Pittsburgh. This is the same church where other daughters of Francis were baptized. Some of the descendants of Francis, Jr., have been detailed as much as extant records will permit. Descendants of William Pitt Alsip will be continued from Alsop's Tables, Volume II, page 180 at this point.

Samuel Alsip, son of William Pitt and wife Mary Ann Meeker Alsip, was living with his wife Margaret Sheffield and six children in Jackson Co., Missouri in 1880. On 26 Aug. 1881, their seventh child Albert A. was born. Additional research has revealed that Samuel left his wife and family soon after this and went to Salt Lake City, Utah to marry another woman. One of the present day descendants of one of Samuel and Margaret's sons has the ceremonial sword that Sam would have been buried with if he had not left the family.

The census of 1900 for Salt Lake City lists Samuel R. Alsip as living in the 1st Precinct at 761 Third St. with his wife Rose and their children Ernest F., born Aug. 1891, and Walter Samuel, born 14 May 1896. This second wife Rose was listed as being born in Switzerland in Aug. 1861. The next enumeration in 1910 informs us that Samuel and Rose had been married nineteen years. In 1920 Rose is the head of her household and the address is 346 Cottage Ave. in Salt Lake City. In this same population count she was reported to be a widow, and living with her, in addition to her two sons, was a third son named Peter M. Gray, born in Utah ca. 1884. Rose had immigrated to the U. S. in 1876. Samuel died on 26 April 1914, and was buried in the Salt Lake City Cemetery. By 1930, Rose, who was still listed as a widow and was using the Alsip surname, lived in Los Angeles, California with her three sons who were all still single. Walter Samuel died 16 Jan. 1961, at China Lake, Kern Co., California and was buried in the cemetery in Salt Lake City next to his father.

Most of the children of Samuel Alsip by his first wife Margaret Sheffield left the Kansas City area and by 1883, one of the sons Horace Greeley "Hod" Alsip was living in the suburbs of Chicago in Cook Co., Illinois and married Alice Marie DuChien on 20 May 1883, in Kenosha

Co., Wisconsin. In 1900, Horace and his wife Alice M. and their children Walter, born ca. 1884, Grace, born 15 Feb. 1887, Horace, born ca. 1890, Willard E., born 11 May 1894, and Charles, born 14 Sept. 1896, were living in Calumet Twp. in Cook Co. Horace and Alice Marie had a son named Frank who died young, and he could be the same person as Horace, Jr. This family was still living in this area in 1910, and by 1920, their address was 247 Birdsall St. in Blue Island with only their youngest son Howard S., born 6 May 1904, still at home. Horace "Hod" Alsip died on 22 Nov. 1933, and was buried at Mount Hope Cemetery.

In 1920, Walter had started his own home located at 593 Burr Oak Place in Blue Island. He was living there with his wife Frieda Carolina Volkman (they were married in Cook Co. about 1907) and two sons Russell Warren and Leslie Walter, and he was working in the Alsip Brick Yard in Alsip, Illinois.

Russell Warren married first Letha and their two children were Russell and Richard. Russell son of Russell W. and Letha Alsip married Marge and their progeny consisted of Rusty, Laurie, Scott, and Mike. Richard the other son of Russell W. and Letha wed Lois and they had a son named Richard. Russell Warren Alsip married as his second wife Magarey Casper and they had sons James and Alan. Alan married Carol Nelson and their family consisted of a daughter Julie who married Mark Lindahl and they had a son Britt born 19 Aug. 1991, and Mike who married Nancy Provenzia who was the mother of Calvin, born 5 Nov. 1991, and Peter, born 12 Aug. 1993. James Alsip, son of Russell W. and second wife Magarey married Carolyn and they produced children Scott, Mark, Jaime, Brian, and Jeremy. James "Jim" Alsip told his brother Alan and wife Carol that he could remember his grandfather Walter's uncle visiting from Canada. At last accounting Scott was married with one child, and Mark and his wife had two boys. Russell W. and his third wife Lois Litchfield did not have any children. Russell Warren followed his father Walter by working at the Alsip Brick Yard.

Walter's other son Leslie Walter married Mildred Dorothy Blomberg on 9 July 1931, and was also employed at the family brick company. Leslie and Mildred were the parents of two daughters Myless and Nori.

Myless married Bob Sinise and their son Gary Sinise is a well-known Hollywood actor.

Grace Alsip daughter of Horace and Alice married a man named Aregood, and their daughter Grace Aregood married a man whose surname is Merriman. Their daughter Mary L. Merriman is interested in the family history and wrote an ethnography on a segment of her ancestry in 1997, as a requirement for one of her college courses.

Horace son of Horace Greeley and Alice disappears from all records after the census of 1900. Willard Earl Alsip, brother of Horace, Jr., was living at home when the 1910 census was recorded. By 1930, he and wife Helen were living in the Worth Twp., 5th Ward, Blue Island, Illinois with their two children Robert, 14, and Alice, 6. He is said by relatives to have been employed at the Blue Island High School as a janitor. He died in March 1972 at Tampa, Hillsborough Co., Florida.

Charles H. Alsip brother of Willard and son of Horace G. and Alice was married by 1920 and living with his wife Anna H., age 22, at 223 Greenwald St. in Blue Island. They were the parents of one child, a son named Charles H. Alsip, Jr., who was born about 1927. Anna Alsip widow of Charles H. wrote a letter to Faye Beckman in Florida in May 1979, in which she details a small amount of her family history. Anna told Faye that her husband was named after Charles H. Alsip, son of Frank and Mary Jane Smiley Alsip, who had operated the Alsip Insurance Co. in Chicago. Charles H. Alsip, Sr., and wife Anna had a winter home in Miami, Florida at one time and knew another line of Alsips who owned a motor court in Miami. Charles H. Alsip, Jr., son of Charles and Anna, was also the owner of an insurance company in Chicago, Alsip Insurance Agency. He and his wife were the parents of four children Dawn, born ca. 1954, Kim, born ca. 1957, Guy, born ca. 1961, and Tod, born about 1963. In 1979 they were all living in Palos Park, Illinois. Anna who was living on Highland St. in Blue Island also mentioned that she was the only Alsip living in the area as all others had either died or moved away, and the brick yards started by Frank Alsip no longer existed. She said that she had met Colonel William Alsip when he had visited his relatives from Winnipeg, Canada.

The last child of Horace G. and Alice Alsip was Howard S. who was 25 and still living at home in 1930. His wife was Larue (maiden name not known) and one of their children was named Blaine. Howard became president of the First National Bank in Chicago. Howard died in February 1981 at Palos Heights, Illinois.

William John "Billy" Alsip, the first child of Samuel and wife Margaret Sheffield, was born 26 Dec. 1858, in Prairie Du Chien, Wisconsin. He followed his brother Horace to Chicago where the following announcement appeared in the Chicago newspaper: Mrs. M. H. Benjamin desires your presence at the marriage ceremony of her daughter Birdie and Will J. Alsip, Wednesday afternoon, September Twenty-sixth, Eighteen Hundred and eighty-eight, at Six o'clock, Bethany Church, No. 3532 Hoyne Avenue. Birdie was born in Quincy, Adams Co., Illinois on 3 April 1868.

By 1900, "Billy" and Birdie were living in Calumet Twp. in Cook Co. with their only child a daughter named Edith Lyda who had been born on 13 Jan. 1891. Their second child William John Alsip, Jr., was born in Blue Island, Cook Co. on 14 April 1903. Billy worked in the brick making business as a burner. He relocated to Manteno, Kankakee County, Illinois with the Illinois Brick Co. prior to 1920 and lived the rest of his life there. Billy and his wife were Presbyterian. Margaret Benjamin, mother of Birdie lived with her daughter and son-in-law until her death. Birdie died in St. Mary Hospital in Manteno on 21 Jan. 1940, from complications of diabetes, and her husband died a few days later on Thursday, 1 Feb. 1940. They were both buried in the Elmwood Cemetery in Manteno.

William John Alsip, Jr., spent his teen age years in Manteno where he married Myrna Lois Jackson on 8 July 1929. At the time of his marriage he was employed as a stockbroker. Needless to say this was probably not a very good start. His other occupations included farmer, employee for Curtis Candy Co. and teacher in Puerto Rico after he left college. Their only child was Ann Margaret Alsip, born in Kankakee, Illinois on 12 May 1931, and died in 1941. Myrna died in Manteno on 5 April 1983, and her husband William J. died in Brownsville, Texas on 21 May 1987. They were both buried in Manteno.

William John Alsip-Birdie Benjamin Alsip

Edith Lyda Alsip-8th Grade Graduation

Lucien W. Voorhees-Edith Alsip In Idaho

Lucien, Leslie, and Donald-Sons of Edith

Edith Alsip grew up in Blue Island and graduated from the high school there on 16 June 1908. She married Lucien Whitman Voorhees on 20 Jan. 1909, at Morgan Park, Cook Co., Illinois. He was born 16 Jan. 1888, in Blue Island and after his marriage relocated to Twin Falls, Idaho. Lucien was an automobile dealer for Chevrolet until his unexpected death on 25 June 1929, from a cerebral embolism while riding a bus from Burley to Twin Falls, Idaho. Edith and Lucien were the parents of Lucien Whitman, Jr., born and died Nov. 1912; Marjorie, born and died 3 Aug. 1914; Leslie William, born 14 Feb. 1917; Margaret Ruth, born 14 July 1920; Donald, born 27 Nov. 1926; and Lucien Whitman, III, born 5 March 1929. Edith lived most of her life in Twin Falls and died there on 3 Oct. 1986. She and her husband are buried in the Twin Falls Cemetery.

Margaret Ruth dau. of Edith and Lucien Voorhees married Herb Clark and then second Lawrence Raymond Shively; she was the mother of two children by the Shively union. Her brother Donald Alsip Voorhees married Thelma Ree Reynolds at Twin Falls on 21 Aug. 1949, and they had two children. The last child of Edith and Lucien was Lucien W. Voorhees, III, who married Vera Speights and they were the parents of three children. He died in California on 29 Aug. 1978.

After attending Stanford University, Leslie William Voorhees married Margaret Estella Zerlang at Twin Falls on 25 Dec. 1939. He lived in El Cerrito, California; Reno, Nevada; and Bellingham, Washington among other places. Leslie and Margaret had three children: Lauren, Marc, and Leslie Ann. Leslie Ann was born 28 Sept. 1952, Berkeley, California and married Clyde Hobbs Andersen on 2 Oct. 1971, at Sparks, Nevada and they have one child. Leslie Ann's father Leslie W. was the assistant vice-president and manager of the American Savings and Loan Co. Leslie W. died in Bellingham, Washington on 24 Sept. 2001. Leslie Ann Voorhees Andersen is very interested in family history, and she has provided much of the information and photos for this specific branch of her family tree.

Mary Ann "Mamie" Alsip, sister of William John, married Harry John Flood on 2 Feb. 1888 in the Chicago area and in 1900, they were living at 5921 Indiana Ave. in Chicago. Living with her was her baby brother Albert A., born 26 Aug. 1881. Harry John and wife Mary Ann were the progenitors of Albert Lincoln, born 20 Dec. 1888-died 18 Oct. 1918; Leslie A., born 21 Dec. 1890; and Harry John, Jr., born 21 Feb. 1892-died 29 Dec. 1927. Marnie Alsip Flood died 19 Dec. 1920, and her husband died 27 Oct. 1935.

Oscar N. another son of Samuel and Margaret Sheffield Alsip moved to Chicago where his first daughter Margaret was born 20 May 1892. He and his wife Delia Olatha had been married on 7 June 1891, in Milwaukee Co., Wisconsin (M. B. 23, page 165) and were the parents of additional children who were reported on the 1910 census of Cook Co. as follows: Ruth, born 11 Sept. 1893; Hazel, born 24 Nov. 1896; Helen, 8 April 1902; and Oscar, born 5 April 1906. Margaret dau. of Oscar and Delia O. Alsip married on 19 April 1911, in Bachtown, Illinois William Warren Trier, a son of Henry Harrison Trier, Sr., and Wilhelmina Dorothea Sass. William W. died in Willow Springs, Illinois on 17 Jan. 1969. In 1920, Oscar and wife Delia were still living in Cook Co. in the town of Bloom with their children Oscar, Jr., Ruth, Helen, and Jane, age 7, who was the only new member of the family since the last census. This family was living in Bloom Twp. in 1930, with the only two children still at home being Jane, and Oscar, Jr., who was divorced. Oscar, Sr., died on 2 Feb. 1937. Hazel Alsip died in 1933.

Samuel Alsip and wife Margaret Sheffield had two more children who were Ida May, born 27 May 1874-died 27 Jan. 1877, and Emma Alsip, born 1871, but nothing more has been learned about her.

Another son of William Pitt Alsip and wife Mary Ann Meeker was Francis "Frank" Alsip who was extremely successful in establishing brick making companies in Chicago. The following biographical sketch has been included to help one better understand both the personal and business experiences of Frank Alsip.

> Frank Alsip was born at Pittsburgh, Penn., on November 7, 1827, and is the son of William and Mary A. (Meeker) Alsip. When he was twelve years of age, he went to work in a brick yard at Pittsburgh, where he was employed about five years. He was then apprenticed to a bricklayer for three years, during which time he learned the trade in all its details. He was employed as a journeyman brick mason, in and about Pitts-

> burgh, until 1849, when he went across the plains to the gold mines of California, and worked in the mines two years. He then went to St. Louis, Mo., where he was employed at his trade for about a year, and then he returned to Pittsburgh, and engaged in business as a builder and manufacturer of brick with A. H. McClellan & Alsip. This firm carried on the business four years, when it was dissolved, and Mr. Alsip removed to Prairie du Chien, Wis., where he engaged in the same business with his brother, under the firm name of Alsip Bros. They made brick and erected buildings in Wisconsin, Iowa, and Minnesota, until 1872, when he came to Chicago, where he formed a partnership with Henry C. Hayt, under the style of Hayt and Alsip, brick makers, which firm, last year, turned out more brick than any other firm in Chicago. He is also in business with his son William H., under the firm name of F. and W. H. Alsip, brick manufacturers, and is now fitting up one of the largest factories for the manufacture of brick in the city. Much of the machinery was invented and designed by him, and will be capable of producing one hundred and twenty-five thousand first class brick a day. He was married in January 1854, to Miss Mary Jane Smiley of Pittsburgh.

Many people who lived in the area of the Alsip Brick Yards found employment there as an alternative to farming. Frank Alsip and his son Charles H. established another Alsip Brick Yard in 1885 which was located between 119th and 120th Streets and Cicero and McDaniel Streets. Today, this area is now filled in, and other industries have taken the place of brick production. A subdivision has even been developed nearby. However, the clay hole located on the west side of 120th and Cicero Ave., where it was originally part of the brick yard, still remains, but it is filled with water. The William and Frank Alsip families did not live in the area that was to later bear their name, but lived in a very wealthy and prominent section of Chicago. The village of Alsip (named after its first industry) was incorporated in 1927 and residents elected their first officials that same year.

In 1900, Frank was a widower living in the Chicago area. One of his relatives who visited him from another state described his residence as truly a mansion. His wife Mary Jane Smiley, born 1 Jan. 1834, in Pennsylvania, died 10 Jan. 1896, and was buried in Rosehill Cemetery. Frank died 20 Dec. 1907, and is buried in Chicago next to his wife.

Jane "Jennie" Alsip was born in Pennsylvania on 23 Nov. 1855, and was the first child of Frank and Mary Jane Smiley Alsip. Her childhood consisted of a number of homes in a number of states.

Jennifer Alsip King - 1855 - 1901

By 1872, she was living with her family in Chicago and on 15 July 1878, in Evanston, Cook Co., Illinois, married William Evans King, born 28 Sept. 1847, Vermillion Co., Illinois. Her husband was a big, tall man whose ancestors had come to this country from the Netherlands. He was a Methodist preacher and started the Pacific Garden Mission in Chicago with his wife Jennie playing the piano for the services there. This mission is still in operation. Their first child Mary Jane was born in Evanston on 24 June 1879, and this family moved to western Montana soon after that where William was a circuit riding minister for the Methodist church. Jennie left a very palatial home and a luxurious upbringing to become a frontier preacher's wife. The other children of Jennie and William were Mabel King, b. 1881, who married Charles Donaldson, and Stanley King.

Stanley King was born in 1883 in Windom, Minnesota which was his parent's residence after their move from Montana. He married Gertrude Emery and died in 1920 in Montana where he managed two ranches for the widow of Bill Cody. His death was the result of pneumonia which occurred one year after Stanley was shot in a card game by an Indian.

William and Jennie lived in Caledonia, Houston Co., Minnesota and also in Byron, Minnesota. Both places are located in the south east corner of the state not far above the Iowa state line. Jennie died 24 Nov. 1901, and her husband died 6 Jan. 1910.

Mary Jane King married 19 April 1911, in Fort Benton, Montana, Wilbur Earl Brann and their daughter Mary Jane Brann married Benjamin Bartley Foster. Mary Jane and Bartley were the parents of a son Bartley Hardy Foster who lives in Brighton, Colorado and is very interested in his family history. He has provided much of the information on the descendants of Jennie Alsip King.

William Henry Alsip first son of Frank and Mary Jane Alsip was discussed in detail in the second volume. He and Marcella Cusak, although they both lived in Chicago, were married in Kenosha Co., Wis. as recorded in Book 3, page 263. This small town a few miles north of Chicago and just across the Illinois state line was probably a place for "quickie" marriages as many residents of Chicago seemed to have taken advantage of the more lenient marriage requirements in Wisconsin. He was at the height of his career, age 42, when his unexpected death occurred in Chicago on 13 Jan. 1901.

It is unknown what happened to William Henry Alsip's widow Marcella or his daughter Virginia, but William Henry, Jr., is listed on the 1920 census as living in Mercer Co., New Jersey near Trenton on Titus Mill Road. He had married Beatrice Bryan on 24 Aug. 1914, in Chicago. Why he moved to New Jersey has not been learned, but living in his household in addition to his son William H., Jr., age 2 years, 4 months, was Winifred McGroy, who was listed as his head servant. He also had a 24 year old man from Prussia living in the home and listed as the hired man. By 1930, William H. Alsip had moved his family back to Chicago where he was living with his wife Beatrice, age 34, and only son William H.

Frank B. Alsip third child of Frank and Mary Jane Smiley Alsip was born in McGregor, Clayton Co., Iowa in March 1862. He spent his boyhood days in this town on the banks of the Mississippi River until his parents moved to Chicago in 1872. Life was very different there where he became a young man with family responsibilities after his marriage to Nellie Bell King on 15 Nov. 1887, which was just a couple of months after the marriage of his older brother. In 1900 he was living at 483 Jackson Blvd. in Chicago with his wife Nellie, born Feb. 1868, and daughter Ruth, born March 1895. Also living in his household was his mother-in-law Sarah C. King who had been born in Canada. The next census taken ten years later reports Nellie King Alsip as living in the home of her mother Sarah with her daughter Ruth. Her husband is believed to have died by this time, as he does not appear in any researched records. In 1920, Nellie is living at 688 Irving Park Blvd. in Chicago in the home of her son-in-law Russell H. Pratt. She is not found on any available census reports after this time.

Maude A. Alsip was born on 25 Jan. 1871, to Frank and Mary Jane Smiley just before they left McGregor, Iowa for Chicago. She is believed to have married a man named Weigal but no details have been learned. Maude died 6 April 1929. Mildred Mae "Millie" Alsip, sister of Maude was born in Chicago in 1877 and married George Russell Linn on 27 May 1900, in Chicago. George was born 3 July 1870, and died 20 Nov. 1942. His wife Millie died in 1949.

Charles H. Alsip was the third and last son born into this family. His birth, which occurred on 28 January 1874, was several years after his parents had moved to Chicago. He seems to have married a woman named Frances Walker as the census for 1900 in Cook Co. shows a Frances Alsip, age 26, living on Lexington Ave. with her four year old son Frank W. Alsip in the home of her father Gerry R. Walker. This son is later identified in family records as the son of Charles H. Alsip. Where Charles is when this census is reported has not been determined. He is, however, found in the 1910 census living in Chicago with his wife Lulu (Lula?) M. Malschaider, age 33, and his fourteen year old son Frank W. Alsip. According to family records, Charles H. and Lulu were married on 10 Nov. 1909. Since the son was living with his father and step-mother, it is more likely that his mother Frances was deceased instead of divorced. By the time that the census of 1920 had been completed Charles and wife Lulu were living in their home at 4646 Magnolia Ave. in Chicago. Also living in the same city at 4908 Greenwood Ave. was the son of Charles H., Frank W. Alsip who was residing in his own home with his wife Helen F., age 23. Ten years later Charles H. Alsip and wife Lula were located in the 6th ward, Evanston, Ill. Family tradition indicates that he left the family brick company to operate an insurance agency. In 1930, his son Frank W. Alsip and wife Helen were found in the 49th ward, Chicago, with their two children Helen G., age 7, and Jane, age 2.

Martha Alsip daughter of William and Mary Ann Meeker Alsip married William Linsay Irwin in 1851, but it was somewhat of a surprise that the marriage record was found in the Cook Co., Illinois records instead of the Pittsburgh, Pennsylvania jurisdiction where they were living at the time. William Irwin was born in Ireland in 1824, and died 8 Sept. 1904, in Lancaster, Wisconsin. The town of Lancaster is located in the south west corner of the state of Wisconsin a few miles across the Mississippi River from Dubuque, Iowa and a few miles south and east of McGregor, Iowa and Prairie Du Chien, Wisconsin.

The other daughters of William and Mary Ann Meeker Alsip, other than Elizabeth Ann, did not leave much of a genealogical trail. Vanelia married John Cupps in the 1870's in Wisconsin, but little else is known about her. Her sisters Harriet Jane and Mary Margaret did not leave many records after their earlier days when they were listed in the census enumerations. Family information tells us that Harriet Jane married a man named Scott and Mary Margaret married a Mr. Dobson, but nothing has been learned concerning their progeny.

John H. Alsip, youngest child of William and Mary A. Alsip, moved to Chicago with his parents and there on 5 June 1878, married Catherine "Kittie" Lipscomb. The 1900 census of Milwaukee Co., Wis. reports that Catherine Alsip was living with her brother-in-law Edward Voss in the town of Greenfield which is today a suburb of Milwaukee. Living with her were her two children Charles, age 18, and Mabel, age 12. What happened to John has not yet been learned, but the Federal census of 1910 lists his family as living in Milwaukee Co. with the son Charles as the head of the household. John's wife Kate is living with her son and is listed as a widow. The census of 1920 again lists Catherine in Milwaukee living with her mother Susan Lipscomb at 591 Washington St. Her son Charles A. has his own home in the same city at 375 18th Ave. where he is living with his wife Jennie O. and their two daughters Gertrude, 4, and Caroline M., four months of age. In 1930, Jennie is listed as the head of the household and married, but Charles is missing from the home. Her two children Gertrude Jane and Caroline are living with her in Milwaukee Co. What caused the death of John prior to 1910 is a project for future research.

The marriage record of William Pitt Alsip, II, and wife Harriet Augusta Ada Craig, daughter of William H. Craig-born 1808 in England, has been located in the Grant Co., Wis. county courthouse at Lancaster. The date of the marriage license is 12 Oct. 1856. After leaving Jackson Co., Missouri in the late 1880's, William and his sons George, Arthur, and Elmer Lee were living in Kittitas Co., Washington by 1890. They had moved the family brick making company to this area to teach the Indians how to make bricks for the state prison. They lived near Ellensburg in the south central part of the state which is in the mountains. William P. and wife Augusta C. Alsip along with two of their sons Arthur and Elmer moved to Winnipeg, Canada in 1898.

Although William was nearing retirement age, he and his wife Augusta established their own home in Winnipeg until his death which occurred 23

June 1912. Augusta then lived with her son Elmer until her death on 8 July 1915. They were both buried in the Elmwood Cemetery in Winnipeg.

George married Harriet "Hattie" Craig on 21 Aug. 1889, at South Portland Precinct, County of Multnomah, Oregon. Harriet was his first cousin as her father William H. Craig, Jr., was the brother of William P. Alsip's wife Harriet Augusta Craig. The children of George and Harriet were Myron, born 1890, in Ellensburg, Wa., Lailah Marie, born 7 Sept. 1893, in Ellensburg, Wa., and Pearlys Harriet, born 4 Dec. 1906, in Fort William, Ontario, Canada. It has not yet been determined whether George and family went to Canada with his parents and two brothers in 1898, or if they joined them several years later. George lived at Fort William until his death on 13 Oct. 1917, and was buried near his parents at Elmwood Cemetery. Hattie his wife was still living at Fort William when her death took place on 8 Feb. 1955.

Myron Alsip son of George and Hattie Alsip married Mary McGregor in 1923 at Ft. William, and they were the parents of David and George. It is unknown what happened to David, but George died in Sunnyvale, California on 23 Feb. 1942. Lailah M. sister of Myron married James G. Biggs at Fort William on 10 Mar. 1919, and died at Thunder Bay, Ontario 10 Nov. 1973. Her sister Pearlys H. Alsip married George Burke in 1927 and died at Fort William on 23 May 1939. They had two children Pearlys Marilyn Burke, born 5 Feb. 1928, and George William Burke, born 28 July 1930.

Also a son of William P. Alsip, II, and Augusta Craig Alsip was Roy B. Alsip. When his parents moved to Canada, Roy established permanent residence in Lead, Lawrence County, South Dakota. This town is located in the south west corner of the state near the Wyoming border, and the county seat is Deadwood which is only about four miles east of Lead. By 1900, Roy and his partner Edward Brock owned and operated a mercantile store and gambling casino in Lead. Roy never married and lived in this area for the rest of his life. In 1920 he was living alone at 45 Gold St. in Lead, and he died there on 12 Feb. 1929. His brothers had his body transported to Winnipeg, Canada where he was buried in Elmwood Cemetery where his parents were buried.

Samuel Henry Alsip, brother of Roy B. above, did not follow his family to Washington, but left home after 1880 and married about 1887, Alice "Allie" Cronan who was born in Ohio. In 1900 Samuel and his wife were living in St. Clair Co., Illinois at 614 Church St., in Belleville. Living with them was Alice's mother Mary Cronan who had been born in Ireland. Samuel and wife moved to Menomonie, Dunn Co., Wisconsin where they were living in 1920. Very little has been learned about the later life of Samuel, but it is known that he died in 1950.

Another son of William and Augusta Craig Alsip was Elmer Lee who accompanied his parents to Canada. Elmer was single when he arrived in Winnipeg. He soon met and married on 10 April 1903, in Winnipeg Alexandria Black, born 23 Jan. 1877, in Quebec. She was the daughter of Alexander Black and wife Margaret DeWar. Alexandria and Elmer were the parents of William Alexander, born 9 Sept. 1904-died 7 May 1944; Margaret Augusta, born 12 March 1907-died 3 Feb. 1964; and Norman Elmer, born 12 Feb. 1911-died 3 Feb. 1929. On 27 Oct. 1912, Alexandria and her sister-in-law Lydia Eliza Jane "Lilly" Talman Alsip, wife of Elmer's brother Arthur Augustus Alsip, decided to take the family car for a short trip. With Lilly in the car, Alexandria attempted to start the vehicle by turning the crank sticking out of the front of the automobile. When the Ford car started, the gears accidentally engaged and the machine, which was still in its infancy and far from being perfected, ran over Alexandria and caused her death. Augusta Craig Alsip had moved into the home of her son Elmer Lee just a couple of months before the tragic mishap, and helped with Alexandria's young ones, as much as her health would allow, until her death three years later.

On 2 November 1915, Elmer Lee married as his second wife Lily Harrison, daughter of Frank and Mary Hourd Harrison, at Birtle, Manitoba. Elmer and Lily had a family of two sons and one daughter. They were Frank Arthur, born 30 Aug. 1916, who married Audrey Eileen Anderson on 11 Oct. 1941, at Westminster Church; Roy Harrison, born 1 Oct. 1921, and wed Ethna Gertrude Mitten on 26 July 1943, at St. Matthews; and Gwenyth May, born 12 Sept. 1929, and married Peter Rattray at St. Andrews Church on 6 Oct. 1951.

William Alexander Alsip son of Elmer and Alexandria married Elsie Mae Oliver in Winnipeg on 15 Oct. 1927, and they were the parents of Norman Lee, born 13 Oct. 1928, and Glenn Arthur, born 14 Aug. 1941. William died in Winnipeg on 7 May 1944, and was buried in the Elmwood Cemetery. His sister Margaret Augusta became the wife of Cedric Robert Hopper on 27 June 1936, in Winnipeg. Norman Elmer Alsip, the third child of this union died as a teenager and was never married.

Frank Arthur Alsip, son of Elmer Lee and second wife Lily, and wife Audrey, born in Winnipeg on 29 Nov. 1917, had three children who were Gordon Anderson, born 4 June 1943; Frank Wayne, born 16 March 1946; and Robert Arthur, born 2 June 1949.

Elmer and Lily Harrison Alsip had a second son named Roy Harrison Alsip who has been very interested in the history of his specific branch of the family tree and has sent me a lot of the data concerning his particular lineage. The following photo was taken at the 50th wedding anniversary of Roy and his wife Ethna in Calgary, Alberta. Roy and Ethna started going together when they were fifteen years old.

Roy and Ethna had progeny as follows: a daughter Terry Lee who was born 3 July 1946, and married in Calgary on 12 April 1969, David Robert Stephenson, and a son Richard Brian Alsip, born 3 April 1948, who married Marsha Lee Duncan on 22 Dec. 1969, at Calgary. Roy was born at 163 River Ave. in Winnipeg and lived in that city until he left during World War II to serve his country in the Canadian Navy. His wife Ethna was the daughter of Joseph William Mitten and wife Kathleen Mary Nicholl. Roy and Ethna moved from Winnipeg to Calgary in the 1950's.

One of the two remaining sons of William Pitt Alsip, II, and his wife Augusta, who has not been covered yet, is Arthur Augustus Alsip, born in Decorah, Iowa on 27 July 1868. He moved with his parents and several of his brothers to Washington and then on to Winnipeg, Canada. Before the death of Harriet Augusta Alsip, widow of William Alsip, II, her family employed a lady's companion to care for her health and social needs. The young lady was Lydia Eliza Jane "Lily" Talman who had been born in Aldershot, England in 1884. She and her brother came to Canada from England in 1905. One morning not long after her arrival in Canada she awoke and discovered that she was totally deaf. She seemed to have been able to attend to her duties as the companion of Augusta, although the handicap must have made her task much more difficult. The situation, however, did not keep Arthur from falling in love with Lily and they were soon married. Their only child who lived to adulthood was a daughter Ruby Florence Alsip, born 11 April 1908.

Arthur Alsip joined his brothers William Pitt, III, George, and Elmer Lee in 1905 when the Alsip Brick Company was established, and they all participated in the ownership and operation of the business. William Pitt Alsip, IV, in a letter to the author dated 1984, states that up until that time the family business was known as William Alsip Brick Manufacturer. However, in the past it had been known as Alsip Brothers, etc. Arthur was named as the treasurer of the company. Arthur put a notice of appreciation in the newspaper in connection with his "beloved aunt, Hortense Sanford" when she died in Ethan, South Dakota. She was the sister of his mother Augusta. Arthur died on 21 May 1930 in Winnipeg and was buried in the Elmwood Cemetery near other family members. William Pitt, III, who was always call "W. P." by his relatives, was very disturbed when his brother Elmer's wife Alexandria died in the car accident, and seemed to have placed a lot of the blame on Lily who was sitting in the car at the time because she had not been able to stop the vehicle. Although Lily was deaf and had never learned to drive, he felt that she should have been able to prevent the accident. After her husband's death Lily and her daughter Ruby and her daughter's husband Harold decided to move to California because of the intense cold winters in Canada. By 1949-50 Lily had sold her share of the company to her brother-in-law William P. Alsip so that the family would have enough money to make the transition to the United States. Ruby Alsip had married Harold Edward Caldwell Hough, born 1907, and their only child Gretchen Diane was born in Canada on 10 May 1941. This family of four left Winnipeg in 1951 and established their permanent residence in California. Ruby died on 13 Aug. 1988.

Gretchen Diane Hough is a present day descendant of this specific lineage and is very interested in the history of the Alsop-Alsip family. She has done extensive research on her specific branch of the family tree and has been very gracious in providing extensive information on Francis Alsop of Ireland and his progeny. Gretchen is an airline stewardess and had taken advantage of her travels to dig into the courthouse records in many parts of the country. Gretchen married Johnny Arley King, born 1934-died 16 Oct. 2002, and was buried in Oaklawn Cemetery in Decatur, Wise Co., Texas. Their only child was Karen Sue King, born 1966, who married Aaron Wayne Alcorn, born 1962, and they have a son Marc Andrew, born 1990.

The oldest son of William and Augusta Craig Alsip was William Pitt Alsip, III, who was living in Waukon, Iowa in 1880 with his wife Mary(maiden name not yet learned) who family tradition says was his cousin, and his daughter Lottie "Lotta" who was three months old, having been born in Feb. of that year. The place and date of his marriage has yet to be determined. He moved to Grand Forks, North Dakota in 1882 in connection with his brick making profession. The Federal census of 1900 lists "W. P." and family as still living in Grand Forks, although his first wife Mary had died in the late 1880's and he had remarried about 1890 to Isabella Shepherd. Lotta who had been born in Iowa was age 20 and still living with her father and step-mother. Isabella, born 10 Aug. 1869, in Scotland was the mother of Gladys A., born Jan. 1891, and Marguerite I., born Feb. 1894.

By 1905, W. P. and Isabella and their three children had located their residence in Winnipeg, Canada where his parents and several of his brothers were living. He and three of his brothers set up the brick company which was to supply employment for much of the family for several generations. Isabella died on 15 Feb. 1919, and sometime in late 1919, W. P. married as his third wife Mrs. Eva Stanley Campbell. In a letter written by William Pitt Alsip, IV, he states that when his father married his mother he was sixty years of age and she was thirty-two. Eva S. Alsip had a son named Jack who was born about 1918, and then a son by her husband W. P. Alsip who was named William Pitt Alsip, IV, born 22 Dec. 1920. W. P. was a multi-talented person with a praiseworthy intellect who was able to accomplish much during his lifetime. Not only was he a very successful business man, but he enjoyed life to its fullest and took educational vacation trips to many parts of the U. S. with his family and then wrote detailed descriptions of his experiences. He would send relatives copies of these accounts of his travels once a year in letter form with one of them being presented in an earlier part of this chapter. This foresight on his part has preserved a lot of family history that would otherwise have disappeared. W. P. died in 1944 and was buried in the family plot at the Elmwood Cemetery in Winnipeg.

William Pitt Alsip, IV, son of Eva and W. P. Alsip, III, was another member of this branch of the family tree who enjoyed every day of his life. When he died, the Winnipeg Sun of 16 July 1986, detailed his life which follows.

WILLIAM PITT ALSIP
"ALPINE ALSIP"

Obituary of William Pitt Alsip

Peacefully on July 15, 1986 at Victoria General Hospital after a valiant struggle with cancer. Born in Los Angeles, California December 22, 1920, son of William Pitt Alsip and Eva Stanley Campbell, he resided in Winnipeg, from 1921 until his passing, mostly in the family home on McMillan Ave. He enjoyed a 47 year career in various executive positions, most recently vice-president with Alsip Brick, Tile & Lumber Company Limited, a firm founded by his father, William Pitt Alsip, Sr., in 1905.

An active sportsman since his childhood, he built the first of a society of shooting lodges out of Passawa Bay on Netley Marsh in 1932 with Glenn "Mudhen" Massey. He later was a founding member of the Manitoba Gun Dog Association and occupied the position of treasurer for a number of years. He was a former member of the Granite Curling Club and the Winnipeg Canoe Club and a member of the Frontier Wildlife Association.

He felt most at home in the Pembina Valley at La Riviere where he pioneered a colony of boxcar ski lodges.

An avid fisherman, skier, and unbelievable cook, his passion was hunting game birds and deer to which he was extraordinarily well suited, being both a crack shot and a true raconteur with hundreds of exploits handy to his mind.

Alpine was blessed with an indomitable life living spirit that his family and friends of all ages and walks of life will always cherish.

He was predeceased by his parents and a brother Jack Campbell Alsip. He is survived by his truest passion, his loving wife Louise; his son William Pitt, Jr., of Nanaimo, B. C.; his son Steve and his wife Mags; his son Dick and his wife Elizabeth; his daughter Janet and her husband Lakhdar; his daughter Marilyn and his like son nephew Jack Campbell Alsip, Jr. and his granddaughters Jenny and Kathy Mihill and Lisa and Alarey Alsip, all of Winnipeg.

Kind thanks to Helen Hudson, Kathy, Bonnie and Julie of the Oncology Department, Ms. Jody Toogood of the Chaplain's office, all the wonderful nursing staff of Unit 5 at the Victoria General Hospital and especially Dr. Ian Maxwell, for truly caring. Also, thanks to the many friends who visited Alpine so faithfully both at home and in the hospital.

Funeral services will be on Friday, July 18 at noon at Thomson's Funeral Chapels with Elizabeth Alsip's father, Reverend Garfield Barber officiating. Services will terminate at the Chapels with cremation to follow. Honorary pallbearers will be Joseph Telford, Walter Prystayko, Myrt Comberbach, Gerald P. Dennehy, Glenn Massey, Roy Alsip, Pat Aseltine, Paul Sweatman, Rob Fenton, and Jake MacDonald.

In lieu of flowers, if friends so desire, donations made to the Victoria General Hospital Research and Services Funds would be greatly appreciated.

****

The Winnipeg Sun of 20 July 1986, ran another article on William Pitt Alsip, IV, giving us additional insight into the life of this remarkable man.

Who's going to ski down Holiday Mountain in his underwear now that "Alpine" Alsip is gone?

Bill Alsip, much loved by skiers and rafts of Winnipeggers who knew the hospitality of his boxcar cabin at La Riviere Hills, died this week of cancer.

Alpine, whom many people might know from Alsip Brick and Tile, was one of Winnipeg's fabulous characters. Life was a banquet and he was the emcee. Kids adored him because he treated them like real people as soon as they could say boo.

He loved to go hunting with his own buddies. But his son's friends loved to take him along with them to hear his marvelous stories. Many of them (like his yarn about being a song and dance man in Las Vegas) came straight out of his fertile imagination.

Such a kidder.

Any young person who came in contact with Alpine learned a lot about love through seeing his open affection for his wife Louise, or "Squeezy Louisey" as he called her. This was the kind of guy who still called his wife from the office for dates years after they were married.

What a man! What a happy life he lived! We could all learn from him.

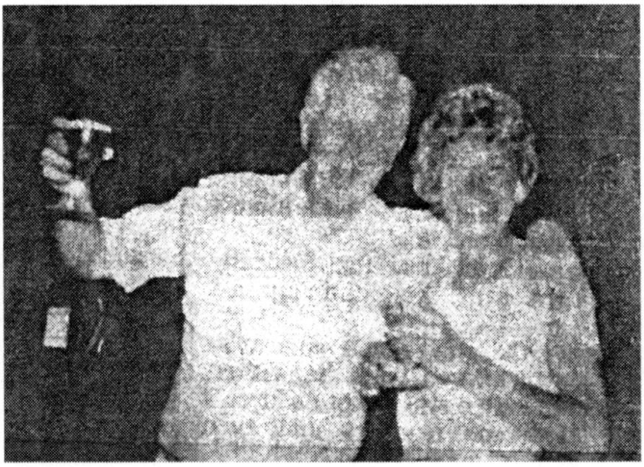

Bill Alsip gives his wife "Squeezy Louisey" a squeeze.

The Alsip Farm in Brookings County, South Dakota east of the town of Aurora. Aaron Henry is shown on the right and son Thomas J. is the third one from the left. Note the nice brick chimney built by "Henry."

Aaron Henry Alsip son of William Pitt Alsip and wife Mary Ann Meeker lived near Brookings, South Dakota until he and his wife joined their son Thomas J. Alsip in Tacoma, Washington in 1908. He was staying at 1014 14th Street in Tacoma when he received a statement from the Bank of Volga located in Volga, South Dakota which reported that his note on a second mortgage was due. It was dated 28 May 1892; therefore, he must have been visiting his son who had moved to Washington by that time. Aaron Henry Alsip died in Tacoma on Saturday, 10 Feb. 1912, after failing to recover from an operation which he had about a year earlier. The funeral was held on the following Tuesday and he was buried in the Tacoma Mausoleum.

Aaron Henry Alsip, his wife Mary Ellen, son
Thomas J. and daughter Belle

Mary Ellen "Ellie" Vedder Alsip died at the home of her son Thomas J. in Mistleton District, near Monmouth, Oregon in Polk Co. on Monday, 24 Feb. 1930. She had moved from Tacoma in 1925 to make her permanent home with her son and his family. Funeral services were held at Smith Chapel on Wednesday afternoon and the remains were forwarded to Tacoma, Washington for burial at the mausoleum there.

Following is a letter received by Ellie from her brother Jefferson W. Vedder who was a soldier in the Civil War. The letter was dated a few months after her marriage to Henry Alsip.

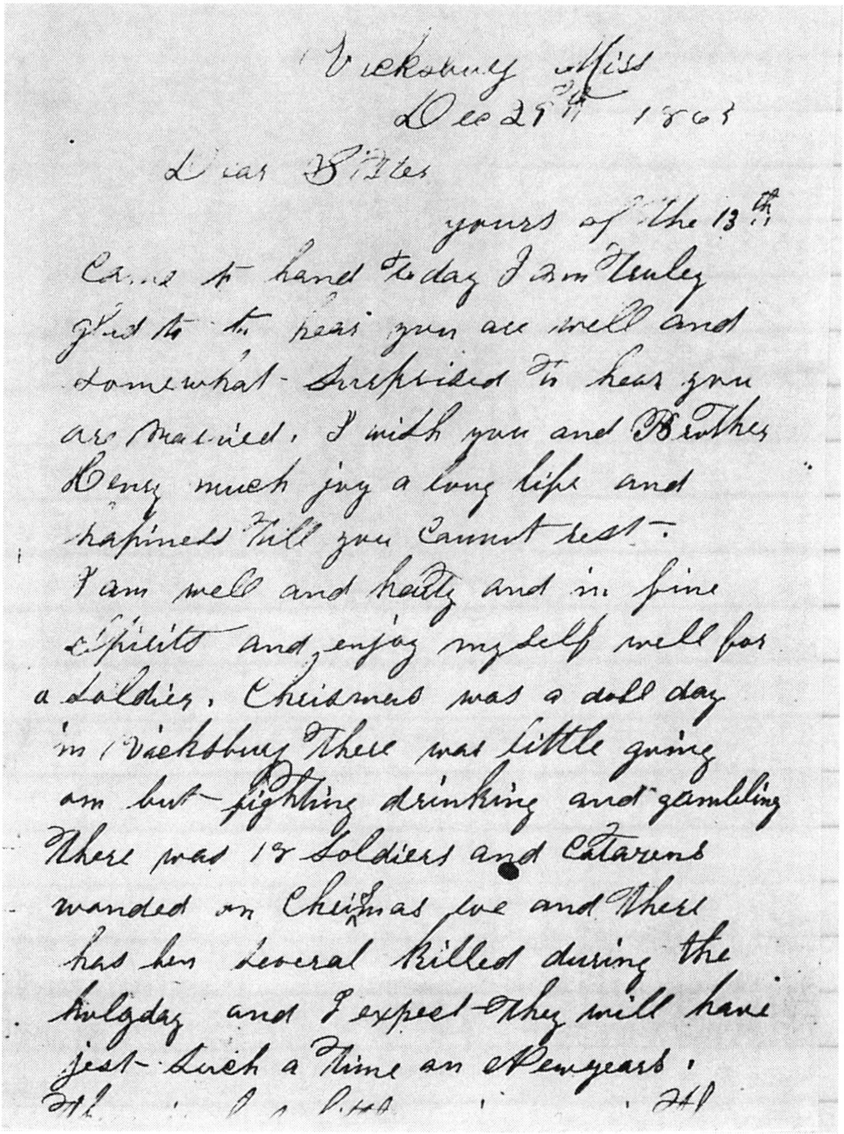

Vicksburg Miss
Dec 25th 1863

Dear Sister

yours of the 13th
Came to hand today I am truly
glad to to hear you are well and
somewhat surprised to hear you
are married. I wish you and Brother
Henry much joy a long life and
happiness till you cannot rest.
I am well and hearty and in fine
spirits and enjoy myself well for
a soldier. Christmas was a dull day
in Vicksburg There was little going
on but fighting drinking and gambling
There was 18 soldiers and Citizens
wounded on Christmas eve and there
has been several killed during the
holyday and I expect they will have
just such a time on Newyears.
[illegible]

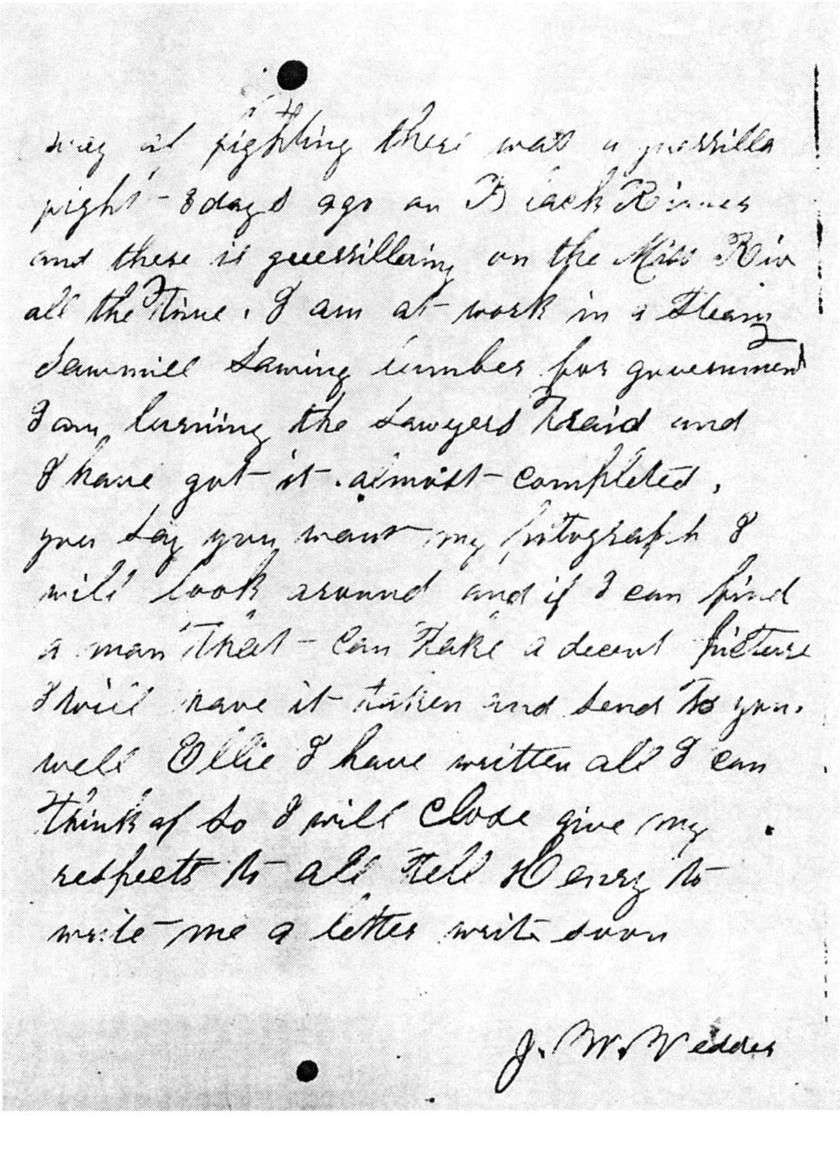
way at fighting there was a guerrilla
fight 8 days ago on Black River
and there is guerrillaing on the Miss River
all the time. I am at work in a steam
sawmill sawing lumber for government
I am learning the sawyers trade and
I have got it almost completed,
you say you want my photograph I
will look around and if I can find
a man that can take a decent picture
I will have it taken and send to you.
well Ellie I have written all I can
think of so I will close give my
respects to all tell Henry to
write me a letter write soon

J. W. Weddes

Susan Belle Alsip, only daughter of Aaron Henry and Ellie Alsip, married William J. "Bill" Stratton and they left South Dakota and moved to Tacoma, Washington as verified by a letter written from Belle and Bill to her parents in January 1896. A portion of this letter is now presented:

Tacoma Wash.
Jan 18-96

Dear Folks

Will brought your letter this
after noon I was awfull
sorry to here Ma was sick
and hope you are well
by this time you bet I
wish I was there to talk
and visite I have wished
lots of times when I felt
bad that if I could only
have Pa and Ma with me
or be where they was how
much better I would
feel, you bet it is tuff
to be so far a part I have
cryed more than once about
it Will says he will come
just when ever you say
the word he is awfull

anxious to leave here he
is getting awfull tired of
carry-ing mail we are
coming sure and sertain
there is no use of talking
I haint going to live cleare
out here right at the
jumping off place and
you cleare to the other end
of the world, if we have
to walk I guess we could
beat our way through
and maby we could catch
a ride part of the way
I might pass my self of
for a single girl and make
a mash on the Engineears
and pass Will off as my brother
and tell them how hard
up we was and that
we could not get work, to
earn a dollar so we thought
we would try walking

Bill and Belle Alsip Stratten continued to live in Tacoma and were the parents of a son Earl G. Stratten. Their struggle to earn a living lingered, and Belle tried to help by utilizing her talents as an artist to help bring in additional family income. She had a business card printed which listed her abilities as landscape and china painting, photo tinting, china firing, and art lessons taught. Their address at the time was 2002 S. Union Ave.

Belle Alsip Stratten

This photo was taken in Brookings, S. D. ca. 1890. Left to right: Thomas J. Alsip, Mary Susan Alsip, Belle Alsip Stratten, and unknown.

Earl, son of Bill and Belle wrote a letter to his maternal grandmother Mary Ellen Alsip and a couple of parts of the letter have been duplicated and are shown for their genealogical content.

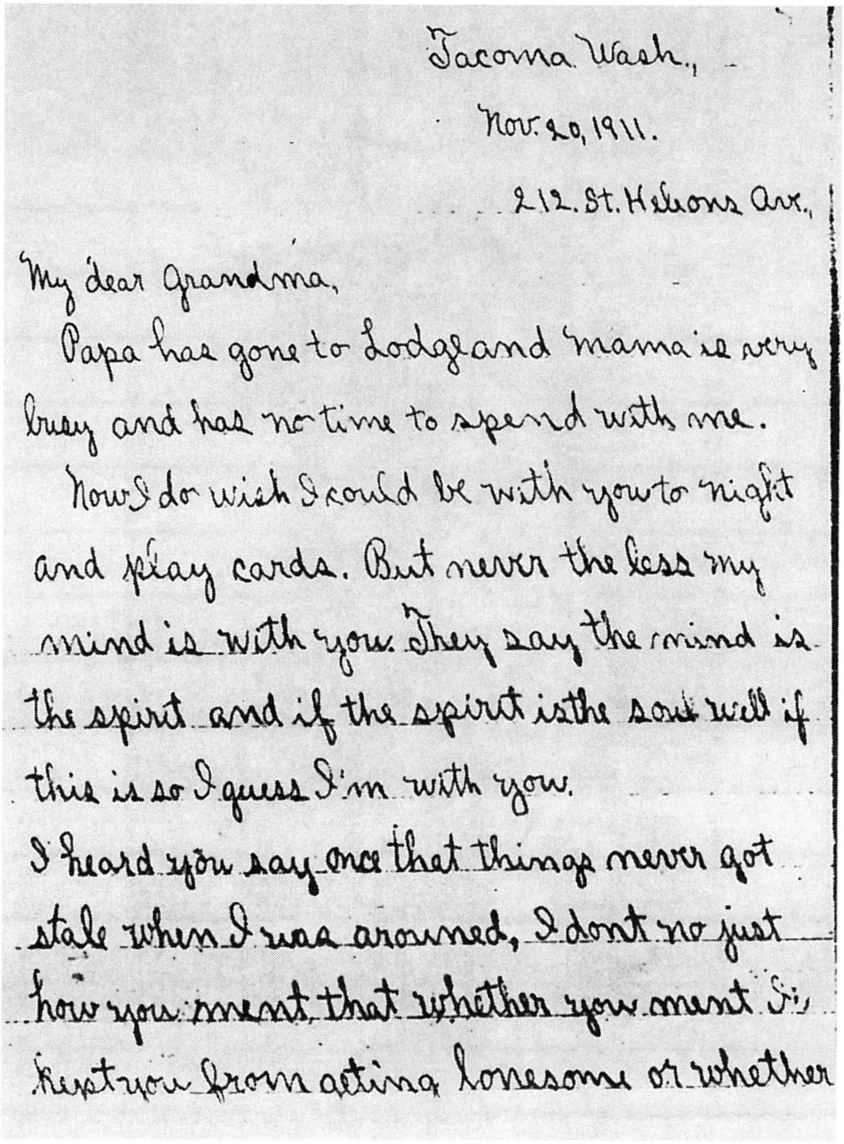

Tacoma Wash.,

Nov. 20, 1911.

212. St. Helens Ave.,

My dear Grandma,

Papa has gone to Lodge and Mama is very busy and has no time to spend with me.

Now I do wish I could be with you to night and play cards. But never the less my mind is with you. They say the mind is the spirit and if the spirit is the soul well if this is so I guess I'm with you.

I heard you say once that things never got stale when I was arouned, I dont no just how you ment that whether you ment I kept you from geting lonesome or whether

I'm glad that Thanksgiving is so near I'm thinging of that nice dinner I am going to have over there. well grandma I guess I will close this with a little rhyme.

Oh! the bulldog on the bank,
And the bullfrog in the pool.
The bulldog call'd the bullfrog
A green old water fool.

Oh! the bulldog stooped to catch him,
And the snapper caught his paw;
The pollywog died a laughing
To see him wag his jaw.

from your grandson
Earl Stratton.

P. S. when can I come over and stay all night

On 24 July 1912, only about five months after the death of her father, Belle went to the hospital and was operated on the next day. She died an early and tragic death at the hospital on July 28 at the age of 37. She was listed in her obituary as the wife of William J. Stratton, a patrolman on the Tacoma police department. Belle was living at 210 St. Helens Ave. at the time of her death. The funeral was held on 30 July 1912, at the L. M. Gaffney Company's chapel. The remains were entombed in the Tacoma Mausoleum. Mary Ellen Alsip wrote a letter to a relative a couple of years later and reported that Bill Stratton had married a woman with five children ranging from four years up. She commented that it was no wonder that Earl was in the hospital. Earl, only son of Belle, also died an early death as reported by William Pitt Alsip, III, in his family letter of 1927.

Thomas Jefferson Alsip brother of Belle and son of Mary Ellen and Aaron Henry Alsip moved with his family at age 10 to Brookings County, South Dakota where he grew up and married in 1894 Mary Susan Davis. Mary Susan, born in Springville, Minnesota on 31 Aug. 1873, the daughter of Alexander Warwick Davis and wife Caroline McClary, moved with her parents from her place of birth in 1878 to a homestead in eastern Brookings Co., which at the time was Dakota Territory. As she grew up she helped as a clerk in her father's store and post office at Bushnell, S. D. Thomas J. and wife Mary Susan lived on a farm near Bushnell after their marriage, but moved to Albany, Oregon in 1902. Three of their sons were born in S. D. and the other three in Oregon. These children will be discussed thoroughly in Volume IV of Alsop's Tables. The Alsips moved to Dallas, Polk Co., Oregon in 1909, living in the North Dallas area first and then relocating to a farm which they had purchased in the Mistleton District.

T. J. and wife Mary Susan lived at the Mistleton area farm where they were in the prune growing and drying business. The climate and soil of this area was conducive to the raising of an Italian prune which was tart, sweet, and especially suited for drying for the market.

Mary Susan Davis (are those pierced earrings?)

Thomas J. Alsip and Mary Susan Alsip

Mary Susan Alsip and her husband T. J. were very successful farmers and owned two farms in the Monmouth, Oregon area. One was a cattle and grain farm while the other was a vast prune orchard farm. They also owned and operated a commercial prune dryer in Monmouth. The Alsips were members of the Co-operative Prune Growers who had their own packing house and sold through the local exchange. Their brand was known as the "Mistland Prunes." T. J. and Mary Susan took an active interest in the welfare work of their county. They were early day Graingers, and also charter members of the Farmer's Union.

It was in 1930 that T. J. Alsip, as a member of the Polk County Cooperative Prune Growers, and sons Frank and Russell made a trip to Brookings, South Dakota to determine what success might be obtained in direct marketing of their prunes. The following newspaper article describes the situation as the Alsip party was returning home:

WRECK ATTENDS RETURN OF ALSIP

Fatality near Boardman as Fruit Man Neared Home From Dakota Trip

T. J. Alsip, well known farmer and fruit grower of the Mistletoe district, died Wednesday morning in the Hermiston Hospital as the result of injuries received in an automobile accident Monday night. Mr. Alsip was returning from a prune selling trip to South Dakota started last spring. His party was traveling in two cars. Mr. Alsip and his daughter-in-law, Mrs. Gladys Alsip and the latter's small daughter, Irene were ahead in his Model A Ford tudor sedan. Behind were Russell Alsip and a young man they had picked up at Twin Falls, Idaho. There had been delays and they were behind on their schedule. Expecting to be home Monday night, 6:30 that evening found them between Irrigon and Boardman 176 miles east of Portland.

Traveling fast, at the crest of a hill they came directly on a man who seems to have been traveling faster still. The result was a head-on collision. Despite bumpers both cars were telescoped wrenching the wiring into a short circuit which set both cars on fire. Mr. Alsip who was driving had his breast caved in. His daughter-in-law was struck on the head resulting in a long scalp wound and was unconscious until after she reached the hospital. Wilbur Staver of Irrigon, who was driving the other car was also taken to the hospital with cuts and bruises.

Responding to a telegram Mrs. Alsip and Ruth Meeker with Henry Alsip driving started Monday night for Hermiston arriving there in the morning. Mrs. Alsip stayed but Henry and Ruth and the girl, Irene returned Wednesday morning. News that Mr. Alsip had passed away reached home about the time they did.

Mr. Alsip was born in Decorah, Iowa sixty three years ago January 30. He lived at Austin, Minnesota and at Brookings, South Dakota and in Montana and came to Oregon about fifteen years ago.

As a business man of Monmouth, Alsip will be missed. He was the owner of the Monmouth prune dryer which he operated each year. He was a member of the grange and prominent in the councils of the Farmers Union. He was a fair minded man, thrifty and enterprising and will be missed in many ways in Polk County.

Beside his widow he is survived by four sons: Russell of Eugene; Vern, Henry and Frank, all of the Mistletoe district.

Harry Keeney, who is to have charge of the funeral services, left this afternoon for Hermiston to bring back the body. Funeral arrangements have not been made but the funeral will probably be held Sunday.

The accident happened on Monday 28 July 1930, and T. J.'s death occurred on Wednesday, 30 July at the hospital in Hermiston, Oregon. Funeral services were held Sunday, 3 August 1930, at the Monmouth Christian Church. Burial was in the Brown Cemetery, near Dallas, Oregon.

The widow of T. J. Alsip, Mary Susan continued to live on the family farm in the Mistletoe District and this remarkable woman spent her final years in numerous projects and activities. She loved her flowers and produced a marvelous flower garden in her yard which was the wonder of area residents. She was an exhibitor and a consistent winner at the Polk Co. Fair. She attended the last eight conventions of the Farmer's Union and was on the way home from the last one in Sheridan, Oregon when she stopped to visit her son Henry Alsip who lived north west of Monmouth. She became ill while there and pneumonia developed taking her life on 5 June 1938. Funeral services were conducted on Wednesday, 8 June 1938, at 2:00 P. M. in the Monmouth Christian Church with Rev. W. A. Elkins officiating. She was buried next to her husband in the Brown Cemetery.

****

Thomas McOuBerg (McCousberg?) Alsip son of William Alsip and wife Mary Ann Meeker Alsip settled permanently in Escambia Co., Florida. The children of Thomas M. and wife Almira "Ella" Cupps Alsip were Guy T., born 28 April 1872; Carl Victor, born 13 Dec. 1875; Ray Thomas, born 25 March 1885; and William George Alsip. Thomas M. was listed as a farmer on the 1900 enumeration. The Federal census of 1920 for Escambia Co. lists the households of Thomas M. Alsip, Guy T. Alsip, Ray Alsip, and William George Alsip. Also living in the home of Thomas M. was his wife Ella, his son Carl V., and his grandson William G. Alsip. Thomas died in Escambia Co., Florida near the town of Pensacola in the community of Brent on 21 Feb. 1935, and was buried in Clopton Cemetery next to his wife Ella who had died in 1925.

The above photo was made ca. 1920 of Thomas M. Alsip and wife Almira "Ella" Cupps Alsip

Guy T. Alsip married on 14 Aug. 1907, in Pensacola Pearl Herrmann who was the daughter of Frederick Hermann and wife Mary Elizabeth Stokes. Pearl had been born in Memphis, Tennessee on 4 November 1890. Their first child was Mildred Faye, born 7 January 1909, in Pensacola. The only other child born to Guy and Pearl was a son named Fred T., who was born on 9 Sept. 1917, and lived about two hours. He was the first of his family to be buried in the Clopton Cemetery. Guy Alsip died in Pensacola, Florida on 3 April 1949, and was interred at Clopton Cemetery. His widow Pearl Alsip remarried on 16 March 1960, to J. D. Renfroe as recorded in Marriage Book 4, page 438, in Brewton, Escambia County, Alabama. Pearl died 15 November 1974, and was laid to rest next to her first husband in the Clopton Cemetery with her tombstone listing her name as Pearl Herrmann Alsip Renfroe.

Back Row: Guy T. Alsip, Margaret Pate Alsip, Pearl H. Alsip, Mary Elizabeth Stokes Herrmann, Frederick Herrmann, Thomas M. Alsip. Front Row: Mildred Faye Alsip, Grace Almira Alsip, William George Alsip, Jr., and Almira Cupps Alsip.

Carl Victor Alsip never married and was living at home with his parents in Escambia Co., Florida when the Federal enumeration was completed in 1920. He died in 1926, and was buried near his mother in the Alsip family plot in Clopton Cemetery.

One of the younger brothers of Guy and Carl Alsip was Ray Thomas Alsip. He married Nellie Mozelle Harper, born 26 April 1890, in Pensacola and in the 1920 census Ray and Mozelle had a three year old daughter named Jewel. Ray died an early death on 6 July 1924, and was buried in the Clopton

Cemetery near Pensacola. Jewell had health problems all of her childhood days and after graduation from high school died having never been married. Her mother Mozelle married as her second husband William P. Brewton and their household was listed in 1930 showing William as having a step-daughter named Jewel. Mozelle continued to live in the Pensacola area and died 24 July 1961, although the burial site in not yet known.

The last child born to Thomas M. Alsip and wife Ella Cupps Alsip was William George Alsip, Sr., who moved from Chicago, Ill. to Florida with his parents while still a boy. He was a good athlete as proven by the photo shown below in which he is the first baseball player on the left.

In Pensacola William G. married as his first wife Margaret Pate, born 29 July 1893, and they were the parents of William George, Jr., born 7 Sept. 1909, and Grace Almira, born 14 Nov. 1910. Margaret died on 2 May 1917, and was buried in St. John's Cemetery in Pensacola. William G. then married the niece of his first wife who was Mary LeRotha Pate, born ca. 1901. The census of 1920 for Escambia Co. reports William and wife Mary as living in the Pensacola area with Grace, one of William's children by his wife Margaret. The other child William George, Jr., was living with his paternal grandparents Thomas M. and Ella Cupps Alsip in the same county. On 9 April 1921, William G. and Mary had a son named Jack Dan Alsip. William George Alsip, Sr., died in Escambia Co. on 22 June 1926, and was buried next to his first wife Margaret. The cause of this unexpected death has not yet been learned. Mary Pate Alsip, second wife of William, died 23 Nov. 1970.

Mildred Faye Alsip grew up in the Pensacola area and on 5 March 1928, married Walter Joseph Beckman, born 3 Feb. 1905 in Philadelphia, Pennsylvania. The census of 1930 determines that Walter and his wife Faye were living with her parents. Faye and Walter were the parents of three children Barbara Faye, Walter Eugene, and Glenn Alvin. Walter Joseph Beckman died in Pensacola on 11 Aug. 1975. Faye continued to live in the Pensacola vicinity and worked for many years on the Alsip family history. I have corresponded with her since the late 1970's and she had supplied me with much valuable family data and historic photos. This photo of Faye Alsip Beckman was taken on Mother's day 1990, when she was age 81.

I received a letter dated 3 June 1995, from Barbara Beckman Burns, daughter of Faye Alsip Beckman informing me that her mother had died on 15 May 1995. She was a diligent Alsip researcher and a wonderful human being, and I will miss her very much. Barbara told me that she had lived with her mother for the previous nine years and was planning to continue her mother's family history research project which she had grown to appreciate.

(This family will be continued in Alsop's Tables, Volume IV)

CHAPTER XII

Samuel Allsop of Derbyshire

(This family is continued from page 188, Vol. II, Alsop's Tables)

Samuel Alsop and his wife Salina Pegg came to America in 1834 and eventually settled in Madison Co., Illinois near the town of New Douglas. Their two oldest daughters married shortly after arriving in Madison Co. Sarah Jane married William J. Griffith on 6 Oct. 1853, and her sister Hannah Marie was wed to James Milton Robb on 15 Oct. 1857, as found in the court records of Madison Co. Salina Alsop another daughter of Samuel and Salina married John R. Long on 22 Feb. 1863. James M. Alsop a son of Samuel and Salina married in Bond Co., Illinois on 9 March 1876, Elizabeth "Libbie" Knowlson as recorded in Book "A", page 93.

William Alsop was the first son of Samuel and Salina Allsop-Alsop, having been born in Jersey County, Illinois on 29 July 1844. He was living with his parents and brothers and sisters when he volunteered for military service during the Civil War. He served in Co. "G", 150th Ill. Infantry (19th?), from 2 Feb. 1865 until 16 Jan. 1866. Returning home after the war, he married in Montgomery Co., Ill. on 17 March 1868, Mary Jones, born 15 Feb. 1846. Montgomery Co., Illinois is the county that joins Madison Co. on the north east corner. William and Mary lived in the small town of Litchfield, Montgomery Co. after their marriage, and their first child, a daughter named Ada Alice, was born on 14 March 1869. They then moved back to New Douglas in Madison Co. where their second daughter Lottie Mae was born on 3 March 1871. They were again living in Litchfield when their third child Josie Estella was born on 19 April 1875.

Hannah Marie Alsop Robb sister of William had relocated to Bourbon Co., Kansas ca. 1859. From his sister's glowing descriptions of the living conditions in Kansas, William decided to establish his permanent residence in that area.

With his wife and three children, William left Illinois in a covered wagon during the year of 1878 (it is believed that his brother John and his family accompanied them on this pioneer journey) and relocated to Kansas according to William's obituary. One family record says that they lived in Funston, Ks. first. They were living in Uniontown, Bourbon County, Kansas by Christmas of 1878, as their son Willis Rosell (Roscoe?) Alsop was born on 25 Dec. of that year (some records give his birth as the 26th). By 1880, William had moved across the Bourbon Co. line to Elsmore Township in Allen Co. which was only about a dozen miles from Uniontown. He lived there for the next 26 years.

Mary Jones Alsop, wife of William, died at their family farm on 10 Jan. 1892. She was buried in the Moran Cemetery which is located in the town of Moran, Allen Co., Kansas.

Working all of his life as a farmer, William continued to live on the home place after the death of his first wife. On 10 August 1897, he married as his second wife Mrs. Minnie B. Larkins, born in Nov. 1864, in Ohio. She brought to the marriage a daughter Silvia E., born in Nov. 1889, by her first union, and she and William were the parents of a son Alonzo "Lonnie" Oscar, born in June , 1899. Prior to his second marriage, William had moved to a farm in Elm Township located four miles south east of LaHarpe which was also in Allen County. The census of 1910 lists William and family as living on this farm and living in the household with them was a man Harry D. Alsop who was single and age 29. He has not yet been identified in this specific branch of the family tree but was probably a cousin.

William was known in the community as a consistent Christian, a member of the Adventist Church, a loving husband, a kind father, a generous neighbor, and a loyal friend who was held in high regard by all who knew him. He had not been well during the final weeks of 1910, with the chief cause being much trouble with pleurisy. On Monday, 9 January 1911, William visited his granddaughter Edna R. Walker Felkins, the daughter of Ada Alsop and her husband Willis Walker. Edna and husband Claude lived near LaHarpe where they entertained her grandfather with a special dinner. Tuesday he brought a load of hogs to Iola, the county seat of Allen Co., and upon returning home had difficulty breathing. He died at his home on Thursday evening, 12 January 1911, at the age of 66. His three daughters were all present when death came.

The funeral was held at Golden Valley Church at two o'clock on Saturday afternoon, 14 January. Rev. Dutro of Iola preached the sermon with burial following at the Moran Cemetery.

William Alsop in a photo taken at Moran, Kansas

The oldest child of William and first wife Mary was Ada Alice Alsop. She came to Kansas with her parents in a covered wagon when she was only 9 years old and grew up in Allen Co. On 21 June 1886, at Iola, Kansas Ada married Willis Cline Walker, born in Battleground, Indiana on 28 Dec. 1860, he being the son of George Walker and Caroline McKillip.

A daughter Gladys Walker Gilbert was interviewed when she was 94 years old and revealed many intimate details about her parents. Gladys said that her mother Ada made peace with God at an early age and followed Him closely all through the years. When her parents first married, her father Willis homesteaded west of Prairie Hall in Allen Co., breaking the sod with oxen drawn plows. Their only transportation was by wagon and Willis told the story that when they had eggs to sell, he would stand up all the way to town so the eggs wouldn't get broken on the way in. Ada was a member of the Prairie Hall Methodist Rural Church and was active in the Ladies Aid of that church until it closed down because of lack of membership. She then transferred her membership to the Golden Valley Evangelical Church. As of 1995, both churches were gone.

Willis and Ada Alsop Walker were the parents of seven children as follows: (1) Mary Cecil Walker, born 8 March 1887, at Elsmore, Kansas, died 27 Nov. 1966, at Turlock, California; (2) Edna Rayborne Walker, born 23 Nov. 1888, at Elsmore, Ks., died 24 Dec. 1989, buried at Colorado Springs, Colorado; (3) Hazel May Walker, born 1 Oct. 1891, at LaHarpe, Ks., died 19 May 1948, at Amarillo, Texas and buried at Moran, Kansas; (4) George Stingley Walker, born 27 Oct. 1894, at LaHarpe, Ks., died 20 Nov. 1947, at Modesto, Ca., and buried at Moran, Ks.; (5) Beulah Gladys Walker, born 20 March 1901, at LaHarpe, Kansas, died 18 March 1995, at Amarillo, TX. and buried at Moran, Kansas; (6) Frederick Lynn Walker, born 19 Feb. 1907, at Moran, Ks., died 5 March 1910, at Moran; (7) and Lois Arlene Walker, born 16 July 1909, at Moran, Ks., died 21 Nov. 1991, at Iola, Ks., and buried in LaHarpe, Kansas Cemetery.

Ada Alsop Walker died 5 June 1949, at Moran, Kansas and was buried in the south west section of the Old Moran Cemetery. Her husband Willis died at Moran on 3 May 1958, and was buried next to his wife.

Lottie Mae Alsop, sister of Ada and daughter of William and Mary Alsop, left Illinois for Kansas with her parents and lived in Allen Co. until her marriage on 17 March 1893, to Dresden Wayne Isaac, son of Allen Isaac and wife Paulina Seger. She and her husband had progeny as follows: (1) Lawrence Allen Isaac, born 8 April 1899, at Moran, Ks., died 25 April 1987, at Oklahoma City, Ok.; (2) William Lester Isaac, born April 1894, at Moran, Ks., died 19 Nov. 1977, at Tracy, California; (3) Bernice Ladine Isaac, born 20 Dec. 1895, at Moran, Ks., died 15 Sept. 1987, at Oklahoma City, Ok.; (4) and Arnold Wayne Isaac, born 31 March 1906, at Shawnee, Ok., married Lois Garten 4 Oct. 1930, died 9 March 1992, at Glendale, Arizona.

Lottie Mae Alsop Isaac

This photo of Lottie Mae was sent to me by Robert L. Issac, a present day resident of Tucson, Arizona and a grandson through Lawrence Allen

Isaac. Bob also sent the photo of William Alsop, father of Lottie Mae, and he has photos of Samuel and Salina Pegg Alsop, his immigrant ancestors, but they are not of a reproducible quality. He had generously supplied much of the detailed information on the descendants of William Alsop who was born in Jersey Co., Illinois.

Lottie Mae Alsop Isaac moved with her husband and family to Oklahoma and died there at Oklahoma City on 29 July 1956. She was buried in the Rose Hill Cemetery at that location. One of her sons Lawrence Allen Isaac married Mintie Mae Combs, daughter of Hugh and Rebecca McAdoo Combs, on 6 Jan. 1924, in Shawnee, Oklahoma. They produced Helen Ruth, Marjorie Ann, and Robert L. Isaac who married Cleta Rosell Mobbs. Another son of Lottie Mae was William Lester Isaac who married Rilla Appeline Combs, sister of Mintie Mae. Their children were Wanda Mae, William Lester, Jr., and Barbara Marie.

The third daughter born to William Alsop and wife Mary was Josie Estella. She married Millard Williams on 27 November 1895, in Kansas and died in Turlock, California on 21 June 1945. Nothing else has been learned about the descendants of Millard and Josie Estella.

William Alsop was the father of two sons, one by his first wife and another by his second wife. The first son was Willis R. who had left home and was living in Sioux Co., Plato Twp., Iowa when the 1900 census was completed. He was reported to be an employee of John Grossenbury in whose household he was living. By 1910 Willis had moved to Fresno, Township 3, California where he was enumerated with his wife Maud M. who was listed as 28 years of age. Willis gave his age as 29, said that he was the head of his household, and reported that he had been married for two years with it being his first marriage. Maud his wife stated that she had been married two times and listed her only child as a son, Orlas W. Nays, age 11. There were no known offspring by Willis and Maud Alsop. They are again found in this same location in 1920 and 1930. Willis died in Fresno in 1943.

The second son of William and last wife Minnie B. Larkins Alsop was Alonzo "Lonnie" Oscar who was living in the family home when his father died in 1911. After this date no information has been found relating to this last son of William.

John Alsop, son of Samuel and Salina Pegg Alsop, is believed to have been the John Alsop who married on 5 Dec. 1870, in Bond Co., Illinois to Almira C. Michels as recorded in Marriage Book "B", page 61. Family records indicate that John married Kate Kleinman so the middle initial in the name of Almira Michels was probably for Catherine. After the death of her husband John Alsop, Kate must have married a man named Kleinman, but this has not yet been substantiated. This family settled in Kansas about 1878. John and Kate's three children had been born in Illinois. John was confined to a mental institution in Topeka, Kansas by 1900. A check of the Moran, Allen Co., Kansas Cemetery proves that John died in 1913 and was buried there as was his wife Kate. She died in 1934, and was buried next to her husband near the grave site of his brother William. William M. Alsop, one of the sons of John and Kate, returned to the area in Illinois where his father had previous lived and married in Bond Co., Illinois on 26 Nov. 1896, Cordelia A. Stallard. This marriage is found in Book 2, page 64. William and wife Cordie were living in Collinsville, Madison Co., Illinois at 403 Clinton St. with their two year old son Earl William according to the 1900 census. This family had moved to Douglas Co., Illinois by 1910, and was living in Defiance Co., Ohio in 1920. William and Cordelia were back in Bond Co. in Pocahontas Village, Illinois in 1930, but their son Earl was no longer living at home.

A younger brother of William and John Alsop and son of Samuel and Salina Alsop was Robert Alsop who lived his entire life in Illinois and most of it in or near New Douglas, Madison Co. The census of 1880 locates Robert, his wife Sarah E., children Leon Franklin, age 10, Arthur H., age 8, Hattie, age 4, Robert Alvin, age 2, and Tressie, age 3 months, as living in New Douglas. Also in their home was a fifteen year old girl Amanda Young who was listed as a servant. Robert Alsop owned and operated a grocery store and also ran an undertaking establishment. The building in which these businesses were located was known as the Robert Alsop **B**uilding and was later used as a telephone office and operated by Mrs. Mae Bunn Schoenmetzler for 35 years. It was torn down a few years after this.

The "Edwardsville Republican" newspaper of Wednesday, 27 Feb. 1907, reported that Arthur H. and his brother Robert Alvin had come out from St. Louis on Saturday 23 Feb. to visit with their father who was sick. Robert had died on Tuesday, 26 Feb. 1907, which was the day before this weekly newspaper came out. The next week the paper published the following notice:

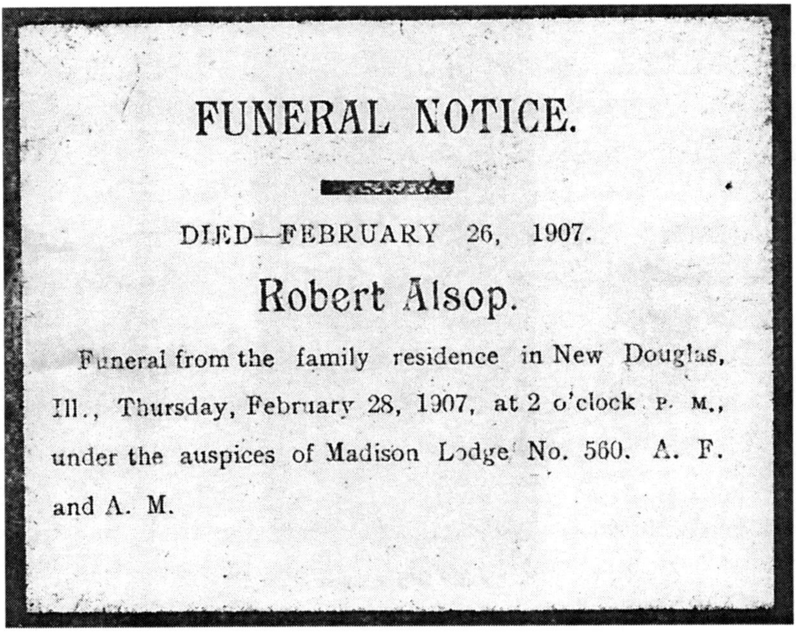

FUNERAL NOTICE.

DIED—FEBRUARY 26, 1907.

Robert Alsop.

Funeral from the family residence in New Douglas, Ill., Thursday, February 28, 1907, at 2 o'clock P. M., under the auspices of Madison Lodge No. 560. A. F. and A. M.

The same newspaper of Wednesday, 8 March 1907, informed its readers that Robert Alsop had given a warranty deed on Lot 8, Block 4, located in New Douglas to Sarah Alsop just prior to his death. Robert was buried in the New Douglas Cemetery. The cemetery reveals the tombstones of two of the children of Robert and Sarah who died as infants. They were Sarah Alsop, died 17 May 1885, age twenty days, and an unnamed baby daughter, born 24 Nov. 1882, with death date the same day.

The New Douglas Cemetery is in the north part of town and has been enlarged a couple of times. It is situated on a slightly elevated rise of ground which was donated by the city founder Alonzo Foster who laid out the city on 5 Sept. 1860.

Sarah E. Young Alsop, widow of Robert, was appointed on 13 March 1907, by the County Court of Madison Co., Illinois, Administratrix of her deceased husband's estate. She was issued letters of administration which was appropriate when no will had been left. As required by the Court, Sarah rendered a true and just account of the personal estate and debts of the said deceased. She determined that Robert had an estate valued at $ 727. 61 and debts allowed against the estate as $ 1113. 60. Since there was a deficiency of personal property to pay the debts of the deceased, Sarah was required to sell the real estate belonging to her husband at the time of his death and apply the proceeds to the existing debts. She filed the appropriate petition dated 24 August 1907, listing the real estate as follows:

Lots numbered Three (3) Six (6) and Seven (7) in Block Number Three (3); also Fifty-two and one half (52 1/2) feet off of the north part of Lot Number Five (5), Block Number Five (5), all in the Original Town of New Douglas, and also, Lots Numbered Five and Eight (5 & 8) in Block Number Twenty-nine (29) in Alonzo Foster's Addition to the town of New Douglas.

This same petition also stated that the said deceased left him surviving Sarah E. Alsop as his widow, having a dower interest in his real estate and the following named children:

Leon F. Alsop; Arthur H. Alsop; Robert Alsop Jr.; Tressie (Alsop) Foster; and Stanley Olive, a minor son of Hattie (Alsop) Olive. and deceased daughter of said intestate.

The real estate of Robert Alsop was sold on 24 August 1907, at the courthouse in Edwardsville with the highest bidder being John F. Stillwell who bid the sum of $ 600.00 for the property described in an above paragraph. The purchaser paid all cash for the real estate.

Sarah Alsop kept a diary and a portion of it was found in an old cookbook by descendants. This specific page from her diary described the wedding of her daughter Hattie and is now presented.

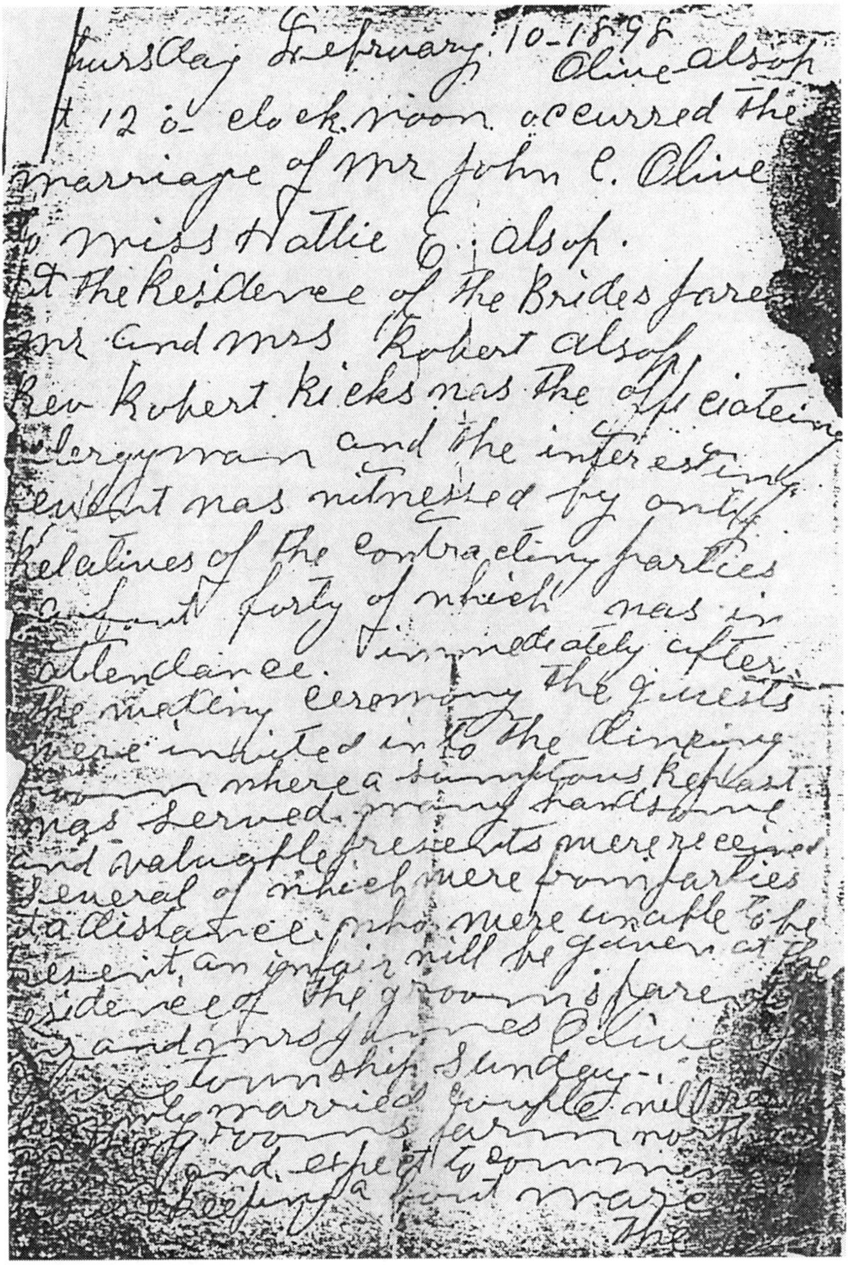

Thursday February 10-1898 Olive-Alsop
At 12 o'clock noon occurred the
marriage of Mr John C. Olive
to Miss Hattie E. Alsop.
At the Residence of the Brides parents
Mr and Mrs Robert Alsop
Rev Robert Ricks was the officiateing
clergyman and the interesting
event was witnessed by only
Relatives of the contracting parties
about forty of which was in
attendance. immediately after
the wedding ceremony the guests
were invited into the dining
room where a sumptuous Repast
was Served. many handsome
and valuable presents were received
several of which were from parties
at a distance who were unable to be
present. an infair will be given at the
residence of the grooms parents
Mr and Mrs James Olive
[illegible] township Sunday.
The young married couple will [illegible]
[illegible] grooms farm north
[illegible] and expect to commence
housekeeping a [illegible]
the

Sarah E. Young Alsop continued to live in New Douglas, and in 1910, she was the head of her household and a grandson Stanley E. Olive, age 10, was living with her. She resided alone on 5th St. in New Douglas in 1920, died on 1 October 1927, and was buried next to her husband. Fairly recent tombstones have been placed at each burial site of Robert and Sarah. The funeral was held on 3 Oct. and the records of the local funeral home have provided us with some of the details of the services. An itemized list follows:

To Transport Box-1.00
Opening Grave-8.00
Funeral Car-15.00
Personal Services-10.00
M. T. Box-8.00.
Total Cost of Funeral- 42.00

Leon Franklin "Frank" Alsop son of Robert and Sarah Alsop married Hattie A. Lane in Montgomery Co., Illinois on 14 Oct. 1890, as recorded in Book 1, page 175. Frank and his family lived their earlier years in New Douglas where he was involved in a number of activities. He was the postmaster of New Douglas and also operated and published a weekly newspaper as verified by the following receipt for advertising concerning the death and disposition of the estate of Alonzo Foster:

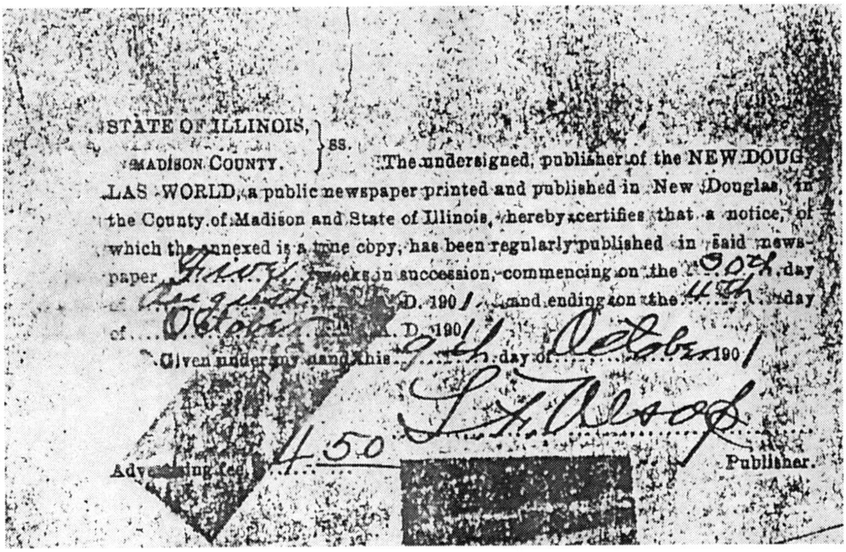

STATE OF ILLINOIS, } ss.
MADISON COUNTY. }

The undersigned, publisher of the NEW DOUGLAS WORLD, a public newspaper printed and published in New Douglas, in the County of Madison and State of Illinois, hereby certifies that a notice, of which the annexed is a true copy, has been regularly published in said newspaper [illegible] weeks in succession, commencing on the 30th day of August A. D. 1901, and ending on the 4th day of October A. D. 1901.

Given under my hand this 9th day of October 1901

L. F. Alsop, Publisher.

Advertising fee, $4.50

Frank and Hattie made their home in New Douglas in 1910, with their six children. Leon, usually called "Frank", seems to be missing during the next two census enumerations but was buried next to his wife in the New Douglas Cemetery with the dates of birth and death listed on his tombstone as 1871, and 1932. His wife Hattie had died on 23 April 1923, and was interred on 25 April. Her date of birth was inscribed on her marker as 1872. At a time near the end of her life Hattie was horribly burned, and her grandson Cullom visited her in the hospital room. The sight of her shocking condition left a lifetime impression on him. The only expense for Hattie shown in the local funeral home records was ten dollars for use of the funeral car.

After the death of his first wife, Leon "Frank" Alsop married Josephine, maiden name not yet learned, and in 1930, they were living in St. Louis in Central Twp. Frank's grandson Cullom L. Alsup remembered his grandfather as a large man with a prominent belly. He described from his boyhood remembrances the gold watch with a gold chain which draped around the protruding midsection of his ancestor. Cullom L. said that his grandfather was not a very responsible person, as he spent all of the money that his second wife had made as the owner of a hardware store in St. Louis, and also all that he had made. He died of a heart attack at the age of 61.

Leon Merlin R. Alsop, first born son of Frank and Hattie married Helen M. Colomb in St. Louis, Missouri on 21 March 1918, as found in Book 20, page 171. The 1920 census of St. Louis Co. records Leon and Helen as living at 3110 Clifton Place with his four step-daughters Norine, Leona, Erma, and Ethel. By 1930, Helen was living alone in St. Louis, and Leon was living in the same city but had remarried to a woman named Louise, age 20. Blanche A. Alsop sister of Leon Merlin was married in St. Louis on 27 Feb. 1912, to Charles Mohme with the marriage listed in Book 15, page 44. She is believed to have remarried to Earl Kaler and moved to San Antonio, Texas.

Virginia Irene Alsop youngest daughter of Frank and Hattie married Charles W. Bierdeman of Anglum, Mo. in St. Louis on 27 Aug. 1924, and they were the parents of a son Charles W., Jr., and a daughter Rosemary born in 1935. The girl was born a blue baby and had to live in an iron lung until she died at less than a year of age. Virginia became mentally ill about that time and had to be sent off to an institution in the St. Louis area. Her son Charles was about five or six years of age when his mother had to leave home, and he never saw her again. Virginia died on Tuesday, 23 Feb. 1943, and her obituary gave her age as 39 with her address as 4471 Olive Street in St. Louis. The funeral was held at the Lawrence Mullen Funeral Chapel at 5165 Delmar Blvd. on Friday, 26 Feb. with internment at 1:00 P. M. on the same day in New Douglas, Illinois. This information was provided by Charles W. Bierdeman, Jr., who is working on his family history and has uncovered many interesting facts about his grandmother.

Cullom Vivian Alsop, born 24 Dec. 1897, was another son of Leon Franklin and wife Hattie Alsop. He grew up in New Douglas, Illinois and in 1920, was serving in the U. S. Army as a wagoner where he was stationed at Ehremburutchen, Germany. While a soldier in Germany, Cullom met and married Theresea Muerer, born 23 Feb. 1897, a native of that country. He and his wife returned to the U. S. A. and in 1930, had established their residence at 23 Amhearst Place in Wellston, a suburb of St. Louis, Missouri located in St. Louis Co. near the north west edge of the city. Living in their home with them were Cullom L., age 9, Steven R., age 7, William J., age 6, John S., age 4, Virginia, age 2, and Charles, age 2. Other children born to Cullom and Theresea were Harrison and Theresea. Cullom V. had various kinds of employment during his lifetime and worked once for the post office in St. Louis driving a motorcycle with a sidecar delivering mail and packages. He was an experienced carpenter. Cullom and his wife Theresea were living in Cuba, Missouri when he died of a heart attack on 20 May 1962. Theresea died in a nursing home in St. Louis on 1 Dec. 1989. They were both buried at Jefferson Barracks National Cemetery in St. Louis.

John S. Alsop, born 3 Sept. 1925, was one of the sons of Cullom and Thresea who grew up in the St. Louis area. He married and was later divorced. His two children were Mitzi G. who married Michael Steel and moved to Columbia, Missouri and John, Jr. who was living in St. Charles, Missouri at last report. John S. dropped out of school after the eighth grade and worked as an auto mechanic most of his life and was self-employed at this occupation when death occurred. He died on 14 Dec. 1990, at the Barnes Hospital where he was an inpatient. His residence at this time was 1548 Gieseking Lane in St. Louis. Doctor Thomas Spray listed the time of death at 3:20 P. M. with the causes of death as respiratory insufficiency, pulmonary fibrosis, and adult respiratory distress syndrome. He was buried in the New Douglas Cemetery on 17 Dec. 1990, with the Lesicko Funeral Home providing the appropriate services.

Steven Robert Alsop another son of Cullom and wife Theresea married Evelyn Eugenia "Jeanne" Lechtenburg, and they lived at 522 Highway "M", Villa Ridge, Missouri for many years. Steven Robert Alsop, Sr., died 27 Sept. 2003. Jeanne Alsop, Steven's wife, obtained a copy of Alsop's Tables a few years ago to help her learn more about the history of the Alsop family. Steven and Jeanne had three sons born near Washington, Missouri: John who married Kimberly, Tom whose wife is Patricia, and Steven Robert, Jr., who died 15 Jan. 2004. I visited Tom and his family a few years ago and was given a very enthusiastic welcome. They lived in Windy Hills Estates on the edge of town and Tom was operating a home building company and also owned an auto repair shop.

Cullom L. Alsop was the oldest son of Cullom V. and Theresea and grew up in St. Louis during the depression days of the late 20's and 30's. He experienced an unhappy home environment and left at the age of sixteen to join the Navy. He made a career of the military service and retired to Maine when he was discharged. Cullom L. was married twice and had two different sets of children and also step-children. Today he lives at 49 Houlton Rd., Fort Fairfield, Maine in a very nice home with acreage. He has been very helpful in providing family information relating to his grandparents, parents, and siblings.

Other brothers and sisters of Cullom L. Alsop were Virginia who married and established her home in Florida; Theresea who first moved to Los Angeles, California and now lives in Salinas, Ca.; Charles who moved to the state of Washington and now lives in Oregon; William J., who was a diabetic and who spent four years in the navy and then lived in many places in the country including Arkansas; and Harrison D. "Harry", the baby of the family.

Even though Harry was the favorite of his mother, he was not a happy person, and as he grew up he found himself in perpetual situations of unmanageable proportions. He married and had children, but his domestic problems also proved to be pernicious in nature. Harry was born in St. Louis on 25 Jan. 1935, and died from the effect of a gunshot wound on 21 May 1961.

Arthur H. Alsop second son of Robert and Sarah Young Alsop moved from New Douglas to Granite City, Illinois where he married Jessie W. Donkin on 11 Feb. 1903, as recorded in Marriage Book 7, page 380 of the St. Louis Co., Missouri court records. He married as his second wife Miss Clara Graf (f) in St. Louis, Mo. on 23 Dec. 1909, and they were the parents of three sons.

One of the sons of Arthur and Clara, Robert Arthur Alsop wrote a letter to me dated 9 Sept. 1983, in which he related some of the family history of his immediate family. Robert was living in Princeton, Indiana at the time he wrote to me, having moved there from Granite City, Illinois after his retirement in 1977, to help his wife take care of her mother who was 97 years old in 1983. Robert worked as a head clerk in one of the

Granite City steel foundries for over thirty years. He also mentioned that he visited his first cousin Donald Alsop in Duluth, Minnesota in 1959.

During the height of the depression, Arthur and his family experienced extreme difficulties, as he was unable to obtain employment that would properly sustain his wife and three children. It was only because of the benevolence of some of his relatives the he was able to make it during the bad times. Arthur died just as this country was coming out of the depression. The Edwardsville newspaper ran the following announcement: Arthur Alsop died on Monday, January 15, 1940 in Granite City at his home. He had been in poor health for some time. His body was brought to the New Douglas Cemetery for burial on Wednesday afternoon, arriving about 2:00 P. M.

The preceding photo was taken in 1928, in Granite City, Illinois. The three boys from l. to r. are Thomas, born 1922; James, born 1918; and Robert, born 1913. They are the sons of Arthur and Clara Graff Alsop.

A younger brother of Leon Frank and Arthur H. was Robert Alvin Alsop who was born in New Douglas to Robert and Sarah Young Alsop on 30 Sept. 1877. Robert left home in the early 1900's and lived in St. Louis where he became an employee of the Bell Telephone Company. Family tradition informs us that Robert A. took a wife in this area, but no valid information has been discovered which would give us any details on this first marriage. By 1920, Robert was a roomer in the Belle Stewart boarding house located on 164th Ave., S. W., in Minot, Ward Co., N. D., and his occupation was still reported to be with the Bell Telephone Co. where he was a line superintendent.

While living in Minot, Robert met and married Mathilda Aaseng, a school teacher, whose family had come to this country from Norway. Robert and his wife were transferred to Hibbing, Minnesota by his employer and then on to Duluth, St. Louis Co., Mn. where they were living in 1930, with their two sons Robert Alvin, Jr., born 1924, and Donald Douglas, born 28 August 1927. Robert lived the remainder of his life in Duluth, Mn. working for the telephone company until his retirement. He died there on 29 October 1954.

Robert Alvin Alsop

Robert Alvin, Jr., son of Robert and Mathilda grew up in Duluth and there married June Hansen. They were the parents of Karen who married John Crandall; Susan who married Steven Asp; Marilyn who married Chris Hull; and a son Robert Alvin Alsop.

Donald Douglas Alsop, brother of Robert Alvin, Jr., and son of Robert and Mathilda also grew up in Duluth and served two years in the army, 1945-46, being discharged at the rank of P. F. C. He then entered the University of Minnesota, receiving a bachelor's degree in 1950, and earning his LL.B. in 1952. During the time he was working on his graduate degree, Donald served as Law clerk to Hon. Thomas Gallagher at the Minnesota Supreme Court. He then entered private practice in St. Paul for two years. Donald married Jean Lois Tweeten on 16 August 1952, and their children were David D. who married Mary Koll; Marcia; and Robert Alan.

Henry Conor, now deceased, was the publisher of the "Allsup Update", a family newsletter, and a portion of an article which he wrote on Donald Alsop follows:

In 1954, Donald moved to New Ulm, Minnesota, where he practiced law with the firm of Gisalon, Alsop, Dosland and Hunter. He and his wife Jean raised their three children in New Ulm during the 21 years they lived there. Twice in 1968, he was offered the position of U. S. attorney, a common step to the position of federal judge. Both offers were turned down. He and his family were satisfied with their location in New Ulm, and he enjoyed working with his law partners.

When U. S. District Court Judge Phillip Neville died in 1974, his judgeship was opened to a new appointee. Donald was now 47 years old, his children had finished high school, and it was a good time for a career change. His friends in the Republican Party were contacted, and their influence resulted in his consideration for the position. President Nixon appointed him to the U. S. District Court on 8 Aug 1974, the same day Nixon resigned. Gerald Ford was president when he was sworn in on 17 Jan. 1975, as Minnesota's 23rd federal judge.

A room adjacent to his office in St. Paul contains mementoes to his years in New Ulm, including law books, legal papers, a key to the city, with plaques and tapestries defining the history of the city and his years as an outstanding citizen. In nearly 18 years on the federal bench, Donald lent his name to several significant and high profile cases, presiding over some of the early abortion rulings and trying two Dalkon Shield cases in the 1980s. On 28 Aug 1992, he took senior status, with the option of choosing the cases he would try.

Donald Douglas Alsop lives in North Oaks, St. Paul, Minnesota where he is semi-retired. He still works on a somewhat part time basis, but maintains his status as a senior judge with his office being in the U. S. District Court at 754 Federal Courts Building located in St. Paul at 316 N. Robert St. He and his wife enjoy a winter home in Peoria, Arizona. I have enjoyed correspondence with Donald for a number of years as he is interested in his "roots" and has been very cooperative in sending historical photos of his specific lineage as well as significant information. His career achievements have been recognized by many of the members of the various lines of this family tree and are genuinely esteemed.

Donald Douglas Alsop

Robert Alvin Alsop, and sons Robert and Donald

Robert and Sarah Young Alsop had two daughters who were Harriet E. "Hattie" Alsop and Teresa Elizabeth "Tressie" Alsop. Hattie must have died not long after her son Stanley Olive was born, as he was living with his grandmother Sarah Y. Alsop in New Douglas when the 1910 census was taken. Tressie and husband Alonzo Foster had a daughter Dorothy Elizabeth who married John Driscoll and a son Merrill A. who married Virginia Lee Rogers. Dorothy and John were the parents of Judith Ann who married Richard Brown and their children were Michael Richard and Matthew John. Dorothy and John also had another daughter Jane Elizabeth whose husband was Peter Fairchild Slaughter, and they produced two children who were James Craig Slaughter and Samantha Elizabeth Slaughter. Merrill and Virginia had a daughter Sara who married John Crowder.

Thomas Henry Alsop last child of Samuel and Salina Juliann Pegg Alsop married Melvina J. Evans on 5 Nov. 1881, in Madison Co., Illinois as found in Book 1, page 73. They were the progenitors of five children who were all living at home on the Alsop farm in Madison Co. when the census was reported in May 1900. By 1910 Lulu M. was missing from the Alsop household and no additional information has yet been found on her. The other children were unmarried and still living with their parents as revealed in the 1910 census.

Ten years later Estella M., born 17 Aug. 1882, and her sister Viola P., were counted twice in the Federal census, first as living on Main St. in Glen Carbon, Illinois in Madison Co. and also as living with their parents near New Douglas. Also living with them in their parent's home was their brother William Oren who was listed as age 27 in 1920. Viola P. Alsop died in 1922, and was buried in the New Douglas Cemetery. Her father Thomas Henry died in 1926, and was buried in a site near his young daughter. The widow of Thomas H., Melvina, was living with her unmarried son William Oren Alsop at the family farm in 1930. When I visited New Douglas in 1992, I found residents who remembered William Oren, and they told me that he had been a farmer with his farm being located at Sorento which was a small community seven miles north east of New Douglas in Bond Co. near the boundary line of Montgomery Co. Estella M. "Stella" Alsop was still single in 1930 and living in the home of George W. and Florence

Ingles at Glen Carbon, Illinois. Stella Alsop died on 11 June 1959, while living at the Rupert Nursing Home in Litchfield, Illinois and was buried in New Douglas Cemetery next to her sister Viola with their names being engraved on the same stone. The services were conducted by the Burgett Funeral Home with the clergyman being Rev. Ralph Ellsworth. Charges for the funeral were: casket, vault, and services- $ 528.00; clothing-23.49; cemetery charges-25.00; minister-10.00; and certificate-1.00.

Sometime after 1930, William Oren Alsop was united in wedlock to a lady named Olive, although her maiden name has not yet been determined. He and his wife and his mother Melvina lived at Sorento until William Oren died on 9 Dec. 1951, at Jefferson Barracks Hospital. He was buried at the New Douglas Cemetery. His wife Olive M., born 1904, lived on until 1970, and was buried next to her husband.

Melvina Evans Alsop wife of Thomas H. Alsop lived in New Douglas until her death in 1956, at the advanced age of 94 years. She was buried next to her husband.

Thomas V. Alsop son of Thomas Henry and Melvina left home before 1920 and married Gertrude, born 1897, whose maiden name is unknown at this time. Thomas and his family are not found in Madison Co. in 1920 or 1930. Thomas died in 1950 and was buried in the New Douglas Cemetery. Where he and his wife spent most of their married life has not been learned. His wife died in 1970 and was buried in a site adjoining her husband.

(This family will be continued in Alsop's Tables, Volume IV)

Chapter XIII

James and John Alsop of Derbyshire

James Alsop, Sr., and wife, name unknown, had a son James Alsop, Jr., who was born in Glossop, Derbyshire, England ca. 1770. Glossop, both a village and the parish in which the village is found, is located in the north west corner of Derbyshire just inside the border. It is on the main A57 road between Manchester and Sheffield. The ancient parish of Glossop was one of the largest in the county as it covered a lot of the rural areas.

The marriage of James Alsop, Jr., and Sarah Bowden occurred on 4 August 1799, at Glossop in Derbyshire. The children of James and Sarah, all born in Glossop, were Hannah, born 19 Nov. 1803; John, born 18 July 1805; James, born 30 September 1807; Ann, born 6 March 1810; Alvin, born 17 September 1811; Millicent, baptized 12 Sept. 1814; Nancy, born 1818; and Sarah, baptized 19 April 1820. A George Alsop, born 1799, in Glossop and baptized 1 Jan. 1800, was a son of James and Sarah according to some records, but alternate records claim that the mother was Martha Platt.

Alvin Alsop son of James and Sarah Bowden Alsop married on 13 January 1836, in Glossop, Derbyshire, Jane Sandham, born 1807, at New Mills. They were the parents of Sarah Hannah Alsop, born 1836; Harriet Alsop, born 1838; John Alsop, born 1840; and George B. Alsop, born 1846. The English census of 1841 reports Alvin as living in Glossop and working as a cotton weaver. In 1851 he was living on Chapel St. in Howard

Town with his wife Jane and their children, except John who had died as an infant. Alvin and Jane and family were also listed in the next two census reports for Glossop living at 27 George Street. Alvin died in June 1771, in Glossop at the age of 59. His wife Jane died after the census of 1881, in which she was reported as a widow with daughter Sarah Hannah Greenwood still living at home along with two grandchildren George B. and James. Sarah, Harriet, and George B. were all cotton weavers.

Alvin's sister Millicent Alsop had a daughter Ann Morehouse Alsop, born 9 Feb. 1840, and Millicent and her child both died in June 1840. The youngest sister of Alvin was Sarah who was the mother of three children: Samuel Alsop; Ann Alsop, born 26 August 1834, in Glossop; and Hannah Alsop.

John Alsop a son of James and Sarah Bowden Alsop married Mary Fielding who was born in Glossop on 25 April 1808, the daughter of Samuel Fielding and wife Mary Heggenbottom (Higginbottom). The census of 1831 lists John, Mary, and family as living in Hadfield. The 1841 enumeration reported that John was working as a cotton spinner, and his eleven year old son Levi was employed as a cotton piecer. Several years later this couple moved to the U. S. A. where many of their descendants through their son Levi still reside.

As listed above, John had a brother named James Alsop who married as his first wife on 3 September 1834, in Glossop, Derbyshire, Hannah Hadfield, born 21 March 1805, daughter of John Hadfield and Martha Robinson. James and Hannah Hadfield Alsop produced children as follows: Ann Grant Bowden Alsop, b. ca. 1835; John Hadfield Alsop, baptized 15 March 1836; Zipporah Alsop, b. 1838; Sarah Alsop, b. 1842; and Charles James Alsop, baptized 21 April 1845-died September1845 in Glossop. James was employed in Glossop during 1841 and 1842 as a joiner. The census of 1841 places him in Glossop with his wife and two children John and Zipporah, as daughter Ann was already dead. Hannah Hadfield Alsop worked as a school mistress. James left his family in England and went to DeWitt Co., Illinois in the United States. When his wife Hannah died in England is not known for certain, but dates vary from 1846 before James left all the way up to 1855. At any rate, James married two more times in DeWitt County and had four children by his third wife.

John Hadfield Alsop son of James and Hannah Hadfield Alsop married Millicent Garlick daughter of Joseph Garlick and Martha Moss on 6 April 1856, in Glossop. Millicent was born in Glossop in 1836, and became the mother of eight children, all of them born in Glossop except the last one. The children were: George J., born 1857; Mary E., born 1859; Joe Garlick, born 1862; John Edwin, born 1865; Arthur William, born 1867; Ada Fanny, born 1869; Cecil H., born 1874; and Percy H., born in 1875, after the family had moved to Hindley, Lancs., England. In 1851, John H. Alsop was working as a coal porter. John was dead when the census of 1881 was tabulated.

Sarah Alsop daughter of James and Hannah H. Alsop married in 1866, Kenneth McLennan, Jr., b. 1827, in London, Middlesex, England, son of Kenneth McLennan and Jane Mann. She left Southampton, England on 11 June 1863, as an assisted passenger on the ship "Robert Small" and arrived in Melbourne, Australia on 16 September 1863, to work as a nurse maid for a well-known doctor, Lt. Harrington of Warrnambool, Australia. She received a weekly wage of 20 shillings. Sarah was the only member of her family to immigrate to Australia, and she could also read and write which was unusual for most women of her time. She and her husband Kenneth had children as follows: Sarah, born 1866; Hannah, born 1867; William, born 1869; Zipporah, born 1870; Charles James, born 1872; Kenneth, born 1875; Ernest, born 1876; K. Penfold, born 1878; and George Augustus, born 1881.

A letter was received by Sarah Alsop McLennan from her father James Alsop mailed from Illinois dated 16 May 1864, to her home in Warrnambool, Australia. He stated in his letter that he was in Chicago, Illinois "to patent the world's first propeller of power". In this letter he referred to Julius James Alsop, John Hadfield Alsop, and Ann Grant Bowden Alsop. His Australian family never heard from him again after the great Chicago fire which occurred on the 8th and 9th of October, 1871.

Sarah Alsop McLennan's husband Kenneth, Jr., died in Warrnambool, Victoria, Australia in 1901, and was buried in the Warrnambool Cemetery. Sarah died 7 May 1909, and was buried in the plot adjacent to that of her husband.

Sarah Alsop McLennan

Kenneth McLennan-
Husband of Sarah

Zipporah McLennan Jones

Ernest, Margaret, Ivy, and Marjorie

Zipporah McLennan daughter of Sarah and Kenneth married 28 May 1898, in Durban, South Africa, James Stretton Jones, b. 29 April 1871, son of Evan Jones and Elizabeth Stretton. They had become engaged in Warrnambool, and he went to Durban where he was able to find employment as a foreman builder. The wedding took place at the Wesleyan Methodist Church in Durban. James Jones and wife Zipporah were the parents of Ernest, Margaret, Ivy, and Marjorie. After their marriage in Durban, this family lived in Germiston for a while, but then returned to Durban where Zipporah died on 3 Dec. 1920, of the flu. She was buried the following day in West Street Cemetery, Durban. Her husband died 24 Feb. 1942, and was buried in the same cemetery next to Zipporah.

Ivy Myrtle Jones was a daughter of Zipporah and James Jones. She was born 26 Dec. 1906, at Germiston, South Africa, and married in 1932, in Durban, Victor Theodore Larsen, and they had one child David Victor Larsen, born 15 September 1933. Ivy died 2 Jan. 1987, in Durban, South Africa, and was buried in Stellawood Cemetery.

David Larsen married (l) in 1958, Angela Joan Hoch. He married (2) on 26 September 1964, in Pretoria, South Africa, Ursula Hedwig Nolting. David had children by his second marriage as follows: James, Gernot, Mark, and Verena. Mark and Debbie Larsen are the parents of Amy and Dean Mark. David Larsen has become an active family history researcher and has contributed generously with photos and information on his specific branch of the family tree.

The children of John Hadfield Alsop son of James and Hannah Hadfield Alsop continued to live in the Derbyshire area of England, and the oldest son George J. worked as a carder in a cotton mill. His sister Mary E. was working as a domestic servant in 1881. Joe Garlick Alsop brother of George was employed as a colliery (coal mine machinery) mechanic, while two other brothers John Edwin and Arthur William were professional bookkeepers.

James Alsop, father of John Hadfield Alsop joined his brother John Alsop in the U. S. A. and married Mary Ann Malson after the death of Hannah, his first wife. He then married as his third wife Mrs. Eliza M. Stallman who had two children, Harry and Alice, at the time of their marriage. Harry and Alice were children of the previous marriage of Eliza M. Keller, born April 1827, in Pennsylvania, to Henry Stallman on 19 June 1850, in Allegany Co., Maryland. Henry Stallman had moved to Illinois where he died ca. 1857.

In the late 1860's James moved his family to Chicago where he had business interests. The census of 1870 lists James and his family as living in South Chicago with the family consisting of his wife Eliza and step-children Harry and Alice Stallman, and children Julius Alsop, Anna Alsop, Sherman Alsop, and Hattie Alsop. James died in Chicago in the early part of 1880, as he was missing from his household when the census was taken in the middle of the year. James' tombstone can be found in the Oak Wood Cemetery in the family burial site, but only the years of his birth and death are given. Eliza Alsop was listed as a widow and the head of her household in the 1880 enumeration with her occupation given as keeping boarders. Eliza died in Chicago on 7 April 1908, age 81, and was buried in the family plot. There are a number of the members of James immediate family buried in the same area. Anna Grant Bowden Alsop, one of the daughters of James and Eliza Stallman Alsop, married on 22 Jan. 1890, in Chicago, Cook Co., Illinois, Elmer Ellsworth Tansey. Her sister Harriet "Hattie" S. Alsop, b. Feb. 1869, married 14 Feb. 1907, in Lake County, Indiana, Eugene S. Campbell.

Sherman Ulysses S. Grant Alsop son of James and Eliza Stallman Alsop was, according to family records, born 16 April 1868. He married in Chicago on 29 Nov. 1893, Mary "Mae" Elizabeth Clark, born March 1871, in Illinois, and then moved to Michigan in connection with his occupation as a locomotive engineer for the Santa Fe Railroad. Their only child, a son Philip Clark, was born 9 November 1902, in New Mexico. By 1910, Mary, who liked to travel and had free railroad transportation, and her son Clark were living in Los Angeles, California, but Sherman was rooming in the home of Edward and Emely Jones at Raton, New Mexico as necessitated by his employment. However, in 1920, Sherman, wife Mary and son Clark were all reported in the Federal census as residing at 314 Pine St., Los Animas County, Trinidad, Colorado. This location was only a few miles north of Raton. When the 1930 census was enumerated,

Sherman and his wife and only son were back living in Raton, Colfax Co., New Mexico. Clark was listed as age 26, and still single.

Sherman U. Alsop spent his working life operating a steam locomotive which consisted of thirty-four years with the Santa Fe Railroad. He was active in the Masons most of his life. His obituary in the "Topeka Daily Capital Newspaper" indicated that he retired on a pension and was a patient at the Santa Fe Hospital in Topeka when he died on Monday, 13 April 1936, at the age of 68. Sherman's body was taken to Chicago for burial in the family plot at Oak Wood Cemetery located at 1065 E. 67th Street. This historic old cemetery is located near the Chicago suburb of Calumet City. Mary, wife of Sherman, was the daughter of a mother and a father who were both born in the Irish Free State. She died in 1953, and was buried in Denver, Colorado.

Philip Clark Alsop son of Sherman and Eliza Alsop was living with his parents when the 1930 census for Colfax Co., New Mexico was completed, and he gave his occupation as a stenographer for the U. S. Freight Co. Clark became interested in the field of foreign service, and pursued and earned a degree at Georgetown University in Washington, D. C. which prepared him for this type of profession. However, he married Claudia Marie Ford in 1935, and ended up living in Denver, Colorado where he worked the rest of his life for the Colorado State Department as an unemployment compensation specialist. He and Claudia were the parents of Sherman Ford, b. 9 Nov. 1939; Daniel Philip, b. 22 May 1941; John and James (twins), b. 9 September 1948; and Beverly Ann, b. 26 December 1949. In 1986, Clark Alsop was residing in Arvada, Colorado which is in the north west edge of Denver. He died 20 January 1987, and was buried on the 26th at Ft. Logan National Cemetery in Denver.

John Alsop lived in DeWitt Co., Illinois near Clinton after arriving in the U. S. from Glossop, Derbyshire, England. Following the death of his first wife Mary, John Alsop married on 6 October 1861, Mrs. Hannah Wilkinson as recorded in Book "B", page 290, DeWitt Co., Illinois.

John's only son Levi Alsop left DeWitt Co., Illinois with his wife Mary Barber (marriage license gives her maiden name as Barger) and six children born in Illinois and relocated to Bourbon Co., Kansas. Only a year or two after the Alsop family settled in Kansas, the Civil War began. Levi enlisted in the Third Regiment, Kansas Volunteers, Company "K", Cavalry, at Fort Lincoln on 1 September 1861, and was transferred the following year to Company "I", Sixth Regiment. He served honorably and bravely for the duration of his enlistment.

Levi Alsop-Union Army-
Kansas Cavalry

Mary M. Alsop-Levi's Wife

Family records indicate that Mary was born in Spotsylvania Co., Virginia 25 May 1830, the daughter of Pleasant Barber, who was also born in Spotsylvania Co., and his wife Sarah Markey, who was born in Germany. Mary continued to live in Bronson Co. after the death of her husband and life appeared to be rather prosperous. Records reveal that in her final years, she was able to help her children financially by managing her affairs in a businesslike manner. In the 1900 Federal census, Mary related to the enumerator that she had had nineteen children and that eleven of them were still living. She left a will dated 1 July 1902, in which she left an equal share of her estate to her nine living children and one share to May, daughter of her deceased son Andrew J. Alsop.

Mary M. Alsop died 26 July 1902, and was buried in the family burial site along side of her husband. The following photo shows Mary standing outside of the front door of her farm home on the porch with her sons, daughters, sons-in-law, daughters-in-law, and grandchildren. It is believed that Virgil Alsop is the boy on the front row, left end.

Pleasant Alsop the eldest son of Levi and Mary Alsop moved to California in his later life, although his reason for the relocation and his connection to this area is as yet unknown. He was living in Alameda County, California when his death occurred. He had also lived in Butte Co., California where probate records were filed.

The next son born to Levi and Mary Alsop was Samuel Fielding Alsop who was the father of four children who reached adulthood and the following children who died as infants: Oliver Alsop, died 21 June 1880, age 10 months, 9 days; Viola J. Alsop, died 13 June 1883, age 5 months, 8 days; and Edmond R. Alsop, died 20 June 1883, age 1 year, 9 months. These three infants are buried in the Walnut Hill Cemetery near Bronson.

Samuel and wife Mary lived on the farm that she had inherited from her parents. The agricultural census of Bourbon Co., Kansas for the farm year ending 1March 1885, reported that Samuel had rented 680 acres in addition to his own farm and had a cash value of $ 9,000 for his total investment. His farm machinery was valued at $ 200 and total wages paid for the year was $400.

Samuel F. Alsop, wife Mary, and daughter Marie
at their residence in Bourbon Co., Kansas

The death of Samuel Alsop is described in the following obituary which was in the local Ft. Scott, Kansas newspaper.

Mr. Samuel Alsop said or did nothing on the day before his death to indicate to his family that he was contemplating taking his own life. He went to bed at the normal time and fell asleep quickly. He slept as well as usual last night and when he arose this morning at the usual hour seemed to be in a perfectly normal condition. Neither his son, daughter nor wife, during the time that he was in the yard near the house, and in the house prior to the time he went into his room to commit the rash act, noticed anything in his actions at all tending to arouse suspicion that he was contemplating the rash act.

It was just before 8 o'clock that Mr. Alsop returned to his room. As he entered the room and stretched himself on the bed, Virgil, his young son, was standing near the door. "Son," he said, "close that door: I believe I can sleep a little." The lad obeyed.

It was not more than five minutes later that Virgil returned to the room to find that his father had shot himself. Just why the lad returned to the room is not known, for none of the family had heard the report of the small .22 rifle.

Dr. Lambeth of Bronson was at once called and arrived within a short time. He found that although Mr. Alsop was not dead the wound was a fatal one. He said that death within a few hours was imminent.

Mr. Alsop was found by his son lying flat on his back on the bed, with a bullet hole almost exactly in the center of his forehead. A small .22 caliber single shot Stevens rifle, resting between his limbs, with the muzzle pointing toward the wounded man's face, yielded incontrovertible evidence of attempted suicide. It appeared that Mr. Alsop after cocking the rifle, had placed the butt of the weapon between his knees, and holding the stock with his right hand, had pressed the muzzle against his forehead, and pressed the trigger with his left hand. The bullet penetrated the skull and entered the brain.

It was about twelve years ago that Mr. Alsop suffered an attack of the grippe, which developed into pneumonia. For many weeks he was dangerously ill, and although at length he was able to leave his bed, and to resume his work to some extent the illness had greatly injured him physically and his health since that time has been very poor. Mrs. Alsop, always a frail woman, became ill about two years ago, and although she has been able to attend to her housework, her health ever since has been very poor. About nine months ago her condition became much aggravated, and since that time she has been in extremely poor health.

And to add to all of these troubles, it is said that Mr. Alsop's crop like many of those in the neighborhood of Bronson, has been practically destroyed by the drouth.

Mr. Alsop has a wife, one daughter, Marie and two sons, Virgil and Floyd. Marie and Virgil are unmarried, and make their home with their parents. Floyd is married and makes his home at Uniontown. William H. Alsop, the grocer of this city, is also a brother of Samuel Alsop, and he immediately went to Bronson, upon hearing of the tragedy. Mr. Alsop also has a sister, Mrs. Mary Jennings, who lives at Bronson. Mrs. Alsop is a niece of both Mrs. Charles Love, and A. N. Allen of this city. (end of obit)

The funeral services for Samuel F. Alsop, who died 18 August 1916, were held on Saturday afternoon at 2:00 at the family home. Rev. Hooten pastor of the Baptist Church of Xenia and M. D. Morris of Xenia conducted the rites with interment in the Bronson Cemetery.

Mary Miller Alsop widow of Samuel lived on the same farm in the Dry Ridge community seven miles north east of Bronson, Bourbon Co., Kansas from the age of three until her death of valvular heart disease on Monday, 7 July 1924, at the age of 65. She came from Lindly, Grundy Co., Mo. with her parents at the age of three. Mary died at 8:00 P. M. at the home of her daughter Marie Defebaugh of 723 Short St., in Fort Scott. The attending physician was L. W. Griffin. She was a faithful member of the Methodist Episcopal Church and also a member of the Royal Neighbors. Funeral services were held at the Methodist Episcopal Church in Bronson at 11:00 A. M. on Wednesday, 9 July 1924. The sermon was preached by Dr. B. F. Gaither of the Methodist church of Ft. Scott who read consoling scriptures and eulogized her Christian life. He recognized Mary's devotion to her family, home, and neighbors with a text from Hebrews 9. Burial in the Bronson Cemetery took place next with her remains being placed in the family lot beside her husband.

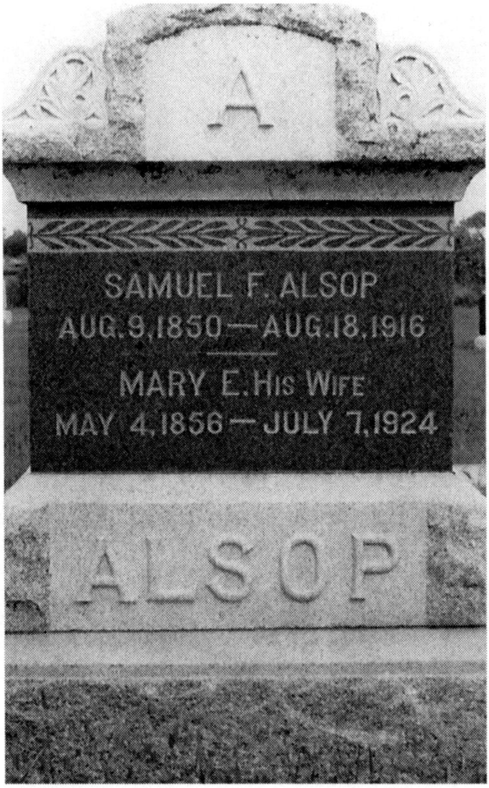

One of the four children of Samuel and Mary Alsop to grow to adulthood was Leo Dane "Dana" who was born October 1884, and died in Bourbon Co. on 16 Dec. 1911. Very little has been learned about his life.

Virgil Faye Alsop brother of Dana and son of Samuel and Mary Alsop was born on the family farm at Dry Creek on 15 April 1891. Virgil was about 24 years old at the time of his father's death. He inherited the family home and about half of the farm land. Fern Alsop Pickerill who lives in Clearwater, Kansas is the daughter of Floyd Allen Alsop, and she told me that when her grandfather died Virgil and Floyd and their sister Marie agreed that Virgil would have the house and some of the farm land, while Floyd would get the 80 acres across the road from the Alsop house. Marie got all of the cash money that Samuel had left as she was not interested in land.

Virgil Faye Alsop

Virgil Alsop, Opal Burt Alsop,
Harold Dean Alsop

Virgil Alsop, born at Dry Ridge near Bronson, married Opal Belle Burt, born 29 July 1898, of Uniontown, Kansas on 20 August 1916, at Fort Scott with the ceremony being conducted by W. W. Padgett, Probate Judge. Virgil took his bride to the family home at Dry Ridge which he had inherited the previous year, and he and Opal lived the first years of their marriage in this old two story house with a newer section being added. This more recent addition was built lower than the original part. The old house was torn down a number of years ago. Virgil and Opal had only one child, Harold Dean, who was born 31 July 1917, in the old Samuel Alsop home place.

Harold Dean Alsop-about 9 years of age

Virgil died 3l March 1962, and was buried in the Bronson Cemetery. His wife Opal, just a few months before her death on 4 Jan.1983, told her grandson Ron Alsop that one of their Alsop relatives had made a ring while serving a sentence in Wyoming Territorial Prison located in Laramie, Wyoming. She had somehow come into possession of the ring and gave it to Ron because of his interest in the family history. This Alsop will be discussed later in this chapter. Opal Burt Alsop was also buried in the Bronson Cem.

Harold Dean Alsop

The following obituary recounts the life of Harold Dean Alsop in impressive detail:

Harold Dean Alsop, 79, Fort Scott, Kansas, died Wednesday, June 18, 1997, at Fort Scott Merry Hospital.

He was born July 31, 1917, in Bronson. Kansas, the son of Virgil and Opal Burt Alsop.

He married Polly Gordon February 8, 1941, in Gerard, Kansas. She survives of the home.

He was a veteran of the U. S. Army, serving during World War II, where he received the American Theater Campaign Ribbon, the European Campaign Ribbon with one Bronze Star, the Good Conduct Medal, the Victory Ribbon and one Overseas Service Bar.

He worked for 30 years for Herrman Lumber Company, serving as manager for many of those years. He later worked for Leek's Clothing and most recently was employed by the Konantz-Cheney Funeral Home for more than 10 years.

He was a member of the First United Methodist Church, the Olson-Fray-Burkhart Post 1165 Veterans of Foreign Wars, a 50-year member of the Rising Sun Lodge #8 AF & AM, a member of the Scottish Rite and Mirza Shrine.

Survivors include his wife, Polly, of the home; two sons, Gordon Dean Alsop, Overland Park, Kansas, and Ronald Dale Alsop, Clinton; one daughter, Paula Sue Black, Stanley, Kansas, and five grandchildren, Kimberly Alsop, Michael Alsop, Spencer Alsop, Morgan Alsop and Hayley Black.

Rev. Jan Hayen conducted funeral services Friday, June 20, 1:3O p.m. at the Konantz-Cheney Funeral Home. Burial was in the U.S. National Cemetery. Masonic services were conducted at the cemetery by the Rising Sun Lodge. Military rites were conducted at the cemetery by the Olson-Fray-Burkhart Post 1165 Veterans of Foreign Wars. Memorials may be made to the First United Methodist Church or the Shrine Crippled Children's Transportation Fund, and left in care of the funeral home, 15 W. Wall, Fort Scott, Kansas. (end of obit)

Floyd Allen Alsop, brother of Virgil Alsop, was born 19 March 1893, at Dry Creek near Bronson at the Samuel and Mary Alsop home place. He married Minnie F. Nutter, born 6 May 1895, and built a house across the road from the home of his widowed mother on land that he had inherited from his father. Fern Alsop grew up in this house and has filled in many details on her father and his brother and sister. She said that the family was very musical as Floyd sang bass, Virgil tenor, and Marie alto.

Floyd Allen Alsop and wife Minnie Nutter Alsop

Floyd and Minnie were the parents of four children as follows: Robert, died 4 Feb. 1914; Russell E., born ca. 1915; Fern E., born ca. 1919; and Eugene, born ca. 1922. Floyd spent his life farming in the Bronson area and died February 1987. His wife Minnie died 8 June 1974, and is buried with her husband in the Bronson Cemetery. Russell died about 1998; Gene is living in Renton, Washington; and Fern married J. F. Pickerill and lives in Clearwater, Kansas.

Cora Marie Alsop, the last child born to Samuel and Mary Miller Alsop, came into this world in March 1896, and lived at home with her parents until her father's death in 1916, and then with her widowed mother and brother who inherited the family farm. On 18 May 1924, she married in Fort Scott, Walter E. Defebaugh, age 27, who was a resident of Fort Scott with the wedding service conducted by Rev. B. F. Gaither, a Methodist minister. Walter and Marie had sons George and Walter. Marie and her husband lived in Ft. Scott and Marie died sometime before 1999.

Andrew Jackson Alsop was born to Levi and Mary Alsop and died in Bourbon Co., Kansas at the age of 34. He was buried in the Bronson

Cemetery in Section "B", Row 6, and his tombstone is unique enough that it is shown below:

Andrew J. Alsop's widow Emma Augusta, born in Illinois in April 1852, was the mother of his only child Edna May Alsop, born in May 1885. Augusta was appointed the guardian of her child after the death of her husband. Andrew Alsop owned a house and lot in Bronson, and 80 acres of land located S1/2 NE 1/4 Section 13, Twp. 24, Range 22, which were sold on 17 Dec. 1894, to H. C. Hinen. Augusta remarried in 1888, and moved with her second husband and daughter to 2520 Dirr Ave. in Parsons, Kansas. The census of 1900 for Labette County, Parsons, Kansas reports the household of Theodore H. Learned located on Briggs Ave. Living with him was his wife Emma Augusta and step-daughter Edna May Alsop who was a school student.

Another son of Levi and Mary Barber Alsop was John E. Alsop who was one of the administrators of his mother's will. John worked all of his life as a farmer and lived back and forth between Blue Mound in Linn Co. and Bourbon Co. The 1885 census of Bourbon Co. reports them as living in Franklin Twp. and in their household were John, 31, Rhoda J., 21, and R. E. Withers, 9. Rhoda J. Withers was the wife of John but was incorrectly named Rhonda in the second volume of "Alsop's Tables". On 3 March 1892, John bought 1/2 of E. 4/5 of Lot 6, Block 10 in Blue Mound. In 1900, John, Rhoda, and their first son George E. were living in Blue Mound, Lynn Co., Kansas which became their permanent home. George had been born in February 1888.

The census of 1910 for Linn Co. reports the Alsops as still living in Blue Mound with the family consisting of John, Rhoda, George, and a new son John Russell L. Alsop, born in 1905. While living in Blue Mound, John purchased several other pieces of real estate. He died at Blue Mound on 21 August 1914, and was buried in Section "D", Row 4, Bronson Cemetery. Rhoda J. Withers Alsop petitioned the court of Linn Co., Kansas on 12 Jan. 1920, concerning her second son Russell who was still a minor. She was living on Walnut St. in Blue Mound during the summer of 1920, with her son Russell. In 1930, Rhoda and Russell were still living in Blue Mound as Russell was single and had not yet left home. Rhoda died on 18 June 1933, and both of her sons were living in Kalispell, Montana by this time. George E. Alsop, first son of John E. and Rhoda married Annie G. (maiden name unknown) who was born in 1884, in Minnesota then married as his second wife Evelyn N. (maiden name not known) born ca. 1898, in North Dakota. He was a resident of Havre, Montana when the 1930 census was taken. George was living there with his wife Evelyn. By 1933, he had moved to Kalispell where his younger brother Russell was living with him.

Horace Lilbern Jennings son of Hiriam and May Jennings and wife Mary Hannah Alsop daughter of Levi and Mary Barber Alsop lived in Franklin Township in Bourbon Co. after their marriage. Horace had been born in Illinois in Nov. 1860, and moved with his parents to Bourbon Co., Kansas after 1870. Horace and Mary were the parents of Roy, Isaac, Loren, William, and Edith. At the time of his death in 1907, Horace owned 160 acres located in S 17, T 24, R 22. The Bruce Marble Co. took one bay mare valued at $ 50 as partial payment for his head stone with the balance being $ 15. Mary also paid $ 90. to her brother John E. Alsop for room and board that Horace received while ill. Horace was buried in Section "D", Row "1", of Bronson Cemetery.

Mary Hannah died 12 December 1934, while living with her daughter Edith Magdelene Jennings Porter at 624 South Crawford St. in Fort Scott, and was buried with her husband Horace Lilbern Jennings. Her obituary gives her age as 79 years, 1 month, and 15 days.

Mary Hannah Alsop Jennings

Horace Lilbern Jennings

Edith Jennings daughter of Horace and Mary Hannah Alsop was born 15 Aug. 1896, near Bronson and married Ralph Porter on 17 May 1919, and when she died in Oshkosh, Wis. at the age of 96, she left two surviving sons Dr. Harold Porter, and Neal Porter. I have corresponded with Neal, and he has researched his family lines which produced the photo of Levi Alsop and also the pictures of Mary Hannah and husband Horace. He sent the photos to Ron Alsop of Clinton, Mo. and Ron generously gave me copies.

Sarah Jane Alsop was another daughter of Levi and Mary Alsop who moved with her parents from Illinois to Kansas as an infant. She grew up on the family farm and wed on 1 July 1877, Ambrose Green Dye as recorded in Marriage Book "C", page 37. She was married in her home by G. W. Timmons, Baptist Minister. The state census of 1885 lists Sarah, age 24, and husband Ambrose, age 36, as living in Zennia, Franklin Twp., Bourbon Co., with their children Selvanis, 6, Teiddia G., 5, Samuel F., 3, M.M., 8 months, female. Ambrose had come from Missouri to Kansas and lived the remainder of his life in either Bourbon or Linn Counties. He died of chronic myocarditis on 9 Sept. 1925, while living at 401 Scott St. and was buried in Pleasant View Cemetery in Blue Mound, Kansas. Sarah Jane died in 1923, and was buried in Lot 57 next to where her husband would later be buried.

Rose Anna Alsop Owens and husband Francis Marion Owens lived on a farm after their marriage performed by G. J. Abbey, justice of the peace in Bourbon Co., where Francis was renting 72 acres valued at $ 1500. In 1885, they were living near Zennia not far from her sister Sarah Jane Dye and her husband. They had a daughter Alma at the time who was one year old. Francis was the son of John and Julia A. Owens who had both been born in Indiana. After her divorce, Rose Anna lived near her family and was buried in the Bronson Cemetery in Section "B", Row 6, near her parents.

The first son to be born to Levi and Mary after their arrival in Kansas was Levi Henry who was born in December 1863, and lived at home until he became irreversibly infected with gold fever. All of the stories that he had heard about the gold rush while growing up in Bourbon Co.

became more than Henry could manage, so in his late teens he left for gold country.

He first lived near Weiser, Washington Co., Idaho where he became a prospector. Later he tried his luck in California and by 1900, he was living back in Idaho where he boarded in the Stephen Holman household. This was in Idaho Co., Warren Precinct, near the Snake River.

How much gold Henry found during his lifetime is not known, but by 1910, he was living in Bronson, Bourbon County, Kansas with his sister Mary Jennings and her family.

Henry had returned to the area of his birth after the early death of Horace Jennings, husband of his sister Mary Hannah, and helped to look after her family. In his later years Henry practiced the trade of a barber in Bourbon Co. While in California, Henry had become involved in some kind of business and when he died his brother's son Floyd Alsop got a one hundred dollar check as his part of his Uncle Henry's estate. It is unknown if Henry died in California or Kansas. His date of death was 1932, and he was buried in the Bronson Cemetery in Section "D", Row l, which was the family plot of his sister Mary Jennings.

Charles Alsop, brother of Levi Henry, usually called "Charley", grew up at the home place in Bourbon County and after leaving home, secured a farm in Uniontown about five miles southeast of Bronson. Charley, at the age of 30, married Addie L. Ward on 5 May 1896. Addie was 19 and had lived on a neighboring farm until her marital union to Charley. The ceremony was conducted by Rev. G. W. Trout.

By 1900, Charles and Addie were the parents of Rissie, born April 1897, and Mildred, born May 1899. Three other children born to them were Darwin, Flave, and Charles, Jr. Charles, Sr., farmed after he first married, but then gave up this occupation and became a barber in Bourbon County.

The 1900 census for Bourbon Co. lists Charles as living in Marion Twp. with his wife and two oldest children. After his last three children were born in Marion Twp., Charles life came to an early and unexpected end on 17 Feb. 1908. He was buried in the Bronson Cemetery in Section "D', Row "3" near his brother Henry and sister Mary Hannah.

When the 1910 census for Bourbon Co., Kansas was completed, Addie and her five children were still living in Bourbon Co. On 11 Feb. 1911, the estate of Charles Alsop was appraised with the Probate Court appointing Charlie Konantz, Sherman Ramsay, and Dr. Helman to perform this service. At some time before 19 May 1915, Addie moved with her five children to Colorado, as on that date the Probate Court of Bourbon Co., Kansas located in Fort Scott wrote a letter to Mrs. Addie Alsop of Maybell, Moffat Co., Colorado, informing her that her account as guardian of "Rissie" Alsop was due.

Tombstone of Charles L. Alsop in the Bronson
Cemetery near Bronson, Kansas

By 1920, Addie Alsop had married a man named Joseph Minks, and they were living in Rawlings, Carbon Co., Wyoming, with four of her children: Narcissa, 22, Darwin, 19, Flave, 16, and Charles, 14. Darwin was counted twice in this census, as he was also reported as living in the household of Jessie C. Gasney of 226 6th St. in Rawlings.

Darwin W. Alsop, born 8 April 1901, Flave Alsop, born 22 September 1903, and Charles Alsop, Jr., born 22 Dec. 1906, continued to live in the Rawlings, Wyoming area, although their mother Addie Ward Alsop Minks moved to Denver, Colorado where she operated a boarding house. Following are two photos of Addie made in the 1930's during her residence in Denver, Colorado.

Flave Alsop got a job in 1924 working for the Rio Blanco Coal Mining Co., located at Nine Mile Hill in Rio Blanco Co., Colorado which was about one hundred and fifty miles south west of his home in Rawlings, Wyoming. While working there, Flave met a seventeen year old girl Maryann "Mamie" Allen who on 11 November 1925 became the mother of his child. She was named Beatrice Ruth Alsop on the Colorado birth certificate, although Flave and Mamie were never married. Flave returned home to Rawlings and Mamie married another man who provided the name that Ruth grew up with. Ruth's mother and her Allen grandparents would never tell her who her biological father was, although she asked many times.

In 1930, Flave "Pud" Alsop was still single and boarding in the home of Fred and Jessie Hansen located in Albany Co., Wyoming. Darwin, brother of Flave was still living in Rawlings where he was married and was living with his wife Josephine. Of the two girls and three boys that Charles and Addie Alsop had, only Flave and Darwin produced offspring and that consisted of one daughter each. However, this family got together many times in later years for family reunions.

Charles "Chad", Addie, Flave "Pud", Mildred "Mid", Narcissa "Rissie", and Darwin W. Alsop-1940's

"Rissie", "Pud", Grandma, "Mid", Darwin, and "Chad"- 1950's

Flave's cabin that he built in the Snowy Mountain range, Wyoming for hunting.

Barbara Alsop Larson, Darwin's daughter, and
Ruth Alsop Stokvis, Flave's daughter.

Flave Alsop married Mary, maiden name not known, and worked as a jeweler. He was very skilled in the art of crafting rings, necklaces, etc. He died in Wyoming in December 1984. His brother Darwin also lived in Wyoming until his death in June 1985. Charles Alsop, Jr., known by the family as "Chad" died on 23 February 1992 in Rawlings.

Benjamin Franklin Alsop was born in Bourbon Co., Kansas to Levi and Mary Alsop after they had removed from Dewitt Co., Illinois. Known by his family as "Frank", he grew up working on the family farm. After discovering that he had Bright's Disease (kidney problems), Frank traveled through the South and West hoping to gain relief from the problem. In 1900, he was living in Flagstaff, Coconino Co., Arizona as a lodger in the household of George Haxworth. He had moved to Kingman, Arizona in Mohave Co. by the next census where he was boarding and working as a barber.

He soon returned home to Ft. Scott, Kansas in Bourbon Co. as the western environment gave him very little relief from the disease. Back home, he entered the hospital, but would have times in which his health would be much improved, and he was able to go down town and visit with his friends. During his good health, Frank followed the barber trade and was a successful business man. He was an excellent musician, and was always prominent in musical circles where ever he lived. His brothers Sam, Henry, and William and sisters Mary Hannah and Sarah Jane were still living when Frank died on 28 February 1911. He died at the Mercy Hospital in Fort Scott, and the following afternoon a short funeral service was held at l: 30 at the Konantz undertaking parlor, conducted by Rev. Satterlee. At 3:00 the body was taken to his sister's house in Bronson where a service was held the following day. His remains were buried in the Bronson Cemetery in the family burying ground near his parents. Innumerable floral arrangements were offered at both services by his many friends and relatives. Frank left no will and his estate was evaluated at $ 500. There was no money left after his debts were removed.

William H. "Willie" was the last child born to Levi and Mary Barger Alsop, and he was only nine years old when his father died. He was raised by his mother with the help of older brothers and sisters. He evidently did not like farming chores, as he stayed away from this occupation entirely when he reached maturity. As a young man, he moved into Fort Scott, which was the largest town in the county, and worked as a clerk.

The state census of 1895 for Bourbon County records Will Alsop as age 22 and living with the B.C. Atterberry family. His landlord owned a livery stable and Will worked for him as a day laborer. The Federal census of 1900 reports Will as living in the household of James H. Spencer in Ft. Scott. He was still working as a clerk.

Marriage Book "J", page 134, contains the record of the union of William H. Alsop, age 35, to Miss Eva Pearl Garlock, age 25, who gave her age on the license as over eighteen. They applied for the marriage license on 18 December 1906, and were married the following day by E.M. Evans, Minister of the Methodist Episcopal Church of Fort Scott. "Willie" and Eva lived their entire married lives in Fort Scott - at one time residing at

117 N. Judson. For many years they operated a grocery at 2 East Oak. William and Eva were never blessed with children.

When Will Alsop's mother Mary Barber Alsop died, he was named co-executor along with his brother John E. Alsop. His mother, who was evidently well established financially, had lent most of her children money, and Will owed to her estate two loans of $350 and $ 150. His brothers Charles, Sam and John also owed loans of a few hundred dollars each.

Later in life Will had trouble with the blood circulation in his legs. His attending physician in the final years of his life was Dr. C. F. Young. His death would be primarily caused by gangrene of the right lower leg, thrombosis, and popliteal artery.

On 23 March 1927, Will and Eva Alsop had a dual will drawn up which left all to the survivor of the two. Will H. died on 19 June 1932, and his wife Eva Pearl was named executrix of the will. He was a patient at the Main Street Mercy Hospital at the time of his death and was buried at the Evergreen Cemetery in Fort Scott. Estate records show that William's personal property was worth $700 and that the value of his entire estate totaled $4,172.00. He owned, as part of the estate, half interest in the equipment in the Courtland Hotel of Fort Scott which was evaluated at $600. After her death, Eva was buried next to her husband.

(This family will be continued in Alsop's Tables, Volume IV)

CHAPTER XIV

From Belper To The Prairie

(Continued from Page 204, Alsop's Tables, Volume II)

Additional family research has determined that John Allsop, born in Belper, Derbyshire, England in 1804, was the son of Samuel Allsop and wife Sarah Webster who were married in Belper on 15 Feb. 1790. John Allsop and wife Mary Ann Slater who was the daughter of William Anthony Slater, born 1775, and wife Hannah "Ann" Stone, born 1776, left England for the U. S. A. in 1845. John and Mary's children grew up in the Moccasin community located in the north west corner of Effingham Co., Illinois.

When John Allsop completed his fall harvest in 1848, he was experiencing financial difficulties which he hoped to eliminate by returning to England to sell his business. He left his twenty-two year old daughter Sarah Elizabeth Allsop and his foster daughter Julia Martin in charge of his younger children during his absence. In November 1848, after the departure of John Allsop, John Sturgeon and two of his Shelby Co., Illinois neighbors initiated attachment proceedings in a justice of the peace court against the property of John Allsop. These three men claimed that John Allsop owed them $ 124. Since John Allsop was out of the country, he could not appear to answer the charges, thus a justice of the peace entered judgment against him. Court records indicate that a constable probably seized John's property and enough was sold at auction to pay the judgment.

After John Allsop returned from England in the spring of 1849, he sued Sturgeon, Smith, and Light for forcibly seizing his personal property. Allsop won a $ 102 judgment. Then, in November 1849, Sarah Allsop, a resident of Effingham Co. sued John Sturgeon for slander in the Circuit Court of Shelby Co. She stated that Sturgeon, a resident of Shelby Co., Illinois, had in the fall of 1848, in the presence of her brother, called her and her sister "whores" and adulterers. Sturgeon claimed that someone from Washington City had written to someone in Shelby Co. and told them that John Allsop kept a "whore house" there, and that he would prove it by producing the letter on the day of the sale of the seized property.

In February 1850, Sarah E. Allsop and Thomas D. Tennery were married which was during the course of her slander case and which caused the name of the case to be changed to Tennery et ux. v. Sturgeon. Sturgeon made every effort to win his case and sought the services of the best known young attorney in the area, a well thought of counsel named Abraham Lincoln. In spite of the representation of the man who would one day become the president of the United States, Sarah Elizabeth Allsop Tennery was the victor and Abraham Lincoln's client the loser. Sarah and her husband were awarded a $ 500 judgment, although in a deal probably worked out by the attorneys, they remitted $ 300. This was not uncommon as most slander cases never got to a jury, and in many of those that resulted in awards, all or some of the judgment was waived. The principal purpose in bringing a slander suit was to clear the reputation of the accused.

Thomas D. Tennery, husband of Sarah Elizabeth Allsop served in the Mexican War and was wounded in the battle of Cerro Gordo. Thomas had kept a diary during the war of his travels and experiences. This diary was later printed in book form and a photo dated about 1884, similar to the one displayed below, was shown in the publication. The following photo shows Sarah Allsop Tennery and her husband Thomas seated on the front row on the extreme left. Also in the photo are some of their children.

Thomas Allsop (1838-1895)

William C. Allsop, son of John and Mary Slater Allsop and brother of Thomas Allsop, had a son, Charles William. Charles William Allsop, the eldest child and only son of William C. Allsop and his first wife Sarah Helen, did not move to Nebraska with his father, but stayed in the area where he was born and on 17 March 1886, married Normandy Isabell Riley. Lillie May Allsop, only daughter of William and Sarah H., was married on 13 March 1888, to Harry James Dugdale. William C. and his second wife Mary Jane Marshall were to have a daughter, Ida Estelle, who grew up and married on 25 December 1891, Alfred Charles White. Lillie May and Jim Dugdale were the parents of Ralph and Thelma, while Ida Estelle and Al White had three daughters Mayme, Kitty, and Florence, and one son, Oliver. Lillie May Dugdale died 15 June 1943, while her half-sister, Ida Estelle died 27 April 1950.

The 1900 census enumeration of Fayette Co., Illinois (the county adjoining Effingham Co. to the west) reports the Charles W. Allsop family as living in Bowling Green Township.

Included in this household in addition to the father were Normandy Isabell, b. September 1869; Lilly Ella, b. February 1887; Ivan Victor, b. July 1888; Nellie Edith, b. 1890; Lula Bell, b. July 1892; Cloe lvaloo, b. June 1895; Alice Cora, b. 1897; and Katie Evelyn, b. May 1900, who was one month old when the census taker stopped at their house. Other children born to this family were Everett Charles, b. 1902; William James Bryan, b. 1904; Riley Samuel; Leora Wilma, b. 1909; and Roy Ralph, b. 1911.

(James and Phoeba Riley Family) Front Row: Phoeba (Angel) Riley; Lloyd Riley; Charlie Riley; Belle Riley Allsop; James Riley. Back Row: Hester Taylor; George D. Riley; Cora Smith; and Ben Riley.

Riley Samuel Allsop was born on 30 October 1906, in Red Cloud, Nebraska, where Charles and "Bell" had temporarily moved their family to be near Charles' father William. William died the following year, and the family moved back to Fayette Co., Illinois where all of the children were born except Riley Samuel.

The census report for 1920 proves that Charles "Charley" William Allsop and wife Isabelle were living in Cowden, Shelby County, Illinois where they had moved sometime after 1910 from Fayette Co., Illinois. Living with them were their youngest children Everette C., 17, Willie, 15, Riley, 13, Lenora, 11, and Roy, 8. By 1930, Charley and Belle had moved to the unincorporated community of Holliday, Shelby Co., Illinois. All of their children were grown and had left home. Charles died 14 March 1934.

Mary Allsop, the last child of John and Mary Slater Allsop, was married to George Eccles on 7 January 1866, and she and her husband lived on the family homestead in Moccasin Township, where they could help care for John in his later years. George was a member of one of the families that John Allsop had met in 1849 on the boat sailing from England to America.

George and Mary were active in operating her father's farm, and it was there that their two children, Mary Lillian, 1867, and John, 1869, were born. John died ca. age 1, and his mother Mary died on 2 December 1872. After the death of his wife, George moved to a farm of his own where he remarried. Mary Lilian "Lillie" Eccles married J. Mark Brown, and their children were Rollie, Roy and Glen.

Thomas Allsop, the only child of John and Mary S. Allsop not discussed in detail, had his biography published in 1883, in the History of Effingham Co., Illinois with the last part now presented as it appears in the 19th century county history.

Thomas remained with his father until he was twenty-one, then began in business for himself in 1859, locating where he now resides. He was married for the first time to Elizabeth Hunt, born in Manchester, England, daughter of John Hunt and Elizabeth Mapplebeck.

She died April 2, 1873, leaving six children. The oldest daughter Lizzie resides in Moccasin Township, this county, wife of Joseph Syfert. His second wife was Sarah Getz, of Ohio, daughter of William Getz; she died leaving one child Bertha. Last wife was Sarah Mahin, born in this county, daughter of Edward and Elizabeth (Powell) Mahin, he, of Ohio, and she of Tennessee. By last marriage two children - Clarence and Nellie. He has 200 acres in this township, 150 acres in Shelby County, and a farm in Moccasin Township. He has done much toward encouraging the breeding of fine stock. Democrat, and of the Southern Methodist Church. He has put all the substantial improvements on his farm.

Thomas and Elizabeth Hunt were married 4 June 1857, with their first child, Mary Elizabeth "Lizzie" born in 1858. Lizzie married Joseph Syfert on 4 August 1877, which union produced Thomas, Milton, Walter, Laurence, Edd, Minnie, and Becky. Other children of Thomas and Elizabeth Hunt Allsop were as follows: William Henry, died 1860 in infancy; John Thomas, b. January 1862, d. 1949, married Mary Etta Bartscht, and their only son

Dean was wed to Lucile Smith which matrimony produced Carolyn and Fred; Emma Jane, b. 1864, d.1931, became the wife of Milton Fitch, and they were the parents of John and Archy; Sarah, b. 1868, d. 1953, married Joseph N. Richards with issue of Arthur who was espoused to Lucile Coslet and the father of Ray and Ruth; and Martha Alice, b. February 1870, d. 1923, who was the wife of Noble Slifer andthe mother of Violet, Florence, Clayton, and Harry Martin.

Thomas was married to Sarah Ellen Getz on 2 October 1874, in Effingham Co. Their only child Bertha Viola was born in 1876, and died at the age of 18 years. After Thomas' second wife's death on 15 November 1876, while giving birth to Bertha, he married Sarah Catherine Mahin on 7 May 1878.

The children born to this third union were Clarence, b. 1879; Nellie May, b. 1881, wed Charles Richards and they were the parents of Leo, Earnest, Kathryn, Helen, Flossye, Naomi, Nell, Calvin, and Raymond; Roy Leslie, b. 1883, died 1885; Cleveland Samuel, b. 2 April 1885; and Florence Nightingale, b. January 1888, married Rollin Oliver with issue of Donald, Helen, and Duane.

Thomas Allsop helped build the first church organized at Moccasin, Illinois which was named the Pleasant Grove Methodist Church. Thomas, who was a very successful farmer, as well as a talented woodworker, made a beautiful bookcase with a built in lock for the church. This artistically crafted piece of furniture still exists in almost original condition and helps to remind us that these sometimes obscure ancestors of ours were actually flesh and blood individuals who went about their daily lives doing the same type of things that we, as descendants, still do.

Thomas never returned to England, even for a visit, and lived all of his remaining years in the prairie country chosen for him by his parents while he was still a small boy. Here he accepted and embraced this land which provided a basis for the interaction of his existence with the environment and his fellowman. Thomas' last wife Sarah Catherine died 24 August 1890, and Thomas departed this earth five years later on July 4. He was buried near his parents and other family members in the Pleasant Grove Cemetery.

When Sarah Catherine Mahin Allsop died at age 42, she left behind under the care of her husband Thomas and several of her stepchildren, four children whose ages ranged from 11 to 2 years. When Thomas died in 1895, these young children found a home with their stepsister Sarah Allsop Richards, wife of Joseph.

Cleveland Samuel, 15, and Florence N., were still living in the Richard's home when the 1900 census was taken. The other two children, Clarence and Nellie May, had reached adulthood by this time. Clarence was reported living in Shelby County, Illinois, Dry Point Twp., in the household of John Hendricks where he was employed as a servant.

By 1910, Cleveland Samuel Allsop, son of Thomas and Sarah Catherine, was living on a part of the original John Allsop homestead, having married Zoa Elizabeth Hunt on 5 December 1905. They had one child by this time, a daughter Ethel Catherine, b. l0 April 1908, who was the author of the book Prairie Boy, mentioned previously. That Ethel was born on the family farm settled by John and Mary Slater Allsop, becomes clearly evident from this Federal census enumeration.

Clarence, older brother of Cleveland Samuel, continued to live in nearby Shelby Co., Illinois with his family consisting in 1910 of wife Bertha Wiley and children Russell, Ula and Thomas.

(This family will be continued in Alsop's Tables, Volume IV)

CHAPTER XV

The Gilbert Alsop Family

(Continued from Page 220, Alsop's Tables, Vol. II)

Gilbert Alsop was born in England and immigrated to Stafford Co., Virginia probably in the late 1600's. He is found on the Stafford Co., courthouse records dated 1701-1702, as being a private soldier in the Virginia colonial militia, "Company of horse troops," under the command of Captain Richard Fossaker and Lieutenant Dade Massey.

A neighbor and good friend of the Alsop family was Thomas Ellis who, together with two of his brother Charles' sons-in-law, witnessed the will of Gilbert Alsop in 1705. This Charles Ellis, previously mentioned as the brother of Thomas Ellis above, had a son Charles, Jr., who in Stafford Co. on 29 Sept. 1734, bequeathed to his friend John Alsop, son of Gilbert, his chest and all of his wearing clothes. The Ellis, Dade, and Buckner families were reported in early county records as living on the western side of the Upper Machotick Neck near the Machotick Dam in Stafford Co. As the Alsops were neighbors and friends of these several families, this information helps to locate the Alsop family during the early 1700's.

Several generations of this specific branch of the Alsop family were discussed in the previous two volumes, but their direct line of descent has yet to be clearly defined. What is definitely known is that Gilbert had three sons who were Gilbert, John, and Edward. John, son of the first Gilbert, was the father of an only son Edward who was the last proven descendant of Gilbert Alsop, Sr.

Other Alsops living in King George County from 1782 until 1822 were George, William, Robert, and Ritchie, but recent records from the Caroline Co., Virginia courthouse located by David P. Alsup of Long Beach, California prove that Ritchie and Robert Alsop were not descendants of Gilbert Alsop, but sons of Benjamin and wife Nellie Alsop of Caroline Co. George Alsop was reported to be a brother of Benjamin Alsop in the first two volumes of Alsop's Tables, but additional information indicates that he could possibly be the son of Benjamin. The ancestry of William Alsop and John Alsop is not certain.

The Robert and Ritchie Alsop families were incorrectly placed in the Gilbert Alsop chapter in volumes one and two of Alsop's Tables but are being correctly relocated to the "George Alsop Family" chapter in this third volume. Thus, it appears that the line of Gilbert Alsop ended with his grandson Edward unless William Alsop, born 1761, or John Alsop who was mentioned on page 144 of the original volume of Alsop's Tables, should prove to be sons of Edward. Additional information will have to be found before any change is made in the family relationships of William Alsop and John Alsop.

William Alsop listed in the previous paragraph as born in 1761, in Caroline Co., Virginia and who served in the Revolutionary War as reported on page 140 of Alsop's Tables, Volume I, was reported to have been the father of Henry M. Alsop, born ca. 1810. Newly discovered marriage records of Caroline Co., Virginia have been found which prove that Henry's parents were Ritchie and Mary Ann Alsop and not William Alsop and wife. This correction on Henry M. Alsop will be presented in the chapter entitled "The George Alsop Family."

CHAPTER XVI

The George Alsop Family

(Continued from page 352, Alsop's Tables, Volume II)

The numbers in parentheses refer to individuals assigned those numbers in Chapter 15 of the first volume and Chapter 16 of the second volume. These individuals are then named and followed by additional information.

(1) George Alsop, immigrant ancestor of this specific branch of the family, was transported to Accomack County, Virginia in 1664, by Colonel Edward Scarburgh who also transported a woman named Jane Ossett to the same area in 1663. She came as a headright of the same person who transported George Alsop, so the probability that her name should have been spelled Alsop is likely, as a similar misspelling of the name of George Alsop's wife Ann was committed. She was probably a close relative of John and George Alsop, but nothing else has been learned about her at this time.

(4) William Alsop, grandson of George the immigrant ancestor, was a witness to an indenture involving Samuel Hoyle and Samuel Skinker, both of King George County, Virginia which was dated 29 June 1726. This indenture related to 119 acres of land that Samuel Hoyle had obtained from his parents Edward and Ann Cobham Hoyle.

William Alsop was one of the appraisers of the estate of Thomas Boyles which was evaluated at 39 pounds, 7 shillings, 5 1/2 pence and approved by the King George Court on 3 October 1729. William Alsop was required to post a bond of 100 pounds as the executor of the will of Margaret Boyles which was recorded in King George County D. B. 3, page 5 B and dated 2 Feb. 1732.

He, Joseph Berry, and James Greecion were appointed by the King George Court as appraisers for the estate of Richard Price. The date was 5 March 1735/36, and the estate was valued at 63-1-7 and approved and recorded in W. B. 1, pages 208-209.

Joseph Berry, James Jones, and William Alsop were the appraisers of the estate of Thomas Traverse, dec., which was approved on 2 April 1736, for the amount of 157-19-2. This was recorded in W. B. 1, pages 211-214, in the records of King George Co.

The inventory and appraisement of James Greecion, dec., was conducted by Robert Benson, William Alsop, and Alex Snelling on 6 Mar. 1740/41, and the value was set at 35-0-2. It was recorded in W. B. 1, page 261.

The marriage record of one of the daughters of William Alsop, Elizabeth who married Wm Jones, is to be found in the courthouse at King George County, Virginia. Listed in the Marriage Register of St. Paul's Parish, this event took place 9 February 1749/50.

(6) Sarah Jones Alsop, widow of William Alsop, Jr., was reported as head of the household on the 1782 tax list of Spotsylvania County, Virginia. She also was listed as having no white male tithables, but was credited with three slaves.

Elizabeth Alsop, daughter of William and Sarah Jones Alsop, married Bartlett Collins about 1780, in Caroline Co., Virginia. Bartlett Collins was the son of Thomas Collins and wife Susannah Bartlett Collins. Susannah was the daughter of William Bartlett and Susanna Davis. Henry Bartlett, brother of William Bartlett, married Sarah Crane, and their daughter Anne Bartlett married George Alsop, the son of George and Mary Wise Alsop of Caroline Co., Virginia. Sarah Bartlett, a sibling of Henry and William Bartlett, married Thomas Perry. Sarah and Thomas had a son Bartlett Perry whose son Greenville Perry married Nancy Alsop on 11August 1841, in Scott Co., Kentucky. Nancy Alsop was the daughter of William and Amy Scott Alsop. William was born in Spotsylvania Co., Virginia ca. 1772, and is listed as number (12), page 167, in Volume 1 of Alsop's Tables.

Benjamin Alsop and John Wood were named the guardians of Polly Holladay after the death of her parents ca. 1787. Polly's mother was Martha Alsop, daughter of William and Sarah Jones Alsop and sister of Benjamin Alsop.

(7) Benjamin who married Nellie, maiden name not yet known, was the son of William Alsop (4) who was the head of the first Alsop family to move into Caroline Co. Benjamin lived the rest of his life in this part of Virginia and died in Caroline Co. in 1777. His widow was listed on the tax list of that same county in 1782, and charged with two tithables and three slaves. Since the second volume of Alsop's Tables was published in 1994, a number of court records have been discovered on Benjamin Alsop, born ca. 1710, and George Alsop(9), born 1735, which shed much more light on their lives.

A Caroline Co. executor's accounting record of the will of Benjamin Alsop dated April 1787, lists George Alsop as the executor. The purpose of this document was an order to allot to Mrs. Elender Griffin, late wife of Benjamin Alsop, deceased, her dower lands of the said Benjamin Alsop. Circumstantial evidence indicates that Elender "Nellie" Alsop had married Roy Griffin and was the Miss Griffin listed as the mother of George Alsop who married Margaret Wise as recorded in the "Pilcher Family Genealogy" authored by J. M. Pilcher. Since Elender "Nellie" Alsop Griffin was the mother of George Alsop, this is the proof that is needed to establish the fact that Benjamin was the father of George Alsop and not his brother. On page 225 of Alsop's Tables, Volume I, George Alsop is reported to be the son of William Alsop, but the recently discovered information about Miss Griffin being George's mother would make William Alsop his grandfather.

A second court document of Caroline Co., Virginia dated June 1789, indicates that the estate settlement of Benjamin Alsop was still being processed by George Alsop, son of Benjamin and executor of the estate.

George Alsop, son of Benjamin and Nellie Alsop, was dead by October 1795, as proven by a court record of Caroline Co. for that date in which Delphia, second wife of George, is listed as the guardian for her daughter Fanny and the father is verified to be George.

In November of 1796, the Caroline County, Virginia court records reveal that in a court suit entitled Alsop vs. Alsop, George Alsop, executor of George Alsop who was executor of Benjamin Alsop, deceased, was ordered to pay out of the estate of Benjamin Alsop: James Alsop, Littleton Jeter in right of his wife Jane, formerly Jane Alsop, Robert Alsop, Susannah Alsop, and Richie Alsop. These were the living brothers and sisters of George Alsop, Sr., deceased, who was the son of Benjamin Alsop and wife Nellie, and the father of George Alsop, Jr., who was the executor in the estate distribution of his grandfather.

In Alsop's Tables, Volume I, page 157, a list of the children of Benjamin and Nellie Alsop was presented as circumstantial evidence would allow at the time. Court records of Caroline Co. and District Court Records of Fredericksburg in Spotsylvania Co. as discovered by David P. Alsop, Lynette Vinet, and your author have made it possible to correct some of the identification errors related to the progeny of Benjamin and Nellie as follows: Elizabeth Alsop who married John Darnaby was listed as the first daughter of Benjamin and Nellie, but could possibly have been the daughter of Joseph Alsop of Pittsylvania Co., Virginia. Additional information is necessary to be able to assign her to the correct branch of the Alsop family tree. (15) Joseph Alsop was listed as the first son of Benjamin and Nellie Alsop. He could have been the son of Joseph Alsop of Pittsylvania Co., Virginia and will be discussed in Chapter XVII, "William Alsop and Descendants" which follows this chapter in Alsop's Tables, Part II. (16) George Alsop, second son listed for Benjamin and Nellie Alsop could also have been a son of Joseph Alsop of Pittsylvania Co., although no additional information has been found on him other than that found on page 173 of Vol. I. (17) James Alsop is a proven son of Benjamin and Nellie. (18) Reuben Alsop, (19) Thomas Alsop, and (20) John Alsop are believed to be sons of Benjamin and Nellie, but this has not yet been proven. Other children of Benjamin and Nellie Alsop which were not on the original list, but have now been genealogically proven are Robert, Richie, Susannah, and Jane Alsop Jeter. George Alsop listed in the first volume of this genealogy on pages 157-158 as the brother of Benjamin was actually his son.

Several records of the District Court of Fredericksburg, Virginia for the years 1803 and 1807 contain Alsop information which has proven to be helpful in solving a few of this family's mysteries. In one lawsuit styled Alsop vs. Taylor & c and dated 1803, Robert Alsop, Susanna Alsop, and Ritchie Alsop are listed as plaintiffs in the case and James Alsop is listed along with the plaintiffs as "next friend" which is a legal term meaning one who is not appointed a guardian for a minor, but one who acts for their benefit. This would indicate that James was probably an older brother who was of age when the father Benjamin Alsop died in 1777, and a guardian was appointed for these three minor children. The suit was filed against the Justices of Caroline Co. and was related to the guardianship of the children of Benjamin Alsop.

A second lawsuit dated 1807, and titled Nelson vs. Taylor & c in which William Nelson was the plaintiff and James Taylor and Anthony Thornton were Justices of Caroline Co., was presented before this District Court in Fredericksburg, Va. The guardian of Robert, Ritchie and Susannah was named as Roy Griffin, and the suit was brought concerning an alleged debt to the Alsops when they were still minors. Caroline Co. was the only place mentioned in the case.

Legal application had also been made to the Fredericksburg, Virginia District Court in 1792, in which Thomas Berry was suing John Skinker, Jr., concerning a land boundary dispute. George Alsop, age 59, was listed as a deponent in the cause. A deponent is usually a witness who can give pertinent information related to the situation. This George is believed to be the one listed as number nine on page 157, Alsop's Tables, Volume I, making him the son of Benjamin Alsop and the brother of Robert, Ritchie, Susanna, etc.

Benjamin Alsop, proven father of Robert, Ritchie, and Susannah Alsop was very likely the father of William Alsop. John Alsop could also have been Benjamin's son, but no definite proof has been found which would substantiate this.

William Alsop and wife Emaline Broaddus were reported in both volumes of Alsop's Tables as having a son Henry M. Alsop who moved to Sparta in Caroline Co., Virginia. Henry M. Alsop's parents were not William and Emaline, but Ritchie and Mary Ann Alsop as reported on several of his marriage licenses.

Henry M. Alsop of Caroline Co., sold on 9 Sept. 1839, land to a man named Houston as recorded in Deed Book 40, page 427.

Henry M. Alsop lived on a plantation named "Mount E(c)oleus," although whether he owned this property or just worked there is debatable. One source of information relates that Mount E(c)oleus was an Alsop homestead for several generations. It was located in a community that is today known as Chase which is near the town of Milford, Virginia.

A picture of the house in which Henry M. lived and where his daughter Emma Jane was born was shown on page 141 of the first volume of Alsop's Tables. This photo was taken in 1963, and at that time the house had been vacant for twenty years or more. It burned several years later when a homeless person was taking shelter there and set the fire. Mrs. Elizabeth Pitts of Sparta, Virginia has provided much information about the house and the grounds, as she has recorded a large amount of the history of the area. She describes the residence as a frame house built ca. 1850, in two parts of 1 1/2 and 2 stories with 10 rooms, and located (in 1937) on the north side of Route 14, near the post office. She said that the three windows clearly seen in the previously mentioned snapshot were on a portion of the house that originally was a porch, later enclosed. Part of the porch to the right of the two windows can still be seen in the photo. The big chimney adjoined the living room, and back of that was a bedroom. One or two bedrooms were back of that, and all rooms and the hall from the front porch opened on a back porch.

Pam Beazley Benson, great-granddaughter of Emma Jane Alsop and daughter of William Oswald Beazley, Jr., read Mrs. Pitts description of the home of her father's grandparents to her father, and he was able to verify the information. He had visited the house often during his youth, and he especially remembered the tall part of the house on the right which had a large room upstairs. He always stayed in that room when he visited his grandmother during his teenage years. Two other areas of the house that he remembered were the parlor directly below his bedroom, and a basement dining room below the parlor. Originally the kitchen was located in a separate building, but was later attached to the house, and stairs were built leading to the basement dining room and a large storage room just past the dining room.

Oswald remembered that his grandmother Emma Jane loved flowers and plants, and kept many plants in the enclosed porch room during cold weather. She also had many flower beds and borders outside, and had a moon and stars edged with cement in the front yard for flowers. Emma Jane and William Franklin Beazley were the parents of William Oswald, Laura L., James Henry, Emma Blanche, and Frank B.

William Oswald Beazley married and had one son William Oswald, Jr., who moved to Texas where he was the executive vice-president of Hardin -Simmons University in Abilene, Texas. He was also an ordained Baptist minister. He was raised in a strict Southern Baptist environment and was somewhat taken aback when his daughter Pam informed him that his direct ancestors had owned slaves. Pam has been very helpful in supplying information and photos of her specific lineage. She has also been very interested in family history and has researched several of her other lines.

Family tradition indicates that Henry M. was buried in his own front yard in what is listed in the Caroline Co., records as the Mount E(c)oleus Cemetery. In a book written by Herbert Ridgeway Collins of Great Falls, Caroline Co., Virginia, Mount E(c)oleus is mentioned as the old Alsop home place and later the home of William F. Beazley and wife Emma Jane Alsop at Sparta. Mr. Collins also wrote that the graveyard was directly in front of the house but was cleared and plowed over in the 1950's by tenants working the property. Although there are no stones in this cemetery, several members of the Alsop, Bell, and Beazley families were reported to have been buried there.

When Henry B. Alsop died, his daughter Emma Jane Alsop was twelve years of age, and the court records of Caroline Co. show that Robert S. Loving was appointed her guardian on 8 March 1875. Her father Henry

B. Alsop left a will which stated that he left all of his property, both real and personal, to his daughter Emma Jane after the death of his third wife Columbia Taylor Alsop. He also stated in his will that his grandchildren by a daughter of his first marriage were to receive nothing, as he had already provided for them in an adequate manner from his estate prior to drawing up his will.

The wedding of Emma Jane Alsop and William Franklin Beazley took place when she was sixteen years old and he was twenty-seven. The following picture was made at that occasion.

Kathleen Rhodes Coleman daughter of Emma Blanche Beazley Rhodes who was the daughter of Emma Jane Alsop Beazley who was the daughter of Henry B. Alsop wrote me a letter telling me much detailed information on her grandmother Emma Jane and her great-grandfather Henry B. Alsop. She sent me photos of a big chest and a little chest that Henry Alsop had made in the 1800's for his first wife. She also sent me photos of Emma Jane's trunk where she kept her family photos and other pictures of her furniture.

Photos in Emma Jane's Trunk

Other Photos in Lower Part of Emma Jane's Trunk

Big Chest

Little Chest

Emma Jane's Loveseat

Chair From Emma Jane's Living Room

Chest in Which Emma Jane Kept Photos

Pie Safe From Grandma's Kitchen

Chicken Incubator Used By Emma Jane

In the letter written to me by the granddaughter of Emma Jane Alsop Beazley, Kathleen described some of her memories while spending time at her Grandmother Beazley's house. She recalled that her grandmother was always a workaholic and expected everyone around her to be the same way. She had some favorite sayings that were deeply imprinted in Kathleen's mind. Several of them were "She could see just as far in the stone as the one who picked it", and "You are not cutting any ice with me." If she had something and a person would ask her what it was, she would say "Lassos Catch Meddlers." Kathleen also told me that she never heard her grandmother say any bad word unless you count "devil." She said that any time she was visiting Emma Jane, she would have to tramp all over her grandmother's hundred acre farm, which she had inherited from her father, and get the six cows up and milk and feed them twice a day. Kathleen also had to get up very early to feed two mules and two horses which were used by the hired hands to work the fields.

Grandma Beazley, according to Kathleen, was very slow to accept new innovations such as electricity and never let it come into her house.

However, she did overcome her suspicions where a telephone was concerned and was one of the first people in her community to have one.

Kathleen's grandfather William Franklin Beazley was a good carpenter, and she remembers when he added two bedrooms to the back of the house and enclosed the front porch so that her grandma could have a flower room. She said that the flower room was the place where her grandpa died. He liked to sleep in the flower room in the summer and died there on 11 August 1925. He was buried in the Salem Church Cemetery in Sparta, Virginia.

The above photo was found in an old picture album in the bottom of an old trunk by Pam Beazley Benson at the home of her parents. Written on the back of the photo was "Grandma Beazley with Rajah; Addie in background....Summer, 1930". Emma Jane was described by her granddaughter Kathleen as a very small lady who wore long dresses, long aprons, and sweaters. She was said by Kathleen to have weighed only about a hundred pounds, but you certainly knew that she was there. Emma Jane died on 3 April 1944, and almost twenty years after the death of her husband, was buried next to him. Most of the antiques that belonged to Emma Jane Alsop Beazley are now in the possession of Polly Southworth who is another granddaughter of Emma and William F. Beazley. She lives in Milford, Virginia near Kathleen Coleman and graciously allowed Kathleen to photograph the family heirlooms.

When Henry B. Alsop moved to Sparta, Virginia, circumstantial evidence indicates that he brought with him Fenton, a Negro slave woman who was the daughter of Truelove. Fenton was incorrectly identified as Mingo in Alsop's Tables, Vol. II, page 210 and 211. Henry Alsop had evidently acquired Fenton from his Uncle Robert Alsop. Fenton's son Simon grew up in Newtown, King and Queen County, and some of his descendants were detailed in the second volume of Alsop's Tables. Simon's marriage license lists his parents as Fenton and Dick.

Thomas "William" Aaron Alsop son of Simon and Lydia Bank Alsop and wife Bessie Vessels Alsop were the parents of eight children. Their first child was a son named William Arthur who was born 3 March 1922, and died 3 November 1939. He died at the age of 17 and had no progeny.

The next child of Thomas "William" and Bessie Alsop was Simon Lewis, born 1 July 1923, who married on 11 July 1949, Iris Hairston of Roanoke, Virginia. They have two children Alonso Lewis, born 27 May 1954, and Adrienne, born 18 June 1960. Simon and Iris live in Washington, D. C., as does their daughter Adrienne. Their son Alonso married Aleta Gladden of Philadelphia, Pennsylvania on 12 March 1983, and they make their home in Silver Spring, Maryland.

James Douglas Alsop was born 9 February 1925 to William and Bessie Vessels Alsop. He and Etta Campbell of White Stone, Virginia were married 9 April 1955, and they presently live in Ellicott City, Maryland. They have a son James Douglas, Jr., who was born 15 September 1957, and married on 10 July 1982, Marlene Hurd who was born in Brooklyn, New York. They now reside in Plano, Texas.

Melvin Pain Alsop, another son of "William" Alsop and wife Bessie was born 3 Jan. 1927, and died 14 Jan. 1946. He had no descendants.

Robert Abraham Alsop, the fifth child of Thomas "William" Aaron Alsop and Bessie Alsop, was born 29 November 1928, and married Adell Byrd of Newtown, Virginia on 7 December 1957. They now live in Silver Spring, Maryland/Newtown, Virginia. Robert and Adell have no children.

Roberta May Alsop, daughter of Bessie and William, was born 17 May 1931, and died as an infant the following year on 27 June.

Raymond Franklin was the last son in the family of Thomas "William" Alsop and wife. He was born 7 April 1933, and married Myrtle Johnson of Newtown, Virginia on 4 February 1956. Raymond and Myrtle still live in Newtown where their three children were born. The first child was Pamela Alsop, born 27 February 1957, who married Bert Green of Suitland, Maryland on 19 March 1975, and they are now residents of Hillcrest Heights, Maryland. Pamela and Bert were blessed on 22 March 1976, with one son named Chad. Raymond and Myrtle Alsop were also the parents of Angela, born 22 July 1961, who resides in Landover, Maryland, and Sherin, born 26 July 1965, who still lives in the Newtown area.

The last child born to Thomas "William" Alsop and Bessie Vessels Alsop was Bessie Irene Alsop, date of birth 24 September 1935, the only daughter to live to adulthood. She and Willard Stanback of Portsmouth, Virginia were married on 1 February 1958, and established their residence in his home town. Their first child was Willard Alonso who was born 3 March 1963, and from the most recent information, was living in Charlottesville, Virginia. The second son and last child was William Anthony Alsop, born 27 October 1966, and died as a youth on 16 October 1978.

Bessie Irene Alsop Stanback, after graduation from high school in 1953, in which she was the class valedictorian, attended Virginia Union University of Richmond, Virginia and received her B. S. with a major in biology in 1957. She began her career that year as a classroom teacher for the Portsmouth Public Schools with the specific assignment of a junior high science teacher and continued in that position until she removed to the Princess Anne County Public Schools in 1961. There she taught courses in general biology and general mathematics for a year before returning to the Portsmouth Public Schools to teach science, mathematics, algebra, geometry, and trigonometry. She remained in this position from 1963-

1975. In 1960 she attended classes in advanced study in earth sciences and mathematics at Virginia State University at Petersburg. The following year she obtained her M. A. T. in science education from Michigan State University located at East Lansing, Michigan. She attended classes in advanced study in mathematics in 1967-68 at Old Dominion University at Norfolk, Virginia. Bessie next became an administrative assistant at Syracuse University in Syracuse, New York from 1976-78. In 1977, she became a candidate for the doctoral program at Syracuse University. In 1978, she was employed as a graduate assistant working in the Division for the Study of Teaching. During the summer sessions of 1980-81, she was an instructor at LeMoyne College, Syracuse, New York, teaching special biology courses. She received her Ph. D. in science education in 1981, from Syracuse University and then in the spring of 1982, returned to her home area as a mathematics instructor at Norfolk State University.

In September of 1982, Bessie Alsop Stanback rejoined the Portsmouth Public Schools as Chairman of the Mathematics Department, Woodrow Wilson High School where she taught a number of high school math classes and was also responsible for the administration of a twelve-member department. She continued to teach as an adjunct instructor at the Norfolk State University in both the mathematics department and the interdisciplinary studies department. She was promoted to Coordinator of Gifted and Talented Programs for the Portsmouth Public Schools in 1985, and is presently a mathematics specialist for the same school system. This position entails developing and monitoring the curriculum and assisting teachers in the teaching of mathematics. During her career, she has been recognized with many awards and academic honors

The 1930 Federal census for King and Queen County, Virginia reports the family of James L. Alsop as still living in that same county, although James was missing from the family and his wife Lucy had remarried to Willie Braxton. What happened to James, a son of Simon Alsop, has not yet been determined. James' children were living with their mother and step-father. The children as listed were: Carrie E., 13; Louise, 11; and James O., 8.

Simon L. Alsop, Jr., had moved from King and Queen Co., where he was enumerated in 1920, to Caroline Co., Virginia where he was counted in

1930. In his household were his wife Elizabeth, 41, and children Charlotte L., 12, Frederick M., 10, Wilfred A., 8, Henrietta M., 7, L. Elizabeth, 5, and S. Naomi, 1.

Thomas "William" Aaron Alsop, son of Simon L., Sr., and wife Lydia Bank Alsop and brother of Simon L. Alsop, Jr., and James L. Alsop, was living in King and Queen Co. when the 1930 census was tallied. Living with him, in addition to his widowed mother Lydia, were his wife Bessie L., 27, and his children William A., 8, Simon L., 6, James D., 5, Melvin P., 3, and Robert A., 1.

(9) George Alsop, Sr., son of Benjamin and Elender "Nellie" Alsop, was listed in Alsop's Tables, Volume I, pages 156-157 as the brother of Benjamin and son of William Alsop who died in 1761, in Caroline Co., Virginia. Supplementary information from Caroline and Spotsylvania Cos. Court Records has genealogically proven that this ancestral identification of George was in error, and that he was actually the son of Benjamin and the grandson of William.

In the Caroline County Court Records, November 1796, is found a legal document which was initiated by the complainant Delphia Alsop. In this suit entitled Alsop vs. Alsop, Delphia Alsop, widow of George Alsop, Sr. was complaining about the executorship of her deceased husband George's estate as handled by her stepson George Alsop, Jr. On the motion of the complainant on behalf of herself and Walker, Fanny, Almond, and Sally Alsop, infant children of George Alsop of whom she is guardian and by consent of the defendants George in his proper person and of Thomas Alsop, Elliott Alsop, William Murrow (Murray?) and wife Elizabeth, Frederick Pilcher and wife Margaret, Mary Alsop, Nancy Alsop, Jane Alsop, and Spencer Alsop, infants by Reuben Row who was appointed their guardian, the court ordered the defendant George, Jr., do make up an accounting of his executorship.

From the information in the preceding paragraph plus other circumstantial evidence, the following family relationships have been determined. George Alsop, Sr., son of Benjamin and Nellie Alsop, married as his first wife Mary Wise ca. 1760. The first known birth for George and wife Mary was George, Jr., b. 1763. Other children were Thomas, b. ca. 1771, Elliott, b. ca. 1773, Elizabeth, b. ca. 1766, Margaret, b. ca. 1775, Mary, b. ca. 1777, Nancy, b. ca. 1780, Jane, b. ca. 1782, and Spencer Alsop b. 1785. George married a second wife Delphia, maiden name not yet learned, about 1786, and they were the parents of Walker, b. ca. 1786, Fanny, b. ca. 1789, Sally, b. ca. 1792, and Almond Alsop, b. ca. 1790.

The second son born to George and Mary Wise Alsop was Thomas Alsop, mistakenly reported in Alsop's Tables, Volume I, page 157, to be the son of Benjamin(7). Thomas is found on pages 176-177 where he is given the number (19) and his life is narrated in some detail.

Elliott Alsop, another son of George Alsop, Sr., and first wife Mary, was reported on page 229 of Alsop's Tables, Volume I, as possibly the son of Major Benjamin Alsop of "Snowhill." This has proven to be incorrect.

George Alsop and wife Mary Wise Alsop's youngest son was Spencer Alsop who was erroneously listed as a son of Reuben and Peggy Alsop on page 175 of the first volume of Alsop's Tables. On page 195 of the same volume he is given the number (35), but the names of his parents are again in error.

On page 158 of the first book of this genealogy, Jane Alsop was given the number (23) and shown as the daughter of George and Mary W. Alsop. She was actually the daughter of Benjamin and Nellie Alsop and the sister of George Alsop, Sr. Under her family number more details are given on page 183 about her married life. George and wife Mary also had a daughter named Jane who married Bennett Hutcheson on 11 Dec. 1799, in Caroline Co., Virginia. No research has been attempted on her and her family after her marriage.

George and Mary Wise Alsop's daughter Mary, b. ca. 1777, could have been the one who married James Petty in Culpepper Co., Va. on 19 January 1797, but proof has not been found. Another daughter Nancy Alsop left a very impressive paper trail. Her marriage to John Fisher is of record in Caroline Co., Va. dated 25 Feb. 1802, with the ceremony being performed by John Sorrill, minister. John and Nancy Alsop Fisher moved from Caroline Co. to Culpepper Co., Virginia soon after their marriage and lived near the boundary line of Fauquier Co. John McEndree married Dolly Alsop on 24 March 1804, and the bondsman was listed as John Fisher. Dolly was the daughter of Reuben Alsop (18) as revealed on page

175 of the first volume of Alsop's Tables. John Fisher and wife had many children with most of them born in Kentucky where they moved from Culpepper Co. In 1857, Robert Fisher, son of John and Nancy, was listed as receiving an inheritance from one of his ancestors. Robert's sister Dorothea "Dolly" Fisher married on 23 May 1825, William S. Pilcher, in Fauquier Co., Virginia, and they moved to Jefferson Co., Kentucky as proven by the Federal census of 1850. Other children of John and Nancy Alsop Fisher were Patsey, Susan, and Mildred Fisher.

George Fisher, brother of John Fisher, and Dorothea "Dolly" Alsop were married on 24 Oct. 1804 in Culpepper Co., Virginia. This seems to have been the same person who was reported as having married John McEndree earlier that same year. What happened to Dolly's first husband or even if the first marriage took place is uncertain. More information on Dolly Alsop Fisher and her family can be found later in this chapter under Reuben Alsop (18).

The first child born to George Alsop, Sr., and second wife Delphia was a son Walker who was incorrectly named as a son of Robert Alsop of King George Co., Virginia in Alsop's Tables, Volume II, pages 213-220, but the rest of the narration about his life in Kentucky is accurate. Walker died in Louisville, Jefferson Co., Kentucky, and his widow Hester Ann Gardner Alsop remarried on 28 Dec. 1842, to John Hikes in Jefferson Co.

The other children of George and Delphia were Sally, Fanny, and Almond Alsop. Very little has been learned about Almond, but this child was probably a son. In 1806, in a Lexington, Fayette Co., Kentucky deed from Reuben Alsop to John Fisher, mention is made of Alderman Alsop which could have been a misspelling of the name Almond Alsop. He was recorded as entering an apprenticeship in which he would learn to be a brick layer. In Alsop's Tables, Volume I, page 175, the other two daughters of George and Delphia were mistakenly identified as the children of Reuben and Peggy Sale Alsop.

Robert Alsop, brother of George Alsop, Sr., and son of Benjamin and Nellie Alsop, had a son named John who took two of his father's slaves and moved to New Orleans at an early age. Robert's dreadful financial situation was very likely the reason that John took this dubious course of action.

Robert Alsop of King George Co., Virginia and certain members of his family were narrated in Alsop's Tables, Volume II, pages 213-220, and will be continued at this point. Benjamin Alsop, one of the sons of Robert, moved to Daviess Co., Kentucky where he left many descendants.

Benjamin had a son named James M. Alsop who owned and operated a large farm near the outskirts of Owensboro, Kentucky. The census of 1880 for Daviess Co., Ky. reported that James was living with his wife Mary and his children Benjamin, Ada C., William T., Henry, James Nathaniel, Catherine D., and Charles V. on their farm in the Uppertown area of Owensboro.

James Madison Alsop, born 1 January 1823, died in Owensboro on 22 February 1897, where he was buried in the Elmwood Cemetery. His widow Mary continued to live at the family farm with the children who had not yet married. In 1900, she was listed as the head of the household located in District 8, Uppertown, Daviess Co., Kentucky, and the children still at home were William Taylor, age 40, James Nathaniel, age 33, and Charles V., age 29. Mary A. Very Alsop, born 29 November 1836, died 9 April 1911, was buried next to James at Elmwood Cemetery.

The census of 1910 for Daviess Co., Kentucky reported that James Nathaniel Alsop, 42, had married Jennie Mae Black, 22, and they were living on the Alsop family farm. Where Mary mother of James Nathaniel was during this time has not been learned, although she did not die until the following year. By the next census James Nathaniel "Nat" Alsop and wife Jennie Mae had a son James Nathaniel Alsop, Jr., who was born 14 September 1917, in the big Alsop farmhouse in the Uppertown area of Owensboro.

James "Nat" Alsop, Sr., like his father, was a very successful farmer and shrewd businessman. In the early 1900's, he invented a portable feed mill which he manufactured and marketed by opening a machine shop and supervising all aspects of the operation. He employed many people in the production of this anglo-sweet feed mill with the headquarters being located in Owensboro on 18th Street. His manager was a man named Freeman Little. James Nathaniel "Nat" was a flamboyant character who enjoyed driving through town in his new Stanley steamer automobile to the appreciation of his admiring and approving friends and neighbors. Toward the end of his life, James N. Sr., according to family tradition, lost all of his wealth, although the details have not yet been learned. His marriage to Jennie Mae also ran into problems, and James and Jennie Mae separated in the early 1920's. Another family legend handed down is that James, Sr., took his young son James, Jr., and ran away with him from Owensboro to London, England.

Jennie Mae Black Alsop, described by present day relatives as "short and dumpy and not an easy person to live with" liked everything her way and expected it to happen. She was described as pretty intimidating and the opposite of the "demure southern lady." When James Alsop, Sr., ran off with their young son, Jennie, who was not the type of person to let that happen, traveled to London and managed to regain possession of "Jimmy". The details of this affair would probably be fascinating, but they have faded down through the decades. It has been learned that she returned to Kentucky with her infant son and moved into her parents' home.

Ada C. Alsop daughter of James M and Mary V. Alsop was born in Jeffersonville, Clark Co., Indiana ca. 1858, but soon moved to Daviess Co., Ky. near Owensboro with her family. She grew up there, and in 1892, married in Covington, Kentucky James William Hunter, born 30 April 1858, in Alexandria, Louisiana, a son of Joseph and Nancy Horrell Hunter. Ada and James Hunter moved to Jackson, Missouri where they were living in Cape Girardeau Co., during the 1910 census. Also living in her husband's household was her brother Charles V. Alsop whose age was given as 39, and his marital status as single.

William and Ada Alsop Hunter had no issue, and lived the rest of their lives in Jackson, Missouri where William was an employee of the Cape County Milling Co. in a high level administrative position. William died 17 June 1945, and was buried in Jackson. Details of the death of Ada Alsop Hunter have not yet been determined. Charles V. Alsop was still single and living with his sister and brother-in-law when both the 1920 and 1930 census reports were completed.

Family tradition indicates that William Taylor Alsop another son of James and Mary Very Alsop moved to Ocala, Florida and kept close contact with his sister Kate Alsop. His brother Benjamin F. Alsop, first born son of James and Mary V. Alsop, was living in the Lowertown area of Owensboro when the 1900 census enumeration was completed. He and wife Lulu, maiden name as yet unknown, were listed as renting a home in District 2 of Daviess Co., and he reported that he worked for the Milk Exchange. No information has been discovered on Benjamin after this time.

Jennie Mae Alsop, while living with her parents in 1924, went to visit her sister who lived in Silent Shade, Mississippi in Humphreys Co. which was between the towns of Cruger and Belzoni. Her sister had married a man named John Miller who was the owner and operator of a large cotton farm and had made her permanent home in this part of the South.

While Jennie was visiting her sister she was introduced to Abram Barnes Archer who was a friend of her sister's husband. At this time, Jennie was either divorced from or a widow of her first husband James N. Alsop, Sr. During that same year Jennie Mae and Abram Barnes Archer were married, and she moved into the Archer home place as the new mistress of the 1600 acre "Archerletta Plantation."

At the time of the 1930 Federal census , Barnes and Jennie Mae were living on their Holmes Co., Mississippi farm. Also living in her husband's household were her twelve year old son James Nathaniel Alsop, Jr., her younger son Abram Barnes Archer, Jr., age 2, and her widowed mother Mary Adair, age 75, who was born in Kentucky. Located about four miles west and a little north of the small town of Cruger and about fifteen miles south of Greenwood, this large southern plantation offered a new environment for Jennie and her son James Nathaniel Alsop, Jr.

James N. Alsop grew up on this farm, but proved to be quite a challenge for his mother and stepfather, as he was a very inquisitive and adventuresome youth by nature. To help combat some of his lack of self-control, he was shipped off to several different boarding schools which did little to calm down his energetic actions during his formative years. He eventually graduated from high school at the Chamberlain-Hunt Military Academy in Port Gibson, Ms. He attended Southwestern College of Memphis, University of the South at Sewanee, Tennessee, Centre College of Danville, Kentucky, Ole Miss at Oxford, and Baylor University at Waco, Texas.

After completing two years of college courses, James entered the military service in 1940 as a member of the Greenwood National Guard, Headquarters

Battery, 114th Field Artillery. His civilian occupation while serving in this part time military organization was newspaper reporter. While living at home in Cruger, James entered active duty in the army on 11 September 1942. He attended Infantry Officer's Candidate School at Ft. Benning, Georgia and was appointed a first lieutenant on 16 October 1942. His organization was Service Company, 164th Infantry Regiment, American Division and his military occupational specialty was Infantry Unit Commander. James N. was described in his military records as 5 ' 11" in height, 215 lbs. in weight, color of eyes hazel, and color of hair brown. He served 1 year, 10 months, and 20 days of foreign service in the Pacific Theater and participated in the battles of the Southern Philippines and the Northern Solomons, where he was wounded on 5 June 1944, at the battle of Bougainville. He was awarded the following medals: the Purple Heart; the Asiatic-Pacific Ribbon with 2 Battle Stars; the Philippines Liberation Ribbon; the Combat Infantry Badge; and the American Defense Service Ribbon. He left for foreign service on 16 Oct. 1943, and returned to the continental United States on 6 Sept. 1945. He was discharged on 17 January 1946, at Foster General Hospital in Jackson, Mississippi.

Edward G. Robinson listens to a real story as told by James Nathaniel Alsop, Jr. who was just back from the war front where he had had a leading role.

First Lieutenant James Nathaniel Alsop, Jr.

Jennie Mae Black Alsop Archer

James Nathaniel Alsop, Jr., shown in a snapshot with Bob Hope who was on a USO tour during WWII

After returning home from military service, James Alsop was recognized in the community for the mature, responsible adult that he had become, and he was provided enough initial expense money by his stepfather Barnes Archer, Sr., to start a newspaper in Greenwood, Mississippi. James in return was very dedicated to his new found occupation as editor, publisher, and writer for his newspaper which he named the "Morning Star." He prided himself on the fact that his newspaper would publish any story as long as the facts were true and complete. When he first began his paper, James had no printing presses and drove every night to Greenville to use the presses of his very close friend Hodding Carter who was the Pulitzer prize winning owner and editor of the Greenville newspaper. He printed his papers there and then drove back in the wee hours of the morning in time to send out his daily issue. He worked night and day, but his paper was doing so well after the first six months of operation that on 18 February 1947, he and Elizabeth Lynn Ball were married in Greenwood.

Following is an article written by one of Hodding Carter's best columnist Brodie Crump:

"Greenville Guest Enjoys Evening At Archerletta"

(Taken from Brodie Crump's column "Mostly Old Stuff" in the Delta Democrat Times at Greenville)

We spent last Saturday evening "down on the old plantation," just beyond Cruger, Miss., as dinner guests of Mrs. Barnes Archer. She was entertaining for her son, James Alsop, and his bride-elect Elizabeth Lynn Ball, and we had a glimpse of American family life at its best.

Mrs. Archer played the piano for us, and sang "The Lilac Tree," which should be included in the May Day exercises every year, and Mrs. Ball sang, and Betty Carter got up a square dance, and we "consented" to play the banjo for the dancers, after getting what we considered was the proper amount of urging. (Two requests.)

"Lib" and Jimmy took a good bit of ribbing from editor Carter, and Barnes, Jr., rigged up his recording machine and made records of the conversations and the music. It was the first time we had played for posterity, and our record of "Buffalo-Gal" sounded pretty good, "if we do say so and shouldn't."

There were mountains of fried chicken, salad, buttered rolls, beaten biscuit, baked ham, and ice-cream and cake. Betty Ball Russell counted the rolls we ate, but we were only mildly discomfitted, because we used to do the same thing with the preachers at our grandmother's table in East Tennessee.

It was nice to see the Arthur Jordans again. Arthur was district attorney for two terms, was brave, both politically and physically, and we are sorry that he has retired from public life. His wife, Mabel (Young), asked to be remembered to Minnie Branton, Virginia Lusk, and Camille Sankstone. She agreed with us, that someone should do a book on "Women in Industry," and write up Virginia, who runs the Greenville Oil Works, and Camille, who runs the mill in Hollandale.

It would have been worth the trip down here just to meet Great-grandma Young, mother of Mrs. Ball and Mrs. Jordan, who was, in many ways, "the life of the party." She knows Mary Augusta, our daughter, quite well, and said a lot of mighty nice things about her. She said she was a beautiful girl, in one breath, and with the next one, said she looked like us. Sounds like a paradox there, but we hope that Mrs. Young knows what she is talking about.

Yes, it was a nice party, and we think that Elizabeth and James are off to a flying start. For there is back-ground, ability and good looks a-plenty behind them on both sides of the marriage. May God grant them long lives and happy ones.

B. C.

In a late afternoon wedding of impressive beauty and dignity Miss Elizabeth Lynn Ball became the bride of James N. Alsop, Jr., at the Church of the Nativity in Greenwood, Mississippi on Tuesday, February 18, 1947. The bride was the daughter of Mrs. Robert Alexandria Ball and the late Mr. Ball, and the groom was the son of Mrs. Abram Barnes Archer, Sr., of Cruger, Mississippi and the late Mr. James Nathaniel Alsop, Sr., of Owensboro, Kentucky. The Rev. Jones S. Hamilton, rector, officiated in the double ring ceremony. Serving the bride as maid of honor was her sister Miss Mable Ann Ball. Bridesmaids who attended the bride were Miss Mary Josephine Biggs and Mrs. Fred M. Witty, Jr. Barnes Archer, Jr., attended his brother as best man, and groomsmen were William E. Parker, Jr., Hodding Carter, and Tommy Golding of Greenville. James Alsop wrote an editorial the day of his marriage which was published in the "Morning Star" and which saved for posterity his emotions and attitude concerning the big event.

Our Excuse ---

Today we are getting married.

We offer this as an excuse for any mistakes that might have appeared in the last few days, or those that may appear in the coming weeks.

The wedding itself is not in our hands, in that, being a groom, we are merely a necessary evil. However, even in being in such an involved affair causes quite a bit of personal consternation.

If any person happens to see a dazed-appearing young man walking the streets this morning, calmly smoking matches and throwing the cigarettes away, or perhaps, sitting at one of the usual cafe counters pouring salt in his coffee, please excuse us.

We must admit walking in a complete daze for the past week, for we had no intention of slighting those thousands of people whose names occurred to us only after we had named the three personal friends we could remember and wandered off into a dark corner to shiver and shake.

If any editorials appear advocating the slaying of infants or the organization of a Nazi Youth Corps, it will be entirely due to our temporary condition, and only hope that it will be overlooked.

We are forced to agree with the statement made by a member of the Morning Star mechanical staff: "This is the last time he can say no one can tell him what to do."

J. N. A.

The extremely long hours, the pressure of newspaper deadlines, and the additional responsibilities of being a husband and then a father began to catch up with James. He went to Dr. George Baskervill's office in

Greenwood in December 1947, and asked for a prescription for indigestion and sick stomach which the doctor gave him. The doctor also informed him that if he had any additional trouble, he should return for an examination. According to Dr. Baskervill, James returned to his office about the middle of May 1948, and complained of stomach problems which were tentatively diagnosed as gastric ulcers. He was advised by the doctor as to the appropriate diet and prescription and told to return in a week for gastric analysis if any trouble occurred. The doctor also stated that he instructed the patient not to take any violent exercise. Below is an editorial that Jimmy Alsop wrote just weeks before his death.

THANK YOU, DOCTOR

(Editor's Note: This was the last editorial Jimmy Alsop wrote, after he had been told of his illness. He laughed at himself, which was his way.)

We were overjoyed the other day to hear a good friend, a doctor, announce that the writer was now the proud owner of a set of ulcers. It has long been the rule that a good newspaper publisher could not be without such an asset.

It was a proud moment when the good doctor stated that long hours, nervous tension and worry had developed the little companions of ours. The old refrain "Gee, it must be nice to be an editor," ripped through our mind and we gulped back a laugh that would have been strongly tinged with irony.

They are here, our ulcers are, and we are glad. Too long the cubs who became brilliant geniuses in two weeks have wondered at the gruff words. Now they will be attributed to the medical cause rather than to the evil nature of a man who expects news to be gathered and written during working hours.

Now when someone begins an argument we have a logical excuse for not having to be gentle and refined (something we never accomplished anyway).

Thanks to the Morning Star we have achieved an artistic ambition. In the old, carefree days, bumming around such wonderful places as Acapulco and other nice spots, we would sit with writers and creators who had made their name. Always they had something glamorous. We were healthy. Pitifully healthy. There was no TB to drive us to creation before our numbered days had ended.

There was no cancer hiding in our body to make people wonder at the great work we did under such handicaps. We were just a healthy man who wanted to be a writer.

It was sad. But now we have arrived. Our creative urge has driven us to an unhealthy condition. It is wonderful.
(Jimmy Alsop)

On Friday night at about 9:30 P. M., 28 May 1948, James N. was playing in an exhibition softball game at Greenwood in which he was pitching. He collapsed on the mound after throwing a pitch and died in the ambulance on the way to the hospital. He had a severe bleeding ulcer which doctors determined as the cause of his death. With the advanced medical technology of today, this would probably not have been such a serious problem. Funeral services were held on Saturday, 29 May at 5:30 P. M. at the Church of the Nativity and were conducted by Reverend Jones S. Hamilton. Interment followed at the Odd Fellows Cemetery in Greenwood. James N. "Jimmy" Alsop was borne to his resting place by ten friends: Jimmy Cockrell, Jack Shaw, Shelton Morgan, Jerry Yocom, Franklin Fitzgerald, Claude Keirn, Tol Thomas, Wade Bell, Hodding Carter, and Byron Dela Beckwith. It now seems kind of ironic that the last two men in this list to serve as pall bearers became so well known in the history of Mississippi for such diverse ideologies.

Elizabeth Alsop tried to continue operating the family newspaper, but knew very little about the profession, and about the middle of March 1949, sold the paper. The "Morning Star" dated Friday, 18 March 1949, issued a statement of policy as endorsed by it new owner and publisher.

STATEMENT OF POLICY

Announcement was made last week of the change of ownership of The Morning Star. Yesterday was our first day as a resident of Greenwood. We received a cordial welcome from several citizens.

It will be our policy to give the people of Greenwood and Leflore County a progressive morning paper, dedicated to the upbuilding of the entire community. We covet the cooperation of each and every person interested in the future of our city.

The Morning Star was founded by Jimmy Alsop, a young journalist with high ideals and aspirations. We feel that in a very real sense, he gave his life in the building of a better Greenwood. It will be our aim to complete the task he started and the result should be a real memorial to his unselfish and sacrificial efforts.

It will not be easy to assemble the equipment and staff necessary to produce the kind of morning paper Greenwood deserves. Therefore, we will appreciate your cooperation and patience. We will need a great deal of both. In just one day we have learned that the people of Greenwood are tops in friendliness and helpfulness.

This is your newspaper. We want you to feel free to come in at any time and ask our cooperation of any matter for the public betterment. We want to know each and every citizen of our city and county.

-VIRGIL ADAMS, Publisher

Elizabeth Ball Alsop, born 30 July 1922-died 12 May 2000, in Greenwood was left with a young daughter Lynda Hamilton Alsop when her husband died. She and Lynda, born in Greenwood on 13 November 1947, moved after the death of James N. from 320 Walthall Street in Greenwood to the home of her mother at 312 George Street which was on the adjoining block. Elizabeth lived at her mother's home until her remarriage in 1957, to R. C. Wingate.

Jennie Mae Black Alsop Archer lived on at "Archerletta Plantation" after the death of her second husband Abram Barnes Archer, Sr. She was described by her granddaughter Lynda Alsop Bain as quite a woman who was way ahead of her time. She was said to have traveled extensively on trips all over the world and sometimes a number of world tours in a single year.

About 1954, Jennie Mae moved from the Archer farm in Cruger to Greenwood to live at the Leflore Hotel. Lynda told me that she has such fond memories of going to the hotel in the late 50's and having dinner in the dining room with her paternal grandmother because all of the staff knew us and she really felt that it was a cool thing for a twelve year old girl to do. Jennie Mae moved from the Leflore Hotel in the 1960's and bought a house on Washington Street in Greenwood where she lived until her death.

When Lynda was in the seventh grade, she and her cousin Barbara, daughter of Barnes, Jr., were treated to an extended vacation to California by their grandmother Jennie Mae. They traveled on a train for four days from Mississippi to California and then spent two weeks touring Hollywood and Disneyland. Lynda described her grandmother as just walking in anywhere like she owned the world. Jennie Mae, Lynda, and Barbara went to see the filming of Clint Eastwood's television show "Rawhide" and Lynda remembers her grandmother interrupting the filming to ask Clint to come over and sign autographs for them.

Jennie Mae Alsop Archer died in Greenwood ca. 1966 and was buried there in the Odd Fellows Cemetery near her son James Nathaniel Alsop, Jr., and his wife Elizabeth Ball Alsop Wingate. Although an Alsop for only a few years and that by marriage, she has proven to be one of my favorite research subjects.

(11) Benjamin son of William and Sarah Jones Alsop died in Spotsylvania Co. in 1832, and part of the inventory and appraisement of his estate not shown in Chapter XVI, Alsop's Tables, Vol. II, will be shown at this point.

5 wheat cradles	5		
7 grass scythes	6		
1 wheat fan	4		
1 culling box	5		
6 hay forks	3		
3 saddles	10		
7 riding bridles	2	50	
1 lott odd hames	2		
1 pick axes	1		
2 crow bars		75	$216.75
garden tools	1	50	
25 hogsheads barrels	5		
9 rakes	1		
Tools			
1 whip saw	5		
2 cross cut saws	2		
2 hand saws	1		
2 broad axes, drawing knife,			
adze, augers, planes	5		
1 grind stone	1	35	
l lott odds		?	?

Household Furniture		
Beds		
1 bedstead and furniture (1)	$25	
1 do - do (2)	20	
1 do - do (3)	20	
1 do - do (4)	20	
1 do - do (5)	20	
1 do - do (6)	15	
1 do - do (7)	8	
1 stead and underbed	2	50
1 side board	15	
2 dining tables 12 and 5	17	
1 tea table	5	
2 half round tables	15	
1 work stand	2	
3 small tables	2	50
2 piece do		50
Chairs		
12 Windsor chairs	6	
12 do do	6	
1 brown do		
1 yellow do	6	
12 split do	6	

Household furniture continued			
1 furniture press	2	50	
4 odd bedsteads	2		
1 bureau	15		
1 desk	8		
1 looking glass	1	25	
1 desk		25	
3 chests		75	
1 safe	1	50	
5 pair dog irons and pair			
shovel tongs	4		
knives and forks and bore	3		
plates dishes ten cups			
saucers turren &c	18		
25 barrels mill cotton	10		
4 bushels salt	2	50	$68.75
Sundries			
2 brass kettles, jugs, butter pots			
2 pr. steel yards coffee mill			
brass mortar firkin candle			
moulds gallon pot pewtr &c.	20		

Carpets			
1 scotch carpet	15		
1 rag ditto	5		
1 stair ditto	1	50	
3 pieces ditto		75	
Silverware			
11 table spoons	22		
1 large ladle	8		
12 tea spoons and sugar tongs	12		
Glassware			
7 tumblers, 12 wines, 11 handle			
glasses, 1 salver, 2 preserve plates,			
5 decanter, 4 salt castors &c.	12	50	
Candle service			
1 pr. plated candlesticks	2		
4 brass do do	2		
1 tin stick, 4 snuffers	?		
2 trays	?		
Illegible	?		
drawers	3		
looking glasses	5		$35.00
amount carried over			$314.50

Elizabeth C. Alsop, daughter of Benjamin and wife Frances Boswell Alsop, was born in the late 1780's and married about 1803, in Spotsylvania Co., Virginia William Spindle, Jr., with her second child being Harriet Alsop Spindle who was born on 2 April 1806. The census of 1850 lists Eliza C. Spindle as the head of her household with no husband at home. Still living at home were children Eliza E., 34, John A., 30, and Emily A., 27.

Benjamin Alsop, father of Elizabeth Alsop Spindle who was discussed in the above paragraph, is recorded in the Spotsylvania Co. Minute Book 3, dated 1790, as being paid one day's pay for traveling thirty-five miles to Orange Co., Virginia. The purpose of his trip was to be a witness in the Winslow trial.

(13) John Alsop, husband of Lucy Spindle Alsop and father of James S. Alsop, was the son of William and Sarah Jones Alsop. John's son James died in 1815, and on 1 January 1816, an inventory of his estate was made and recorded in the courthouse records of Spotsylvania County, Virginia.

(18) In 1781, Reuben Alsop, a resident of Caroline Co., Virginia signed a petition to remove the Tories. He was on the 1787 tax list for the same county. However, by 1800, he had relocated to Orange Co., Va. as verified by that county's tax roll.

He had moved to Fayette Co., Kentucky by 7 May 1808, as on that date a newspaper for the area appeared which displayed the following advertisement: "Taken up by Reuben Alsop in Fayette Co. near Estis's tavern, Strodes rnd., a black horse, star and snip in his forehead, near hind foot white, 4 years old, 15 hands high, appraised for $60. by John Darnaby and Francis Preston, this 11th March 1808."

Reuben Alsop who married Peggy Sale also named John Darnaby in a legal document which indicated that the two men had an acquaintanship. John Darnaby married Elizabeth Alsup, believed to have been a daughter of Joseph Alsup of Pittsylvania Co., Virginia who eventually moved to Shelby Co., Kentucky after he became an adult. Thus, John Darnaby from Spotsylvania Co. married an Alsup who could have been from Pittsylvania Co. which possibly created a connection between two different lines of Alsops and/or Alsups.

(19) The 1795 tax list of Culpepper Co., Virginia reports that Thomas Alsop paid tax on 1 white tithe, no slaves over 16, and two horses, but the amount was not given. The following year on 19 April, he again paid tax on 1 white tithable, 1 Black over 16, and two horses. Again, the amount of

tax was not listed, but the tax district was that of Daniel Brown, Comm. Thomas was on the tax rolls of 1799 and 1800 for Culpepper Co. with 1 white tithe, 4 horses, and 1 Black over 16. His tax for the two years was $1.45 and $.44. respectively, and he was in the Aaron Lane District one year and the Daniel Brown District the last year. Thomas Alsop, according to records found in Caroline Co., and Culpepper Co., Virginia, moved to Scott County, Kentucky in 1802.

(22) The Federal census for 1820, Franklin County, Kentucky enumerated the George Alsop, Jr., family which was composed of George, head of the household, wife Ann Bartlett Alsop, and children Sally, 33, Betsy, 32, Guilford Dudley, 28, Parmelia, 26, George T, 21, Louisiana Bartlett, and Nancy, 12.

(27) Boswell Alsop's Tavern and Liberty Hotel burned 29 April 1836. He died in October of that same year, but it is unknown if the fire had anything to do with his death. Quinn's History of Fredericksburg provides an article on Boswell Alsop's Liberty Hotel on page 168.

(28) Elizabeth Alsop, daughter of John Alsop and Lucy Spindle Alsop Luck, and husband John Estes are listed in Deed Book 37, page 220, Orange Co., Virginia as securing a loan from Boswell Alsop's estate. This loan took place in the late 1840's and William Alsop, brother of Boswell and Elizabeth, was executor of Boswell's estate and approved the loan on land located in Orange Co. Lucy Alsop Luck, mother of William, Boswell, and Elizabeth was mentioned in the deed. Deed Book 40, page 332, contains the validation of the loan paid in full.

(29) A son born to William Spindle, b. 1774, d. 1836, and wife Elizabeth Alsop was Jefferson Spindle, b. 1804, d. 1861, who in 1846 bought "Windsor Forest " in Stafford Co., Virginia. Jefferson sold this farm to a man named Bridwell who in turn sold part of it to William Alsop, son of John and Lucy Spindle Alsop. Jefferson Spindle's mother Elizabeth Alsop Spindle was the first cousin of William Alsop and the daughter of Benjamin Alsop and wife Frances Boswell Alsop.

William Alsop and wife Manissa Harding had located from Spotsylvania Co. to Stafford Co. to be near her parents who had lived their entire lives there. She and her husband William Alsop spent the rest of their lives in Stafford Co., Va. and were buried next to each other in the family cemetery on their own farm.

William Alsop-husband of Manissa Harding Alsop

"Snow Hill Cemetery" was the family burying site for Benjamin Alsop, the Revolutionary War soldier and some of his descendants. Additional information can be found on page 165 of the first volume of Alsop's Tables. In addition to his own grave stone, two of the other three burial markers are those of two of his granddaughters through his daughter Elizabeth C. Alsop Spindle and her husband Colonel William Spindle.

One of Eliza's daughters was Harriet Spindle who married Edmund S. Leavell, Esquire, and was buried at "Snow Hill" after her death on 17 April

1860. She was buried next to her husband who had died in Spotsylvania Co. on 17 Nov. 1858, age 54 years. The last visible tombstone in this family cemetery was that of Emily A. Alsop widow of Reverend William G. Cross and also daughter of Col. William and Elizabeth Spindle. Benjamin Alsop died 20 Dec. 1832, and was buried two days later. His burial monument was placed at "Snow Hill" at a later date by the Washington Lewis Chapter, D. A. R.

In 1986, Scott Thomas Horton, fourteen year old son of James and Carole Horton of Spotsylvania County, Virginia, completed his three year climb to become an Eagle Scout. Preserving the heritage of the area has always been a concern of his family. Scott led several other Scouts from Troop 192 and other community members to research and restore about twenty gravesites in "Snow Hill Cemetery." Only the four original gravesites mentioned above had been visible when he and his crew began this project of brush and weed clearance and repairing and replacing fallen headstones and matching up foot stones.

Elizabeth C. Alsop Spindle, as discussed on the previous page, had a son Jefferson Spindle who was a very enterprising individual. Jeff married Maria Tackett and was a school teacher under her father. Later on, he entered politics and was very successful in this field also. He held several county offices in Stafford Co. in later years. Elizabeth Alsop Spindle's other children were Benjamin, 1808-1860 of Spotsylvania, William Warner, b. 1811, Ellen, b. 1815, Frances A., b. ca. 1818---married James Quisenberry of Spotsylvania, and John A., born 1820.

(49) The Caroline Co., Va. tax list for 1782, reports that George Alsop claimed 2 tithables, and 9 slaves. George also was a witness to a will of Caroline Co., dated 10 March 1804, in which John Bell devised to his niece Elizabeth Jones, wife of Robert Jones, her share of his estate. On 18 Dec. 1812, George Alsop was a witness to a land purchase in Caroline Co. in which Thomas Miller sold to William Bernard 241 acres adjoining Port Royal called "Westenton." Mary Alsop of Caroline Co., Va., daughter of George and Lucy Harrison Strother Alsop, received a deed gift from Walker Landrum on 19 March 1824.

(51) John Alsop, son of Samuel Alsop, Sr., was a witness to the marriage of William Martin and Nancy Brumley on 23 June 1803, which took place in Caroline Co., Va. When John passed away in 1811, he and his brother-in-law Thomas Hicks were the owners of property in Spotsylvania County's most distinctive crossroads, which is the present day intersection of Route 208 and Route 613. At this corner a well-known ordinary (combined tavern and hotel) had stood since the 1700's, located diagonally from the site of the Spotsylvania County Courthouse. John's half of this property went to his father Samuel Alsop, Sr., as he died intestate.

(53) In October 1802, Chancery Court, Caroline Co., Virginia, Samuel Alsop, Jr., and wife Dorothea "Dolley" Campbell Alsop were involved in a court suit in which the sons and daughters of Joseph Campbell, dec., and his wife Elizabeth Campbell, dec., were suing Matthew Campbell, administrator of his parents' estate. One result of the suit was that Samuel and wife Dolley received a bed as willed to them by Elizabeth, mother of Dolley.

Samuel Alsop, Jr., paid county taxes on Alsop's Tavern located near the courthouse in Spotsylvania Co. in 1813, and obtained an ordinary operator's license for the same year. He had evidently bought this property from his sister and brother-in-law, Lucy and Thomas Hicks sometime after 1811. Tax records prove that Samuel continued to operate the tavern along with a retail store until 1838. His establishment very likely served travelers on the public road from Richmond to Fredericksburg. Another of the Spotsylvania Co. owners was John Herndon who owned and operated the ordinary from the late 1700's into the early 1800's.

When Samuel Alsop, Jr., and Dorothea "Dolley" Campbell were married, her mother Elizabeth Peatross Campbell, widow of Joseph Campbell who died August 1794, gave them a feather bed as a wedding present. Dolley had been the youngest daughter in the family and her brother Elliott had been the baby.

A chancery suit between Samuel Alsop of Spotsylvania Co. and John Hoskins of Caroline Co., took place on 30 June 1810.

Martha Ann Eliza Alsop, daughter of Samuel and Dolly Alsop, was the mother of Zebulon Anderson, b.1828, in Spotsylvania Co., and Ann

Eliza Anderson whose birth date is listed on page 227 of the first volume of Alsop's Tables. Ann Eliza died ca. 1832, although she is not listed as buried in the Spotsylvania Museum Cemetery. Samuel Alsop, father of Martha Ann Eliza Alsop Anderson, left his grandson Zebulon Anderson, who had moved to Texas, slaves worth $ 3,000 and also $ 2,000 in money. In addition Sam devised to Zebulon all of the estate given to his sister Ann Eliza Herndon if she should die without heirs. This codicil was dated June-July 1852.

On 24 August 1840, Samuel Alsop and his son Joseph were involved in providing a loan of $15,000. to Francis W. Taliaferro and his wife Catherine. All of the participants were residents of Spotsylvania Co. with the grantee securing the loan with 350 acres of land (and other property) which was located at Epsom on the Rappahanock River in Spotsylvania Co. 4 miles south of Fredericksburg.

Samuel Alsop, Jr., added a codicil to his will on 15 October 1853, to the children of his deceased brother James giving them $ 1,000. and two slaves, carpenter Poss and gardener Lewis Mahony. In July 1857, Joseph M. Alsop, son of James Alsop, dec., received a gift from the estate of Samuel Alsop, Jr. In October 1857, John S. Alsop and wife Dorothea Ann Alsop also received personal property from the estate of Samuel Alsop, Jr. Mary C. Alsop, widow of Samuel Alsop, in December 1859, gave 14 slaves valued at $13,100. in trust to: George B. Washington and wife; Mary J. Chandler; Henry H. Chandler; and Selia Z. Anderson. They were to be divided appropriately. She also gave slaves in trust to: John Herndon and wife; Edgar Chancellor and wife; Enseline C. Anderson; and James S. Frazer.

Many of the descendants of Samuel Alsop, Jr., were buried in the Berea Church Cemetery, now known as the Spotsylvania Museum Cemetery. Clementina S. Alsop Chandler, wife of Thomas C. Chandler, was the mother of Elizabeth, James, Nannie, and John all of whom are buried in this cemetery. Other children or grandchildren of Samuel Alsop, Jr., buried in Berea Church Cemetery are Jane P. Anderson, husband Thomas W. Anderson, and their children Euodia L. Anderson, Eusebius C. Anderson, and Clementine Mattie Anderson.

John Franklin Alsop, son of Captain Jack Alsop, was one of the executors of Samuel Alsop's will and as such took a thorough inventory of Sam's estate during the December term of 1859.

SAMUEL ALSOP, JR.
Inventory and appraisement of the personal estate of the late Samuel Alsop, 1859

one grey mare mule called Jenny	20
one bay mare mule called Kildie	20
one black mare mule called Nelly	30
one bay mare mule called Sal	35
one bay horse mule named Rock	100
2 sorrel horse mules named George & Sam	260
2 dark mare mules Martha & Amanda $150 each	300
2 black horse mules Charly & Peter	250
2 bay mules, Ned & Mary $150 each	300
1 bay horse Bil	75
1bay horse Peter	50
1 black horse Bil Brown	130
1 old bay mare	20
2 young mules (twins) $ 75 each	150
1 bay horse mule Peter	125
1 carriage and harness	350
1 rockaway and ditto	175
1 set of old harness	2
1 pied ox called Ball	40
1 ditto called Linsey	30
2 ditto called Davy and Dragon	40
2 ditto called Longside & Ranger	50
1 ditto called John	25
1 Yoke oxen called Buck & Lion	40
1 ditto called Peter & Lion	40

1 ditto called George & Charles	40	
1 ditto called Ned & Prince	40	
1 ditto called Charly & Tom	40	
1 ditto called Bil & Ned	50	
1 ditto no name	40	
1 ditto called Mike and George	50	
1 pied cow and calf	18	
1 white ditto	15	
1 buffalo ditto	20	
1 white ditto	25	
1 ditto called Kale	18	
amount carried forward		3028
1 pied heifer	10	
1 black bull	12	
1 buffalo ditto	12	
2 white ditto at $8. each	16	
1 Red ditto	13	
1 brindle ditto	15	
1 bull	12	
2 red heifers	15	
1 small ditto	3	
43 sheep at $ 3 each	129	
ox cart $12; ditto 2 at $5. Each	22	
2 ox waggons at $20 each	40	
1 horse ditto	65	
1 horse ditto	45	
1 small ditto	25	
1 horse cart	5	
1 ditto	15	
1 ditto	5	
1 old buggy	15	
1 old carryall	5	
1 horse cart & gear	12	

3 two horse ploughs & single trees	18	
4 # 1 cuff & brace; one horse ditto	12	
3 shovel ploughs at $2 each	6	
6 old McCormick #9 ditto at $1. each	6	
6 ditto #5 at .50 each	3	
2 cultivators at $2. each	4	
1 lot old coalters	0.5	
3 side wisses at $2. Each	6	
2 large harrows at $3. each	6	
2 new McCormick mouldboards	0.5	
3 spades $l; 6 shovels $1.50	2.5	
3 mattocks $2.; 3 briarhooks $1.50	3.5	
9 scythes & cradles at $2.50 each	22.5	
3 bramble blades	1.5	
lot of old scythe blades	1	
		584
amount brought forward		3612
2 old mill saws $.50; old steelyards $.25	0.75	
lot old tyers	3	
1 pannel door	1.5	
1 lot rubish plank	2.5	
3 picks .75; hoes $1.	1.75	
9 axes $4.50; 2 hay forks $1.5	5.5	
2 dung forks $1.50; 4 crowbars $3.	4.5	
lot iron	5	
4 pair wedges $3.; 1 log chain $3.	6	
4 lock chains $6; 1 fifth chain $.50	6.5	
4 ox chains	4	
wagon & plough gear	15	
1 old cast mill $1; 1 balance $.50	1.5	
1 bucket $.40; 3 half bushels $1	1.4	
1 wheat fan	10	
1 threshing machine	125	

50 stacks wheat & oat straw at $3.	150	
rye straw	6	
6 stacks hay at $6	36	
1 stack top fodder	30	
19 blade stacks at $5.	95	
270 barrels corn at $13.50 pr barrel	945	
corn sheller	10	
carpenter's tools	25	
plank & timber	15	
4 work benches	5	
2 grind stones	2	
black smith tools	15	
2 old iron axles	3	
2 cross cut saws	1	
6 old whip saws	6	
3 cutting boxes	5	
1 saddle & bridle	3	
1 set cart gear	4	
3 ice hooks	0.5	
		1549.9
amount brought forward		5161.9
Household furniture		
Parlors		
1 Mahogany sofa	15	
1 Cane seat rocking chair	4	
30 ditto chairs @ $1.50 each	45	
1 small Mahogany table	3.5	
1 Spring seat sofa	25	
2 small sofas @ $20. each	40	
2 mahogany rocking chairs @ $8. each	16	
curtains & fixtures for 6 windows	60	
1 carpet & rug	20	
fender, andirons, shovel & tongs	5	

carpet & rug	40	
fender, andirons, & c.	12	
mantle lamps	10	
Hall		
1 Side board	6	
2 lounges $3; 1 chair $5	8	
carpet & matting	5	
2 candle stands	5	
Chamber		
1 wardrobe	20	
1 bureaw $12; looking Glass $2.50	14.5	
1 mantle mirror	3.5	
1 lounge	10	
bed & furniture	40	
6 cane seat chairs	3	
2 rockin ditto	1	
1 small table	1.5	
wash stand & c.	3	
3 window curtains	5	
carpet & rug	10	
Nursery		
1 Bed & furniture	20	
1 lounge $10; 5 flag chairs $2.50	12.5	
1 clock $15; 1 case $1	16	
1 looking glass $1; 1 wardrobe $10.	11	
1 bureaw & medicine stand	3.5	
pine chest, table & candle stand	2.5	
carried forward		489.5
		5651.4
2 pair andirons & fenders	3	
6 sad irons	2	
2 small pine tables	2	
3 old chairs	1	

matting in cross passage	1.5
Upstairs	
Room 1	
3 bedsteads, beds, and beding $35 each	105
1 set draws and looking glass	3.5
1 wash stand, pitcher & Ewer	1.5
1 table & 2 slop buckets	1.25
andirons, fender & c.	3
carpet $5; 4 curtains $2.	7
10 chairs at $ .40 each	4
Room 2	
2 bedsteads, beds & bedding & c.	80
9 chairs at $ .50	4.5
1 wash stand, pitcher & Ewer	3
1 small table, pitcher & Ewer	2.5
1 table and water bucket	0.75
andirons, fender, shovel & tongs	5
mantle mirror & pitcher	5
dressing table and glass	2
carpet and rug	5
window curtains	2
Room 3	
2 beds, beding &c. at $30 each	60
1 trumble bed & c.	10
1 bureaw & mirror	10
1 settee $1.50; 4 chairs $2.	3.5
andirons, fender, and C.	1.5
carpet, rug & c.	3
wash stand, pitcher, basin	2
table and bucket	0.75
window curtains	1.5
Room 4	
2 Beds, bedsteads, and bedding	50

2 chairs $1; table and looking glass $2	3	
wash stand and c.	1.25	
andirons, fender & c.	2.5	
carpet $3; curtains $ .50	3.5	
		397
carried over		6048.4
1 corner table in cross passage	1	
1 wardrobe	12	
2 trunks and stand	2	
Passage		
1 bed and c.	35	
2 wardrobes at $8 each	16	
1 crib and c.	2	
1 walnut chest and one box	4	
matting	1.75	
1 arm chair and 6 common ditto	3.5	
2 half round tables	5	
Cellar		
2 silver ladles @ 12.50 each	25	
22 table spoons	55	
12 desert ditto	25	
3 sugar tongs	8	
2 butter kn. & 2 pickle kn. & forks	10	
4 salt spoons	2	
12 plated forks	3	
2 plated cake baskets	20	
glass $4; castors $15.	19	
12 knives and forks (horn handles)	3	
12 ditto and ditto (buckhorn handles)	5	
24 ivory handle ditto	12.5	
6 plane ditto	2	
tea set, China & glass	18	
common castors	1.5	

ditto cups & saucers	1.5	
2 sets white China	35	
1 set common blue ditto	8	
goblets, wine glasses &c.	2	
Bratania coffee & Tea pots & c.	2.5	
Preserve bowl & salver	1.5	
14 waiters	5	
side board & glass press	7	
3 tin safes at $7. each	21	
1 glass press	4	
		405.75
carried forward		6454.15
1 walnut dinner table and half rounds	8	
1 pine table	2.5	
14 chairs and small table	6.5	
1 clock	0.5	
fender, andirons & shovel and tongs	2	
carpet and mat	2	
6 brass candle sticks	1.5	
tin safe, tables, and water stand	2	
contents of cellar closets	14	
ditto cellar storeroom	15	
ditto small dining room	4	
ditto dairy	6	
ditto kitchen	25	
4022 lbs pork at $8. per hundred	321.96	
beef	40	
bacon & contents of smoke house	25	
1 loom & spinning wheel	10	
54 hogs at mill	278	
18 ditto at house at $10 each	80	
		843.76

Slaves		
Walker	50	
Ben Davis	100	
Jeff. Monroe	100	
Mellford	150	
Jefferson White	800	
Miles	950	
Robin	450	
William	600	
Jacob	1100	
Roy	750	
Edmund Fisher	300	
Gilbert	1100	
Thornton	1250	
Jim Slaughter	650	
Henry Smith	1200	
Tom Black	300	
		9850
amount brought forward		17147.91
Daniel	1350	
Peter	1500	
Michael	1300	
Charles	1250	
Bob	1200	
Tom	1200	
Jack	1400	
Sam	1400	
Wingfield	1300	
Ignacius	1200	
Kesiah	200	
Mary	1000	
Nannie	700	
Robert	600	

Lucy Ann, Eliza and Malvina	1400	
Amanda	800	
Beverly	700	
George	550	
Ellen and Charles	700	
Georgeanna	1150	
Edgar	800	
Susan	450	
Betsy, Emanuel, & Wesley	900	
Minor	900	
Ezekial	700	
Dolly, Milly. Moses & Joshua	1400	
William	1000	
Alice	500	
Joe	450	
Milly	800	
Catherine	1000	
Isaac	1000	
Martha	1100	
Susan, Polly & Phil	1350	
Hariet	550	
James	450	
		35325
Brought forward		52472.91
Georgeanna & infant child,		
& Frank & Emma	1600	
Frances & child Abram	1300	
Sarah	1200	
Mary Willis	1000	
Judith	1000	
Elizabeth	1200	
Adaline	1250	
Maria	1000	

Sarah Carter	1000	
Joe Frazer	450	
Anthony	400	
Billy	1500	
Reuben	1300	
Clara Pendleton & Victoria	900	
Festus	1400	
Lewis	1200	
Henry	600	
Anthony Jr.	600	
Nelly, Arina & Eli	1600	
Margaret & infant	1300	
Susan	900	
Woodson	1500	
Mat	900	
Linsey	1100	
George	750	
Lucy	600	
Jacob	450	
Wesley	250	
Polly, Selina & Killis	500	
Rachael, Mary Ann & Delphia	1200	
Silvy	1300	
		31250
		83722.91

The undersigned acting under the annexed order of the County Court of Spotsylvania being duly qualified by taking the oath prescribed by law appraised the personal estate of the testator Samuel Alsop. Decd. shown to us by the executors as set forth above.

J. P. Gayle
C. M. Harris

Benjn S. Cason
Jno. R. Samuel
John F. Alsop
[1859]

(54) Alsop's Tables, Volume I, page 228, provides interested family history researchers and descendants with information concerning the known children of Benjamin and Lucy Pemberton Alsop. Other children of this couple have been discovered since the first publication in 1986, with one of them being Edward H. Alsop, the youngest son of Benjamin and Lucy. He was probably still in Spotsylvania Co., Va. in 1840 but when the 1850 census was compiled, Edward was enumerated in Yazoo County, Mississippi as a 21 year old male. He was reported to be a "gin wright" who had been born in Virginia and other information informs us that he was working at a cotton gin on farmland owned by Captain "Jack" Alsop and his brother Jesse Alsop.

On 30 November 1852, Emeline C. Foulkes and Edward H. Alsop applied for a marriage license in Yazoo Co., Mississippi which was granted by the Clerk of Yazoo Probate Court. The marriage ceremony was consummated on 13 December 1852, by James A. Harrison, J. P. Nothing has been learned about this couple since their marriage.

(57) After Elizabeth Mitchell Alsop, widow of James Alsop, died in August 1849, the two daughters still living with their parents, Elizabeth P. C. and Amanda, stayed with their sister Mary Jane Alsop Beazley and her husband Charles that she had married the previous year. The census of 1850 for the Eastern District of Spotsylvania Co., Va. listed Charles Beazley, 30, as the head of his household and living with his wife Mary Jane, 26, his only child James T., age 1, and his wife's sister Elizabeth P. C. Alsop, 19. In Will Book "T", page 278, Spotsylvania Co., July, 1851, Charles Beazley was named guardian of Amanda Alsop who was listed in one of the family Bibles as born in 1831. However, census records give various ages for her.

Mary Jane died sometime after 1853, probably in Virginia. Charles, now a widower, soon moved to Mississippi and took Elizabeth P. C. and

Amanda Alsop with him. His new residence was verified by the census of 1860 as Holmes Co., Dark Corner Beat with Charles, 38, as the head. Living with him in his home were his three children by his wife Mary Jane who were listed as James T. Beazley, 10, Charles C. Beazley, 8, Amanda, 6, and also Elizabeth P. C. Alsop, 25, and Amanda Alsop, 20.

Charles Beazley married, after 1865, as his second wife Amanda Alsop who was a younger sister of his first wife Mary Jane Alsop. The 1870 Federal census locates Charles Beazley and his family in Copiah Co., Mississippi near the town of Crystal Springs. They were living in the home of Nancy Smith, 78, although her relationship to Charles, 55, and Amanda, 34, is unknown. Living with Charles and second wife Amanda were James S., 21, son by Mary Jane; Amanda J., 15, daughter by Mary Jane; Susan, 3, child of Amanda; Charlie, 2, son by Amanda; Rhoda, four months, daughter by Amanda; and Elizabeth P. C. Alsop, 35.

In 1880, Amanda M. Alsop Beazley, 43, was reported to be a widow, but was still living in the same area. Children still living at home were Susa May, 12; Charles L., 11, and Rhoda India, 9. Also living with Amanda was her sister Elizabeth P. C. Alsop.

Amanda was probably deceased by 1900, as the census for that year shows her son Charles C. Beazley as the head of his household, although he is reported as still single. Living with Charles is Amanda's sister Elizabeth P. C. Alsop who never married. Also living in this same home was Eadie (Rhoda Endia?), a sister of Charles. Charles' other sister Susa May died leaving her husband John T. Cook a widower who was also living with his brother-in-law.

(59) Thomas and Elizabeth Wharton Alsop were the parents of a large number of children, and all of them were not listed in "Alsop's Tables," Volume I; but several more have been discovered since that time. Also, the first child listed for them, John S. Alsop, has proven to be a son of Benjamin and Lucy Pemberton Alsop.

Additional information has genealogically proven that Thomas J. Alsop, b. ca. 1824, was one of the children of Thomas Alsop, b. 1786, died on 25 Dec. 1856, and wife Betsy Wharton Alsop. On 16 November

1858, Emily J. Stevens Alsop, wife of Thomas J., died after only three years of married life and after having produced no children that lived. Thomas J. remarried to Sarah Ann Proctor 24 December 1858, and they relocated to Alabama where they spent the rest of their lives. A son Walter Alsop, b. ca. 1862, in addition to being enumerated in his parents household in Montgomery Co., Alabama , was reported on the 1880 census as living in the Manly Foster home in Marion, Alabama, Perry County, while attending Judson College in that location.

One of the children of Thomas and Betsy Alsop described in the original volume of this family history was Robert Alsop, who was detailed in the 1860 census. He was also reported in the next census which took place in 1870, but the name was misspelled. Robert was the head of his household, living in Fredericksburg, age given as 50, and occupation related to be that of a carpenter. His last name was spelled "Alford," but it definitely should have been Alsop. His wife was Catherine, age 35, and his children were Ellen, 15, James, 12, and Lucy R., 11. Robert and his family are not found in any census after 1870.

(60) In Volume I of "Alsop's Tables," on page 235 is found Margaret Ann Alsop, child number four of the five children attributed to Henry Bartlett and wife Mary Jones Alsop. The child's name should have been Mildred A. Alsop, and the information about her marriage is incorrect. Margaret Ann Alsop was the progeny of the descendants of John Alsop of Surry Co., England as found in Chapter VIII of the second volume of this family history; and she will be assigned to the correct historical lineage in either this or the next volume. Mildred A. Alsop, 30, was reported in the 1850 census for Bullitt Co., Kentucky as living in the household of her sister Mary Ann Alsop and husband Levi Joseph Troutman. It is believed that Mildred never married and lived with her sister until her death which occurred before 1870.

(61) Walker Alsop, b. ca. 1786, in Caroline Co., Virginia was a son of George Alsop, Sr., and his second wife Delphia Alsop. Delphia was mistakenly listed on page 158, "Alsop's Tables" Volume I, as the daughter of George Alsop,

Sr., and wife Delphia, when in actuality, she was the widow of George Alsop, Sr., and was marrying John Dye as her second husband.

John Dye and his wife Delphia Alsop Dye and their children Walker, Fanny, Sally and Almond left Caroline Co., Va., ca. 1800-05 and moved to Lexington, Fayette Co, Kentucky. Dye, who was apparently a prominent citizen and active merchant, became involved in many enterprises after settling in Lexington. In 1808, Dye ran an ad in "The Reporter," the local newspaper of Lexington, informing the residents of that town that he intended to hold an elegant ball at "Big Pond" on the 4th of July. He explained that he had rented the Russell Farm known as "Big Pond" and was inviting all of the ladies and gentlemen of the area to his celebration. On 17 Oct. 1808, John Dye and Obediah Carter appraised the estate of William Parish in Fayette Co. In 1809, when his two stepdaughters Fanny and Sallie married, he was listed as their stepfather and guardian. The census of 1810 for Fayette Co. lists John Dye and his family consisting of wife Delphia and three young children.

George Alsop, Sr., had by his first wife Mary Wise Alsop a son George Alsop, Jr., who married Ann Bartlett and was a half-brother of Walker Alsop. George Alsop, Jr., was the father of Guilford Dudley Alsop who left his parents' home in Franklin Co., Kentucky ca. 1821, and moved to Louisville, Jefferson Co., Kentucky where his Uncle Walker Alsop had settled a number of years earlier and was a very successful businessman. About that same time Benjamin Alsop, son of Robert Alsop, left his parents' home in Caroline Co., Virginia and joined Walker and Guilford D. Alsop in Louisville, Kentucky.

The earliest date that Walker Alsop can be found on the records of Jefferson Co., Kentucky was 11 May 1814, at which time Walker and his stepfather John Dye, who had moved there from Lexington ca. a year earlier, ran an ad in the local paper in Louisville announcing that they had opened a house of public entertainment located at Cross and Market Streets. Dye ran another ad on the same date announcing that he was opening a bake shop on Main Street. An additional ad ran in the local newspaper of 21 Sept. 1814, by these same men who reported that they had taken over the Louisville Hotel and were ready for business.

James Horsely also placed an ad which gave public notice that he was taking depositions in his behalf at the tavern of Dye and Alsop on the first Saturday in January in 1815. Dye and Alsop dissolved their business partnership on 4 January 1815, and sold all of their merchandise at a public sale. Evidently, Walker and his stepfather John did not get along very well.

Most of the newspapers of the seventeenth and eighteenth centuries in the United States ran a special column which listed the people who had letters at the post office and had not picked them up in a reasonable length of time. The "Louisville Public Advertiser" was no exception, and a number of Alsops were included in this list which now helps us to locate them in certain places at a specific time. Guilford Dudley Alsop, son of George, Jr., had letters to pick up at the post office on Wed., 7 Aug. 1822; Sat., 3 July 1824; Wed, 7 Sept. 1825; Sat. 5 Nov. 1825; Wed. 4 April 1827; and Wed 4 June 1828. Walker Alsop was on this same list which informed him of the need to retrieve letters on Monday 6 February 1815; Wednesday 3 October 1820; Wednesday 7 August 1822; Wed. 5 March 1823; Sat. 7 Feb. 1824; Wed. 1 September 1824; and Saturday 4 October 1828. Benjamin Alsop's name was on the list to pick up an overdue letter on Wednesday 3 September 1828, and John Alsop was also informed on Wed. 5 November 1828, that he should pick up his letter. Other letters were for Rebecca Alsop on Sat. 7 Feb. 1824, Alsop and Schwing on Wed. 3 Oct. 1827, Delphy Dye in Jan. and Sept. 1825, and John Dye in 1827.

On Monday 7 Oct. 1816, Walker Alsop placed an advertisement in the paper informing readers that he wished to hire journeymen carpenters. Guilford Dudley Alsop and Benjamin Alsop ran an ad in the newspaper announcing that they were now partners and that on Wednesday 14 Feb. 1821, they were opening a livery stable. Benjamin Alsop put an ad in the paper dated Wednesday 24 April 1822, indicating that he wished to hire a miller. On Saturday 3 September 1825, the school of Guilford Dudley Alsop and Brooke Hill was reported in the paper as reopening on Monday. No details have been learned concerning the nature of this school, but Guilford D. Alsop was a recognized cabinet and coffin maker.

The Federal census for 1820 for Louisville, Jefferson Co., Kentucky enumerated John Dye and his family of wife and children. The local paper also announced that Dye had opened a tavern in his home which operated from 1818 until 1820.

There is a record of a trust deed in Deed Book 30, page 321, in the Orange County, Virginia courthouse dated 22 March 1824, between Jabes Tuttle the grantee and Walker Alsop the grantor. Walker, who was a resident of Louisville, was lending Jabes $ 223.92 and he was securing his loan with twenty-two acres of land to a third party. No information has been uncovered about the outcome of this loan.

John Dye and his family were gone from Jefferson Co. by the census of 1830. It is unknown what happened to Delphia but her second husband John Dye's death was reported in The Sun, probably a Kentucky newspaper, but whose location has yet to be identified.

> "John Dye, formerly of Louisville, the pilot of the steam boat "Arab" shot and killed himself on 24 July 1837, on his boat near Grand Gulf. Dye placed the muzzle of a musket under his chin and pulled the trigger with his toe."

(63) Austin F. Alsop was the oldest son born to Ignatius "Nacy" Alsop (24) and wife Margaret Farrell and the grandson of William Alsop (12) whose wife was Amy Scott Alsop. Nacy Alsop and Margaret Farrell Alsop were married in Lexington, Kentucky on 7 February 1824, which was incorrectly reported in Volume II, "Alsop's Tables," page 236. Also married in Fayette County, Lexington, Kentucky was Jane Alsop, aunt of Austin F., and sister of Nacy Alsop who wed Alexander James on 10 November 1824. Nacy signed the marriage license as surety, and William Alsop gave consent for his daughter. In the 1850 census Jane Alsop James, 45, was a widow living in Covington, Kenton Co., Kentucky with her birth place listed as Virginia. Living with her were her children America, 18, Alexander, 16, and Mary, 14.

(68) George Lewellyn Alsop, son of Nacy Alsop and wife Margaret Farrell Alsop, married Molly Covington who was born in October 1841, and died

9 November 1936. She is believed to have been buried next to her husband in the Baptist Church Cemetery at Long Lick, Kentucky.

In the index of "History of Scott County, Kentucky," there is information given on George Alsop on page 517. Family information is also given on Boswell "Tobe" Alsop, page 557; Nancy Jane Alsop, 517; J. A. Alsop, 513; and Mrs. Sydney Alsop, 557. George Alsop had a daughter Flora Elizabeth "Lizzie" Alsop who, according to family tradition, lived to be 101.

(71) Sarah Ann Alsop and husband James M. Warring had a family of three children as follows: George L. Warring who married Betty Griffith; Shed Warring who married Margaret Darnell; and John H. Warring who married Mary E. Sprakes. It is not presently known if there were more children.

(73) In "Alsop's Tables," Volume II, page 270, William H. Alsop, son of William S. Alsop and Corilla Hardy Alsop, was mistakenly given the family number of (74). His number should have been (73), as his sister Eliza Alsop was assigned number (74) on the same page.

(75) Benjamin Layton Alsop died in Fayette County, Kentucky on 1 October 1921, and his age was given as 76. His date of birth varies from 1845 to 1848, according to census records and other personal records. He was a patient in the Eastern State Hospital for the Insane at Lexington at the time of his death.

(77) James Edward Alsop, son of William and Manissa Harding Alsop of Stafford Co., Virginia, was enumerated in the 1870 Federal census of Grimes County, Cootney P. O., Texas. James E., 53, was listed as the head of his household and living with him were his wife Elizabeth Chism Alsop, 43, and their children Manissa Uinice, 12, Edwina, 11, and Edwin, 6. Edwina was mistakenly listed as a male by the enumerator.

(79) Albert Benjamin Alsop, another son of William Alsop and wife Manissa Harding, served heroically in the Civil War for the Confederate

Army and fought in a number of battles. Albert was a prisoner of war at the Union prison camp at New Market, Maryland, having been captured on 13 October 1862. He was paroled in one week, but was reported MWIA on 22 May 1864, and died of battle wounds on 1 August 1864.

(80) Additional information on Mary Frances Alsop, daughter of William and Manissa Harding Alsop, and her descendants was sent to me by Sarah Moore Fulford and it was most welcome. Sarah listed one other child born to William F. Moore, Jr., and wife Mary Frances Alsop Moore. This child Ella Moore was born in Stafford Co., Va. On 23 Nov. 1857, and died young as she was not living when the 1860 census was reported.

William Thomas Moore was the great-grandfather of Sarah and married Hope Grace Pearce 21 Dec. 1882, at Boeuf Prairie Methodist Church, Fort Necessity, Louisiana. He was followed to Louisiana by his brother John P. "Frank" Moore and both are listed in 1880 as residents of Fort Necessity, Franklin Parish, La. Several generations of this Moore line lived their whole lives in Fort Necessity until Harold Arthur Moore, father of Sarah, moved to Columbia, South Carolina.

(81) The 1870 census for Stafford Co., Virginia, Post Office Stafford Store, Rockhill Township, disclosed that the enumeration of the Alsop family with Martha W. Alsop as the head of the household was completed. Martha W. Alsop, 44, the oldest living sister of this family, had her real estate value reported as $ 2,500 while her personal evaluation was estimated at $ 530. Living on "Greenwood Farm" with her were her two unmarried sisters Mildred, 42, and Elizabeth, 38. Also living in this home were Manissa Moore, 21, Annie Moore, 18, William T. Moore, 14, and Arthur Moore, 6. These last residents were the orphaned children of Mary Frances Alsop and husband William F. Moore, Jr., and were being provided a home by their mother's sisters who had inherited their parents' home place.

(90) All of the descendants of Joseph and Elizabeth Allsup of Shelby County, Kentucky who were listed in Volume I and II of Alsop's Tables, were mistakenly assigned to the chapter entitled "The George Alsop Family."

Since these two books of the family history were published in 1986 and 1994, new information has indicated that Joseph Allsup of Shelby Co., Ky. may have arrived there from Pittsylvania Co., Virginia and not Spotsylvania Co. Therefore, any information on Joseph Allsup and descendants will be incorporated into the appropriate place in this volume and any additional volumes in the "William Alsop and Descendants" chapter.

(97) George Obadiah Alsop, son of Spencer (35) and Judith Carter Alsop, was the grandson of Obediah Carter, who was a Revolutionary War soldier. Obadiah Carter applied for a pension on 16 June 1818, at age 63 while living in Lexington, Kentucky and reported that he had married Judith in Essex Co., Virginia. Obadiah died 28 July 1820, after being awarded pension W8585. His widow applied for pension benefits on her husband's military service as a soldier in the Continental Line and the Virginia Line. The date of her application was 24 Nov. 1838, when she was 84 years of age and living in Scott Co., Kentucky. She mentioned her grandson George Obadiah Alsop in the application form. Spencer Alsop was the last child of George Alsop, Sr., (9) and his first wife Mary Wise. He was mistakenly identified in earlier volumes of this family history as a son of Reuben Alsop (18).

(98)James Elliot Alsop and wife Sarah A. Miller Alsop moved from Scott Co., Kentucky to LaGrange, Oldham Co., Ky. in time to be counted in the census of 1870. James E. was self-employed as a shoe and boot maker. Living with them were their children Alexander C., 29, Caroline, 23, Thomas, 19, John, 19, Robert Letcher, 16, and James, 15. James E., 63, was still living in LaGrange when the census of 1880 was compiled where he was serving as a justice of the peace. The children still living with their parents at this time were Thomas H., 29, deputy clerk; John M., 29, railroad brakeman; and Robert Letcher, 24, railroad telegrapher operator. James Elliott and wife Sarah Miller Alsop were probably dead by the next census in 1900, as they were not listed in the Alsop household in LaGrange which included John M. Alsop, 49; Tom H. Alsop, 49; and Robert L. Alsop, 45.

Thomas H. Alsop, son of James E, and Sarah Adaline Alsop, on 17 March 1871, while living in Oldham Co., Kentucky, was a witness to a statement for William Jennings in which he claimed bounty land due him for military service in the War of 1812. Thomas H. Alsop, 73, died at the home of his niece, Mrs. Shelby Allen on Saturday 2 July 1927, according to an obituary in the "Lexington Herald" of 4 July 1927. Although Thomas had been ill for several weeks, his death was unexpected, and he was the last of his generation. Mr. Alsop had been connected with the courthouse for 53 years serving in many different capacities. His funeral was held on Sunday afternoon 10 July 1927, from the residence of Mr. Shelby Allen on West Jefferson Street. His burial was in the "Valley of Rest Cemetery."

(102) Jonathan Alsop and wife Ellen Jane Kellogg were the parents of eight children with the youngest being Charles R. Alsop. Nathaniel K. Alsop, 40, a brother of Charley, was born in Gibson Co., Indiana in February 1869, and by 1920, he and his wife Estella McCool that he had married on 28 June 1898, had moved to Denver, Colorado where he lived to be in his nineties. Nathan spent most of his working years as a house painter.

The census of 1920 for Vanderburgh Co., Indiana has Charles and his first wife Katherine Doesser as separated and living in two different areas of Evansville. Charles was living alone while Katherine was living with her children at 329 Elliott St. The children were Blanche, 17; Harold Paul, 15; Vivian Marie, 12; Ellen, 9; Vincent, 5; and Evelyn, born 9 June 1918. All of the children were listed as being born in Indiana except Ellen and Vincent who stated that they were born in Alabama.

By 1930, Charles, 51, was living with his second wife Mary, 38, in Evansville, so he and his first wife Katherine were very likely to have been divorced. One of their daughters Blanche married Sam Lenn, Sr., while her sister Vivian Marie moved to Texas and lived in both Dallas and San Antonio, but was not known to have been married. Ellen Alsop married Robert Plato of Evansville, and her sister Frances Evelyn moved to Baltimore and married a man named Cerwonkan. Their brother Paul also moved to Baltimore.

Charles died on 18 May 1949, in New Salem, Indiana which is a small town about 40 miles south east of Indianapolis, after having spent his life as a shoe maker. Katherine, first wife of Charles, died 21 March 1965, at the Boehne Hospital; her daughter Evelyn moved to Orlando, Florida where she died in Nov. 1995. Very little has been learned about the final years of the other children.

(107) Thomas Dudley Alsop, son of Thomas E. Alsop and first wife Zilpah Anthony Alsop, was reported in the second volume of "Alsop's Tables," page 304 as moving with his family from Gibson Co., Indiana to Union Co., Kentucky ca. 1821. However, a marriage record for Thomas E. Alsop and second wife Elizabeth Talbot dated 27 May 1818 proves that he was in Kentucky by this earlier date. Circumstantial evidence indicates that Thomas' first wife had died and that he remarried in Union Co. so that his three young children Greenberry, Thomas Dudley, and Anna O. Alsop would have a mother.

Thomas E. and Elizabeth Talbot Alsop were the parents of Amanda M. Alsop, Manalcus P. Alsop, and a daughter born ca. 1825 who died young. Thomas E. lost his second wife as indicated by the fact that he married Rachel Talbott on 9 April 1830, as found in the marriage records of Union Co., Kentucky. He and Rachel were the progenitors of Lenah Elizabeth and Spencer W. Alsop. An excerpt from Thomas E. Alsop's will also names the two youngest children of this couple as Raird and Ido. However, I did not find these last two children in the will which is located in W. B. "C", page 198, of the Union Co., Courthouse.

Reuben Alsop (18) and wife Peggy Sale Alsop were the grandparents of Thomas Dudley Alsop and parents of Thomas E., John B., William, Reuben, and Benjamin who eventually moved from Gibson Co., Indiana to Union Co., Kentucky. The first four of these brothers moved to Kentucky ca. 1817-22 and the last brother Benjamin probably didn't arrive in Union Co. until after 1850. In the two earlier versions of this family history, Benjamin Alsop and his brother John B. Alsop were not clearly identified and errors were made concerning some of their family history. Additional information at this point should help to clarify their situations.

Benjamin is mentioned in his father Reuben's will, but is not found in any census or other court records in Gibson Co., Indiana or Union Co., Kentucky until the census of 1860 in Kentucky. In this census Benjamin Alsop, 55, is living in the household of Nathan Ashley where he is working on the Ashley farm as a laborer. Living with him is John Alsop, 27, who is also a farm laborer and is probably the son of Benjamin, although no marriage record has been found for Benjamin and the mother of John.

The courthouse records of Union Co., Ky. dated 2 May 1861, contain the marriage record of Benjamin Alsop, 56, and Rebecca Llewellyn, 43. Rebecca was a widow in 1860 when the census of Union Co. was taken. She was living in her own household with her three children Enick, 18; James, 14; and Franklin, 5. Benjamin Alsop must have been dead by 11 March 1869, as Rebecca Alsop and James McCleland were married on that day as recorded in M. B. D-1, page 351. No details have yet been learned about Benjamin after his marriage to Rebecca.

One of the brothers of Benjamin Alsop, John B. Alsop was mistakenly thought to be the Alsop living with the Ashley family in 1860, but he was already dead by this time. Book "C:, page 319 and 349 of the Union Co. Probate Court Records contain the sale of John Alsop's estate on 18 Feb. 1854, and 4 Dec. 1854. In Book "E", page 217, is found the appraisal and inventory of his estate. The settlement of his estate was dated 1857, and the administrator was Thomas Dudley Alsop, son of Thomas E. and Zilpah Anthony Alsop. James Alsop, son of John B. and wife Theodocia Darby Alsop, died just a couple of months after being enumerated in the Union Co. census of 1870 with his mother Docia. His will is found in Book "F", page 354, with the date of the will being 2 Oct. 1870, and the will probation beginning on 8 Nov. 1870.

(111) Elizabeth J. A. Alsop, daughter of Reuben and Mildred Talbott Alsop, was listed on page 202 of the first volume of "Alsop's Tables" as having married Azariah "Azar" Patrick on 28 March 1846. The 1850 census shows her as still living at home with her parents and siblings with age given as 17. Leanah Elizabeth Alsop, daughter of Thomas E. and wife

Rachel Talbott Alsop, seems to be the only child in this family that had the name Elizabeth and could have been the one who married Azar Patrick. There was another daughter in this family who was born about 1825, but her first name is not known. Family tradition indicates that this daughter with the missing first name died in her youth. Circumstantial evidence suggests that Elizabeth Alsop, daughter of Reuben, was probably the one who married Azar Patrick, but that her age was wrong on the 1850 census. There is no definite proof of this genealogical relationship, but Reuben Alsop states in his will that he left one dollar to the heirs of his daughter Eliza J. Patrick.

(118) George Franklin "Frank" Alsop was the son of John B. and wife Theodocia Darby Alsop, but on page 203 of Volume I of "Alsop's Tables" his mother "Docia" is reported to have died before 1880. The 1880 census for Union Co., Ky. lists Docia Alsop, 70, widow, as living the community of Raleigh in the household of Eliza McCoughtry, relation not shown. This is definite proof that Docia did not died before 1880. Frank Alsop also had a sister Amanda E. Alsop who married D. W. M. Lash on 11 Nov. 1852 in Gallatin Co., Illinois.

(119) In "Alsop's Tables," Volume I, page 203, there is a mistake that needs to be corrected. Clark Chapel Cemetery is the burial place of Elliott and Julia Gum Alsop; however the cemetery that is the site of their interment is not in Boonville, Missouri. Boonville is located across the Missouri River in Cooper Co., south of Howard Co. where the Alsops lived. Clark Chapel Cemetery is located in southwest Howard Co. near the town of New Franklin, and at one time, it was a part of the circuit ministry based on the New Franklin M. E. Church South. Howard Co., county seat Fayette, is one of the most historic areas west of St. Louis. It is known as "The Mother of Counties;" a part of "Little Dixie;" the "Birthplace of the Santa Fe Trail;" the boyhood home of Kit Carson; and an area associated in many ways with Daniel Boone.

Clark Chapel Church and Cemetery

Decorative Window-
Date of Origin

(124) John (20) and wife Eleanor "Nelly" Wren Alsop were the parents of James (43) W. Alsop who married Elizabeth Isabell Poe, and the grandparents of William Alsop who married Parmelia A. Fifield. John Alsop and Nelly Wren were married in Montgomery Co., Kentucky on 23 January 1800, with the ceremony being performed by Rev. Joseph Howe, a Presbyterian minister who came from N. C. to Kentucky in 1794. Howe was ordained by Transylvania Presbytery in 1795 over Little Mountain (Mt. Sterling) and Springfield Churches in Montgomery Co., and the original journals and marriage records are now in the Presbyterian Historical Society Library in Philadelphia; part of the John D. Shane Collection.

John Alsop was reported in earlier volumes of "Alsop's Tables" as being descended from the Alsops of Spotsylvania Co., Virginia, but more recent information indicates that he could have possibly been from the line of Alsops who lived in Pittsylvania Co., Virginia in the late 1700's. More data is needed to resolve this quandary.

Eleanor "Nelly" Wren Alsop, born ca. 1779 in Fairfax Co., Virginia, moved with her parents James Wren, b. Dec. 1755 in Stafford Co., Virginia, d. Sept. 1827 in Montgomery Co., Kentucky, and Verlinda Barry, b. 24 April 1756 in Fairfax Co., died 2 Nov. 1832 in Montgomery Co., Kentucky. James and Verlinda Wren were married in Fairfax Co., Virginia on 17 May 1778, and left that location for Montgomery Co., Ky.

in the early 1790's. Nelly Wren Alsop's brothers and sisters were: James Jasper, b. 1781, married Anna; Catherine "Caty", b. 1783, married John Anderson; Sarah Ann "Sally," b. 1785; Verlinda, b. 1790; Elizabeth "Betsy", b. 1789, married Daniel Shortridge; Hannah, b. 1791, married Hezekiah Magruder; John Barry, b. 1793, married Verlinda Wade Magruder; Hugh B., b. 9 May 1796, married Susan Ramey; Mary "Polly" , b. 1798, married Daniel Harrow; and Washington Wade, b. 24 Oct. 1800, married Maria Frame ca. 1827 in Montgomery Co., Kentucky.

Nicholas Wren, b. 1631, d. 1701, was the immigrant ancestor of Eleanor "Nelly" Wren Alsop. Nicholas married ca. 1670, in Lancaster Co., Virginia Margaret Bell, b. 1650, d. 1701, and in Feb. 1664, they were living on a hundred acres of land in Lancaster Co. which is near what is today the town of Irvington. Eleanor Wren Alsop's other direct ancestors were: Will Wren, b. 1674, d. 1710, married Elizabeth Howard, b. 1679, d. 1741; John Wren, b. ca. 1701, d. 1750, married Hannah Anne Turner, b. 4 Feb. 1691, d. ca. 1760; Col. James Wren, b. 1727, d. 1815, married Catherine Brent, b. 1729, d. 1770, and second wife on 22 May 1771, Verlinda Wade. Col. James Wren was the grandfather of Eleanor "Nelly" Wren Alsop and became widely known in Northern Virginia as a builder and architect, as well as a churchman, politician, and inn keeper. He held the position as Commissioner for Provincial Law in Fairfax Co. during the Revolutionary War and was also appointed Tax Commissioner and Sheriff. He also owned and operated a famous tavern known as Wren's Ordinary which was recommended by Thomas Jefferson to travelers, and President James Madison visited Wren's Tavern after fleeing Washington during the British invasion of 1814.

John Alsop and wife Eleanor Wren and family lived in Montgomery Co. for nearly two decades, but did not appear to own any property, have much live stock, or own many slaves. They lived near Eleanor's father and his family as determined by the census of 1810. However, James Wren and his family gave every indication of being well off with 268 acres of land on Grassey Lake Creek just west of Mt. Sterling, Kentucky, the county seat of Montgomery Co. James Wren was a tobacco farmer and owned 18 slaves. Eleanor "Nelly" seems to have been the oldest child born to James and Verlinda and was mentioned as Nelly Wren Alsop when James died in September 1827, and his will was probated.

The Alsop family consisting of John, Eleanor, and a large number of children left Montgomery Co., Ky. and moved ca. 1816-19 to the small town of Ellettsville, Monroe Co., Indiana which was nine miles north west of Bloomington. By 1848, most of John's children had reached adulthood and relocated to central Illinois in the counties of Macon, DeWitt, and McLean. John Alsop's oldest son James M. Alsop spelled his name "Allsup" after arriving in Illinois and eventually several spellings of the name developed.

William Alsop-Alsup, first born son of James M. and Elizabeth Isabell Poe Allsup, and his wife Parmelia Fifield had a third son James W. Alsop-Alsip who was born 30 July 1860, and not 1861 as reported on page 322 of the second volume of "Alsop's Tables." He was buried in Old Oak Grove Cemetery next to his mother, and his date of death on his mother's tombstone was 1863, although it is unknown how close their death dates were to each other.

After the death of his wife Parmelia Fifield, William moved in 1867 from Le Roy, McLean Co., Illinois to Cole Camp, Benton Co., Missouri where his sister Ann Eliza Alsop Sperry, b. 25 May 1826, and husband William Hugh b. ca. 1824, had established residence in 1861. The Federal census of 1870 locates Eliza Alsop Sperry and her family and William Alsip and his family in Benton Co., Missouri living near each other. Living with Eliza Alsop Sperry in addition to her children was her sister Manda Alsop Farmer, age 24, widow of James Farmer. Living in the household of William Alsip were his two sons John, 16, and Benjamin, 12, who were both mentally deficient.

A Missouri state census was taken in 1876, for Benton Co., and William W. Alsip, age given as between 21 and 45, was reported as living in Township 40, Range 22. Living with him was Martha Alsip who was reported to be in the same age range. This could have been a second wife of William, but no marriage record has been found.

Ann Eliza Alsop Sperry lost her beloved husband 25 Dec. 1881, and from that time made her home with her children. At the time of her death on 12 March 1898, she was living with her son, W. O. Sperry, three miles west of Leesville in Henry Co. which was one county west of Benton Co. She was a member of the Christian Church and her funeral was held at the Tebo Church where her favorite hymn "We Will Never Say Good-Bye in Heaven" was sung. Two of her sisters and two of her brothers were still living in Illinois when her death occurred. On Sunday morning, the 13th, many friends gathered at the home of her son to speak words of condolence to her family and to take the last look at the features of one they had long known and respected. She was buried in the Tebo Church Cemetery.

William W. Alsip-Alsup was back in Illinois by 1878, as proven by court records concerning his two sons and their feeble minded condition. He left a very detailed will and lots of other probate records which help us to better understand his situation in 1885, the year of his death. William was buried in the Woodlawn Cemetery at Clinton, Illinois, and his court records indicate that the executor of his will, A. D. Metz, a store owner in Wapella, paid a workman named P. B. Hildreth $3.50 to dig and fill his grave. William also mentions other companies that he had accounts with in Wapella which were John Pettibone Harness Shop and Newton's Livery Stable. On l0 November 1885, the estate of William Alsup received from the U. S. Pension Agent a payment of $ 72.00 which was the final payment for his service as a corporal in Co. "C", in the 94th Illinois Infantry during the Civil War. Another payment of debt to his estate was made on 1 Dec. 1885, by C. C. Webb of $ 26.00, and a second payment to the estate by the same person on 1 January 1886, of $ 55.00.

Dr. John Wright was paid $ 5.00 for one consultative visit on 3 Sept. 1885, which was the day of William's death. His estate also paid other debts as follows: $ 3.50 for work done by his blacksmith W. S. Roberts on 15 July 1885, $ 22.05 owed to T. W. Davis for merchandise on account paid on 7 Oct. 1885, $9.50 owed to the same man for four visits from 2l Aug. to 3 September; debt for burial equipment dated 4 September 1885 and described as a burial case and box $ 40.00, hearse for funeral $ 10.00, and clothing for dressing body $ 5.00. A. D. Metz, administrator of William's estate, listed two heirs as James Alsup and Mrs. John Alsup with the date given as 7 November 1887.

A total of $ 15.65 was owed to Edgar F. Turner for grocery items. They were 18 June 1885-beans $.25; 24 June-butter $.15; vinegar $.13; curry comb $.15; 29 June-beans $.25; small tobacco $.25; 3 July-flour $1.50; 8 July-butter $.15; small tobacco $.25; 10 July-plug of tobacco $.50; 14 July-small tobacco $.25; 20 July-small tobacco $.25; 30 July-soap $ .25; cloves $.05; flour $1.50; 3l July-sugar $1.00; small tobacco $.25; 4 August-starch $ 25; butter $.30; small tobacco $.25; blac $.10; 10 August-smoking tobacco $.25; 12 August- plug tobacco $.50; 14 August-smoking tobacco $.25; 24 August- (?) $1.75; small tobacco $ .25; 26 August-sugar $1.00; tea $.25; 30 August-flour $1.50; small tobacco $.25; 1 September-butter $.40; l0 September-butter $.19; oil $.13; lard $.25; and meat $.65.

(125) John F. Alsop, son of James M. and wife Elizabeth Isabell Poe, served faithfully during the Civil War and joined the "Soldiers and Sailors Historical and Benevolent Society" located in Washington, D. C. after the completion of his war experiences. His military service has been compiled and certified by this organization and a copy of their report will now be shown.

-: THIS CERTIFIES THAT JOHN F. ALSUP:-

Inlisted from McLean County, Illinois on the 12th day of August, 1861 to serve three years or during the war, and was mustered into the United States service at Chicago, Ill. on the 11th day of October, 1861, as a private of Captain Isaiah W. Wilmeth's Company "B", 39th Regiment, ILLINOIS VOLUNTEER INFANTRY, Colonel Thomas 0. 0sborn commanding.

He was HONORABLY DISCHARGED at Hilton Head., S. C., on the 31st day of December, 1863, by reason of re-enlistlng as 0rderly Sergeant of Captain George T. Heritage's Company "B", 39th Regiment Illinois Volunteer Infantry, Colonel Thomas O. Osborn commanding.

John F. Alsop

This regiment was first known as the "Yates Phalanx" in honor of Governor Richard Yates, and was organized at Camp Mather, Chicago in the fall of 1861. It left the state October 13th, 1861, and during the next eight months was stationed in West Virginia, guarding railroads most of the time. It first served with Shield's Division in the Shenandoah Valley, and was present at the battle of Kernstown, March 23rd, 1862, but was not actively engaged. It was ordered to the Peninsula in June, arriving there just after the battle of Malvern Hill, and was assigned to Peck's Division, 4th Corps. Upon the retreat from the Peninsula the Thirty-ninth was ordered to Suffolk, where it remained for a few months. It was later assigned to the 1st Brigade, 1st Division, 10th Corps, which in December, 1864 became the 24th Corps, Army of the James. During its service the regiment took part in engagements at Cacapon Bridge Bath and Alpine Station, West Va.; Morris Island, Fort Wagner, Fort Moultrie,

S. C.; Drewry's Bluff, Ware Bottom Church, Bermuda Hundred, Deep Bottom, Darbytown Road, (two battles), Fair Oaks, Blackwater, Siege of Petersburg, Fort Gregg, Appomattox C. H., Va.; and a number of minor engagements and skirmishes. The total of killed and wounded in the regiment was five hundred and twenty-two.

The said John F. Alsup was promoted to Corporal in 1862, to Sergeant in June, 1862, and was commissioned Captain of Company "B" April 11th, 1865, but he was in command of his company from December 6th, 1864.

He was wounded in front of Petersburg, Va. by piece of shell in left breast, but remained with his command. He was again wounded at Deep Bottom, Va., August l6th, 1864, by gunshot through left shoulder, sent to hospital at Beverly, N.J., from where he was furloughed home; later reporting to the same hospital, and rejoining his regiment in front of Petersburg, Va. Here he was again wounded in the Assault of Fort Gregg, by gunshot, tearing off the third and fourth fingers of his left hand, the shot passing into left hip at the joint, and causing permanent injury. He was removed to hospital at Fortress Monroe, Va., from where he rejoined his regiment at Richmond, Va.

He was at all other times with his command, participated in all the battles and campaigns of its long and arduous service, except the engagement in Front of Richmond, Va., and while on furlough and in hospital, and, either as a private or an officer, rendered faithful and meritorious service, winning commendation for bravery, soldierly conduct, and efficiency as an officer.

He received a Final HONORABLE DISCHARGE at Norfolk, Va. on the 24th day of September, 1865, by reason of close of war.

His three brothers served in the Union Army: William in the 94th Illinois; James M. in Company "B", of the 39th Illinois; and Robert D. in the 69th and 39th Illinois. He is the son of James M. and Isabelle Poe Alsup, and was born in Monroe County, Indiana, on the 30th day of August, 1840, was united in marriage to Alice Karr in McLean County, Illinois on the 22 day of September, 1871, from which union were born the following children, viz:-Carrie,(wife of Grant Smith), Gertrude, Charles, Hattie (wife of John Howard), Arthur and Clarence.

He is a member of Thomas Riddle Post, No. 230, Department of Illinois, Grand Army of the Republic; assisted in the organization of said post, in which he later served as Commander for two terms.

He was city Marshal of LeRoy, Ill., about twenty-one years; Deputy Sheriff since 1867, with the exception of four years, and Constable one term.

His wife is an active and honored member of Thomas Riddle Corps No.43, W. R. C., of which she has filled many offices, and is, at present, Conductress.

These facts are thus recorded and preserved for the benefit of all those who may be interested.

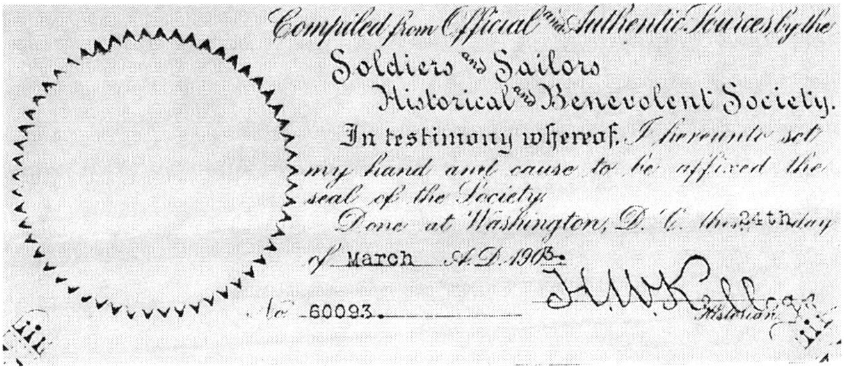
Compiled from Official and Authentic Sources by the
Soldiers and Sailors
Historical and Benevolent Society.
In testimony whereof, I hereunto set my hand and cause to be affixed the seal of the Society.
Done at Washington, D.C. the 24th day of March A.D. 1903.
No. 60093.
Historian.

Captain John F. Alsup and wife Alice Karr Alsup were both buried in the Gilmore Cemetery located three miles west of Le Roy and four miles east of Downs in McLean County. When John F. died on Friday 13 April 1917, his funeral services were held at the family residence. At the time of his death John had no brothers still living, but he had two sisters still living who were Mrs. Martha Melchi and Mrs. Amanda Gallagher, both living in Le Roy. The birth and death dates on the tombstone of Alice K. Alsup are 18 November 1851, and 27 November 1926. John F. Alsup and wife Alice had a daughter Gertrude who could be the Gertrude Alsup who got married in McLean Co. 21 August 1925. She was single when her father died, and she was reported in the 1920 census as living with her mother in Le Roy and still single.

(126) William T. Alsop-Allsup was the son of Thomas (44) and Susanna Newcomb Alsop and the grandson of John (20) Alsop and wife Eleanor Wren Alsop. When Thomas Alsop married Susanna Newcomb and moved from Indiana to Macon Co., Illinois, his son James Andrew (nicknamed Trink), b. 17 Jan. 1832, was the first person born on section 10 in Tunbridge Twp., Macon Co. which became DeWitt Co. in 1839. Among other early settlers of this township was a man named Baron F. Lowry who entered land on section 9, in November, 1830. He married Jane Newcomb, sister of Susanna Newcomb Allsup, and was the official in many of the marriages in the 1830's in this area.

The Thomas Allsup home was located near the town of Kenney which was in the south west part of DeWitt Co., and William and wife Love Randolph Allsup were living on their own farm next door to his parents in 1850. John W. Allsup lived with his parents Thomas and Susanna and also with his brother William after reaching adulthood.

At the time of his death, John W. Allsup was single and still living at home near Kenney with his parents. He left no will, so letters of administration were obtained by petition by James A. Kirby, a family friend. His inventory is listed in Book "A", page 273, and was appraised by Wm C. Humphries, Wm Cantrell, and David Ely.

The John W. Alsup-Allsup estate sale took place on 25 August 1862, with the total being $315. 70. The items were: two plows and rolling cutter-James Kirby for $ .25; one half of ten foot reaper-Jacob Trowbridge for $ 20.00; two log chains-Joseph Missildine for $ .55; one man's saddle-B. F. Allsup for $ 5.00; one silver watch-Mary Allsup Cass for $ 5.00; one two horse waggon-L. D. Gaddis for $ 39.00; one set harness-Susanna Allsup for $ 6.00; one black mare four years old-Susanna Allsup for $ 49.00; three year old black mare-Thomas Allsup, Jr., for $ 70.50; one sucking colt-Amos Trowbridge for $ 18.00; one blind sorrel mare-Wm Brown for $ 40.25; twenty-five bushels of wheat at eighty and a half cents per bushel-Jacob Trowbridge for $ 20.12; twenty-six bushels of wheat at eighty-and a half cents per bushel-Jacob Trowbridge for $ 20.93; one third of five acres of corn-Amos Trowbridge for $ .83 1/3; twenty-five bushels of oats at twelve cents per bushel-James Kirby for $ 3.00; and 17 bushels of oats at twelve cents per bushel-James Kirby for $ 2.04.

The description and value of the real estate owned by John W. Allsup follows: 30 acres N ½ of NE ¼ of SW frac of ¼ S 19, Twp 19 N, R 1 E; also 20 acres off E side SE ¼ of NW frac ¼ of S 19, Twp 19 N, R 1 E; also nine acres off W side E ½ of W ½ of SW frac of quarter S 7, Twp 19 N, R 1 E; 3 rd Prime Meridian. Timber land valued at $ 7.00 per acre for a total of $ 63.00. Total value of acreage $ 563.00. Final settlement of the estate was on 25 October 1865, and the heirs received a total of $ 274.26.

Thomas Allsup-Alsup and his son William T. Alsup lived on adjoining farms near Kenney after the son was grown. They apparently experienced a very difficult time in earning a living in agriculture as proven by the following documents:

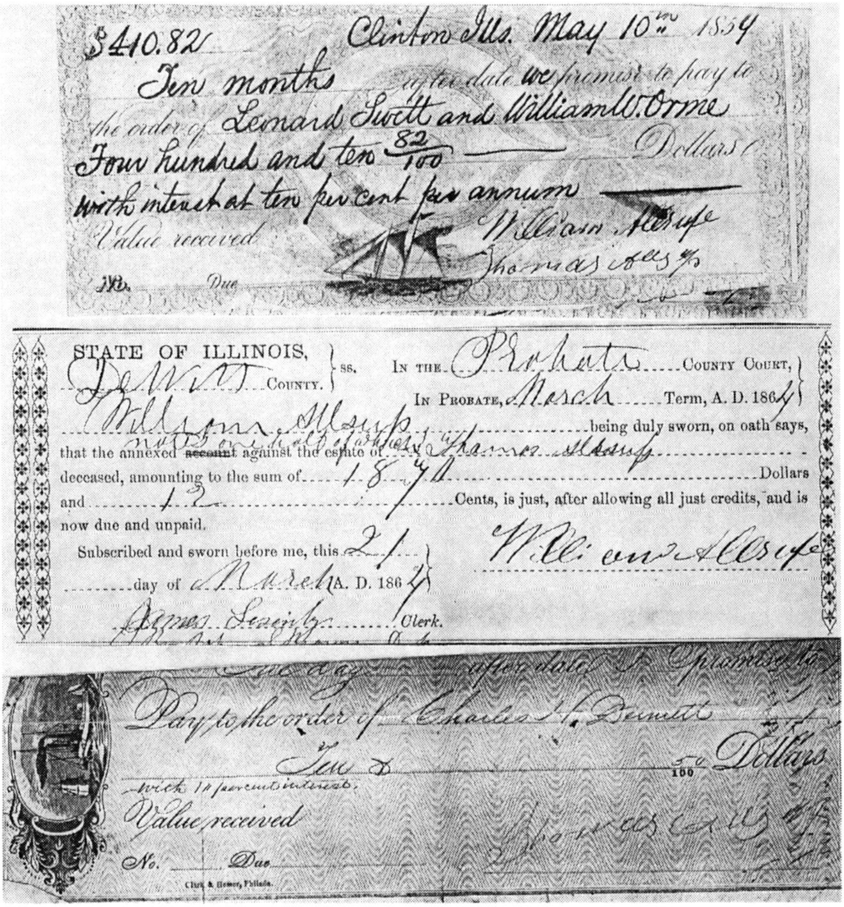
$410.82 Clinton Ills. May 10th 1859

Ten months after date we promise to pay to the order of Leonard Swett and William W. Orme

Four hundred and ten 82/100 Dollars

with interest at ten per cent per annum

Value received William Allsup

Thomas Allsup

No. Due

STATE OF ILLINOIS, DeWitt County. } ss. In the Probate County Court, In Probate, March Term, A. D. 1864

William Allsup being duly sworn, on oath says, that the annexed ~~account~~ against the estate of Thomas Allsup deceased, amounting to the sum of 187 Dollars and 12 Cents, is just, after allowing all just credits, and is now due and unpaid.

Subscribed and sworn before me, this 21 day of March A. D. 1864 William Allsup

James Leavitt Clerk.

One day after date I promise to

Pay to the order of Charles H. Bennett

Ten 50/100 Dollars

with 10 per cent interest

Value received Thomas Allsup

No. Due

Clark & Hemer, Philada.

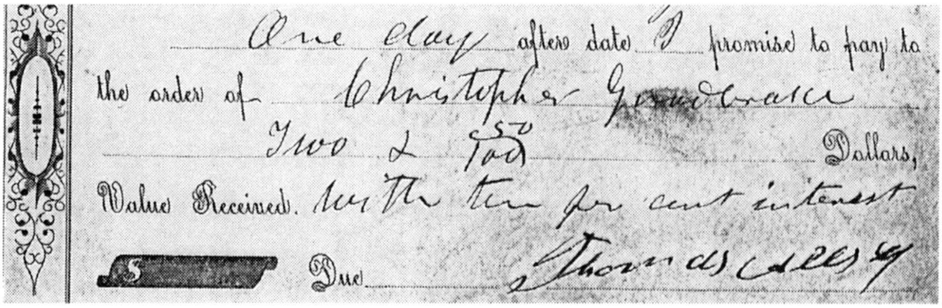
One day after date I promise to pay to the order of Christopher [illegible]
Two & 50/100 Dollars,
Value Received. with ten per cent interest
$ Due Thomas Allsup

The previous notes of indebtedness from either Thomas Alsop-Allsup or his son William were all acquired during the late 1850's or early 1860's when they lived on farms next to each other. William and Thomas borrowed $ 410.82 from Leonard Levett and Wm Orme on 10 May 1859 and also on the same date borrowed $ 1800.00 from Hiram D. Keays.

Thomas died in 1862, at his farm residence but left no will. James A. Kirby, his friend and local J. P. of the Kenney area was his administrator. The petition for letters of administration listed Thomas' living heirs as widow Susanna and children William, Byron F., Thomas G., Jr., Mary Allsup Cass, and Juda Ann Allsup Trowbridge. Probate records prove that Thomas owed $ 1,912.46 at the time of his death. Other debts owed by Thomas and listed by the probate records were (1) owed James A. Lemon $ 44.20 on January 1863 for medicine and attention from 22 December 1861 to 20 June 1862; and (2) coffin for Thomas Allsup, Sr., made by Tidball and Boger for $ 12.00 and charged against the estate on 20 January 1863.

On 26 August 1862, part of the personal property of the estate of Thomas Allsup was sold and an individual list of the items follows: one bedstead to William Allsup for $ .50; five head of hogs to G. W. Butler for $ 3.25; and five head of hogs to Jacob Trowbridge for $ 1.55.

The widow of Thomas Allsup, Susanna Newcomb Allsup, was allowed by law to claim the following articles from his estate: beds $ 15.00; household and kitchen furniture $ 15.00; loom $ 8.00, spinning wheel $ 4.00, cards $ .75, and woman's saddle and bridle $ 15.00; stove $ 10.00; wearing apparel $ 8.00; milch cow $ 20.00; one horse $ 40.00; provision for one year $ 40.50; four sheep and fleeces $ 8.00; stock feed for six months (100 bushels of corn) $ 10.00; fuel for three months $ 3.00; other property $ 60.00; one yearling heifer-brindle with white face $ 10.00; one gray mare $ 60.00; ten head of hogs $ 10.40; twenty-five bushels corn (10 cents per bushel) $ 2.50; twenty-five bushels oats (20 cents per bushel) $ 5.00; cross cut saw $ 3.00; one broad axe $ .50; one spade $. 75; one 17/8 inch auger $ .25; one grubbing hoe $ .25; one cow bell $ .25; one grind stone $ .25; one two horse harrow $ 1.00; and one bedstead $ 3.00. The above items were evaluated at a total of $ 354.40.

James Kirby also petitioned the court of DeWitt Co. for permission to sell the real estate that belonged to Thomas Allsup in order to pay his debts. Some of his land was sold soon after his death but most of it was sold on 15 March 1875, probably after the widow Susanna was deceased. Thomas owned forty acres of land at W ½ of S ½ of lot 1 of N W ¼ of S 19 N, of R 1 E- 3rd P. M. Also E ½ of S ½ of Lot 2 of the N W ¼ of S 19. All of this acreage was bought by Wm C. Humphries for $ 20.00 per acre for a total of $ 800.00.

Thomas Allsup, Sr., and wife Susanna Newcomb Allsup were both buried in the Pleasant Valley Cemetery DeWitt Co., Kenney, Illinois. Also buried in this same cemetery are a number of their children and other relatives.

William T. Allsup and wife Love Randolph had sons Charles, b. 1863, and Frank who were not listed among their children on page 325 of the second volume of "Alsop's Tables." They were probably missing from this list because they were born after the family left DeWitt Co., Illinois for Mapleton, Bourbon Co., Kansas in the early 1860's. William enlisted in the Mexican War and was honorably discharged from Co. "E," 4th Regiment, Illinois Infantry. After William moved to Bourbon Co., Kansas, the state census of 1885 indicates that he remarried to Rachel, maiden name unknown, after his first wife Love died in 1880.

(127) The name of Baron (Byron?) Frank Alsop-Alsup has been discussed in previous volumes of "Alsop's Tables," but it will be examined and the derivation explained according to the information discovered since the last book of this family history was published. The name entered the Alsop family when Jane Newcomb, sister of Susanna Alsop who married Thomas

Alsop, married on 2 Feb. 1826, Baron F. Lowry in Monroe Co., Indiana. When Thomas Alsop and his family moved to DeWitt Co. near Kenney, Baron F. Lowry and his family were already living in the area. Susanna Alsop-Allsup named her third son Baron Frank Alsop after her sister's husband. The 1850 Federal census for DeWitt Co., Illinois has Baron F. Lowry and family living next to Mary Ellen Alsop Cass and husband William. However, Baron Frank Alsop did not seem to like his first name even though it had strong family connections. He evidently utilized his prerogative to use the name that he preferred and thus, was called Byron by one and all after reaching adulthood. I have interviewed present day living direct descendants, and they are all question his being known as Baron.

Ann Maria Fifield-Widow of Byron Frank Alsup-
Born 1831-Died 1885-Photo Made 1879

Family tradition has handed down the story that Byron F. Alsup died during a blizzard in DeWitt Co., Illinois where he and his family were living near Kenney. Byron was in extremely poor health with what was then called "quick consumption." During the blizzard he became much worse and his son Thomas Beniah, age ca. 17 at the time, boarded him on a makeshift stretcher and tried to take him into Kenney to see the doctor. However, Byron died very quickly, and the weather was so bad that Thomas ended up burying his father in the snow behind the house until the family could get to the undertaker with the body.

Oscar and John C. Alsup
-Sons of Byron F.

John C. Alsup, Molly Alsup
Van Atta, Ernest Alsup,
Mrs. Thomas Beniah Alsup,
and friend.

Ellenor "Ellen" Alsup, daughter of Byron F. and Ann Maria Alsup, and husband Emanuel Ensminger, b. 21 May 1838 in Stark, Ohio, son of Henry Ensminger and Maria Moyer, were the parents of Bessie, b. Nov. 1875; Lou, b. April 1877; Phillip, b. Sept. 1878; Frederick, b. Aug. 1886; and Edna, b. March 1891.

Ellen Alsup Between Sisters
Molly and Susie

Thomas B. Alsup-Son of
Byron F. Alsup

John Alsup, son of Byron F. and Ann M. Fifield Alsup, was born in McLean Co., Illinois near Le Roy and married Mary Yocum on 20 Dec. 1894, in the same area. They had a son Charles who was born in 1915, in McLean County. They were listed on the census report of 1900 for McLean Co., Downs Precinct with John's birth date given as Feb. 1867, and his wife Mary's birth as Oct. 1871 in Oregon. In 1910, John and Mary were living in their home in McLean Co. with their two children Adille, 4, and Charles, 2. By 1920, they were living in Hayworth, Illinois in McLean Co. where John was farming, but there were no children in the household. John was residing in Hayworth Village in 1930, but his wife was listed as Anna who had been born in Illinois, so his first wife must have died by this time.

Wesley Alsop, brother of Thomas Alsop who married Susanna Newcomb, and uncle of Byron Frank Alsop-Alsup, was married several times and had a number of children. His first wife Lydia Cooper was the mother of his first four children who were Eleanor "Ellen," Isabelle J., b.

Monroe Co., Indiana, Mary, b. DeWitt Co., Illinois, and Eliza, b. Edgar Co., Illinois. On 18 May 1850, in Vigo Co., Indiana, Wesley married as his second wife Alley Crabile, age 27, with the wedding services held by John Burnam, J. P. Alley had four children by her first husband at the time of her second marriage.

Very little has been learned about the third marriage of Wesley to Louisa Leland, but by 1860, she was living in Cave Creek, Bates Co., Missouri with no husband in the household. She had three children living with her who were Caroline, 11, A. Cora, 7, and Wesley, 4. Records indicate that she also had children as follows: George, b. 1838; John W., b. 1839; Sarah E., b. 1844; and Verlinda, b. 1845. These last four were born in Indiana. The children by Louisa were born in Illinois.

Eliza Allsop married 18 Sept. 1864, in Edgar Co., Illinois John Black with the ceremony being performed by G. R. S. McElfresh, Minister of the Gospel. Records show that she also married Issac Wilson. Mary married William Coppage. Her sister Isabelle J. Allsop married William H. Larimer, on 12 Dec. 1858, in Edgar Co. with the wedding conducted by N. B. Bastion, M. G.

William H. Larimer

Isabelle Alsop Larimer

(128) Thomas Sylvester Alsup was born in DeWitt Co., Illinois and married as his first wife Mary, maiden name not yet known, who was born in 1846. Thomas and Mary Alsup were the parents of Ida, b. 1862, Frank, b. 1866, and Mary b. 1869. It is unknown what happened to Mary, his first wife, but on 1 October 1865 (?), Thomas married as his second wife Mrs. Sarah Huffmann in DeWitt Co. Their first child was Amos B. Alsup. What happened to Amos and to the other two children that Thomas S. and his two wives produced is not known at this time.

(129) William W. Alsup was the son of John B. Alsop-Allsup and wife Mary McDonald and John B. was the son of John Alsop and wife Eleanor "Nelly" Wren. John and Eleanor Wren Alsop and family moved to Monroe Co., Indiana prior to 1820 where they lived near the small town of Ellettsville. When they crossed the Ohio River, John Alsop freed his slaves. Family tradition says that the slaves followed at a distance and made camp at night when the Alsops did. Whether they followed them all the way to Ellettsville, Indiana is not known. There, one of John and Eleanor's sons John (Baynard?) Alsop (the marriage license spelled the name "Allsup"), born 14 January 1814, met and married Mary Ann McDonald, a daughter of William McDonald, who had moved with his family to Clay Township, Owen Co., Indiana about the same time.

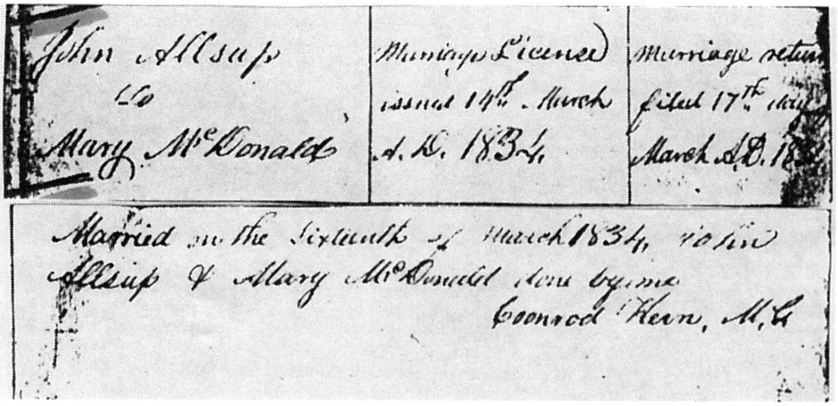
John Allsup
to
Mary McDonald

Marriage License
issued 14th. March
A.D. 1834

Marriage return
filed 17th day
March A.D. 18[illegible]

Married on the Sixteenth of March 1834, John
Allsup & Mary McDonald done by me
Conrad Kern, M.G

William McDonald, Jr., married Ruthy McFadden in Bracken County, Kentucky on 27 May 1812, with the license being taken out two days earlier in Maysville, Mason Co. which borders Bracken Co. on the east. William McDonald, Jr. was the father of Mary Ann McDonald Allsup and the son of William McDonald, Sr., and wife Charity MacFaden who were married in Maysville, Kentucky on 20 Jan. 1791. William McDonald, Sr., fought in the Revolutionary War, enlisting on 10 April 1775.

William McDonald, Jr., purchased 160 acres of government land in Clay Twp., Owen County, Indiana on 5 May 1818, He and his family plus his parents moved from Mason Co., Kentucky to Indiana just before the "Panic of 1819." There, along with three other prominent families, he settled in an area of almost unbroken wilderness. The Stansberys, the Ellets, and the Gilberts joined the McDonalds as land owners who were relatively wealthy and exhibited aristocratic pride and honest hard-working attitudes in their daily life. The first graveyard was started on the McDonald farm, and William, Jr., was an early township officer and also served two terms as a Justice of the Peace.

Nine daughters were born to William and Ruthy McDonald; four of them before leaving Kentucky and the other five after their arrival in Indiana. The children in addition to Mary Ann were: Sarah Ann "Sally" , married Andrew W. Reeves on 20 March 1832; Eliza Ellen, married William R. Reeves on 11 Sept. 1834; Charity, married Joel A. Coffey on 12 Dec. 1847; Harriet Newell, married Wiley H. Coffey on 10 Jan. 1849; Elizabeth, married John J. Cooper on 10 Oct. 1839; Nancy, married Henry M. Cooper on 1 Jan. 1844; Matilda, married Zephaniah Dowden on 25 July 1844; and Martha J., married William H. Dowden on 21 Sept. 1845.

Zephaniah Dowden and his brother William Harrod Dowden were born in Jackson Co., Indiana to Zachariah and Catherine Herrod Dowden. Zachariah was born ca. 1794, in North Carolina and Catherine ca. 1797, in Kentucky, and they were married 28 May 1817, in Jackson Co., Indiana. Zachariah had an older brother named Zephaniah Dowden, so it should not be surprising that this name was handed down in the Allsup family by Mary Ann McDonald Allsup. The photo below shows Mary Ann in her later years.

John B. Allsup-Alsip was named the administrator of his father, John Alsop, who died in August 1838, (day not given) according to a document of Macon Co., Illinois dated 1 October 1838. This same record relates that John Alsop died intestate with personal property which needed to be collected and processed by the administrator to those who had a legal right or interest therein. John B. was authorized to carry out the necessary procedures of distributing property and collecting debts as required of him by law. On the 20th day of October 1838, John B. Allsup, administrator of his father's estate, held an auction at the late residence of the said Allsup between the hours of 10 A. M. and 5 P. M. The following items, which had been inventoried a few days earlier, were sold at the family auction: one broad axe-Thomas Allsup for $ 3.00; one drawing knife-Lewis Jackson for $ .50; one matock-Thomas Allsup for $ 1.00; one plow-Eleanor Allsup for $ 1.00; one yoke of oxen-John B. Allsup for $ 22.00; one yoke of oxen-Melven Lowery for $ 60.00; one log chain-Obadiah Hooper for $ 3.00;

one pair of streachers-Eleanor Allsup for $ 1.50; one pair of gears-John B. Allsup for $ 2.50; one clock-Verlinda Allsup for $ 4.00; one saddle-Tolbert Allsup for $ 7.25; one colt-Thomas Allsup for $ 12.25; six sheep-Eleanor Allsup for $ 3.00; one waggon-Eleanor Allsup for $ 67.12 ½.

The inventory and appraisal of the estate of John Allsup by his son John B. Allsup, Jr., is shown next: one colt $ 10.00; one bed and bedding $ 10.00; one table $ 4.00; six chairs $ 2.50; cubbert ware and looking glass $ 10.00; one lot of palmettae $ 8.00; one clock $ 10.00; one man's saddle $ 7.00; one pair of gears $ 3.00; one pair of strechers $ 3.00; one broad axe and one drawing knife $ 3.00; six head of sheep $ 6.00; one waggon and hand gear $ 65.00; one large yoke of steers $ 65.00; one small yoke of oxen $ 30.00; one muley cow $ 12.00; one dunn mare $ 50.00; two wheat shocks $ 12.00; one log chain $ 3.00; twelve acres of corn $ 72.00; and one plow $ 3.00.

John B. Allsup, Jr., son of John and Eleanor Wren Alsop, was appointed by the Macon Co. Court to handle the estate of his father. In the probate record of Macon Co. dated 29 October 1840, John B. Allsup, Jr., listed the legal heirs of his father as the widow Eleanor, children James, Thomas, Verlinda, Wesley, Eliza Allsup daughter of Eliza Allsup and granddaughter of John, deceased, Washington, Tolbert, and the affiant John B. Allsup, Jr.

All of the children of John and Eleanor "Nelly" Wren Alsop have been pretty thoroughly narrated in this family history, but very little information has ever been found on William Allsup, son of John and Eleanor Wren Alsop. He was reported, along with his brothers, on the 1840 tax list of Clinton Precinct, DeWitt Co., Illinois proving that he was living in that area. It has also been determined that he was born in Kentucky ca. 1813, and married Elisha, place unknown, b. ca. 1813, in Kentucky. They were the parents of George, b. 1838 in Indiana; John W., b. 1839 in Indiana; Sarah E., b. 1844 in Indiana; and Verlinda E., b. 1845 in Indiana.

On 1 June 1848, John Alsop, assignee of Thomas Hutchin, was granted by the United States the South West Quarter of Section Twenty-Five in Township Nineteen North, of Range One East, in the District of Lands subject to sale at Danville, Illinois containing one hundred and sixty acres in DeWitt Co., Illinois. This land patent was signed by President of the United States James K. Polk. Thomas Hutchin a private of Captain Newcomb's Company, Fourth Regiment, Illinois Volunteers, having deposited in the General Land Office a warrant in his favor numbered 10,391 did assign this warrant to John Alsop. This John Alsop was John B. Allsup-Alsip who was the son of John Alsop and Eleanor Wren Alsop.

Family tradition has handed down the story about the death of John B. Allsup-Alsip in a detailed fashion, but how true it is can be open to conjecture. According to Allsup-Alsip historical legend, John B. Alsip fell from his horse and hit his head on the rail of a horse tank which broke his neck. A broken neck at that time in our country's medical history meant almost certain death. John B. was well known in the community for his ability to imbibe large quantities of spirits and, it was probably this condition that was at least partly responsible for his fall from his horse and his almost immediate death. The following obituary appeared in the "Champaign Co. Gazette" on Wednesday 22 Dec. 1880, with the date of the decease of John B. Alsip being 18 December 1880.

> FATAL FALL.-Last Saturday, John B. Alsip, a respected farmer, aged 69 years, who lives near Leverett, in Somer, fell on the ice while watering his horses and dislocated his neck, from the effects of which he died almost instantly. Coroner Buch held an inquest and the jury returned a verdict in accordance with the above fact. Mr. Alsip was buried in Mt. Hope Cemetery on Monday, a large number of his neighbors testifying their respect by following his remains to the grave.

After the death of her husband John B. Alsip, Mary McDonald Alsip, born in Indiana 7 April 1817, made her home with her youngest son Zephaniah Dowden Alsip at or near Ogden, Illinois in Champaign Co. where she was a member of the Ogden Methodist Church. The exact date of death of Mary McDonald Alsip is unknown, but she was buried in Mt. Hope Cemetery next to her husband.

Mt. Hope Cemetery Burials and Marker Inscriptions-24 November 1997 (cemetery founded 25 October 1856)

LAST NAME, GIVEN NAME	BORN & SOURCE	DIED & SOURCE	INTERRED	SE	BK	R
Alsip, John B.	14 Jan 1814-CALC	18 Dec 1880-DAR	20 Dec 1880	BB	5	2
Alsip, Jesse L.	1883-DAR	1949-DAR	28 Aug 1949	MH	22	4
Alsip, Jessie Edward	21 Apr 1924			MH	20	43
Alsip, John F.	1879-DAR	1950-DAR	5 Mar 1950	MH	22	4
Alsip, Laura Pauline	13 Aug 1848-DAR	25 Jan 1925-DAR	28 Jan 1925	MH	23	47
Alsip, Marietta	3 Oct 1846-CALC	5 Jan 1865-DAR	7 Jan 1865	BB	5	2
Alsip, Mary Ann				BB	5	2

John B. Allsup-Alsip and Wife Mary McDonald Allsup-Alsip

Verlinda B. Allsup-Alsip, b. 4 January 1834, was the first child of John B. Allsup-Alsip and wife Mary McDonald Allsup-Alsip and married on 30 October 1851, John Cross in DeWitt Co., Illinois as found in M. B. "A," page 90. The 1870 census record for DeWitt Co., P. O. Clinton, reports the household of John Cross, 46, farmer, as containing wife Verlinda B., 36, and child Frankie W., 1 year of age. By 1880, John and Verlinda B. Cross were living in Ogden, Champaign Co. with their two children John F., 11, and Corry E., 8.

There was another Verlinda Alsop-Allsup, the daughter of John and Eleanor Wren Alsop who was born ca. 1812, who was incorrectly identified in the first volume of "Alsop's Tables," page 179 as the wife of Harden Tolbert Alsop. Also in the same volume on page 210, Verlinda is erroneously identified as the wife of Tolbert who was actually her brother. This sister of John B. Allsup and wife Mary Ann McDonald was listed on the census of 1850 for Sangamon Co., Illinois as the wife of Clement Clifton, 54, with their marriage having taken place on 5 October 1848. Clement had first married Nancy Martin, who died in 1845, and then he married Mrs. Sarah Williams, nee Huckleberry, and they had one child Elias. Sarah died 1846, and her son Elias died 3 Jan. 1853. Verlinda Alsop Clifton died in 1855 and her husband in 1857.

Harriet Jane Allsup-Alsop, sibling of Verlinda and daughter of John B., was born 7 November 1835, and she and husband Andrew Jackson Clifton, son of George and Betsy Price Clifton, were the progenitors of Verlinda, ca. 1858; Laura Ann, ca. 1859; Matilda, ca. 1862; George Andrew, 28 Feb. 1864, married Evaline Matilda Hedges in Homer, Vermillion Co. on 8 July 1886, d. 4 Feb. 1942, at Spencer, Clay Co., Iowa; Margaret, 11 Nov. 1866, married Washington Taylor Hedges on 28 March 1881, d. ca. 1927; Ada, ca. 1870; John Oscar, ca. 1871; Mary, ca. 1874; and Charity, ca. 1876. On 18 September 1868, Andrew and wife Harriet Jane Allsup Clifton sold to her uncle, Washington T. Allsup, for $ 1,250.00 a tract of farm land described as N W ¼ of the S E ¼ of Section twenty-nine, of Twp nineteen, N of R 2 E of the 3rd P. M. in DeWitt Co., Illinois. This land was sold to Harriet Jane's father's brother with the condition that she and her family could still harvest the crop now standing and growing on the land previously described. She and her husband also exempted from the sale one acre of land in the S E corner of the involved tract.

John B. and wife Mary McDonald Allsup-Alsip had other daughters who were Margaret Anne, b. 16 October 1847; Mary Ellen, b. 2 April 1850; and Charity, b. 22 December 1853. The two older sisters were living with their parents at home when the census reports of 1850-60 were completed. The youngest sister Charity was enumerated in the John B. Allsup household in 1860 and died in 1869, before the next census was taken. Margaret Anne died in 1865, and both are believed to have been buried in the Mt. Hope Cemetery. Mary Ellen was living with her parents when the 1870 census was recorded and married Beynard "Doc" Pettyjohn, although they never had any children.

Harden Thomas "Richard" Allsup-Alsip, b. 14 February 1845, in Kenney, DeWitt Co., was the son of John B. Allsup-Alsip and wife Mary McDonald Allsup. Charlotte Minerva Stringfield, b. ca. 1850, and died November 1880, as she was experiencing the birth of her last child Herbert, was the first wife of Richard. Richard married Laura Pauline Baldwin Sherman, b. 13 August 1848, in Ohio, as his next wife. Richard died 5 January 1908, and was buried in the Mt. Hope Cemetery three days later. His last wife Pauline died 25 January 1925, and was buried next to her husband Richard in Mt. Hope Cemetery.

Their son, Roy Waldo Alsip, b. 26 Feb. 1889, was reported in the 1930 census as living with his wife Gertrude Lee Baker (West) b. 28 May 1886, in Danville, Vermillion Co., Illinois. They were married in Champaign Co., Champaign, Illinois in 1914, which was the birth place of Roy. Gertrude died in Champaign on 19 August 1952, and was buried three days later in Roselawn Cemetery in that city. Roy died 26 Feb. 1969, and was buried next to his wife. He began service with the Champaign Fire Department on 6 June 1906, at age 17, and was appointed "Chief" on 1 October 1940. Roy retired 1 September 1951 after 45 years of service. During his working years he was elected secretary of the Illinois Firemen's Association in 1918 and served until 1964. He established the first Fire College at the University of Illinois in 1925.

John Fletcher Allsup, b. 4 August 1840, in DeWitt Co., Illinois near the town of Kenney, the son of John B. and wife Mary McDonald Allsup-Alsip, was mistakenly given the middle name of Franklin in the second volume of "Alsop's Tables," page 250. John F. married on 7 April 1864, Cordelia Swiger, born 4 November 1844, and they were the parents of Mary May, b. 1867; Grace D., b. Feb. 1874; Herbert Swiger, b. 21 Nov. 1880; Hattie, died at 15 months; and Hamilton, d. at age of 8 years. John Fletcher died 10 June 1920 and his wife Cordelia died 29 January 1922.

Grace D. Alsip was born in DeWitt Co. and married after 1920, in Decatur, Macon Co., Illinois William J. Hiller. Grace died after 1932. Her sister Mary May was born in DeWitt Co., married (1) 20 Nov. 1884, in Champaign Co., Illinois James McElwee, and (2) George Grimes before 1932. The children of Mary May and James McElwee were Pearl and Madeline "Madge" who married Marion Roberts.

Herbert Swiger Alsop-Alsip was born at Delavan, Tazewell Co., Illinois and married on 27 September 1908 in Lovington, Moultrie Co., Illinois, Julia Evelyn Potts, daughter of Philip Bennett Potts and Catherine Melissa Huss. Herbert died after 1932, and was buried in Cerro Gordo, Piatt Co., Illinois as was his wife Julia. Herbert graduated from the University of Illinois Dental School in 1905 and established the first practice in Lovington. Herbert and Julia raised two children who were Katherine, b. 30 May 1910, and Janet Elizabeth, b. 27 August 1915. Katherine married William Robert Moore and had Stephen Michael and Thomas Sean, while her sister Janet Elizabeth married Howard R. Newcomb, Jr., and their children were Howard, III, David, and Nancy. Stephen Michael Moore married Suzanne McCulloch and they were the parents of Melissa and Jason.

Zephaniah Dowden Allsup-Alsip, son of John B. and wife Mary M. Allsup-Alsip, married Eliza Ellen Woodrum who was born in Green Co., Iowa, the daughter of Louis and Susan Albright. Louis was born in Putnam Co., Indiana and lived in Iowa and them moved back to Indiana where he was mustered into military service on 15 July 1863, at Indianapolis. He wrote a letter home on the 13th of July during the process of joining the Union army and described his health as excellent. On 26 July 1863, after serving only eleven days after mustering in he died of dysentery.

The farm that Zeph and Eliza Ellen bought was swampy and poorly drained. However, Zeph and his family set up drainage districts, and oxen hitched to capstans were used to pull huge "V" plows to form drainage ditches. After the land had been drained, rich, dark fertile soil was the result. Zephaniah's judgment in purchasing swampy land was questioned by some of the local residents, but later on, his grandchildren thought that his judgment had been fully justified and wished that he had invested in more of the worthless, swampy land.

An opportunity arose once for Zeph to buy additional farm land in Mayview, Illinois. His sorrel mare "Patty" was so old and so slow that someone else bought the land before he could arrive at the land site. He was sure that he had miss the chance of a lifetime until shortly thereafter, a serious economic recession occurred and farm prices declined drastically. It was immediately apparent that Patty had saved Zeph from financial ruin including the loss of all of his other land, and to show his appreciation when Patty died, he buried her in a prime location in the pasture where she had spent her final years after she was too old for farm work. Another incident remembered by Zeph and his progeny was the time a very thirsty oxen team pulled the work wagon with driver and farm laborers right into the river because they didn't give the men time to remove the yoke. No amount of dissuasion kept the situation from happening, and the oxen refused to leave the river for the bank until they had completely quenched their thirst.

Zepheniah Dowden Allsup-Alsip- father of John Franklin Alsip and grandfather of John F. Alsip

Eliza Ellen Woodrum and husband Zepheniah Alsip were buried next to each other in the Mt. Hope Cemetery with Eliza dying on 21 March 1936, and the burial taking place on 23 March 1936. Zeph died on 1 July 1933, twenty-five years after the death of his brother Richard whose grave site was nearby.

Effie Rosella, first child of Zepheniah and Eliza Ellen Alsip moved to State Line, Indiana and lived the rest of her life there with her husband Gus Hendricks. The road that ran along in front of their house was the dividing line between Indiana and Illinois. Effie died 18 July 1946.

Jesse Lewis Alsip lived on a farm that he purchased from his father Zepheniah. It was located about a mile west of Zeph and Eliza's home place and the first house east of his brother John "Frank" Alsip. He died 26 August 1949, and was buried in the Mt. Hope Cemetery which was started on 25 October 1856.

Elsie Pearl Alsip died 20 February 1960, and was buried in the Mt. Hope Cemetery. Her brother Chester Preston Alsip lived his whole life at the home place of his parents and died of a heart attack at the age of fifty-two. He was buried in the Mt. Hope Cemetery on 3 August 1949, two days after his death. Although he never married, Chester was the father of a boy and a girl who were later put up for adoption.

The oldest son of Zeph and Eliza was John Franklin Alsop who seldom used his first name and was usually known as "Frank." Frank farmed one of his father Zeph's farms and also helped operate Z. D.'s oats threshing machine and corn sheller. Frank's specific duty was to operate the steam engine that powered the two machines. Frank, Sr., also taught at a country school near Royal, Illinois known as Pleasant Valley School, although he only had the schooling that he was able to obtain in the Ogden area. After he quit farming, Frank cut meat at the William Hiller Meat Market in Ogden for a number of years.

I visited John Franklin Alsip, Jr., his wife, two sons James and Jeff and daughter Jane in Onarga, Illinois a few years ago, and he most generously supplied most of the detailed information on Z. D. Alsip and descendants. He and his wife Betty researched his specific branch of the family tree and wrote a fifteen page summary of their findings. This valuable document has saved many historical facts on this particular lineage. John Franklin, Jr., also told me about some of the memories of his boyhood days. He said that he and his brothers spent many a long day threshing oats and shelling corn. He said that they developed a love for that old steam engine which they called "Abe." John Frank remembered as a youngster what a fine day it was when he would see the old steamer come smoking up the road to thresh at his family's farm. John F. told me that his father John Frank, Sr., died of heart complications and his mother Etta Carrie died exactly two years to the day later. She was born in 1877, died 5 March 1952, and was buried next to her husband in Mt. Hope Cemetery on the same plot with Chester, Jesse, Elsie, Zepheniah, and Eliza Ellen Alsip.

John Franklin Alsip, Jr., was the last of twelve children and was named after his father at the request and suggestion of his older sisters. He attended Hickory Grove and Ogden Grade Schools and graduated from Ogden High

School. He was in the U. S. Air Force during World War II, having served in Germany, France, England, and Belgium with discharge in January 1945. He graduated from the University of Illinois, College of Agriculture in 1951, and then taught Vocational Agriculture in Paxton, Illinois for a semester. He was sales supervisor or managed Farm Supply companies in several Illinois counties before moving to Onarga on Labor Day 1960. There he worked for the Illinois Department of Agriculture until he retired in 1985.

William W. Allsup-Alsip, b. 4 November 1842, was the son of John B. and wife Mary McDonald Allsup-Alsip, and grandson of John and Eleanor Wren Alsop with the birth date being a correction of the one given in an earlier volume of this family genealogy. He served as a private in the Civil War and official records show that he deserted on 1 September 1862. William married on 18 November 1878, in Henry County, Missouri to Middie Lutticie Phelps, b. 4 January 1858, in Illinois, daughter of William Richard Phelps and Sarah May Bridges. In 1887, William and Middie Alsip moved from Sedalia, Pettis County, Missouri to Ft. Scott, Bourbon County, Kansas with their two sons.

William W. Alsip-Son of John B. Allsup-Alsip
and Wife Mary Ann McDonald Alsip

William W. Alsip, who worked for the railroad, was killed in a railroad accident on 4 October 1893, in Fort Scott, Bourbon County, Kansas and was buried in Evergreen Cemetery. His wife Middie Lutticie Alsip died 7 July 1910, in Tacoma, Washington and was buried in Fort Scott, Kansas. Much of this information plus additional data on later descendants of William W. and Middie L. Alsip was sent to me by John Franklin Alsip, great-grandson of William W. Alsip.

(130) The birth of Warner O. Allsup, son of Washington T. and Margaret H. Allsup, occurred on 18 July 1858, and he lived his entire life in either DeWitt, the location of his birth, or Macon Counties, Illinois. Margaret Havely, mother of Warner and his brother and two sisters, was the daughter of Samuel D. Havely, farmer of Cerro Gordo in Piatt Co, Illinois who had been born in 1800 in Pennsylvania. Sam moved to Ohio next where he married Elizabeth Wiley in 1826, and then to Piatt Co. by 1837. Elizabeth died in 1850 leaving four children of which Margaret had married Washington Allsup three years earlier, and they were living in Maroa, in Macon Co.

Washington T. Allsup and wife Margaret, in addition to four children who reached adulthood, had three children who died in their infancy. They are all buried in the Maroa Cemetery next to their parents. The children were Loretta, William J., and Sarah L. They all have small stones, but no dates. On 3 January 1881, four years after the death of her first husband, Margaret married Lorenzo Hobbs in Macon Co.

Warner Allsup, like his father, was interested in acquiring as much farm land as possible. His father Washington T. Allsup was very wealthy due mostly to his ability and interest in owning real estate. On the day that Washington died, he bought his wife Margaret sixty acres of land near Maroa. The two sons of Washington and Margaret were Warner and Minor R. with this second son being named for his mother's brother Minor Havely. Minor Allsup was one of the heirs of Washington and on 18 March 1879, the court records of DeWitt and Macon Counties show that he inherited land described as SE-S29-Twp 19, R 2, NE-S32, Twp 19, R 2, SE SE S 20, Twp 19, R 2. This land was evaluated at $ 600.00 with Margaret Allsup, Minor's mother as his guardian. The death record of Minor is found in Bk. 10, page 253, Macon County.

The "Decatur Herald" dated Tuesday Evening, 18 September 1928, presented an article that informed its readers that Warner Allsup, executor and also trustee of the estate of Minor R. Allsup, had asked the circuit court to clear the title of the Allsup estate which indicated that some of the heirs of Minor had involved the title by assignments of interest. At the time of the death of Minor Allsup in 1919, he owned 5,650 acres of farm land in Macon and DeWitt Counties, Washington, Texas, and Canada. The assignments of interest or execution of mortgages of the trust estate by grandchildren of the testator created the clouding of the title. Grandchildren of Minor Allsup mentioned in the article were Harold M., Orval, and Tuffolia Allsup Butler. A second article in the same newspaper dated Tuesday Evening, 17 September 1929, related that Warner O. Allsup, 71, of Maroa had been adjudged insane by a commission sitting in Maroa on Monday morning. He was taken to the hospital for the insane in Jacksonville later in the day. Nervous strain brought on by his handling of his estate evaluated at over $ 100,000.00 as well as operating a grain business, managing large landholdings and looking after other personal property are thought to have brought on his derangement. The petition for examination was filed by Warner's wife Mrs. Alice Belle Davis Allsup.

On Monday evening, 17 February 1930, The "Decatur Herald" reported that the administrator of the Warner Allsup estate would prepare his final report as trustee of the Minor Allsup estate. Arthur C. Ammann, new trustee of the Minor Allsup estate has filed an inventory of this estate following his appointment. This final inventory shows the Minor Allsup estate to consist of 1,430 acres of land in Macon Co., 760 acres of land in DeWitt Co., 674 acres on Texas, and 880 acres in Canada. Other real estate consists of lots and other business properties in Maroa, some of which have accumulated rentals due over a period of years. Personal notes and liberty loans total about $ 83,000.00 plus bank deposits of ca. $ 11,000.00 and grain and farming equipment complete the inventory. No dispute is expected among the heirs of the two estates as they are largely identical.

Two other newspaper articles from the "Decatur Herald" have been discovered with the first one having a date of Friday Evening, 4 July 1930. The land inventoried as part of the estate of Warner Allsup, according to this article, will not have to be sold or distributed by the circuit court of Macon Co. The estate consisted of 500 acres of land in Macon and DeWitt Counties and $ 65,000.00 in personal property. Alice Belle Allsup filed a petition in court soon after the death of her husband to take a dower interest instead of an absolute one-third undivided interest in her husband's real estate. She then transferred her entire interest in the estate to her children and grandchildren by means of a quit claim deed which divided the estate in proportion to the interest held by the heirs as their distributive shares of the entire estate. As a result of this transfer, each child of Warner received a one-fifth share of the estate which became the absolute property of the four children and the other one-fifth share was divided among the three grandchildren, children of Warner's deceased son Fred Allsup.

The second and later article verified that the land of Warner had been fairly distributed. All of the land was located in Texas Twp., DeWitt Co., except for 80 acres which was in Maroa Twp., Macon Co. The division was as follows: Orvil-160 acres; Mrs. George Butler-160; Mrs. B. F. Caplinger-160 acres; Mrs. G. T. Smart-160 acres; and the grandsons Harold, Dwight, and Roy each received one-third of the one-fifth 160 acre share.

(131) Washington Thomas Allsup, son of Hardin Tolbert Allsup and wife Emily Davenport, was reported as either the son of Hardin Thomas Allsup or Hardin Tolbert Allsup in the first two volumes of "Alsop's Tables." Washington T. Allsup's father has been proven to be Hardin Tolbert Allsup and not Hardin Thomas Allsup. Harden Tolbert Allsup-Alsop was a son of John and Eleanor Wren Alsop, and additional genealogical information indicates that John and Eleanor did not have a son named Hardin Thomas Allsup-Alsop. Washington T. Alsup married Minerva Jacobs in Jackson Co., Missouri on 16 May 1869, and they were in Pulaski Co., Illinois by ca. 1872. At some time after 1880, Washington and wife and three boys moved from Pulaski Co. across the county line into Alexander Co. where Minerva Jacobs Alsup died prior to 1892. No information has been found concerning the death of Minerva or the exact date.

The court records of Alexander Co., county seat Cairo, reveal that W. T. Alsup and wife obtained from Con Maubry and I. C. D. on 5 May 1898, for

$ 125.00, at Sandusky, Freezes 2nd Addition, Lots 3 and 4, in Block 5. This is recorded in Deed Book 33, page 536. Sandusky is a small town located in central Alexander Co. just south of Elco and Tamms and about three or four miles southwest of Ullin which is in Pulaski Co. The wife listed in this deed would be Victoria "Victor" Hugo McRaven who was the second wife of Washington Alsup. Victor had also been previously married as the Alexander Co. marriage records contain in Bk. "F", page 269, the marriage of Victa H. McRaven to Marshall Augustine on 8 March 1887.

Washington T. and family have not been found on the 1900 census enumeration. After last being documented in Alexander Co. in 1898, Washington and wife next moved to New Madrid Co., Missouri, although it is unknown if any of his children moved to Missouri with them. Their next move to Scott Co., Missouri was to provide the location of their residence for the rest of their lives. Living in the Alsup household in 1910 with Washington and wife Victor were her mother Elizabeth Daniel McRaven, and Victor's brother John F. McRaven. Elizabeth was widowed after marrying Thomas G. McRaven, and they were the parents of Belle, b. 1862; Victoria Hugo, b. 1868, and John F., b. 1875.

Belle McRaven, sister of Victoria Hugo McRaven Alsup, married Joseph Bouschard on 12 December 1885, in Alexander Co., Illinois as found in M. B. "F", page 249. They had a son Thomas Bernard Bushard, b. 16 August 1886, in Miner's Switch, Missouri, Scott Co. who was raised by his grandmother Elizabeth after his mother Belle died as a young adult. The Bushards, before and after the death of Belle, enjoyed visiting the Alsup family who lived near them in Chaffee, Missouri. Eugene Bushard, present day descendant of Belle, remembers his father's Aunt "Hu" and Uncle Tom from visits to the Alsup home when he was about eight or ten years old. One thing that he was curious about was why his great-uncle Washington Thomas Alsup had a wooden leg. He told his niece Lonna Baugher that he remembered the leg was wooden from the knee on down. Although Washington Thomas fought in the Civil War, the grandchildren knew that his leg injury came late in life. He also was impressed that his great-uncle Tom was retired and in his spare time, made money by owning the first "hot air popcorn popper in Chaffee or probably in the whole state.

Victoria Hugo McRaven Alsup was the daughter of Thomas G. McRaven, and her father was an avid reader and a fan of the works of Victor Hugo. He planned for a boy when Victoria was born, but he still used a form of the name of his favorite writer when this child was a girl. She was usually called "Victor."

About 1920, the Bushards (Lonna Baugher's grandparents and their oldest three children) moved out of the city limits of Chaffee to a dairy farm, but their regular visits to the Alsup residence continued for some time. The dairy farm was located next to the Union Park Cemetery, just to the east of the Chaffee city limits. Lonna, who provided most of the information on her relatives, said that her uncles had bicycles equipped with special devices to carry a large number of milk bottles so that they could deliver all of the milk prepared for sale by her grandfather for customers living in Chaffee or surroundings areas.

(132) John Franklin Allsup-Alsup, son of Hardin Tolbert Allsup and wife Emily Davenport, had a daughter Jane, b. 1855.who married William Scott in 1880, location unknown. She was born in DeWitt Co., Illinois, but nothing is yet known about her death. Pictured below are John Franklin Allsup's son George and great-grandson James F. Allsup.

George Thomas Allsup (1884-1962)

James Francis Allsup (Born 1953)

(133) Hardin Tolbert (Pony) Allsup, son of Hardin Tolbert Allsup and wife Emily Davenport, was incorrectly listed as the son of Hardin Thomas Allsup in the second volume of Alsop's Tables on page 332. The descendants of Hardin T. "Pony" Allsup spelled their surname with either one "L" or two "L's," and both spellings are commonly found in the present generation. Mary Allsup, daughter of Hardin Tolbert and wife Emily Davenport and sister of Hardin Tolbert "Pony" Allsup, was married to Milford W. Walker on 29 June 1876, when she was only sixteen years of age. The record of the marriage is to be found in the Macon Co., Illinois court records, M. B. "A," page 58.

(Individuals numbered 134, 135, 136, 137,138, and 139 were omitted in Alsop's Tables, Volume II, Chapter XVI, which was entitled "The George Alsop Family." They will now be described in as much detail as present research will allow.)

134. John[7] J. Alsop (George,[6] Samuel,[5] John,[4] William ,[3] George,[2] George[1])was the oldest child of George and Lucy Strother Alsop, and he was born in Caroline Co., Va. on 8 April 1787. He grew to manhood at his parents' residence in Caroline Co. called "Glen Mary." John was a member of Captain William F. Gray's Co., 30th Regiment, Virginia Militia, Caroline Co., during part of the year of 1813. From 22 July 1814, to 17 August 1814, John served in the Virginia Militia, Co. A. (Lieut. Benjamin Clark's Co. of Infantry), 16th Regiment, as a private with his rate of pay being 8 dollars per month. From 29 August 1814, to 22 September 1814, he was a mattross in Captain William F. Gray's Co. of Artillery (Co. "A"), 16th Regiment commanded by Lt. Colonel Aylett Waller. John Alsop entered the service, which took place during the War of 1812, at Camp Selden near Fredericksburg, Va.

After his return home from the war, John J. lived at home with his family and helped his father with the operation of the extensive land holdings, most of it used for farming. John married as his first wife on 18 December 1817, Elizabeth Hampton Jones who died the following year. John then married Mary "Polly" Purvis Leavell, b. 10 September 1801, the daughter of Burwell Leavell and his first wife Mary Purvis who are buried in the Leavell Cemetery in Spotsylvania Co., Va. As a wedding gift, the ceremony took place on 23 December 1819, George and Lucy S. Alsop gave their son and daughter-in-law the brick mansion "LaVue" which was thoroughly described in Vol. I, Alsop's Tables, page 265. John J. Alsop, known by everyone as "Captain Jack" and his wife Polly lived their entire lives at "LaVue," and it was there that their seven children were born.

"Capt. Jack" was a very successful business man and farmer, as he was able to add substantial amounts of land to his estate during his lifetime. "Eastern View," located on Route 608 near the Richmond, Fredericksburg, and Potomac R.R. at Massaponax Creek, was a part of the "LaVue" residence of John Alsop. Part of "Eastern View" became a Pratt property in 1842. It was sold to Musterfield Sand and Gravel Co. in 1912, and then to Massaponax Sand and Gravel Co. A 150 acre tract of "LaVue" was sold to the Richmond, Fredericksburg, and Potomac R.R. in 1975. "Hunter's Lodge" was also a part of "Captain Jack's" land which was located on Route 608 near the Richmond, Fredericksburg and Petersburg R.R. adjoining a part of "LaVue."

"LaVue," built by George Alsop on some of his Spotsylvania land, was officially bequeathed to John his son, along with 337 acres in 1839, which was the year that George died.

Three years after John and Polly Alsop established their residence at "LaVue," they were taxed (1822) on seventy acres of land at $.28, seven slaves and three horses at $4.11-1/2, seven levies at $5.11, and overseer of the poor at $3.90 for a total tax amount of $13.40-1 /2. Deed Book "Y", p. 256, Spotsylvania Co., Va., dated 6 October 1823, records the sale of real estate, as required by the will of Daniel Starke which was advertised by Hugh Mercer, sheriff of Spotsylvania Co., and 100 acres of it as sold on 10 September 1823 at public sale to John "Capt. Jack" Alsop and Henry F. Phillips at the price of $1.70 per acre. The land was bound by acreage owned by James Owens and Mr. Bullock. Other property obtained during his residency at "LaVue" by Captain Jack were the present day farms of "Redfield," which was a 169 acre tract adjoining "LaVue," and "Musterfield" which also bounded a part of the Alsop homestead. Both of these properties are located near Route 608 at the R.F. and P. Railroad near Massaponax Creek. "Musterfield" was acquired from the Alsop family by the Musterfield Sand and Gravel Co. which in turn sold it to the Massaponax Sand and Gravel Co.

On 7 February 1846, Mary "Polly" Alsop, wife of "Captain Jack," received from the will of her deceased brother George Purvis Leavell all of the interest that he held in the dower land then in the possession of their mother Mary Purvis Leavell who was still living.

Captain Jack and Polly were living at "LaVue" when the Civil War began. During the Battle of Fredericksburg, "LaVue" was offered by the Alsops as a shelter for refugees from Fredericksburg. The displaced citizens who accepted the protection offered by the sanctuary in the Alsop home were also able to see the progress at the Hamilton Crossing end of the Battle of Fredericksburg which was only a mile and half away, as "LaVue" was on a high hill which afforded excellent observation.

Many family stories were remembered and passed down to succeeding generations about experiences that occurred during the refugees' stay at "LaVue." Blanche Alsop Hansen, great granddaughter of Captain Jack and Polly, told me several interesting tales that originated at "LaVue" during the refugee period (December 1862). She titled these comical developments as follows: (1) The Parrot From Fredericksburg, (2) Harriet, the Cook, (3) Great grandmother's Boot (4) and Mr. Lacy's Whole Family.

Polly Alsop died 18 October 1863, and Captain Jack Alsop passed away on 30 April 1866. The inventory and appraisement of the estate of Captain John J. Alsop is found in the Spotsylvania Co. probate records dated 18 May 1866.

Children of John J. Alsop and wife Mary "Polly" Purvis Leavell:

237. i. George W. Alsop
238. ii. John Franklin Alsop
239. iii. William Samuel Alsop
240. iv. James Addison Alsop

v. Elizabeth H. Alsop, the first daughter born to this family at "LaVue" in Spotsylvania Co., Va., arrived 23 December 1829, but died in childhood.

241. vi. Thomas Burwell Alsop
vii. Eliza Byrd Alsop was discussed in Vol. I, "Alsop's Tables," page 268.

John "Captain Jack" Alsop Not Long Before His Death

135. Jesse[7] Alsop (George,[6] Samuel,[5] John,[4] William,[3] George,[2] George[1]), the youngest son of George and Lucy H. Strother Alsop, was born in Spotsylvania Co., Va. according to the inscription on his tombstone. It would seem that his parents were living on some of their property located in Spotsylvania Co. at the time Jesse was born, but returned to one of their Caroline Co. farms where Jesse grew to manhood. He helped his father George operate the agricultural acreage which over the years grew to be extensive with the Alsops owning and utilizing a large number of slaves.

Jesse never married, but ca. 1830, he had a mulatto child Virginia by one of his father's slaves named Mary. By 1832, Jesse had bought farm land from the government in Yazoo Co., Mississippi and relocated to this farm taking the Alsop family slave Mary and their daughter Virginia with him. He also bought other farm acreage available from the government in 1833 and 1834. Jesse Alsop is recorded in Yazoo Co. literature as being one of the original landowners of this area. Much of the land bought by Jesse was acquired in partnership with his brother John "Captain Jack" Alsop of Spotsylvania Co., Va. as recorded in the deed books of Yazoo Co., Ms.

On 31 August 1840, Jesse Alsop gave a bill of sale to his brother John Alsop as found in the deed books of Yazoo Co. for that year as follows:

Whereas John Alsop residing in Spotsylvania County in the State of Virginia and his brother Jesse Alsop residing in Yazoo County in the State of Mississippi are now and for several years past have been engaged in the cultivation of lands in the last mentioned county and state in partnership under the superintendence and management of the said Jesse Alsop. And whereas the said John and Jesse Alsop now jointly and equally own upon the lands of aforesaid the following named slaves viz: Henry (short), Henry (long), Henry Garnett, John Griffin, Jenny, Armstead, Andrew, Clesby, Ben, William, George, Henderson, Solomon, Griffin Jur., Phillip, Daniel, Newman, Stephen, Albert, Middleton, Presley, Mima (big), Mima (little) and child, Mary Clinn and child, Mary Jackson, Silvey and child, Nancy, Hermey and child, Abby, Fanny (old) and child, Fanny (young), Jenny, Harriett, Eb and Anthony. Also eleven mules, five horses, sixteen oxen, about twelve head of other cattle - about seventy head of hogs - and farming and plantation utensils and whereas the said Jesse Alsop hath this day bargained and sold to the said John Alsop, his the said Jesse Alsop's undivided moiety of the said slaves, mules, horses, oxen, & other cattle, hogs, and farming and plantation utensils - and also hath bargained and sold to the said John Alsop a Negro woman named Mary Lee and her five children, and a Negro girl named Marie, belonging entirely to the said Jesse Alsop, and also in the said county of Yazoo. Now therefore the said Jesse Alsop, for and in consideration of the sum of Fifteen Thousand Dollars to him in hand paid by the said John Alsop, the receipt of which is hereby acknowledged, will pay one half of all outstanding debts due by the said John and Jesse Alsop on account of their partnership in the purchase & cultivation of laws of Mississippi.

After applying to that object the proceeds of the crops of the present year, which still to remain their joint property, and subject to the payments of said partnership debts.

In witness whereof the said Jesse Alsop hath here unto set his hand and seal this 31st day of August, 1840.

Witness Moncure, RCL

Jesse Alsop

Jesse Alsop sold all of the land that he and his brother John had purchased in partnership as described in the following indenture:

This indenture made the 31st day of August 1840 between Jesse Alsop of the County of Yazoo in the State of Mississippi of the one part and John Alsop of the County of Spotsylvania in the State of Virginia of the other part: witnesseth that where-as the said Jesse Alsop has heretofore purchased of different persons, at different times various tracts or lots of land in the County of Yazoo in the State of Mississippi, for the joint and equal benefit of himself and his brother the said John Alsop who has fully paid his portion of the purchase money, but the legal title of the said tract or lots of land was conveyed by the several vendors thereof to the said Jesse Alsop alone: and whereas the said John Alsop has purchased from the said Jesse the latters moiety of the said tracts or lots of land and is therefore now entitled to a conveyance from the said Jesse of the whole of the said laws - this indenture therefore further witnesseth that the said Jesse Alsop in consideration of the premises and of the sum of Ten Thousand Dollars to him in hand paid by the said John Alsop the receipt whereof is hereby acknowledged doth sell to said John Alsop all of the tracts or lots of land containing about one thousand acres which are described as follows:

North west quarter - the west half of the South quarter - the West half of the North East quarter - and North half of the East half of the South West quarter of Section No. thirteen - North East quarter of Section No. fourteen - The East half of the South East quarter of Section No. fourteen - the East half of the North East quarter of Section No. twenty-three, the

South half of the East half of the South East quarter - the South half of the West half of the South East quarter of Section No. eleven - the West half of the South West quarter of Section No. twelve, and lot no. two of Section No. twenty-four (containing Eighty Acres) all in Township No. Ten of Range No. One East, and an other lot containing forty acres lying on Big Black River but the number not recollected - and the other of which said bodies or tracts of land consists of the several lots known and described as follows to wit: The East half of the South West quarter of Section No. twenty-five. The South half of the East half of the North West quarter of Section No. twenty-five. The East half of the South East quarter of Section No. twenty-five - The North East quarter, and the East half of the South East quarter of Section No. twenty-four.

The North East quarter, and West half of the'South East quarter, and North half of the East half of the North West quarter of Section No. twenty-five. The West half of the South East quarter; the East half of the South West quarter of Section No. twenty-four -the West half of the North West quarter and the West half of the South West_ quarter of Section No. twenty-five, all in Township No. Eleven of Range No. One East.
Witness: Robert L. Moncure

Jesse Alsop continued to live in Yazoo Co., MS where he owned extensive farm land and slowly acquired additional acreage in both Yazoo Co. and adjoining Madison Co., MS. The 1850 census places Jesse in Yazoo Co. near the present day community of Lynnwood and several miles from Yazoo City. John, brother of Jesse, acquired more land in 1846 in Yazoo Co., and he employed his cousin Edward Alsop to help operate his cotton gin and manage the farming operations in Mississippi. At some point in the early 1850's, Jesse left Mississippi and entered into a business partnership with a friend in Kentucky which is more fully disclosed in the will of Jesse Alsop. This will is recorded in W. B. "A", page 217, in Yazoo Co., MS, and also in W. B. "J", page 456, in Washington Co., Kentucky. Excerpts from the will follow.

Item 2d- I Give, Will and bequeath to my esteemed nephew James A. Alsop twenty-five hundred dollars to be paid him as soon as convenient out of my estate in Mississippi, but as he is Indebted to me for money loaned and a horse. That five hundred dollars be deducted from said devise, and he is not to bring any charge against my Estate for services or other accounts.

Item 3d- It is my Will and desire that after the payment of my debts and said Legacy as above directed that all the remaining part of my Estate in the State of Mississippi both real and personal be sold by my Executor herein after named and converted into money and soon as practicable, at such time and upon such conditions as my Executor may think best for the interest of my Estate and said money to be applied by my Executor to buy land and Real Estate in the State of Ohio to settle Mary and her six children. Viz: Virginia, Milina Ann (Called Puss), Mortimer, Sam, Celia and Elizabeth, whom I have heretofore emancipated and set free in said state of Ohio, and who now resides in Clemount County, Ohio, and that I may not be misunderstood. It is my Will and intention that after all my just debts are paid and the before mentioned Legacy that all the Estate I own in the Counties of Yazoo and Madison in the State of Mississippi or in any other county in said State of Mississippi, shall be converted into money, and the money invested in lands and other real estate in the State of Ohio by my Executor herein after named, the same to be conveyed to the said Mary and her six children above named Equally, the portion conveyed to Mary to go to her said six children or their heirs equally after her death, and I do hope that my Executor or whoever may act in that capacity, should the Executor appointed by me die or fail to act, carry out my wishes in this clause of my Will as it is the great desire of my heart.

Item 4th- I will and bequeath to Mrs. Neomie Redding for her kindness to me out of my Estate in Kentucky for her own use Three Hundred Dollars.

Item 5th- I will and bequeath to my friend Samuel Redding for his attention and kindness to me all my Estate in the State of Kentucky both real, personel and mixed after the payment of all our partnership debts.

Item 6th- My boy Israel I now have with me to go to Mississippi and be embraced with my estate there.

Item 7th- I direct my Executor take special care of my watch and specks and to give my watch to Sam, and my specks to Mary devises named in the 2d clause of this my Will, and I will and bequeath to Mortimer a brother of Sam, One Hundred and Twenty-Five dollars in cash to be paid to him and of the money arising from the sale of my Estate in Mississippi before the same is vested in Real Estate and lands in Ohio as is directed in this Will in addition to his part of said investment.

Lastly I nominate, constitute and appoint my friend Samuel Redding of the County of Washington and State of Kentucky Executor of this my last Will and Testament hereby revoking and annulling all other will or wills by me heretofore made.

In Testimony where I have hereunto set my hand and affixed my seal this 2d day of January 1856.

Jesse Alsop

Witnessed:
W. Wharton
John B. Starr

Jesse Alsop died 3 September 1856, and was buried in the Pleasant Grove Presbyterian Church Cemetery. The inscription on his tombstone disclosed that he was a successful planter in MS for twenty years and died a citizen of Washington Co., KY. The inscription closed by stating that he died in full assurance of eternal happiness. Pleasant Grove Church was founded in 1833, and is still in full operation. It is located on Highway 555 about eight miles north of Springfield, Ky.

Burial Site of Jesse Alsop -Pleasant Grove
Cemetery in Washington Co., Ky.

At the meeting held for the Washington County Court at the courthouse in Springfield on Monday 22 September 1856, the last will and testament of Jesse Alsop was presented. Samuel Redding was approved as the executor and all provisions of the will were instituted.

Mary Alsop, the Virginia slave of Jesse Alsop and the mother of his six children, was living in Clermont Co., Ohio in Wayne and Miami twp. when the census of 1860 was reported.

Living in her household were her six children and a seventh child named Francis Lucian Alsop, born 1853 in Yazoo Co., MS who may also have been a son of Jesse Alsop but was not recognized as such in the will previously discussed. Jesse may have left Mississippi for Kentucky prior to the birth of this last son and omitted him from the will because he never knew of his existence.

Mary Alsop was still living in 1879, as she and her children gave power of attorney to a lawyer named T.B. Sheldon to determine what legal claim they might have to property belonging to Jesse Alsop's estate and located in Madison Co., Ky. near Richmond. This situation is recorded in Book 24, page 601, and is dated 12 April 1879. Listed in this record as heirs of Jesse Alsop were Mary, Virginia, Samuel, Mortimer, George Ann, Marcelia and Elizabeth. No record was found which divulged the outcome of this court action. The date of Mary's death is unknown.

Known issue of Jesse Alsop and Mary:

i. Virginia Alsop, the daughter of Jesse Alsop and Mary, a slave owned by the Alsop family in Caroline Co., Va., was born either in Virginia or in Yazoo Co., MS after Jesse moved there to manage farm lands that he had bought from the government. Virginia shared in the provisions of her father's will and in 1860, was living with her mother, brothers, and sisters in Clermont Co., Ohio. The census of 1880 locates her in Brown Co., Ohio as a widow with a seven year old son named Edward Tunsel. She disappeared from any known records after this time.

ii. Milina Georgia Ann "Puss" Alsop was born in Yazoo Co., MS ca. 1832, and grew up on the cotton plantation owned by her father. About 1853, she and her mother and brothers and sisters were emancipated by Jesse Alsop and relocated to Clermont, Ohio where she was living with her family in 1860. Her death date is unknown, but she was still living in 1879, when she signed a power of attorney to give a lawyer in Madison Co., Kentucky the authority to pursue her claim to property belonging to her father's estate.

242. iii. Mortimer Alsop

243. iv. Samuel Alsop

v. Marcella Alsop was born in Yazoo Co., MS ca. 1848, and lived her first five years as a slave before being liberated by Jesse Alsop. In 1860, "Celia," was living in Clermont Co., Ohio with her family. The census of 1880 places Celia, her husband Timothy Ballard, age 40, and their children John, 10, Elizabeth, 9, William, 7, Rosanna, 6, Sarah, 5, Jacob, 4, and George, 5 mo., as living in Brown Co., Ohio, Sterling Twp., in the household of her widowed sister Virginia.

vi. Elizabeth Alsop was born ca. 1850 in Yazoo Co., MS into slavery on the cotton plantation of her father Jesse Alsop. When she was about three

years old, she was liberated and sent to Ohio with the rest of her family. She lived in Clermont, Co., and later in Brown Co. where she married George Burr as proven by a court record in Madison Co., Ky. dated 12 April 1879, and found in Bk. 24, page 601. No records have been located after this.
244. vii. Francis Lucian Alsop

135-B. Joseph[7] M. Alsop (Samuel,[6] Samuel,[5] John,[4] William,[3] George,[2] George[1]), a son of Samuel Alsop and his first wife Dorothea "Dolly" Campbell, was erroneously assigned number 135 on page 226 of Vol. I, Alsop's Tables, which had already been given to Jesse Alsop on page 214 of the original volume. Therefore, to help eliminate any confusion, Joseph has been designated as family number 135B in this volume. Joseph was born in Spotsylvania Co., Va. in September 1805, and grew to adulthood as the only son of one of the wealthiest and most influential men in north eastern Virginia. From a very early age Joseph was interested and active in his father's many enterprises. He too, was a very successful and affluent citizen of Spotsylvania Co. Not only was he active in business pursuits, but he also had strong civic interests and was a Justice of the Spotsylvania Court by 1833.

Joseph lived at his parent's residence called "Fairview" until his marriage to Sarah Ann French, the eldest daughter of Dr. William French and Elizabeth Maxwell Trippe Barton. Although no marriage record has been found in the court records, Joseph and Sarah were married ca. 1836, and their first child was born in 1838. Sarah Ann French Alsop was born in Spotsylvania Co. in November 1816 at her parents' home located next door to "Fairview," the home of Samuel Alsop, father of her husband. She was the granddaughter of Dr. George French and wife Anne Brayne Benger.

The Culpepper Co., Va. deeds, dated 13 March 1833, contain the sale of land by George Alsop and Mary of that county to Joseph Alsop of Spotsylvania Co. This land adjoined land owned by Samuel Alsop and William Brooke. Samuel was the father of Joseph, and George Alsop's identity is uncertain, as there were several George Alsops living in the vicinity. The following year on 1 May, D.B. 2, pages 267, 272, and 274, Joseph Alsop and several other men created a stock company to mine portions of land that he had bought in Culpepper Co. He also leased other parts of this property.

The 1850 Federal census reported Joseph, Sarah Ann, their five children and his mother-in-law as living in the Eastern District of Spotsylvania Co. at their residence known as "Kenilworth" which later was named "Hunter's Lodge." John Lacy bought the property in 1857, which was located on the present day Route 608 at the Richmond, Fredericksburg and Petersburg R. R. near "LaVue" the home of John "Capt. Jack"Alsop, first cousin of Joseph. The home was destroyed by fire while Mr. Lacy was living there.

After selling his Spotsylvania Co. farm, Joseph and his family moved into the town of Fredericksburg in May 1857, and resided on Princess Ann St., located between Fauquier and Lewis Streets, at their new home which was bought from Thomas F. Knox who had obtained it from a man named Seddon in 1846. Tradition says that the house was built by Sam Alsop of "Fairview." The property later became known as the "Shepherd House" as George Shepherd acquired it from the Alsop estate. Today it is called the "Prince Frederick Arms."

Another interesting property owned by Joseph Alsop was "New Post" which is located east of present day Highway 1 at the river and three tenths of a mile from Gravel Pit Road. The land was sold to the Massaponax Sand and Gravel Co. in 1916, and workers uncovered the old brick foundation of the principal residence in 1931, it having disappeared several generations earlier. Careful excavation of the foundation revealed the tomb and remains of John, the eldest son of Governor Spotswood. John had died in 1756, and was buried by his wife and two sons at "New Post" which had belonged to his father.

In 1850, Joseph Alsop's real estate was evaluated at $34,000 and his father's was only $2,500 indicating that his father turned over most of his business interests to his only son a number of years before his death. The census of 1860 evaluates Joseph's real estate as $65,000 and his personal wealth at $72,000 of which slaves constituted some portion.

The five children that lived to adulthood were all still at home in 1860, although, the two oldest sons were college students. Joseph, Sarah, and most of their children continued to live on Princess Anne St. during the Civil War. By 1870, only the two youngest children were at home with their parents.

Joseph was still in excellent financial condition following the Civil War, as in 1870, his real estate was reported to be $50,000 and his personal wealth was evaluated at $60,000, although the slaves had all been freed. Joseph Alsop died at his home in Fredericksburg on 24 June 1872 at 2 o'clock a.m. He was recognized in his obituary as one of the leading citizens of Spotsylvania Co., and mention was made of his long years of service as a magistrate. During his residence in Fredericksburg, Joseph was also a member of the Hustings Court. His funeral was held at 11:00 A.M. on 25 June from the Fredericksburg Baptist Church, and his burial occurred at the Confederate Cemetery in Fredericksburg.

Sarah French Alsop, widow of Joseph, was living in the household of her son George Edward when the 1880 census was enumerated. This residence was located on North Charles St. in Fredericksburg where George Edward Alsop was a physician. Sarah continued to live in Fredericksburg until her death on 12 August 1885. She was buried beside her husband.

Issue of Joseph M. Alsop and wife Sarah Ann French:
245. i. William S. Alsop
246. ii. George Edward Alsop

iii. Nannie Clementina Alsop was born in Spotsylvania Co., Va. ca. 1844 at the family home "Kenilworth" located several miles southeast of Fredericksburg. At age 13, she moved with her family to their new residence in Fredericksburg on Princess Ann St. She married Carter M. Braxton who had served as a Col. of Artillery for the Confederate States of America. Their children were Nannie Mayo Braxton who first married Archibald Peachy and then Franklin G. Power, as her second husband; Josephine Braxton; Elizabeth Maxwell Braxton who married Edward E. Patteson; Susan Taylor Braxton who married V.D. Barclay; Sallie Moore Braxton who first married Lew Saunders and second Edmund Christian.

Elizabeth Maxwell Braxton and Edward E. Patteson were the parents of Richard Lee, Scotta Elizabeth, Nannie Braxton, Dorothea French, Mary Warden and Edward E., Jr. Sallie Moore Braxton and her first husband Lew Saunders were the parents of Sallie Braxton Saunders who married

Lyndon Burr and their two children were Braxton and Lyndon II. Sallie Moore Braxton Saunders then married Edmund Christian, and they had a daughter Loulie C. Christian who married T.S. Bailey, and they produced Carter Braxton, Jack and Carrol.

Nannie Clementina Alsop and Carter Braxton also had a son named William C. Braxton and a daughter Josephine Braxton who married Robert Brenneman.

247. iv. Elizabeth Maxwell Alsop

v. Emmilly Browne Alsop was born in 1851 at "Kenilworth" but grew to womanhood at the Alsop home in Fredericksburg. She was still living at home with her parents when the 1870 census was recorded. "Emma" married Frederick D. Power on 17 March 1874. She and her husband had no children.

vi. Joseph Alsop died in infancy.

vii. Barton Alsop died in infancy.

viii. Susan B. Alsop was born in 1850 and died in infancy.

ix. Dorothea Alsop died 9 August 1855, age 2 years, 9 months.

x. Seth Alsop died in infancy.

136. Samuel[7] S. Alsop (Benjamin,[6] Samuel,[5] John,[4] William,[3] George,[2] George[1]), born in Spotsylvania Co., Va. in 1810, was a son of Benjamin and Lucy Pemberton Alsop. His youth was spent on his parent's farm, "Pine Forest" located in the Eastern District near "LaVue," home of "Captain Jack" Alsop. He lived at home and helped his father with the family homestead until his marriage ca. 1840 to Mary H. Purvis. In 1850, he was living on part of the Benjamin Alsop farm which had been willed to him when his father died in 1847, and this acreage was valued at $2,000.

By 1860, Samuel and Mary's family had grown from five children in the previous census to seven. They were living in St. George's Parish, Courthouse, Virginia on farm land purchased by Samuel since the last census and evaluated at $3,000. He estimated his personal worth at $8,000. The farm of Samuel was located near Spotsylvania Courthouse which gave him an opportunity to be more involved in county affairs, and he was appointed a justice for Spotsylvania Co., Va. in 1865. Only a daughter, Mary P., was left at home by 1870.

Samuel continued to operate his farm in Spotsylvania Co. Va., but he also acquired an additional residence in Halifax Co., Enfield, N.C. known as "Woodside" which was located in the area where several of his sons had established their homes. He lived back and forth between his Spotsylvania farm and his "Woodside" property until his death which occurred about 1880. His will dated 1 October 1878, and recorded in Halifax, N.C. stated that he formerly lived in Spotsylvania Co., Va. He left his real estate in N.C., to his wife Mary H. Purvis Alsop and to his daughter Mary P. The will was witnessed by his son Samuel S., Jr. The census of 1880 reported that Samuel S. and Mary Purvis Alsop were living on their Spotsylvania Co., Va. farm, and also living in their household were Samuel S., Jr., his wife Molly and their three children. The death of Mary Purvis Alsop has not been determined nor the place of burial of her or her husband.

Known children of Samuel S. Alsop and wife Mary H. Purvis:
248. i. Richard B. Alsop
249. ii. John Thomas Alsop

iii. Henry P. Alsop was born in Spotsylvania Co., Va. in 1844, and was reported as living at the family residence in 1850 and 1860. He enlisted in the Confederate forces on 23 May 1861, as a seventeen year old student. He was a member of Co. "C", 30th Virginia Regiment, and he was promoted on 1 September 1861 to corporal for bravery at the first Battle of Bull Run (Manassas) won by the Confederate troops on 21 July 1861. At the Battle of Antietam (Sharpsburg) on 17 September 1862, the Confederates under Gen. Robert E. Lee retreated after a bloody fight in which many of their men were killed or wounded. Henry P. was one of the Confederate soldiers wounded in the battle and captured by Union troops who took him about fifteen miles north to Hagerstown, Maryland where he died a few days later. He was buried in Samuel Beeler's barn field along the fence running east from the barn about fifteen feet from a small locust tree near a rock quarry. The grave was reported still there in 1869, but it was plowed over in later years. This area is located today in Rose Hill Cemetery, District

22, Hagerstown, Md. This Confederate mass grave has a plaque which lists all of the known soldiers buried there, among them is found the name of Henry P. Alsop.

iv. Margaret "Peggy" L. Alsop, the oldest daughter of Samuel and Mary, was born in Spotsylvania Co., in 1845, and grew up on the family farm located near the county courthouse. She lived at home until her marriage on 24 October 1867 to Lawrence Bataille Pendleton, age 27, a son of John T. Pendleton of Fredericksburg. Nothing is known about her issue.

250. v. Samuel S. Alsop, Jr.

vi. Mary P. Alsop was born in Spotsylvania Co., Va. ca. 1851 to Samuel and Mary Purvis Alsop. She remained at home and was single until at least October 1878, which was the year that her father mentioned her in his will. Her parents were living in Spotsylvania Co., Va. in 1880, but she was not reported as living in the household by the census enumerator. She disappears from all known records about this time.

251. vii. Othneil Alsop

137. George[7] B. Alsop (Benjamin,[6] Samuel,[5] John,[4] William,[3] George,[2] George[1]) was a son of Benjamin and Lucy Pemberton Alsop who was born in Spotsylvania Co., Va., although the date is unknown. Deed Book II, page 37, of Madison Co., Tennessee contains proof of the identification of George's father as found in Vol. I, <u>Alsop's Tables</u>, page 228, and that George was still living on 27 August 1846. He has not been found on any other existing records researched at this time. The "Richmond Whig" carried the obituary of a Benjamin Alsop, Jr., who died on 26 July 1833 in Spotsylvania Co. of billious fever at the residence of his father. This could possibly have been a son of Benjamin and Lucy Alsop and a brother of George B. Alsop but proof has not been found. In the first volume of this family history on page 164, this Benjamin, Jr., was discussed as a possible son of Major Benjamin Alsop of "Snow Hill."

138. William[7] Pemberton Alsop (Benjamin,[6] Samuel,[5] John,[4] William,[3] George,[2] George[1]), born in Spotsylvania Co., Va. ca. 1817 to Benjamin and Lucy Pemberton Alsop, lived on the family farm during his childhood

and youth, but left home at an early age and found employment as a railroad trainee. This type of work required that William travel frequently, and his residence during the 1840's changed many times.

On 22 September 1840, William P. Alsop and Margaret D. Hamilton, born ca. 1825, were married in Orange Co., Gordonsville, Va. which was the location of the residence of James Hamilton, father of Margaret. She was the only child of James who had moved to Virginia from Little Rock, Arkansas. William rose to the position of train engineer and was soon transferred to Wilmington, New Hanover Co., N.C. He and his family were living there when his wife's father died ca. 1848 in Gordonsville, VA. and left all of his estate to his daughter Margaret. D.B. 41, page 131, Orange Co., Va., dated 16 April 1849, contains the sale of the inheritance left Margaret by her father which she and William Alsop sold to William Hamilton, Jr., of Baltimore, Maryland. The census of 1850 verified that the Alsop family was still living in Wilmington, N.C. and that William was still employed as a train engineer. By this time William and Margaret had been blessed with two children, Mary, age 6, and Cornelius, age 1 year.

Very little has been learned about what happened to William's wife and two children, but in 1860, he was back in Spotsylvania Co. living with his widowed mother and managing the farm left to her by her husband. Also living in the household was the seven-year old son of William whose name was William W. Alsop. Whether Margaret was the mother of this child is unknown. William continued to live in Spotsylvaniaas proven by a deed found in D.B. 48, page 44S, Orange Co., Va. which recorded the sale of seven acres of land in that county by E.H. Taliaferro to William P. Alsop, both parties of Fredericksburg, Va. The significance of this purchase may have been sentimental, as William purchased this land on 2 August 1873 for $120.00 and sold the same property, as found in D. B. 50, page 314, to George W. Wright for $36.09 on 2 April 1880.

The census verified the fact that William was living on Main Street near Commerce Street in Fredericksburg in June 1880. He was reported to be widowed and employed as a machinist. His obituary appeared in the local newspaper on 7 May 1895.

> "William Pemberton Alsop, age 77, died from heart trouble, Saturday at the home of his son-in-law, Charles W. Small of Melvale, Md. He was an engineer on the Petersburg & Richmond Railroad for many years. His daughter survives him."

Known issue of William Pemberton Alsop and wife Margaret D. Hamilton:

252. i. Mary Alsop

ii. Cornelius Alsop, born in New Hanover Co., Wilmington, N.C., about 1849, was listed in the Federal census report the following year living in the family household. He disappears at that time from any records yet researched.

Issue of William Pemberton Alsop, mother uncertain:

253. iii. William W. Alsop

139. Ignatius[7] Alsop (Benjamin,[6] Samuel,[5] John,[4] William,[3] George,[2] George[1]), born ca. 1822 in Spotsylvania Co., Va. to Benjamin and Lucy Pemberton Alsop, lived in his parent's household near Spotsylvania Courthouse until he left home to work for the railroad. He moved many times with this transient employment until the Federal census of 1850 places him in the Upper Division of Chesterfield Co., Va. living with his wife Martha, age 21, and his three year old son, George. His specific duties by this time were those of a train engineer. He was still living in this area in the town of Manchester with his wife Martha S. when the census was repeated ten years later. He gave his vocation as blacksmith and stated that he owned no real estate but had a personal worth of forty dollars. There were no children reported as living with his wife and him.

This family was not found in the next census, but the 1880 enumeration reported Martha S. Alsop as a widow, living in the home of her son George whose location was still Manchester, Va. in Chesterfield Co. No details have been learned about either the death dates or burial sites of Ignatius or his wife Martha.

Known children of Ignatius Alsop and wife Martha S. Alsop:
254. i. George Alsop
255. ii. Walter Alsop

iii. Ida Alsop was born in Manchester, Chesterfield Co., Va. ca. 1865, and was living with her widowed mother in the home of her brother George and his family when the 1880 Federal count was held for Chesterfield Co., Va.

(This concludes the information on individuals 134, 135, 136, 137, 138, and 139 who were inadvertently omitted in Volume II of Alsop's Tables. The second volume for this specific branch of the Alsop family tree ended on page 352, so this third volume will continue with information on William Samuel Alsop, number 142, the son of James and Elizabeth Mitchell Alsop.)

Issue of William Samuel Alsop and first wife Mary F. Woodall:
265. i. James Carl Alsop

ii. Jesse R. Alsop, born at his parents' farm in Hinds Co., Dry Grove, MS on 1 November 1859, grew up there and helped his father with the farming operations until his death on 13 July 1885. He was buried at Bethesda Baptist Cemetery near Dry Grove.

iii. Alice Alsop was born ca. 1862 at the Dry Grove farm of her parents. In 1870, she was a member of her father's household along with her two older brothers. She was missing from the next census and not mentioned in her father's will, so it is presumed that she was dead by 1880.

Children of William S. Alsop and second wife Bettie McClelland Alsop:

iv. Mary Fannie Alsop, the first child of William and Bettie, was born in Dry Grove, Hinds, Co., MS on the Alsop homestead on 7 December 1872. She was listed as an eight-year old daughter in her parents household when the Federal census of 1880 was enumerated. Fannie married Thomas Owen Curtis on 31 October 1894. The census of 1910 lists the Curtis household as Thomas (the father), Fannie (the mother), (and children) Hattie, 14, Willie, 12, Thomas A., 11, Vancy M., 9, Earl, 7, Treadwell, 5,

Bessie, 3, and Marse, 1. They were living in Hinds Co., MS, R4W, Twp. 3, Beat 3, on their farm near the town of Edwards. They also lived at Utica, MS and later at Vicksburg, MS where Fannie Alsop Curtis died on 21 February 1954.

v. Gertrude Alsop was born in October 1875, and was listed in the Federal count for Hinds Co. in 1880, as living with her parents, a half-brother, and three sisters at their farm near Dry Grove. She was single and still living at home with her family in 1900. At some point before 1910, she married a man named Beazley and they established their home in Crystal Springs, MS, Copiah Co. Also living in Copiah Co. when the 1900 census was taken was Bettie Alsop, sister of Gertrude's father William S. She was living in the home of Charles L. Beazley who was 30 years of age and single. More research should determine if this is the Beazley that Gertrude married.

vi. Willie Alsop, born in Dry Grove, Hinds Co., MS, ca. 1877, was three years of age when the census for Hinds Co. was reported in 1880. She was living in the farm home built by her father William S. Alsop on several hundred acres. She married William Henry Brady about 1900, and she was listed with her husband and children when the 1910 census report for Beat 4, Twp. 3, R2W, Hinds Co., MS. was completed. William, husband of Willie, was a farmer, who was born in MS. ca. 1875 after his parents relocated there from South Carolina. The children of William and Willie Alsop Brady were listed in the enumeration as Alice, 9, Robert, 8, Frank, 7, Neil, 5, and Clyde, 10 months. Willie lived in Jackson, Miss. later in her life.

vii. Maud Alsop was born on the William S. Alsop farm in Dry Grove, MS., Hinds Co., 19 May 1878, and was reported in her parents household in both 1880 and 1900, which were the dates of the first two Federal enumerations taken after her birth. After the death of her parents, Maud continued to live on the home place with her brother William Samuel, Jr., and her sister Bessie. In 1910, she was living at home, single, and teaching at the Dry Grove School. She and Bessie were good friends of Maggie and Mamie Hollingsworth who lived nearby.

After Maud quit teaching to get married, the two Hollingsworth sisters taught at Dry Grove School with Miss Maggie starting in 1916.

The Hollingsworth sisters and the Alsop sisters were very close friends and visited in the homes of each other frequently.

Maud married T. I. Greer, date unknown, and they made their home in Dry Grove. She remained good friends with the Hollingsworth sisters, and in later years she would visit them and spend weeks at a time in their home. It is not known if Maud had issue. She died 8 November 1934, and is buried in Bethesda Baptist Cemetery in Dry Grove.

266. viii. William Samuel Alsop, Jr.

ix. Bessie Alsop was born November 1882 on the family homestead where she lived with her parents, a brother, and several sisters. After her parent's deaths, she continued to live with her brother and a sister, Maud, on the home place. She married at some point after 1910 to J. S. Hand and moved to Franklin, Texas where she and her husband made their permanent home. Additional research is needed to determine more about her life in Texas.

143. Edward[7] Alsop (William,[6] Samuel,[5] John,[4] William,[3] George,[2] George[1]), born in Spotsylvania Co., Va. ca. 1808, was the son of William G. Alsop and wife Susan. Edward's father died in 1815, and left Edward and his other son Samuel S. 162-1/2 acres of land. Both sons gave up their inheritance rights to the estate of their grandfather Samuel Alsop, Sr., in 1832, as detailed in Vol. I, Alsop's Tables, page 232. Edward Alsop disappeared from all known records after 1832.

Susan Alsop, widow of William G., remarried in 1817, Pearson W. Payne, b. 1796, and their only child was Jessie W. Payne. Jessie wed Catherine Virginia Hicks on 6 January 1852, and was given 35 acres of land by his father which was named Stoney Point. This land is now the location of the Stoney Brook subdivision near the Spotsylvania Courthouse. Jessie and Catherine were the parents of Tom Payne who lived in Spotsylvania Co. and had issue.

Edward's brother Samuel S. left Virginia and lived in Texas. The court records of Martin Co., Indiana reveal the marriage of Samuel Alsop, b. 1812 in Virginia, to a Mrs. Mary Smith, age 35, on 9 November 1836. This Samuel Alsop is thought to be the brother of Edward Alsop but definite proof has not been found. The 1840 census of Martin Co., Ind. lists Samuel, wife, a step-son, and a daughter under five years of age. The next census lists only Samuel and Mary in their household in Perry Twp., Martin Co., Ind. where Samuel is farming. By 1860, Samuel had moved to Evansville, Indiana in Vandenburg Co. which was about 80 miles southwest of his farm in Martin Co. Samuel was living in the household of Henry Hawkins. No additional records have been discovered on this family.

144. John^{7} S. Alsop (Benjamin,^{6} Samuel,^{5} John,^{4} William,^{3}George,^{2} George^{1}) was erroneously listed in Vol. 1, Alsop's Tables, page 233, as a son of Thomas and Elizabeth Wharton Alsop. Since the publication of the original volume of this family history, genealogical proof has been found which proves that he was a son of Thomas' brother Benjamin and his wife Lucy Pemberton Alsop. Since he married his cousin Dorothea Alsop, daughter of James Alsop who was a brother of John S. Alsop's father Benjamin, the narration of his life is combined with that of his wife which can be found earlier in this chapter under family number 140.

145. Joseph^{7} W. Alsop (Thomas,^{6} Samuel,^{5} John,^{4} William,^{3} George,^{2} George^{1}), a son of Thomas and Elizabeth Wharton Alsop, was born in Spotsylvania Co., Va. ca.1826. He was reared at "Locust Grove" which was the name of his parents' farm located near the estate of his father's brother, Samuel Alsop. Joseph learned farming skills as a youth and by the census of 1850, he was employed as an overseer on the farm of a neighbor. Over the next ten years Joseph was able to acquire enough money to buy his own farm in St. George Parish, Spotsylvania Co., near Fredericksburg. He evaluated his farm land to be worth $1,000 and his personal worth $3,600 in 1860.

Joseph had married Martha A. Wilson, daughter of Ben and M. Wilson, about 1850, but the marriage record has not been found in either the Spotsylvania Courthouse or the Fredericksburg marriage records. Joseph and Martha were living with their five children, ages from 8 years to 1 year when the Federal count was compiled the year before the Civil War began. After the birth of his last child Josey in 1862, Joseph Alsop died, but whether it was as a result of the War Between the States or from other causes cannot be determined without additional research.

Martha Wilson Alsop married second John A. Grayson, age 27, of Lafayette Co., Miss., son of Joel and D. Grayson. The wedding date was 23 March 1866, and John reported that he was a farmer and had never been married. Martha, born about 1832, was listed as a widow and the ceremony was conducted by G.W. Lightner. Their two children were Magnita, b. 1867, and Robert, b. 1871. Living with Martha and her second husband in 1880 were Ella and Josey Alsop, both daughters of Martha and Joseph Alsop. Martha Alsop Grayson was living with her son Lawrence H. Alsop in Washington, D.C. in 1900. Her death date is unknown.

Known children of Joseph W. Alsop and wife Martha A. Wilson:
267. i. Samuel B. Alsop
268. ii. Thaddeus Alsop

iii. Nannie B. Alsop, born in St. George Parish, Spotsylvania Co., Va., ca. 1855, was living with her parents, three brothers and a sister when the census of 1860 was enumerated. She was not living with her mother and step-father after their marriage in 1866, and her residence until she became an adult is unknown. On 9 January 1879, Nannie and C.A. Perry, age 23, a son of E. and S. A. Perry of Caroline Co., Va., were married in Spotsylvania Co. by M. S. Chancellor. After their marriage, Nannie and C.A. lived on a farm in the area.

269. iv. Lawrence H. Alsop

v. Ella Alsop, born in Spotsylvania Co., ca. 1859, was the baby in the family of Joseph and Martha Alsop when the 1860 census was reported. After her father's death she lived in Spotsylvania Co. with her mother and step-father. When she left home is unknown, but she was living in Washington, D.C. at 1012 "K" Street, N.W. when the 1900 census was completed. She listed her employment as a servant in the house of Frederick Eberly. In 1920, Ella was again reported as a maid in the home of Robert V. Fleming located at 1470 Howard St. in Washington, D.C.

vi. Josey Alsop was born on her father's farm in Spotsylvania Co., Va. near Fredericksburg about 1862. In 1880, she was reported living in the home of her mother and step-father.

146. William[7] R. Alsop (Thomas,[6] Samuel,[5] John,[4] William,[3] George,[2] George[1]) was born in Spotsylvania Co. on 7 May 1827 at the farm of his parents Thomas and Elizabeth Wharton Alsop. He followed his father's example and engaged in farming just as soon as he was old enough. At age 22, he was working as a farm overseer in Spotsylvania Co., Eastern District. On 21 November 1850, William and Martha Belle Lowry, b. 12 October 1834, were married by S. Smith in their home county.

Ten years later William was still working as an overseer in St. George Parish, on a farm located between Spotsylvania Courthouse and Fredericksburg. He fought for the South during the Civil War as a soldier in Co. "A", 30th Virginia Regt.

Returning to Spotsylvania Co., William acquired his own farm which was made possible in some degree by his share of his parents' estate which was divided among the children after the mother's death. William Alsop's farm, located about two or three miles west of Fredericksburg near the Salem Baptist Church on the Plank Road, was known as "Apple Grove." It was here that all of their children were reared in a farming environment that was typical of most families in the 1860's and 1870's. The 1880 census records William, Martha B., and six of their ten children as living on the home place in Courtland District, Spotsylvania Co. with the head of the household listed as a farmer. Also living with them was Jane F. Lowry, age 70, widowed mother of Martha B. Alsop. The Federal count was taken every ten years, but nearly all of the 1890 records were destroyed, so the next extant records, in 1900, reveal that the Alsop family was still living at the same residence with only two children at home. William reported to the enumerator that he and Martha B. had been married 49 + years, nine of their ten children were still living, and that he owned his farm.

William died at his farm on Monday night, 11 March 1907, after suffering from asthma the last sixteen years of his life. The funeral services was held at Salem Baptist Church on Wednesday at 2:30 p.m., 13 March, where he and his family were members, and he was buried in the church cemetery immediately following the rites. This church is located at the intersection of Route 3 and Route 639 between Fredericksburg and Chancellorsville.

Martha Belle Lowry Alsop, widow of William, continued to live at the farm home "Apple Grove" where she was located in 1910. Living in her household, in addition to her single daughter, Martha Belle, were her son George Samuel Alsop's widow Anna M. and her two small daughters, Della S. and Georgia S. Martha B. also died at "Apple Grove" and was buried next to her husband on 9 February 1921.

Children of William R. Alsop and wife Martha Belle Lowry:

i. Emma O. Eurlalia Alsop, the first child in this family, was born ca. 1852 in Spotsylvania Co., Va. and in 1860, was living with her family on a farm between Spotsylvania Courthouse and Fredericksburg in St. George Parish. Emma was living in 1880 with her father's sister Jane F. Alsop Curtis and husband John. She was reported to be single, age 27, and niece of the head of the household. The marriage records of Spotsylvania Co., Va. contain the information that Emma O. Alsop, single, age 32, was married on 17 February 1887 to John Stephen Cannon, 42, widower, by J. H. P. Crismond. Stephen had been the overseer for John Franklin "Frank" Alsop, son of Capt. "Jack" Alsop, in 1860. No research has been attempted on Emma after her marriage.

270. ii. William L. Alsop

271. iii. Melvin Broaddus Alsop

iv. Lillian "Lilly" Jane Alsop was born in Spotsylvania Co., Va. in the spring of 1860. She grew up on her parent's farm near Fredericksburg where she was living with her parents, four brothers and a sister when the 1880 Federal census occurred. More research is needed to determine if she had issue.

272. v. Jackson L. Alsop

273. vi. Charles Alsop

vii. Martha Belle Alsop was born in Spotsylvania Co. on 26 January 1866, and lived at the family farm with her parents until their deaths. She never married and her disposition after the death of her mother in 1921 has yet to be learned. Martha Belle Alsop died on 10 September 1948, and was buried in the family burial plot at Salem Baptist Church Cemetery.

274. viii. Benjamin Franklin Alsop

ix. Edward "Ned" S. Alsop was born on 31 March 1871 at "Apple Grove," the residence of his parents William R. and Martha Belle Lowry Alsop. In 1880, he was living at the home of his parents, but no records or information have been found on his life after that date.

x. George Samuel Alsop was born in Spotsylvania Co., Va. in June 1873, and grew up on his parents' farm where he learned the responsibilities of rural life. He was still single and living at home when the 1900 census was recorded. However, on 17 February 1906, George and Myrtle Anna Day, age 22, daughter of W. R. and Maggie Day of Spotsylvania Co., were married in said county. George and Anna were the parents of Della S., b. 1907, and Georgia R., b. 1908. George died about 4 September 1908, leaving a widow and two infants. An extract from his obituary follows:

> "Geo. S. Alsop Found Dead by Wife, Who Heard His Last Call"
>
> Mr. Geo. S. Alsop was found dead in his barn yard in Spotsylvania County, Friday night about 8 o'clock by his wife, who had heard his last call before death. She went in the direction of the sound and found her husband stretched out on the ground dead. Mr. Alsop had just returned from driving up his cows on horseback, and had put his horse in the stable. He started for the house to get the milk bucket and was stricken.

At the time of his death, George had four brothers and two sisters still living. The brothers were William, Jackson, Benjamin and Melvin B. The funeral took place at the Salem Baptist Church with the services conducted by Rev. Hampton Jones. Since George's father William had died just the year before, his widow Martha B. encouraged her daughter-in-law Anna and her two small children to live with her and her daughter Martha B. This Myrtle Anna did, and this is where she was residing when the 1910 census was completed. In 1920, the two daughters of Anna and George were living in the household of their stepfather Virgil L. Williams in Spotsylvania Co. The date of Anna's marriage to her second husband is not known. No additional information has been learned about Della, but Georgia R. and Reginald L. Jones, age 18, son of George W. and Carrie M. Jones, were married on 8 October 1926 by E.V. Peyton. Reginald stated on the marriage license that his occupation was clerk of Jones Store, Virginia, while Georgia said that she had been living at Brokenberg, Va. It is unknown if Georgia and Reginald had issue.

147. Benjamin[7] P. Alsop (Thomas,[6] Samuel,[5] John,[4] William,[3] George,[2] George[1]), the youngest son of Thomas and Elizabeth Wharton Alsop, was born near Courthouse, Va. ca. 1832. In 1850, he was living with his family at their residence "Locust Grove." Benjamin P. and Margaret "Maggie" A. Offort, age 24, were married in Spotsylvania Co. ca. 1852, but the marriage record has not been located.

The 1860 census finds this family, made up of the father, mother, and their three children, living near Fredericksburg in St. George's Parish on their own land which was estimated to be worth $150. Benjamin was earning his living as a farmer, although very few details have been learned about him during these early years of his marriage. It is unknown if he served in the military during the Civil War, but he is living at home in the late 1860's as the birth records of Spotsylvania Co. contain the information that Brinton Alsop, son of Benjamin and Margaret Alsop, was born on 2 November 1867. Another son Philip was born about 1868 or 1869.

The census of 1870 for Spotsylvania Co. places the Alsop family in Chancellor Twp., Fredericksburg, Va. with Margaret Offort Alsop listed as a widow and the head of the household. Nothing has been learned about the death of her husband Benjamin. She evaluated her real estate at $1,000 and her personal property $350. All of her children were living with her which included five sons and two daughters. Margaret Alsop was enumerated twice in the census of 1880, as the earlier dated count describes her as a widow living in Courtland Dist. near "LaVue," the estate of Captain "Jack" which by this time had been inherited by his son, Dr. Samuel Alsop. Living with her in her home were five of her seven children. Also living with her was her mother Mary A. Offort, age 65, who was listed as a widow. When Margaret was counted for the second time in the census which happened a couple of months later, she was reported in the household of Napoleon Curtis as his wife, and the only child who had moved with her into the residence of the new step-father was Benjamin B. Alsop, age 14. No information has been found on Margaret "Maggie" Offort Alsop Curtis after the previously discussed Federal census reports. Genealogical proof that Margaret Offort Alsop married Napoleon Curtis has not been found.

Known children of Benjamin P. Alsop and wife Maggie Offort:
275. i. Thomas Rosser Alsop

ii. Mary "Mollie" E. Alsop, the eldest daughter of Benjamin and Maggie, was born in Spotsylvania Co. ca. 1856, and grew up on the farm operated by her father until his death in the late 1860's. On 25 March 1885, she was married to William C. Farmer, age 27, son of Robert and Nancy Farmer. The groom stated that he was employed as a farmer and rites of matrimony were officiated by J. P. H. Crismond. No research has been attempted on their issue.

276. iii. Charles R. Alsop
277. iv. Joseph W. Alsop

v. Maggie E. Alsop, the last daughter of this family, was born in Spotsylvania Co. ca. 1864, and by the time of the 1870 census, she was living with her widowed mother and her brothers and sisters. N. F. Smith, age 26, a son of Thomas Smith and wife Nancy, and Maggie Alsop were married on 23 December 1885, with the ceremony conducted by J. P. H. Crismond. After marriage, this family lived on a farm in Spotsylvania Co., but no information has been found from this point on.

278. vi. Benjamin Brenton Alsop
279. vii. Phillip Alsop

148. Guilford[7] Dudley Alsop (Henry,[6] George,[5] George,[4] William,[3] George,[2] George[1]), son of Henry Bartlett Alsop and wife Mary Jones, was born in Caroline Co., Va. in 1817, and while still a boy, moved with his family to Franklin Co., Ky. during the year 1828. After three years with his parents in Franklin Co., Guilford D. was apprenticed to his uncle in Jefferson Co., Louisville, Ky., who was also Guilford Dudley Alsop. Guilford D., Sr., taught his nephew Guilford D., Jr. the skills of the cabinet business. Guilford lived with his Uncle Guilford and Aunt Caroline until he completed his required years as an apprentice, and then he and his uncle worked together as designers and builders of quality hand made furniture and beautifully embellished coffins.

His uncle died in 1842, and Guilford was a grateful recipient of the will of this generous and thoughtful relative as detailed in Vol. I., page 235, of Alsop's Tables. Guilford D. and Miss Nancy Harris Moore, granddaughter of Col. James Francis Moore who was an early pioneer in Jefferson Co., were married in 1842. Nancy, a very capable woman, managed her husband's farm lands while Guilford was occupied with his cabinet shop. One family story that has been preserved through several generations tells of how she rode horseback through the fields with her red hair blowing in the wind. The Alsop farm, located near Greenwood Rd. and the Valley Station community, had not long been converted from wilderness as attested by an incident one day in which Nancy was attempting to approach twin fawns when she looked up and realized there were Indians nearby. Her horse had become quite skittish by this time, but she was able to remount and dash safely home.

In 1850, Guilford was living on the farm with his first five children, although Nancy is not listed in the household, and Frances P. Acres, a 22 year-old female servant is reported there. This omission could have been a clerical error by the census taker, but family records indicate that Nancy probably had a health problem, as their last child was only one month old.

Their address ten years later was Laconia, Ky. which was still in the same area of Jefferson Co. The family had grown to seven children and Nancy was listed as the wife of Dudley, age 42. The 1880 census located Guilford Dudley Alsop at his farm which was described as being in

Johnstown District near Valley Station. Nancy was evidently deceased by this time as her husband was reported the head of the household, but she is not listed. He had two of his grown sons living with him, and one of them was married with children. The death date of Guilford is not known, nor is the location of his burial site.

Children of Guilford Dudley Alsop and wife Nancy Harris Moore:
280. i. Gideon Higgins Alsop

ii. Susan Alsop, born in Jefferson Co., Ky. near the community of Valley Station in 1845, was the eldest daughter of this family. In 1850, she was living on the Alsop homestead with her parents, one sister and three brothers. She was still at home, P.O. Laconia, Ky., when the next Federal count was held, but she has not been found in any records after 1860.
281. iii. Mary Alsop
282. iv. Guilford Dudley Alsop, Jr.

v. George M. Alsop was born in the spring of 1850 on the farm of his parents located in Jefferson Co., Ky. about ten miles south of Louisville. The next census finds him still living with his family consisting of his parents, two sisters, and four brothers. In 1880, George is living in his father's household in the Johnstown District near Valley Station. No information has been found about George after this date.
283. vi. William Alsop
284. vii. Hiram Alsop

OLD ALSOP HOME JOINING THE TOM LEWIS PROPERTY

NANCY HOWARD ALSOP (1843-1877)

This was the second Alsop home built on the farm land of Guilford Dudley Alsop and wife Nancy Harris Moore. The original building was a log home whose site was some distance behind this one near the woods.

(This concludes the descendants of George Alsop, emigrant, of Accomack Co., Va. through the seventh generation and also Part I of the Third Volume of Alsop's Tables. See you in Volume III, Part II.)

Index

B

C

D

E

F

G

H

I

J

K

L

M

N

O

P

R

S

T

U

V

W

Z

CPSIA information can be obtained at www.ICGtesting.com
Printed in the USA
BVOW07*2022180614

356695BV00003B/166/P

9 781469 798318